CHARLES
DICKENS
IN
LOVE

CHARLES DICKENS
IN
LOVE

Robert Garnett

PEGASUS BOOKS
NEW YORK LONDON

CHARLES DICKENS IN LOVE

Pegasus Books LLC
80 Broad Street, 5th Floor
New York, NY 10004

First Pegasus Books cloth edition 2012

Interior design by Maria Fernandez

Library of Congress Cataloging-in-Publication Data is available.

ISBN: 978-1-60598-395-0

10 9 8 7 6 5 4 3 2 1

Printed in the United States of America
Distributed by W. W. Norton & Company, Inc.

For Margery
1950–1975

CONTENTS

CHAPTER 1

No discourse, except it be of love

Charles Dickens first visited America in 1842. Not yet thirty when he landed in Boston, he was already famous for half a dozen novels, including the rambling *Pickwick Papers*, the melodrama *Oliver Twist*, and *The Old Curiosity Shop*, in which the death of the girl heroine Little Nell had been a maudlin sensation in both Britain and America. Now America was eager to welcome him, and he in turn arrived with high expectations . . .

. . . only to be disappointed. Americans were coarse, cocky, and money-loving; obtrusive, vain, and ignorant. He reported one of them boasting, "Our people don't think of poetry, sir. Dollars, banks, and cotton are *our* books"—and Dickens agreed: "They certainly are in one sense; for a lower average of general information than exists in this country on all other topics it would be very hard to find." American men chewed tobacco and spit everywhere, incessantly. In four months of touring, from Boston to St. Louis, he found little to admire, much to dislike.

Toward the end of his tour, however, he visited Niagara Falls, and, awed by "nature's greatest altar," he momentarily put aside the annoying Americans. He was seldom sensitive to the presence of the divine, in or out of church, but standing at the foot of the cataract he was moved by powerful intimations of the sacred. "It would be hard for a man to stand nearer God than he does there," he wrote to his close friend John Forster in England:

> There was a bright rainbow at my feet; and from that I looked up to—great Heaven! to *what* a fall of bright green water! The broad, deep, mighty stream seems to die in the act of falling; and, from its unfathomable grave arises that tremendous ghost of spray and mist which is never laid, and has been haunting this place with the same dread solemnity—perhaps from the creation of the world.

In this sublime mood, and with the mighty falls suggesting both Death and Resurrection, his thoughts irresistibly turned to a beloved girl, Mary Hogarth.

His wife's younger sister, Mary Hogarth had died suddenly five years earlier, only seventeen, and since that stunning loss Dickens had revered her as his tutelary angel. In moments of deepest feeling, he sensed "the presence and influence of that spirit which directs my life, and through a heavy sorrow has pointed upwards with unchanging finger for more than four years past."

Now at Niagara Falls, Mary was vividly present, hovering in that "tremendous ghost of spray and mist" which haunted the falls with such "dread solemnity." "When I felt how near to my Creator I was standing," he wrote in *American Notes*, the travel book he wrote about his visit, "the first effect, and the enduring one—instant and lasting—of the tremendous spectacle was Peace. Peace of Mind, tranquillity, calm recollections of the Dead. . . ." The rest of America was well forgotten, but at Niagara he stood on "Enchanted Ground," where the spirit of his beloved Mary was alive and spoke to him:

What voices spoke from out the thundering water; what faces, faded from the earth, looked out upon me from its gleaming depths; what Heavenly promise glistened in those angels' tears, the drops of many hues that showered around, and twined themselves about the gorgeous arches which the changing rainbows made!

Mary's grave was in Kensal Green Cemetery outside London, and from Niagara he wrote to his friend John Forster: "What would I give if the dear girl whose ashes lie in Kensal-green, had lived to come so far along with us—but she has been here many times, I doubt not, since her sweet face faded from my earthly sight."

Dickens survived Mary Hogarth by more than thirty years, and until he died his love for her was inseparable from his strongest religious feelings: indeed, she *was* his religion. Hers was the human face of perfect beatitude, and of his own ultimate longings: "peace of mind—tranquillity—great thoughts of eternal rest and happiness."

A quarter century later, he crossed the Atlantic again, this time to give a series of public readings from his works. During his reading tour, he took time out to make a second visit to Niagara Falls—the only spot he had visited in 1842 that he went out of his way to revisit in 1868. It was March; the upstate New York winter had been, as always, frigid and snowy; but as he traveled toward Niagara from Boston, giving readings in Syracuse and Rochester along the way, a rapid thaw dammed the rivers with ice and caused widespread flooding. Syracuse, he observed glumly, was "a very grim place in a heavy thaw, and a most depressing one." Niagara welcomed him with almost providentially fine weather, however. "We have had two brilliant sunny days at Niagara," he wrote to his daughter back in England, "and have seen that wonderful place under the finest circumstances."

Once again, Niagara stirred his deepest feelings; once again, he sensed the immediacy of God. From a vantage point above the falls:

All away to the horizon on our right was a wonderful confusion of bright green and white water. As we stood watching it with our faces to the top of the Falls, our backs were towards the sun. The majestic valley below the Falls, so seen through the vast cloud of spray, was made of rainbow. The high banks, the riven rocks, the forests, the bridge, the buildings, the air, the sky, were all made of rainbow. Nothing in Turner's finest water-colour drawings, done in his greatest day, is so ethereal, so imaginative, so gorgeous in colour, as what I then beheld. I seemed to be lifted from the earth and to be looking into Heaven.

As before, Niagara gave a glimpse of unearthly power and beauty, raising his soul to a higher pitch of awareness. And once again, he hinted to his friend Forster, the transcendent spectacle awakened him to Mary Hogarth's presence: "What I once said to you, as I witnessed the scene five and twenty years ago, all came back at the most affecting and sublime sight. The 'muddy vesture of our clay,'" he misquoted Shakespeare, "falls from us as we look." Though she had now been gone for more than thirty years, Dickens's most powerful emotions and most exalted, even mystical, aspirations still returned to his beloved Mary Hogarth. The spirit of the dead girl rose from the powerful torrent of water roaring down—"dying"—into the chasm, and the cascade itself suggested the rush of emotions evoked by Mary's ghostly presence. It was characteristic of Dickens to be so deeply moved by the thundering violence of the falls, and at the same time by a gentle, gently remembered girl.

His Niagara thoughts on this second visit were not entirely transcendent, however, nor was all his time spent "looking into Heaven." On the same day that he described the sublimity of the falls to Forster, he dispatched a packet to the sub-editor of his magazine *All the Year Round* in London, enclosing (as he cryptically put it) "another letter from the same to the same." The second "same," the recipient of the letter, was his mistress Ellen Ternan, whom he had been eager to bring with him to America but had reluctantly left behind.

Along with the letter for Ellen, he enclosed a "receipt for a small box from Niagara that is to come to the office addressed to me. Please pay all charges on it, and put it (unopened) in my office bedroom to await *my* coming." His confidant the sub-editor might have wondered about the exact contents of the mysterious package, but would scarcely have doubted that it was a gift for Ellen. Dickens liked to give her jewelry, in particular, and when not standing enraptured by the magnificent prospects at Niagara he had evidently found time to purchase a (probably not inexpensive) bijou. The spirit of Mary Hogarth, suspended in the mists, had encountered a rival in the warmly embodied Ellen Ternan. The two absent women both stirred his strongest emotions—but while Mary drew his thoughts upward, Ellen drew them down to earth, to the moment when, back in England, he could once again embrace her.

Thus the virgin icon and the mistress came together at Niagara Falls—and in this curious meeting, we glimpse some of the contradictions of Dickens in love.

Scarcely two years after this second visit to Niagara Falls, he was dead, buried in Poets' Corner of Westminster Abbey: near the grave of Geoffrey Chaucer, whose bones had lain beneath the Abbey floor for almost five hundred years; of Ben Jonson, Shakespeare's friend and rival; of John Dryden, the first poet laureate; of John Gay, author of *The Beggar's Opera;* of Samuel Johnson, the eighteenth-century monarch of letters. A distinguished company of writers and poets—but none of his silent companions had possessed the fancy and fertility of Dickens. His only peer in that respect was the playwright buried in Stratford.

Three months before his death, Dickens had been honored by a private audience with Queen Victoria: a meeting, it was said, of the most famous woman and most famous man in England. For all his fame, however, and despite the distinction of Poets' Corner, he was buried quietly—indeed, secretly.

Two decades earlier, a million and a half spectators had crowded the streets of London for the Duke of Wellington's funeral procession. With six regiments of infantry, eight squadrons of cavalry, and seventeen rolling guns, the procession took two hours to file past. The duke's body was carried in an ornate eighteen-ton bronze carriage, twenty-seven feet long, drawn by twelve black draft horses; as many as eighteen thousand people jammed into St. Paul's for the service. Dickens had censured the gaudy spectacle: "the more truly great the man," he asserted, "the more truly little the ceremony."

His own body was smuggled into the Abbey surreptitiously, with only a dozen or so mourners and a handful of early-morning tourists in attendance. A plain, private service had been his own dictate, for he detested funeral ostentation; but the modesty of his funeral had a fitting symbolism as well, bringing his life full circle.

He had arrived in the world obscurely. His father had been an unimportant clerk in the Navy pay office; his father's parents had been servants. From modest circumstances, the Dickenses sank even lower, into bankruptcy and embarrassment. When Charles was twelve, his father was imprisoned for debt, and while his mother and younger siblings moved with him into debtors' prison in London, young Charles was sent to work in a shoe-blacking factory, "a crazy, tumble-down old house, abutting of course on the river, and literally overrun with rats." A bright, ambitious boy with hopes for education and gentility, he found himself a working drudge. The poignant tale of the sensitive, neglected boy toiling in the blacking factory and wandering alone and unprotected through the streets of London is well known, for it was related by a master storyteller—Dickens himself, the only source for the story.

This boyhood experience of insecurity, indignity, poverty, and menial employment helped form some of the salient qualities of his character—his determination, his drive, his perseverance, his work ethic, his earnestness. His parents had failed him; he would not fail himself.

A self-made man, he was an exemplary figure of his dynamic, striving times, the age of "steamboats, viaducts and railways," as Wordsworth put it; the age of telegraph, Crystal Palace, and Empire. Victorian writers were no less industrious than the engineers, entrepreneurs, explorers, speculators, and navvies. Dickens's contemporary Anthony Trollope wrote forty-seven novels (three times as many as Dickens, the Trollope Society likes to point out), rising at four each morning and writing without pause from five to eight—before heading off to his full-time job, for he was also a busy bureaucrat in the Post Office. Trollope's mother, Frances, had been a novelist, too; publishing her first book at fifty-two, she went on to publish forty more over the next twenty-five years. Dickens attributed his own success to "a patient and continuous energy." "I have been very fortunate in worldly matters," his autobiographical character David Copperfield remarks; "many men have worked much harder, and not succeeded half so well; but I never could have done what I have done, without the habits of punctuality, order, and diligence, without the determination to concentrate myself on one object at a time."

If in his indefatigable activity Dickens was a man of his times, he was unique in a second and rarer quality—his extraordinary inventive powers. His energy was a steam engine, his imagination the winged horse Pegasus.

This fertile tension between force and fancy was paralleled by other inconsistencies. Like David Copperfield, for example, he was punctual, diligent, and orderly—almost excessively so. He had a rage for tidiness: "There never existed, I think, in all the world, a more thoroughly tidy or methodical creature than was my father," his eldest daughter Mary recollected. "He was tidy in every way—in his mind, in his handsome and graceful person, in his work, in his large correspondence, in fact in his whole life." He was strongly domestic, "full of the kind of interest in a house which is commonly confined to women," inspecting every room daily, "and if a chair was out of place, or a blind not quite straight, or a crumb left on the floor, woe betide the offender." Many years later, his second daughter Katie told a friend that as girls, she and her sister were allowed to arrange and decorate their bedroom as they pleased, "so long as the room was kept tidy and neat." This neatness also applied to their dresser drawers, which their father periodically inspected—at one time every day—in common with his visits to other rooms in the house—"and if their contents were not found to be in apple-pie order they quickly had to be rendered so."

He was dapper in dress, with a penchant for bright, even flashy, waistcoats, admitting "that he had the fondness of a savage for finery." He "liked a tidy head," his daughter Katie recalled, "and if when he went out into the garden a wind blew his hair about, and he caught sight of his dishevelled locks in a mirror, he would 'fly for his hairbrush.'" (A fellow diner at a London restaurant was once amazed when Dickens "took out a pocket-comb and combed his hair and whiskers, or rather his goatee, at the table"; two days later the same observer at the same restaurant "saw Dickens again, and a recapitulation of the comb process.") He couldn't begin his morning writing session until his writing implements and the bric-a-brac on his desk (including an indispensable figurine of two frogs dueling with swords) were perfectly disposed, but in thirty-five years of writing to deadline—all his novels were written as weekly or monthly serials—he missed a deadline only once, and then only because he was stunned by Mary Hogarth's death. "His punctuality," his daughter remembered, "was almost painful."

In 1846, he spent the summer and autumn in Switzerland. Earlier, he had spent a year in Italy, which he found dirty and disorderly. "The condition of the common people here is abject and shocking," he wrote of Naples:

I am afraid the conventional idea of the picturesque is associated with such misery and degradation that a new picturesque will have to be established as the world goes onward. Except Fondi [a town outside Naples], there is nothing on earth that I have seen so dirty as Naples. I don't know what to liken the streets to where the mass of the lazzaroni live. You recollect that favorite pigstye of mine near Broadstairs? They are more like streets of such apartments heaped up story on story, and tumbled house on house, than anything else I can think of, at this moment.

Switzerland, by contrast, was an Eden of tidiness:

The country is delightful in the extreme—as leafy, green, and shady, as England; full of deep glens and branchy places . . . , and bright with all sorts of flowers in profusion. It abounds in singing birds besides—very pleasant after Italy; and the moonlight on the lake is noble. . . . The cultivation is uncommonly rich and profuse. There are all manner of walks, vineyards, green lanes, cornfields, and pastures full of hay. The general neatness is as remarkable as in England. . . . The people appear to be industrious and thriving.

The peasantry were "admirably educated . . . and always prepared to give a civil and pleasant answer." His Swiss servants, "taken at hazard from the people of the town," were exemplary: "I never saw more obliging servants . . . and in point of cleanliness, order, and punctuality to the moment, they are unrivalled."

But even as he loved the trim and tidy, he was fascinated by disorder and uproar, and the placidity of the Swiss began to oppress him. Of Lausanne, he observed that "The Genius of Dullness seems to brood over the town." He missed the noisy jostling streets of London, and found it difficult to write without them. "The absence of any accessible streets continues to worry me," he fretted. "At night, I want them beyond description. I don't seem able to get rid of my spectres unless I can lose them in crowds." His restless energies and lively imagination sought an active, crowded stage. The absence of busy streets caused him "giddiness and headache," he complained, and he began to think the Swiss were made "despondent and sluggish in their spirits by the great mass of still water, Lake Leman." On the other hand, "The sight of the rushing Rhone [in Geneva] seemed to stir my blood again."

His appetite for rush and violence was even more evident in an arduous climb up Mount Vesuvius in 1845, the year before his Swiss sojourn. He had arranged to ascend the mountain at night, to enhance the fiery spectacle within the crater. Nearing the top, he admired the moonlit vista below: sea, Naples, and countryside.

> The whole prospect is in this lovely state when we come upon the platform on the mountain-top—the region of Fire—an exhausted crater formed of great masses of gigantic cinders, like blocks of stone from some tremendous waterfall, burnt up; from every chink and crevice of which, hot sulphurous smoke is pouring out: while, from another conical-shaped hill, the present crater, rising abruptly from this platform at the end, great sheets of fire are streaming forth: reddening the night with flame, blackening it with smoke, and spotting it with red-hot stones and cinders, that fly up into the air like feathers, and fall down like lead. What words can paint the gloom and grandeur of this scene!

He was eager to climb to the higher, active crater: "There is something in the fire and roar, that generates an irresistible desire to get nearer to it. We cannot rest long, without starting off, two of us, on our hands and knees, accompanied by the head-guide, to climb to the brim of the flaming crater, and try to look in." Prudently remaining below, the rest of the climbing party "yell, as with one voice, that it is a dangerous proceeding, and call to us to come back":

What with their noise, and what with the trembling of the thin crust of ground, that seems about to open underneath our feet and plunge us in the burning gulf below (which is the real danger, if there be any); and what with the flashing of the fire in our faces, and the shower of red-hot ashes that is raining down, and the choking smoke and sulphur; we may well feel giddy and irrational like drunken men. But, we contrive to climb up to the brim, and look down, for a moment, into the Hell of boiling fire below.

And yet this was the man whose dueling-frogs figurine had to be precisely in its assigned position before he could dip his pen in the inkwell.

His love of order and fascination with violence often rub against each other in his fiction. Novel after novel presents scenes of tidy, cozy homes. In *David Copperfield*, the Peggotty family lives in a beached boat, snug and shipshape, "beautifully clean inside, and as tidy as possible." Visiting this boat-house, young David Copperfield is shown to his bedroom, "the completest and most desirable bedroom ever seen—in the stern of the vessel; with a little window, where the rudder used to go through; a little looking-glass, just the right height for me, nailed against the wall, and framed with oyster-shells; a little bed, which there was just room enough to get into; and a nosegay of seaweed in a blue mug on the table. The walls were whitewashed as white as milk, and the patchwork counterpane made my eyes quite ache with its brightness." Such snugness appealed deeply to Dickens, satisfying both his need for order and his wistfulness for childhood's small world.

Yet his novels betray, too, his attraction to chaos and violence. In his novel of the French Revolution, *A Tale of Two Cities*, he was both appalled and excited by the fury of the Paris mob:

". . . The Bastille!"
  With a roar that sounded as if all the breath in France had been shaped into the detested word, the living sea

rose, wave on wave, depth on depth, and overflowed the city to that point. Alarm-bells ringing, drums beating, the sea raging and thundering on its new beach, the attack began.

The mob presses the attack: "Flashing weapons, blazing torches, smoking waggon-loads of wet straw, hard work at neighbouring barricades in all directions, shrieks, volleys, execrations, bravery without stint, boom, smash and rattle, and the furious sounding of the living sea." The bloodthirsty Madame Defarge is the harpy-heroine of the assault, and when the governor of the Bastille is hauled out and murdered by a "rain of stabs and blows," she pounces on his corpse: "When he dropped dead . . . she put her foot upon his neck, and with her cruel knife—long ready—hewed off his head." Then "the sea rushed on":

> The sea of black and threatening waters, and of destructive upheaving of wave against wave, whose depths were yet unfathomed and whose forces were yet unknown. The remorseless sea of turbulently swaying shapes, voices of vengeance, and faces hardened in the furnaces of suffering until the touch of pity could make no mark on them.

Dickens the bourgeois Victorian householder was horrified by his own vivid imagining of such mayhem and butchery—and yet sympathetic, too. He could imagine himself one of the mob, but also one of its victims—one of the heads borne aloft on pikes, "whose drooping eyelids and half-seen eyes awaited the Last Day. Impassive faces, yet with a suspended—not an abolished—expression on them; faces, rather, in a fearful pause, as having yet to raise the dropped lids of the eyes, and bear witness with the bloodless lips, 'THOU DIDST IT!'"

Tidiness, punctuality, and domestic coziness . . . volcanoes, storms, rampaging mobs, and murder: such inconsistencies and conflicts fueled his genius.

Other contradictions abound. He admired "the great progress of the country . . . of Railway construction, of Electric Telegraph discovery, of improvements in Machinery." He demanded that his sons "be trained in the spirit of the Time," and thought it would be "horrible" if his eldest son "were to get hold of any conservative or High church notions." He regarded every era before his own as benighted if not barbaric, with the middle ages a particular horror. "Dickens was a pure modernist," John Ruskin scoffed, "a leader of the steam-whistle party *par excellence*—and he had no understanding of any power of antiquity except a sort of jackdaw sentiment for cathedral towers." And yet despite his progressive zeal, he was deeply nostalgic, strongly in the grip of his own past.

He was gregarious and sociable, and an exuberant performer who loved to organize theatricals and act the leading roles, and to read aloud from his own works. Behind his gusto and bonhomie, he maintained a deep reserve, however. He kept his childhood employment in the blacking factory a close secret for a quarter of a century, even from his wife. He admitted to being "chary of shewing my affections, even to my children, except when they are very young." One of his sons, Henry, testified to his father's "intense dislike of 'letting himself go' in private life or of using language which might be deemed strained or over-effusive," and recalled an example. After his first year at Cambridge, Henry won a scholarship from his college. Driving a carriage to the train station near their home in Kent, Gad's Hill, to meet his father, arriving on the train from London, Henry announced the triumph. Dickens's congratulations were perfunctory:

He said, "Capital! capital!"—nothing more. Disappointed to find that he received the news apparently so lightly, I took my seat beside him in the pony carriage he was driving. Nothing more happened until we had got halfway to Gad's Hill, when he broke down completely. Turning towards me with tears in his eyes and giving me a warm grip of the hand, he said, "God bless you, my boy; God bless you!"

Though reluctant to betray emotion to his son, Dickens wept openly at the theater and delighted in extracting tears from his own audiences when he read or acted.

He could in fact be highly sentimental, and none of his novels is wholly free of lachrymose indulgences. One of his most notable triumphs in this way was the death of the heroine Little Nell in his fourth novel, *The Old Curiosity Shop*. Thousands of readers wept as Nell languished—as did Dickens himself. "I am breaking my heart over this story, and cannot bear to finish it," he wrote as Nell lay dying, and two weeks later (it took her many chapters to die), he lamented that "I am slowly murdering that poor child, and grow wretched over it. It wrings my heart." As Nell's end grew yet closer, he felt himself "the most wretched of the wretched":

> It casts the most horrible shadow upon me, and it is as much as I can do to keep moving at all. I tremble to approach the place. . . . I shan't recover it for a long time. Nobody will miss her like I shall. It is such a painful thing to me, that I really cannot express my sorrow.

And finally having dispatched Little Nell, he sighed: "I am, for the time being, nearly dead with work—and grief for the loss of my child."

One reader deeply touched by Nell's death was William Bradbury, a partner in the firm of Bradbury and Evans, Dickens's publishers. A few years earlier, Bradbury had lost a young daughter, and as he narrated Nell's slow dying, Dickens kept people like Bradbury in mind:

"I resolved to try and do something which might be read by people about whom Death had been,—with a softened feeling, and with consolation." He was gratified when Bradbury wrote an appreciative note: "I was moved to have poor Bradbury's note yesterday, and was glad to think he felt as I would have had him."

But he "who wrote so tenderly, so sentimentally, so gushingly," an acquaintance observed, "had a strain of hardness in his nature which was like a rod of iron in his soul." In 1854, Dickens described with comic zest a boy's death in a London street accident:

> You know my man Cooper? Steady stupid sort of highly respectable creature? . . . Eldest boy 13 years old, "working" (I can't conceive how) at a Mathematical Instrument Maker's . . . On Tuesday night, the boy did not come home. Mother half distracted, and getting up at 5 in the morning to go and look for him. Father went out after breakfast, to do likewise. . . . Father conferring with Policeman on disappearance, up comes strange boy saying that how he as eerd tell, as a boy is a lyin in the "Bonus" [bone-house, or mortuary], as was run over. Wretched father goes to the Bonus . . . and finds his child with his head smashed to pieces! . . . He fell under a coal waggon as it was advancing, and was picked up as Dead as Adam.

Just the year before this joking account of a boy's death, Dickens had invited his readers to weep at the pathetic death of another boy, Jo the crossing sweeper, a character in *Bleak House*.

Some years later William Bradbury, who had been consoled for the death of his young daughter by Little Nell's death in *The Old Curiosity Shop*, lost another child—an adult son who took his life by drinking prussic acid. Having in the meantime quarreled with Bradbury, for reasons reflecting badly on himself, Dickens regarded his former friend's new grief with cold vindictiveness, greeting young Bradbury's suicide with gloating satisfaction. "Mr. Henry Bradbury has poisoned himself," he gossiped. "A gloomy professional purchaser of Nos., with a dirty face, ... offered to make oath 'wot he dun it in Cremorne in a bottle o' Soda Water. It wos last Sunday, wot he knowed Mr. Bradbury well, and he dun it there.'" Another version had Bradbury's death occurring at his father's house, and Dickens continued:

> I cannot say which account is correct—probably neither—but the wretched creature is doubtless dead. . . . Nothing having appeared in the papers, I suppose strong influence to have been used in that wise, to keep the dismal story quiet. Holsworth . . . said that he, the deceased, "had been laying it at Miss Evans's door for her getting married." God knows whether any blurred vision of that most undesirable female with the brass-headed eyes, ever crossed his drunken mind.

He could be not only cold but ruthless. When news of the 1857 Indian Mutiny reached England, he blustered that were he Commander in Chief in India, he would give notice of his intention "to exterminate the Race from the face of the earth, which disfigured the earth with the late abominable atrocities." Three years later, following the Second Opium War, he "spoke with great vehemence against the Chinese" and "believed that if we struck off the heads of 500 mandarins we should achieve more than by the greatest of victories." When a few years later the English governor of Jamaica suppressed a native insurrection with much bloodshed, flogging six hundred and summarily executing more than three hundred, Dickens heartily approved.

He was both pragmatic and idealistic. He was a highly successful entrepreneur and businessman. It was more or less an accident that his first novel, *Pickwick Papers*, was published in monthly numbers, but it proved a happy accident, and he seized on the advantages of serial publication and exploited them for the rest of his career. He holds a leading place in a nineteenth-century revolution in publishing, a revolution "brought about by attendant revolutions in literacy, real wages, urbanization, industrialization, technology, commerce, finance, transportation, and law, to be sure," as the leading scholar of Dickens's dealings with his publishers, Robert L. Patten, describes it, "but at critical points fuelled and sparked by one writer, Charles Dickens." His friend and fellow novelist Edward Bulwer-Lytton admitted that Dickens was "one of the greatest geniuses in fiction the world has produced," but noted, with less admiration, that Dickens "understands the practical part of Authorship beyond any writer—[Walter] Scott not excepted." In an interview a few weeks before his death, an aspiring young writer was impressed by his charm but also "found Mr. Dickens very practical. He spoke a great deal of the pecuniary advantages to be derived from his profession." He was aggressive and astute in extracting profit from his writings. Knowing that he was more valuable to his publishers than they to him, Dickens discarded them whenever it suited him. By twenty-five, he had already disposed of two and moved on to a third. His dealings were sometimes barely scrupulous, and certainly not high-minded. In disputes with his publishers, Patten admits, "Dickens behaved outrageously at times."

He wrote for money, enjoyed money, and spent liberally. It is a common misconception that he wrote long novels because he was paid by the word, but he was bent on squeezing shillings and pounds from his writing and reputation. His fecund imagination was a gift, but writing novels was hard work. "I do not regard successful fiction writing as a thing to be achieved in 'leisure moments,'" he once acidly observed to a genteel amateur. Because fiction-writing was a heavy drain on his energies and provided little income between novels, he established a weekly magazine, *Household Words*, with himself as proprietor, editor, and frequent contributor, to provide him with a steadier income. Falling out with *Household Words*' publisher, he promptly discontinued it and began another weekly, *All the Year Round*.

Eventually he realized that he could reap more profit from his fame and histrionic flair by giving public readings from his novels and stories, and for his last dozen years reading tours consumed more of his time, and earned more money, than writing. His letters are full of gleeful financial accountings from these readings, as: "I made last week, clear profit, £340; and have made, in the month of August, a profit of One Thousand Guineas! . . . Pretty well, I think?" He gave generously of time and energy to worthy causes, but his almsgiving was modest. In his will, he bequeathed one thousand pounds to his mistress; nothing to charity.

But focusing on Dickens's hard-edged dealings and business push misses his complexity. He was deeply and ardently idealistic. He entertained romantic notions of the poor and dispossessed—the penniless but cheerful and loving Cratchit family in *A Christmas Carol*, for example. He idealized childhood, and his novels often feature noble-hearted children, preferably orphans, struggling in a world of selfish, rapacious adults; Oliver Twist is only one of many such virtuous orphans.

After his death, eulogies and reminiscences were almost uniformly laudatory, sometimes fulsome. His energetic benevolence was particularly remarked. His best American friend, the Boston publisher J. T. Fields, recalled that in Dickens's presence "there was perpetual sunshine, and gloom was banished. . . . No man suffered more keenly or sympathized more fully than he did with want and misery; but his motto was, 'Don't stand and cry; press forward and help remove the difficulty.'"

But a woman friendly with his mistreated wife was less dazzled by Dickens's radiant virtues: "That man," she declared, "is a brute."

These and other contradictions and conflicts flowed into Dickens's novels: energizing, animating, complicating, enriching them. What did *not* find its way into them was love—or so it would seem. George Orwell, for example, claimed that "sexual love is almost entirely outside his scope."

In 1847, Dickens was in the midst of *Dombey and Son*, his sixth novel, published serially over the course of a year and a half. *Dombey and Son*'s heroine, Florence, is a girl of impeccable purity and virtue who dedicates herself to her sickly young brother and cruel, autocratic father, and who over the course of the novel weeps eighty-eight times, one reader calculated. The novel lacks a hero and features only the most pallid of romances. Meanwhile, during *Dombey*'s month-by-month progress, *Wuthering Heights* was published. For heroine, *Wuthering Heights* features the recklessly eager Catherine Earnshaw; for hero, the savagely passionate Heathcliff. It seems an anomaly that the immaculate young heroine Florence Dombey should have been created by a thirty-five-year-old man, experienced and worldly, father of half a dozen children, while *Wuthering Heights*'s author "Ellis Bell" was a spinster living in a remote Yorkshire parsonage.

Wuthering Heights was Emily Brontë's first and, as it turned out, only novel. Dickens's own first novel, *Pickwick Papers*, published a decade earlier, the year Victoria ascended the throne, could scarcely have been more different. Wholly lacking romance, let alone erotic fury, *Pickwick Papers* chronicled the misadventures of a genial old man and his bumbling chums. It had been a great popular success, making Dickens's reputation, and remained for most of his contemporaries as well as many later readers their favorite among his novels, even as he went on to write fourteen more.

His second novel demonstrated that he was much more than just a comic genius, however. Begun as he was still in the midst of *Pickwick Papers*, *Oliver Twist* was strikingly different: a lurid melodrama set among the criminal underworld of London, with orphan pathos and anti-establishment satire. But the hero of *Oliver Twist* is a young boy, who falls not into love but into drawing-room gentility. One of the novel's two young female characters is, to be sure, a prostitute, compulsively bound to a brutal thug; but *Oliver Twist*'s heroine is an angel, eventually married in the most perfunctory of romances. Oliver Twist the character initiated Dickens's fictional romance with the lonely child and orphan, the outcast and powerless. His novels consistently favored such characters, intermittently expanding the sentiment into a reformist agenda. The sparkling humorist of *Pickwick Papers* proved to be, as well, an earnest Victorian moralist.

A few years later, *A Christmas Carol* added to Dickens's celebrity, casting him in yet another role, as national patron of Christmas cheer and good feeling. But all the various aspects of Dickens, all the busy manifestations of his genius—comic sparkler, reformer and satirist, sentimentalist, champion of the lonely child, purveyor of punchbowl and Christmas turkey—seemed to leave him little time for romance. His energies were expended in so many other directions, perhaps, that he scarcely had time for amorous diversions; or perhaps, one might guess, like many ambitious men he had no capacity for strong personal affections. His early novels, in any event, evince little interest in that powerful engine of human affairs—and of literature—love. The novels' nods to romance, in getting their young heroes and heroines suitably married, are invariably conventional and tepid. Dickens was thirty-one when he wrote *A Christmas Carol*, and from the evidence of his novels and stories to that point, one might have supposed that he had never been in love, had never known any feelings of desire, passion, or urgency.

In fact, he had loved ardently as a young man—and unsuccessfully. After the failure of that early romance, he was reluctant to revisit the painful feelings in his fiction. But there was another reason he found it difficult to deal with the complex emotions of sexual love. His strongest religious feelings held the feminine spirit in high reverence. For Dickens, the essence of femininity was love, but a love that was self-denying and otherworldly, too ethereal to descend into lower regions of impulse and desire. A pure maiden's love was daughterly or sisterly, never erotic, and only reluctantly did he concede romance and marriage to his young heroines. His contemporary John Ruskin accused Dickens of killing *Old Curiosity Shop*'s heroine Little Nell for the market, as a butcher kills a lamb; but it would be more accurate to say that his concession to the market was rather to marry off his heroines. Marriage condemned them to the sorry exigencies of husbands and children; it might gratify the expectations of his readers, but it violated his own idealistic cult of the maiden.

A glance at Shakespeare suggests Dickens's dilemma. With no notion of his heroines as rarefied spirits, Shakespeare made them prompt to fall in love, ready to marry, and quick to seize opportunities. Having known Duke Orsino for only a few days, *Twelfth Night*'s Viola decides that "myself would be his wife" (1.4). Having just met Orlando, *As You Like It*'s Rosalind foresees him as "my child's father" (1.3). Though Rosalind and Viola are irreproachably chaste maidens, Shakespeare did not imagine them possessing any high sanctity or ethereal detachment, nor did he see their sexual warmth opposed to their virtue. By contrast, Dickens savored the celibate sisterly and daughterly vocations of his heroines and shrank from any suggestion of amorous motives. Marriage might be an honorable vocation, as well as a novelist's obligation, but it was nothing he relished, philosophically, and he surrendered his heroines to their earnest suitors with jealous reservations. He would have preferred that they remain vestal.

His religion of feminine self-abnegation had its roots both in his own nature and in the culture of his time, but it was given its specific shape by the death of his beloved young sister-in-law Mary Hogarth when he himself was a young man, a loss affecting him so strongly that for the rest of his life she remained his principal icon of holiness. Dickens critics often disparage his fixation on Mary Hogarth as encouraging his propensity for insipid angelic heroines. Certainly her influence was deep and long-lasting. But even if the saints of his religion were excessively spiritualized maidens—Orwell scoffed at them as "legless angels"—at least they gave Dickens a religion, and one with a generous code of compassion, loyalty, and self-sacrifice. As a theology, it was slight; as an ethic of humility and self-giving, it had much to recommend it. He might have done worse. From time to time he fell into other agitations and enthusiasms, but only in passing;

he never worshiped the gods of politics, prosperity, technology, or science.

Dickens's three loves are three different stories: each revolving about a young woman who had nothing to do with the other two; each occupying a different era of his life; each with a different plot and outcome. And yet taken together, his three loves form a single story, extending across forty years, from his youth to his death.

His first love ended, his second began, in loss. "Does the imagination dwell the most/Upon a woman won or woman lost?" William Butler Yeats would wonder in "The Tower." "If on the lost, admit you turned aside/From a great labyrinth . . ."—the labyrinth, that is, of fully embodied love, with its ambiguous fusion—often confusion—of soul and body. For much of his life, Dickens's imagination brooded tenderly over the two women he had lost, richly poignant memories, sanctified by loss, regret, and time. One became the image of his own vanished youth, the other a ministering angel. Under their charm, his early novels seldom ventured into the labyrinth of Eros. For many years, he loved not a woman, but two vanished spirits.

But twenty years after the death of his young sister-in-law, Dickens fell in love a third time, with revolutionary impact. His affair with a young actress altered his life: fracturing his marriage; rupturing long friendships and business partnerships; drawing him into a double life of public celebrity and esteem on one hand, of guilt, sin, and secrecy on the other. With Ellen Ternan, he entered the labyrinth. This love was no fond memory, no wistful dwelling on a lost ideal, but a passion that possessed him for a dozen years and ended only with his death. Under its influence, his fiction ventured into new regions of feeling. The earlier women he loved gave him models of the Coquette and the Virgin; his later novels probed the mysteries of Venus.

His liaison with Ellen Ternan unsettled basic and longstanding assumptions. His feminine ideal, with the face of Mary Hogarth, had for years inspired him with reverence for maiden devotion and self-surrender. Pure love was a feminine spirit, so chaste and celestial that it could have no sweaty business with male lovers. Soul and body were uneasy partners; the upward-tending spirit did not embrace, but only tolerated, its bondage to the flesh. It was all very well for light coquettes—of the world, worldly—to flirt and allure. But Dickens's fictional heroines enact a divine love, sacrificing themselves, Christ-like, to unworthy and ungrateful males—fathers, grandfathers, brothers. If Orwell's "legless angel" jest oversimplifies these heroines, it is true enough that they seldom seem troubled by desire or temptation; and that they selflessly dedicate themselves to their weak or wretched male kin, rather than wasting their time on lovers.

Dickens never relinquished his cult of the sanctified feminine spirit, but his passion for Ellen Ternan gave flesh to this spirit. She inspired him to devotion, but also enmeshed him in desire; she exalted him, but also entangled him.

Several centuries earlier, John Donne had reflected on love's inter-mixture of soul and flesh:

> Love's not so pure, and abstract, as they use
> To say, which have no mistress but their Muse,
> But as all else, being elemented too,
> Love sometimes would contemplate, sometimes do.
> ("Love's Growth")

For Dickens, Love had never been so fully "elemented"—embodied—as in his desire for Ellen Ternan. The Virgin and Venus, the Muse and the Mistress, love in contemplation and love in action—as these contraries jostled one another in his imagination, his novels grew richer.

Dickens died on a beautiful June afternoon in 1870, at his country house, Gad's Hill, in rural Kent. He had collapsed at dinner the day before, after writing much of the day in the upper story of his summer retreat, a miniature Swiss chalet on the grounds of Gad's Hill.

The next day, he lay unresponsive on a sofa that had been carried into the dining room. Ellen Ternan was summoned. Those of his children within a few hours' reach of Gad's Hill kept vigil; the attending doctors shook their heads gravely. "The sweet scent of the flowers he had so much admired floated in through the open doors of the new conservatory," his daughter Katie recalled. "Just before 6 o'clock the breathing became less, and at ten minutes past that hour he gave a deep sigh, a tear rose to his right eye and trickled down his cheek—and he was gone from this world."

A deep sigh and a tear—for what? For leaving the world on a sunny June day, the air sweet with early summer? For the novel left unfinished? For the inevitable regrets of a busy, crowded life?

There was much to regret, certainly, but much accomplishment too. Westminster Abbey awaited him.

Yet the prospect of a grave in Poets' Corner might have seemed cold consolation, forty years earlier, to a young shorthand reporter who cared for nothing in the world but the pretty, capricious daughter of a London banker. Perhaps his final tear had something to do with that sorrow too.

CHAPTER 2

Deep as first love, and wild with all regret:
Maria Beadnell

In May 1830, the obese and sclerotic King George IV lay dying in Windsor Castle, his approaching end unlamented. Waiting to succeed him was his sixty-four-year-old brother, soon to be William IV. The Duke of Wellington, hero of the Napoleonic era and now prime minister, had turned sixty-one-years-old on the first of May. A few weeks later, the young Princess Victoria turned eleven.

Some time that same month, eighteen-year-old Charles Dickens, a youth of no importance, met a girl named Maria Beadnell.

In F. Scott Fitzgerald's first novel, *This Side of Paradise*, the young hero falls in love with a girl named Rosalind, who eventually jilts him. But:

> Amory had loved Rosalind as he would never love another living person. She had taken the first flush of his youth and brought from his unplumbed depths tenderness that had

surprised him, gentleness and unselfishness that he had never given to another creature. He had later love affairs, but of a different sort. . . . Rosalind had drawn out what was more than passionate admiration; he had a deep, undying affection for Rosalind. (2:2)

Perhaps every man has a Rosalind; in any event, Dickens did, and she was Maria Beadnell. "In his youth," he later wrote of *Little Dorrit*'s Arthur Clennam, "he had ardently loved this woman, and had heaped upon her all the locked-up wealth of his affection and imagination. That wealth had been . . . lying idle in the dark to rust, until he poured it out for her." "This woman" was a character based on Maria; and in Clennam, Dickens was clearly remembering her impact on him a quarter century earlier.

He had pursued her eagerly and earnestly for over three years, until she brusquely sent him on his way. But she lingered in his imagination. "Ever since that memorable time," Dickens (like *Little Dorrit*'s Clennam) "had kept the old fancy of the Past unchanged, in its old sacred place." For years he cherished not only the idea of the girl he had lost, but also the memory of his own younger self in love with her. "When I became a man," St. Paul observed, "I put away childish things"; but Dickens even as a middle-aged man could not untangle himself from his youthful passion for Maria. When, many years later, long out of touch, she wrote to suggest they renew their friendship, he was swept up in excitement, seeing no obstacle to picking up where they had left off two decades earlier—although both were now married. "You open the way to a confidence between us," he replied, "which still once more, in perfect innocence and good faith, may be between ourselves alone." However innocent, the confidence "between ourselves alone" evidently excluded their spouses.

Dickens's biographers generally treat his love for Maria Beadnell as a juvenile folly, ultimately unimportant. When he met Maria again twenty-two years after their youthful rupture, his fascination with her "shivered and broke to pieces" instantly—a sadly comic disillusion that seemed to suggest that his infatuation had been a mere bubble from the start.

There is a more practical reason that the biographers slight Maria: little is known about her, or about Dickens's pursuit of her. Researchers pursue the footprints they can follow, and Maria Beadnell's footprints are few and faint. One indefatigable biographer, Peter Ackroyd, concluded his exhaustive researches with the admission that "information about Maria Beadnell is not easy to acquire." Her very appearance is largely a mystery. Ackroyd's Maria is "dark-haired" with a "slightly plump beauty"; another biographer sees her as "blond, petite, and conventionally pretty." Both Marias—brunette and blonde—are fanciful, however: no reliable portrait or specific description of Maria as a young woman exists. Dickens's only relevant comment, years later, was that "there used to be a tendency in your eyebrows to join together."

He himself is only occasionally visible during the three years he pursued her. There are no missing years in his early biography, as in Shakespeare's; but for the obscure young man courting Maria Beadnell, the sources are fragmentary. It was good fortune that a friend named Henry Kolle, a young man courting Maria's sister and a loyal ally in Dickens's own romance, kept the letters that Dickens wrote him at this time—for at the time almost no one else thought Dickensian ephemera worth saving. Of the thirteen surviving letters that he wrote in 1832, for example, when he was twenty-years-old, nine are to Kolle. He probably wrote dozens or hundreds of notes to Maria herself, but only a few survive, while her letters to him, whatever they amounted to in quantity or interest, he returned to her or later burned.

But as often with Dickens, lack of evidence does not imply lack of importance; while, conversely, mountains of evidence may document a small matter. Dickens the businessman, for example, is visible in hundreds of surviving letters, contracts, account-book entries, and bank records detailing his arrangements with publishers. But in those fertile regions of imagination from which his novels emerged, the petite Maria dwarfed his publishers.

In the spring of 1830, the eighteen-year-old Dickens was a shorthand reporter in an archaic corner of the English judicial system called Doctors' Commons, a medieval relict comprising an overlapping collection of courts with jurisdiction over matters ranging from wills and divorces to collisions at sea. Dickens later described it as "the place where they grant marriage-licenses to love-sick couples, and divorces to unfaithful ones; register the wills of people who have any property to leave, and punish hasty gentlemen who call ladies by unpleasant names." Earlier, clerking in a law office, he had taught himself a difficult shorthand system and with this skill found employment recording and transcribing the proceedings of the Doctors' Commons courts. It was respectable but dreary, glamorless work. He lived at home with his parents, though their address varied from year to year as precarious finances kept them on the move from one house to another. He had written nothing and given no particular indication that he would.

But he was energetic, ambitious, and hopeful, conscious of good abilities and determined to avoid the pecuniary embarrassments of his father. Willing to work hard and impatient of dull employments, he yet lacked a vocation. His early letters show a confident flair, and his hard-earned mastery of shorthand would presently create opportunities in journalism; but even when he became a journalist, it was several more years before he began writing, as opposed to reporting. Although as a boy he had been an eager novel-reader, he was aware that his education was incomplete, and as soon as he became eligible— the day after his eighteenth birthday—he applied for admission as a reader at the British Museum.

Despite their straitened finances, the Dickens home seems to have been congenial. The oldest son, Charles had two sisters and three brothers. He was particularly close to his older sister Fanny, training as a musician. He himself had more vernacular tastes in music. He loved traditional songs and ballads, and his gusto for popular music, as well as the musical vivacity of the Dickens home, is evident in invitations he issued to friends. When he was twenty, for example, he wrote to his friend Kolle: "Are you going out of town next Saturday? Because if you are not we propose to get one or two young men together for the purpose of knocking up a song or two." Another invitation to Kolle, actually a note deferring an invitation because of one of his family's relocations, suggests how central the piano was to their evening entertainment:

> Will you excuse my postponing the pleasure of seeing yourself and Brother until Sunday Week?—My reason is this:—as we are having coals in at the new place, cleaning &c we cannot very well remove until Tuesday or Wednesday next. The Piano will most likely go to Bentinck St. to day & as I have already said we cannot accompany it—So that the Piano will be in one place and we in another.

Dickens himself had no special musical talent but delighted in music-making and singing among friends and family. (Snatches of over two hundred popular songs would appear in his novels.)

Above all, however, he loved the theater, as both spectator and actor. He attended plays whenever possible. One letter to Kolle apologizes for missing an invitation: "I am exceedingly sorry that I was so unfortunate as to select last night for my annual visit to Drury Lane [Theatre] as I should have very much preferred having a chat and Cigar with you." The underscored "annual" no doubt alludes ironically to the frequency of his visits to Drury Lane, one of only two London theaters licensed to stage spoken drama. There were other theaters, however, for operas, operettas, pantomimes, and the like, and he frequented them as well. As a young man he attended hundreds of such performances, and though theater-going was relatively less expensive then, he no doubt spent much of his modest income on theater tickets.

He also enjoyed amateur home theatricals. One of his earliest writings to survive is a fragment of a burlesque he wrote for such an entertainment, titled *O'thello*. Only his father's lines, cues, and songs survive, Mr. Dickens having the foresight to save his handwritten part; later, probably pressed for funds, he sold the manuscript scraps when his son was renowned. The rest of *O'thello* has vanished, and no record of its performance survives. More is known about another theatrical evening, featuring a play called *Clari; or the Maid of Milan*, which Dickens organized soon after he turned twenty-one. By almost every account, he was a talented amateur actor; by some accounts, of professional ability. He was undoubtedly an exuberant performer. Almost every aspect of dramatic presentation excited him. As a spectator he laughed and wept without inhibition, while in his own theatricals he threw himself into the arrangements, the rehearsals, and the acting.

At this point in his life—an eighteen-year-old youth from an erratic family, ambitious and possessing great initiative and vigor, devoted in turn to hard work and theatrical pleasures—came the fateful moment when he met Maria Beadnell.

Unlike his own improvident family, the Beadnells were genteel and stable—perhaps to a fault. Mr. Beadnell was a clerk and later manager with Smith Payne & Smiths, a well-respected bank located in the City, London's financial district; the Beadnells lived next door to the bank, at 2 Lombard Street. The Lord Mayor's mansion was almost across the street; around the corner were the Bank of England and the Royal Exchange. It may be risky to draw inferences from this august neighborhood, but a heavy respectability may have brooded over 2 Lombard Street. Maria, fifteen months older than Dickens, was the youngest of three Beadnell daughters. She was small and attractive, to her family the "pocket Venus." Several amateur, stylized sketches of her as a girl exist, but no credible likeness; this was before the days of photography. Maria was very likely pampered and spoiled, and no doubt vain and flirtatious. She is usually and probably accurately described as a "coquette"; the besotted Dickens himself once accused her of "light butterfly" feelings. Perhaps girlish capriciousness was, initially, one of her charms.

What design or accident brought them together in the spring of 1830 is a mystery, and for the first year of his courtship the evidence is slender. His friend Kolle, courting Maria's sister Anne, may have introduced him to the Beadnells. In any case, Dickens was soon welcomed at 2 Lombard Street and became a frequent visitor. A sketch he wrote a few years later, "The Steam Excursion," features a sociable young bachelor, Percy Noakes, who "seldom dined at his own expense," and its description of Percy probably recalls Dickens's own evenings as a dinner guest at the Beadnells': "He used to talk politics to papas, flatter the vanity of mammas, do the amiable to their daughters. . . . he was always 'willing to make himself generally useful.'"

Young Dickens may at first have been accepted as a suitor, for Maria's parents could scarcely have been blind to the infatuation of the young puppy hanging about their Lombard Street parlor in the evenings. If in doubt, they had only to glance at Maria's album, to which he contributed several verses. The nature of a young lady's album—"a blank book in which to insert autographs, memorial verses, original drawings, or other souvenirs" (*OED*)—fairly guarantees that its contents will be light, complimentary, and often flattering, so that Dickens's contributions must be read in their context. Even so, his special interest in Maria seems plain even in the first of his verses, a strained acrostic on her name, concluding with a trite but probably heartfelt couplet: "Life has no charms, no happiness, no pleasures, now for me/Like those I feel, when 'tis my lot[,] Maria, to gaze on thee."

A second poem, "The Devil's Walk," composed about eighteen months after he had met Maria, describes the Devil, passing "not far from Lombard Street," as struck with contrition by her beauty:

> He saw at a window a face so fair
> That it made him start and weep
> For a passing thought rushed over his brain

Of days now beyond recall,
He thought of the bright angelic train
And of his own wretched fall.

This seems to allude to Milton's Satan admiring Eve in Paradise; perhaps *Paradise Lost* had been on Dickens's reading list at the British Museum.

The most ambitious of his early verses, however, was a contribution to the album of Maria's sister Anne. This poem, "The Bill of Fare," extending to some 350 lines of rhyming couplets—long enough to make its doggerel rhythms quite wearisome—is a comic sketch of the guests at a dinner party at 2 Lombard Street: "a small party," but eighteen people are named and described, concluding with Dickens himself, self-characterized as "a young summer cabbage, without any heart," because he had lost it "a twelve month ago, from last May." As "The Bill of Fare" was written in the autumn of 1831, it gives us Dickens's own dating of his infatuation with Maria as May 1830, as it probably began with their first meeting.

What other facts about Dickens and Maria can be squeezed from "The Bill of Fare"? In describing the dinner guests, Dickens first imagines each one as an item on the menu—that's why he himself is a summer cabbage. Mr. Beadnell is a "good fine Sirloin of beef," Mrs. Beadnell "an excellent Rib of the same," and Maria and her sister Anne "two nice little Ducks." This culinary conceit, borrowed from Oliver Goldsmith's satiric poem "Retaliation," is soon exhausted, however, at which point "The Bill of Fare" turns to a new fancy, also borrowed from "Retaliation." Imagining the assembled diners as dead, Dickens supplies epitaphs for each. (Goldsmith's poem imagines his fellow diners not as dead but as passed out under the table, drunk—but this jest might have seemed too bacchanalian for the bankerly Beadnells.)

Befitting his position at the head of the table, Mr. Beadnell is buried first, with a suitably flattering epitaph: "an excellent man," "most hospitable, friendly and kind," a man without an enemy. Apart from these genial qualities, vaguely sketched, he is "a good politician," with strong political views. Controversy and agitation over electoral reform, culminating in the Reform Bill of 1832, was in the news at the time, and Beadnell *père*'s views were well known to his family and guests:

> His opinions were always sound and sincere
> Come here! ye reformers, o'er him drop a tear
> Come here, and with me weep at his sudden end,
> Ye who're to ballot and freedom a friend.

Beadnell would seem to have been a political bore, and like "The Steam Excursion's" Percy Noakes, Dickens no doubt had "to talk politics to papas"—at least to the tiresome papa at number 2 Lombard Street.

By this time, moreover, Dickens's ears were routinely battered by political rhetoric. From court proceedings at Doctors' Commons, he had advanced to reporting debates in the House of Commons; and thus daily (and often nightly) he was now listening to and recording torrents of Reform Bill oratory. The experience quickly soured him on politicians and their speechifying; and Mr. Beadnell's dinner-table harangues must have seemed an unnecessary extra dose. (After reporting his last debate, Dickens never again entered the House of Commons.) No one deeply in love can care much about politics, more-over; absorbed by Maria, Dickens was unlikely to relish Reform Bill table-talk. "How can I, that girl standing there,/My attention fix/On Roman or on Russian or on Spanish politics?" William Butler Yeats would later ask rhetorically ("Politics"), and listening to Mr. Beadnell hold forth while Maria herself glittered nearby, Dickens would surely have agreed.

Years later, he gently mocked Maria's mother, recalling that she never managed to get his name right ("Mr. Dickin"); and her epitaph in "The Bill of Fare" begins with bland enough praise: ". . . whose conduct through life/As a mother, a woman, a friend, a wife/. . . Can but be summ'd up in one Word—Perfection." Yet the tribute to Mrs. Beadnell then takes a personal turn: ". . . when living she was, I then knew her well./It chances to've been by the fates brought about,/That she was the means of first bringing me out." Exactly what Dickens meant by being brought out is unclear, but the phrase seems to recall a specific kindness. Mrs. Beadnell must at first have welcomed him into the Beadnell household and circle of friends, allowing him to fall in love with Maria. When she actually did die, eighteen years later, Dickens recalled her "many old kindnesses, bestowed upon me when I was a mere boy." "The Bill of Fare" concludes its eulogy of Mrs. Beadnell by stressing the sincerity of his gratitude for her early hospitality and "her kindness since then": "I think what I say—I feel it, that's better." The earnestness of his gratitude, the stress on its authenticity, suggests an esteem for Maria's mother lacking in the eulogy of Mr. Beadnell.

In reading "The Bill of Fare," however, we turn with most interest to the mock epitaph for Maria herself, seeking hints about her personality and Dickens's struggle to win her. Alas, the thirty-four lines devoted to her scarcely yield thirty-four insights. The first dozen lines wind through a hyperbolical lamentation of no particular meaning whatever, unless they constitute a joke. While Maria's sister Anne has just been characterized as good-humored and agreeable, "a truly delightful, and sweet tempered girl," the extravagant rhetoric of Maria's epitaph, following Anne's, suggests that the difficult younger sister demanded a higher pitch of flattery. The poem then elaborates Dickens's grief for Maria's mock death: "My bright hopes and fond wishes were all centered here/Their brightness has vanished, they're now dark and drear." Since other evidence suggests that his courtship of Maria had indeed encountered difficulties, this conventional-sounding lament may have had actual pertinence.

The last ten lines of Maria's epitaph focus on a "small form that she folds to her breast" as she lies in death. Like the pampered Belinda of

Alexander Pope's "Rape of the Lock," Maria seems to have reserved much of her affection for her lapdog Daphne, "the little dog that,/ Would eat mutton chops, if you cut off the fat." This description of the cosseted Daphne may yield our clearest glimpse of Maria herself. Her childlike doting on her spaniel, no doubt a charming whimsy, nonetheless suggests her own petted immaturity. Her devoted suitor can only have been frustrated to see her lapdog enjoying Maria's endearments while he suffered her petulance and neglect.

The poem's eulogy for Maria concludes: "I'd resign all my natural graces,/E'en now, if I could with 'Daphne' change places"—that is, folded to Maria's breast. Did Dickens, one wonders, ever find himself so favored?

His own epitaph comes last: "A sweet pair of eyes sent him home to his grave."

One wonders how Maria's family responded to the amateur verse and satiric banter of "The Bill of Fare." They almost certainly heard it declaimed by its pert young author himself, for he loved to read his own works to an audience, and "The Bill of Fare" probably featured as after-dinner entertainment for the Beadnells and other guests at a dinner party like that described in the poem itself—perhaps a celebration of Maria's twenty-first birthday in the autumn of 1831. Dickens favored dapper clothing and colorful waistcoats, and we may imagine him festively dressed for the occasion as he recited his witty verses in the heavily upholstered and heavily curtained Beadnell drawing room to a well-fed and well-wined audience, most or all of whom figure in the poem and will recognize its many private jokes and allusions. After composing and revising for weeks and rehearsing repeatedly, he has his lines virtually memorized.

As he performs that evening, he has mixed feelings. He is a proud author—Dickens was never modest about his achievements—and his select audience chuckles appreciatively; but he keeps an apprehensive eye on the beautiful Maria, wondering how she will respond to what is, after all, primarily a tribute to her.

When he wrote "The Bill of Fare," Dickens had been doting on Maria for a year and a half, but none of his letters to her from those months survives. The first to do so was probably written soon after "The Bill of Fare," for it mentions that he is returning Anne Beadnell's album, in which he had just transcribed his verses, while in a postscript he hopes Maria likes the poem and urges her to credit its declarations of admiration and affection. The note's ostensible purpose, however, is to request Maria to lend him a glove to serve as a pattern for his glovemaker, whom Dickens has commissioned to make a pair of gloves for Maria. She has already lent one glove for this purpose, but the glovemaker has "made some stupid mistake" about them. When can he present her with the new gloves?—as he is "most anxious indeed to see you." (More than twenty years later, he still remembered these gloves, reminding her that "I once matched a little pair of gloves for you which I recollect were blue ones.")

He is especially eager to deliver the gloves to Maria in person, because he wishes to talk to her about "the Annual." Annuals were small keepsake anthologies of verse, prose, and engravings, published for the New Year and designed as Christmas gifts for daughters or sweethearts. Their seasonal marketing helps to place the glove letter—dated only "Wednesday Morning"—in the closing weeks of 1831. Beginning in the 1820s, the vogue of annuals lasted two or three decades ("the epidemic of illustrated annuals . . . raged with considerable flimsiness and platitude for about twenty years," one contemporary later observed). It is curious to see the great novelist-to-be so eager to give his beloved such a trifling, dilettante literary production as the annuals were. In 1831 they were at the peak of their popularity, however, with more than sixty different volumes published for the following year. With so many on the market, it is impossible to know which one Dickens hoped to give Maria; perhaps that was the very question he wished to discuss with her. He was not at all sure, though, that she would deign to receive such a gift from him. "Let me entreat of you do not refuse so slight a token of regard from me," he urged her; "surely you will not refuse so trivial a present: a mere commonplace trifle; a common present even among the merest 'friends.'" His pleading suggests Maria's power—and, perhaps, her fickleness.

The bracketing of "friends" in quotation marks, as he begs her to accept his gift, implies that Maria and he were rather more than just friends, but the letter also hints at a cooling, or at least a chilly caprice, in her regard. He feels obligated to defend the propriety of asking her for a glove: "Pray do not think this wrong under existing circumstances." The circumspect, underscored phrase evidently alludes to some unhappy alteration in their affairs. Correspondence between them must be kept clandestine—concealed not just from the Beadnells but from his own family as well, for he assures Maria that no one at his own home will know she has sent him either glove or letter: "I shall be very busy at home and alone all day tomorrow as my mother and sister will be in town."

Such hints reveal that Dickens's courtship had once prospered—Maria had tolerated or even encouraged his use of the affectionate "My dear Maria," for example, and he had written verses rejoicing in her favor:

> This charming spot my home shall be
> While dear "Maria" keeps the key,
> I'll settle here, no more I'll roam
> But make this place my happy home.

Evidently the Beadnells had soon developed other ideas about the young shorthand reporter settling down in their Lombard Street parlor, however, and his visits to Maria were now limited and tightly chaperoned. It had become so difficult to speak with her privately, in fact, that he resorted to a secret correspondence, for several notes written in the summer of 1832 ask Kolle to smuggle letters to Maria. One of them suggests stage-comedy action at 2 Lombard Street. Soliciting Kolle to deliver a note to Maria, Dickens explains: "I should not have written it (for I should have communicated it's [*sic*] contents verbally) were it not that I lost the opportunity by keeping the old gentleman out of the way as long as possible last night." Spending an evening at the Beadnells with Kolle, Dickens as loyal friend has drawn off Mr. Beadnell's attention, perhaps feigning interest in his wearisome political opinions, thereby sacrificing his own chance to speak with Maria—so that with papa distracted, Kolle can pay court to Maria's sister Anne. Dickens can't help but feel that Kolle owes him a favor in return: a much-needed favor, for though Dickens can speak to Maria among company, he is forbidden to write her. "You know so well my existing situation," he reminds Kolle, "that you must be almost perfectly aware of the general nature of the note."

That Kolle knew the situation so well is unfortunate, for otherwise Dickens's note might have explained it to us. Probably the "existing situation" was much the same as the *existing circumstances*" of the earlier glove letter, namely a ban on correspondence between Dickens and Maria: such confidential exchanges might be thought to imply an engagement. For now, at least, Maria was willing to violate the ban and receive his contraband letters. Perhaps there were forbidden visits as well. According to a Beadnell family tradition, "Dickens was on several occasions hidden in the china cupboard at No. 2 Lombard Street."

Indeed, if Maria had given him no cause for hope at some point, even the relentless Dickens is unlikely to have persisted in courting her for three years. "The Bill of Fare" had lamented "happy days now pass'd away," and during the waning days of their connection he sadly recalled palmy days in the past: "Situated as we have been once I have . . . too often thought of our earlier correspondence, and too often looked back to happy hopes the loss of which have made me the miserable wretch I am, to breathe the slightest hint to any creature living of one single circumstance that ever passed between us." Later yet, reproaching Maria for chatting too freely to a friend, he wrote that "recollecting what had passed between ourselves I was more than hurt more than annoyed at the bare idea of your confiding the tale to *her* of all people living."

But what exactly was this secret tale? Stolen kisses? A clandestine engagement? Years later, he wrote to her: "How it all happened as it did, we shall never know on this side of Time; but if you had ever told me then what you tell me now, I know myself well enough to be thoroughly assured that the simple truth and energy which were in my love would have overcome everything." Since he later burned every personal letter he had ever received, we will never know just what Maria (now Mrs. Winter) had said to elicit this stirring declaration; but she had apparently claimed that she had rejected him those many years past against her own inclination. Whether this was actually the case will, barring new evidence, forever remain a mystery.

Later accounts of Dickens's courtship of Maria usually assert that her parents were chary of her young suitor, not only because of his own uncertain prospects but also because of his father's chronic financial distress—especially alarming, no doubt, to a banker like Mr. Beadnell. In November 1831, around the time of "The Bill of Fare," Mr. Dickens senior had been summoned to appear in the Court for Relief of Insolvent Debtors, a disgrace which would have furrowed Mr. Beadnell's eyebrows when he saw notice of the summons in *The London Gazette*. Nor was it Mr. Dickens's first appearance at the Insolvent Debtors' Court. Perhaps this latest embarrassment determined Beadnell to scotch his daughter's romance with the son of such a shiftless family. (Years later, when Dickens was prosperous and celebrated, it was Maria's husband who went bankrupt.)

The Beadnells' wish to rid their daughter of her importunate suitor is often cited as the reason that Maria was at some point dispatched to school in Paris. "My existence was once entirely uprooted and my whole Being blighted," Dickens recalled, "by the Angel of my soul being sent there to finish her education!" Just when she left for Paris and how long she stayed are mysteries, however. An early period in Dickens's courtship seems the most likely time for the Angel of his soul sojourning abroad. Maria turned twenty-one in November 1831, and her schooling should have been finished by then, but the removal to Paris might nonetheless have come later. "The Bill of Fare," composed about the time of her twenty-first birthday, makes no discernible allusion to any absence. But she seems curiously missing from letters written to Kolle during the latter months of the following year, 1832, with no requests that letters be smuggled into 2 Lombard Street, and in fact no apparent reference to Maria's being around at all. One despondent note, written during a rainy week, remarks that "my cold is about as bad as a Cold can be, and on the whole I feel tolerably happy and comfortable to day, the state of the weather being so admirably adapted to dispel any gloomy ideas of which I always have a plentiful stock." Perhaps his gloom was owing to Maria's absence abroad.

Her schooling in Paris, whenever it occurred, may have extinguished her flickering interest in Dickens. If so, Mr. Beadnell could have congratulated himself on his strategy—if she had in fact been sent abroad to disengage her from an unwelcome suitor. But there is no specific evidence that the Beadnells sent Maria away to separate them. Dickens's relations with her parents were subject to fluctuations; an undated note to Kolle, possibly from early 1833, suggests the uncertainty: "With our friends the Beadnell's [sic] too you can do no wrong; I am not so sure of coming off well." But he maintained amicable relations with Mr. Beadnell for many years afterward: he was a dinner guest of the Beadnells five or six years later, for example, and on another occasion invited them to attend a play at Covent Garden Theatre with him; and he wrote Beadnell letters of condolence on the deaths of his son in 1839 and his wife in 1849. In 1852, when Dickens was on his way to perform in an amateur theatrical production in Shrewsbury, Mr. Beadnell, now retired and living near Shrewsbury, invited him to visit, and Dickens replied cordially: "Your handwriting is like a breath of my hobbydehoyhood and is delightful to encounter." Beadnell may have been a bore, but Dickens seems to have borne no resentment.

Even if parental disapproval asserted itself, moreover, Dickens's pleas to Maria imply that she herself was much of the problem. In urging her to accept the gift of an annual, he had felt obliged to assure her: "Do not misunderstand me: I am not desirous by making presents or by doing any other act to influence your thoughts, wishes, or feelings in the slightest degree." Did Maria typically receive gifts so ungraciously as to regard them as insidious persuasions, or bribes? That Dickens thought this abject disclaimer necessary suggests that she was a difficult customer. She had forbidden him to see her: "I cannot unless you will grant me an opportunity speak to you either on this, or any other subject;—I hope and trust you will not refuse: consider how long it is since I have seen you." While her parents might discourage visits to Lombard Street, his entreaties suggest that the difficulties of giving Maria a gift and of seeing her had less to do with her scruples as a dutiful daughter than with her own resolve, or caprice: "Surely, surely you will not refuse. . . . I hope and trust you will not refuse."

This chill occurred only about halfway through his three-year pursuit of Maria, and perhaps she soon smiled on him again. But whatever the chronology of their romance—however long and however steadily the sunshine of her favor lasted—she eventually decided to cut him loose. The final crisis arrived in 1833, but had probably been gestating for months, if not longer; the glove letter suggests she had begun to fall away, or at least waver, as early as the autumn of 1831. Later he recalled "many" melancholy late-night perambulations to Lombard Street during their growing estrangement: "When we were falling off from each other, I came from the House of Commons many a night at two or three o'Clock in the morning, only to wander past the place you were asleep in." The Beadnells' by no means lay on his way home from Westminster; his detours to Lombard Street took him about two miles out of his way and left him a hike of another three miles along dark streets to reach his own home. Such melancholy late-night pilgrimages to the shrine of his beloved suggest that his own ardor was scarcely diminished—that the "falling off" was entirely on Maria's part.

In February 1833, Dickens turned twenty-one and his parents, perhaps prompted by Dickens himself, gave a party to celebrate his coming of age. Invitations to a journalist friend and to Henry Kolle and Kolle's two brothers survive; there is no solid evidence that Maria was invited or attended. Thirty years later, however, he wrote a reminiscent essay, "Birthday Celebrations," which purports to describe his twenty-first birthday:

> I gave a party on the occasion. She was there. It is unnecessary to name Her, more particularly; She was older than I, and had pervaded every chink and crevice of my mind for three or four years.

Though "Birthday Celebrations" is hardly reliable autobiography, Maria may have attended the gala, as the essay claims. But by now her interest had vanished. Soon after, he wrote the first of a series of five despairing love letters to her, and moved by sentimentality or vanity she preserved them. Together they show a youthful romance in its waning days, and give us our best glimpse of young Charles Dickens in love.

The first of these letters is dated March 18, 1833, six weeks after his twenty-first birthday. His letter about gloves, a year and a half earlier, had begun "My dear Maria"; now he salutes her as "Dear Miss Beadnell" and plunges into his motive for writing. After a "painful struggle," he has determined to return "the little present"—probably a miniature portrait of herself—which she had given him "sometime since (which I have always prized as I still do far beyond anything I ever possessed)." In addition to this cherished icon, he is also returning other "mementos of our past correspondence" (tied together, he remembered more than twenty years later, "with a blue ribbon, of the color of the gloves"). This reluctant renunciation has been compelled, he explains, by her recent coldness—perhaps a snub at his own birthday party: "Our meetings of late have been little more than so many displays of heartless indifference" on her part, while for him "they have never failed to prove a fertile source of wretchedness and misery." His courtship "has long since been worse than hopeless," and "further perseverance . . . can only expose me to deserved ridicule." Such being the case, it would be "mean and contemptible" of him to "keep by me one gift of yours or to preserve one single line or word of remembrance or affection from you."

He may have felt it chivalrous to return Maria's letters and gifts; such tokens of past entanglements could, after all, be embarrassing, even dangerous (twenty years later, Lady Dedlock of *Bleak House* would be undone by old love letters). But the melodramatic gesture may simply have been an excuse for writing to Maria; as an avid theater-goer, Dickens knew stage protocol for a lover's renunciation. Having explained his return of the mementos, he went on: "I have but one word more to say and I say it in my own vindication," a character-istic swerve into self-justification, for Dickens could not easily admit himself at fault, and "one word more" turned into several hundred, lauding himself—"I deserve the merit of having ever throughout our intercourse acted fairly, intelligibly, and honorably"—and chastising her: "I have never held out encouragement which I knew I never meant; I have never indirectly sanctioned hopes which I well knew I did not intend to fulfil," and so on.

Thinking it unwise to end on a sour note, however, he closed by assuring her of his eternal affection and good wishes: "Nothing will ever afford me more real delight than to hear that you the object of my first, and my last love, are happy. If you are as happy as I hope you may be, you will indeed possess every blessing that this World can afford."

Reading this poignant letter, any right-feeling woman would be moved by the magnanimity of her forlorn lover, stricken by reminders of her own inconsistency and neglect, flattered by the vehemence of his feelings, melted by his unalterable love, and alarmed that she might be about to lose her generous and devoted admirer—or so Dickens might have imagined Maria's response.

She was in fact strongly moved—moved to send his letter straight back to him, with a note complaining of its bitter tone (although before this dramatic gesture, she took the trouble to transcribe a copy for her records).

Her stern rebuff must have seemed promising, however. His own letter had been a desperate attempt to provoke some show of interest—even anger. Any response was better than apathetic silence. In eliciting a reply, even a rebuke, he achieved his purpose. By replying to his fervent rhetoric, Maria became, ironically and accidentally, one of his earliest appreciative critics. Indeed, she seems to have admired his letter more than she admired Dickens himself. Her literary judgment, at any rate, was sound, for in his stagy farewell we may glimpse the embryonic novelist. For all the urgency and even desperation of his feelings, his letter sketches a small romantic melodrama: a beautiful, fickle charmer is confronted by her earnest, devoted lover; remonstrating indignantly, he returns her gifts; and yet, though heartbroken, he shows generosity of spirit and hope for reconciliation.

The only element missing in this story was the heroine's change of heart: her contrition, repentance, and loving embrace of the loyal hero. Several years later, Dickens would write a play, *The Village Coquettes*, with much the same plot, and a happy ending. But though enjoying her leading role in Dickens's melodramatic courtship, Maria refused to write the final happy scene.

Nonetheless, he persisted. Her rebuke had at any rate given him a reason to write again, and he sent her a conciliatory letter, "expressive of the same sentiments as I ever had felt and ever should feel towards you to my dying day." This letter does not survive; once again, in her preferred means of rebuff, Maria sent it straight back "without even the formality of an envelope" (he complained). So promptly did this second letter rebound that she did not even pause to make a copy for her private archive; perhaps she found his epistolary style less interesting in its conciliatory vein. To this second snub, he refrained from responding: "I know what your feelings must have been," he remarked later, "and by them I regulated my conduct."

With this second rejection, his courtship of Maria was apparently over. The following month, April 1833, his friend Kolle became engaged to Maria's sister Anne, and Dickens congratulated him with morose self-pity: "Although unfortunately and unhappily for myself I have no *fellow feeling* with you—no cause to sympathize with your past causes of annoyance, or your present prospects of happiness,—I am not the less disposed to offer my heartfelt congratulations to you because you are, or at all events will be what I never can—happy and contented." Even so, he had not given up hope of seeing Maria again, for he was in the process of organizing and directing an evening of private theatricals which he expected her to attend.

The theatrical evening took place some five weeks after she had rejected his two letters. The Dickens house was elaborately converted into a small theater, and, setting the pattern for many later theatricals, he marshaled the production with vigorous generalship: "The family are busy, the *Corps dramatique* are all anxiety, the scenery is all completing rapidly, the machinery is finished, the Curtain hemmed, the Orchestra complete." Three plays would be performed: an operetta titled *Clari; or the Maid of Milan*, followed by two short farces. Dickens managed the entire production and acted in all three plays. His brothers, sisters, and father were all assigned parts; friends and family connections filled out the cast. A poster advertising the performance was printed. A band, "numerous and complete," was assembled and rehearsed.

To this elaborate event, the Beadnells were invited. If friendship and curiosity were not sufficient inducements, they were likely to attend because Anne Beadnell's fiancé Henry Kolle had a role in *Clari* and had also helped with the scenery.

Clari was a melodrama in three acts, interspersed with songs. It had first been performed ten years earlier, at the Theatre Royal at Covent Garden. Its single lasting contribution to English-speaking culture was the song "Home, Sweet Home":

> 'Mid pleasures and palaces though we may roam,
> Be it ever so humble, there's no place like home!
>> Home, sweet home!
>> There's no place like home.

The plot centers on a country girl, Clari, induced by a false promise of marriage to elope with Duke Vivaldi—a cad with no intention of marrying a peasant maiden. Despite appearances, however, Clari remains chaste, even while closeted at the duke's summer palace waiting for him to fulfill his promise. She longs to return home— hence "Home, Sweet Home"—and when her conscience (like Claudius's in *Hamlet*) is stung by an interlude within the play, she resolves to flee the duke, return home, and throw herself on her parents' mercy. The duke, repentant and remorseful, follows her, and the play ends with Clari reconciled with her parents and betrothed to the reformed duke. Dickens's older sister Fanny played Clari; Dickens played Clari's angry father, Rolamo, who appears only in the last scene, allowing Dickens to devote himself to off-stage management until the end.

When Rolamo does come on stage, however, his melodramatic grief and wrath dominate; it was characteristic of Dickens to give himself a Lear-like role with lavish histrionic emotions—both melting:

> A father's curse is heavy! dreadful his anguish when that curse is wrested from him! Shall I paint this agonizing suffering to you, child? I can do so, for I have *felt* it.—I feel it now. (*Weeps.*) Once I had a daughter.

. . . and raging:

> (*Violently*) Hence, hence! I know you not. My sight rejects you—spurns you. If you have wasted all the spoils of guilt, there, there's gold! your idol, gold, gold, for which you

bartered all your hopes of bliss! (*Dashes down a purse violently on the earth.*)

Dickens had seen *Clari* performed professionally, and his fondness for it reveals his taste for the melodrama on which he had been theatrically suckled. Clari's predicament—a humble maiden's innocence and virtue tempted by love for an upper-class rake—foreshadows several novel plots—the seduction of Little Em'ly in *David Copperfield*, fifteen years later, for example, and later yet the dilemma of Lizzie Hexam in *Our Mutual Friend*. When, as Rolamo, Dickens wept for his daughter Clari, Dickens was only twenty-one; but in his rants and tears, the future was fermenting.

No account of the *Clari* performance exists. Several months later, he wrote a comic sketch, "Mrs. Joseph Porter 'Over the Way,'" about an ambitious family theatrical:

> Most extensive were the preparations . . . as the day fixed for the representation of the Private Play which had been "many months in preparation", approached. The whole family was infected with the mania for Private Theatricals; the house, usually so clean and tidy, was . . . "regularly turned out o' windows"; the dining room, dismantled of its furniture and ornaments, presented a strange jumble of flats, flies, wings, lamps, bridges, clouds, thunder and lightning, festoons and flowers, daggers and foil, and various other messes in theatrical slang included under the comprehensive name of "properties". The bedrooms were crowded with scenery, the kitchen was occupied by carpenters. Rehearsals took place every other night in the drawing room. . . .

In "Mrs. Joseph Porter," this elaborate amateur performance of *Othello* degenerates into a debacle.

Given Dickens's energetic and efficient management, *Clari* probably went off more successfully, but with respect to Maria the evening was another disappointment. A letter he wrote several weeks later implies that she attended, as it casually alludes to an incident of the evening as if she were familiar with it. But if present, she apparently made no attempt to greet him, let alone ingratiate herself, for Dickens complained that "on the night of the play after we went up stairs," he was instead bothered by a close friend of Maria's, one Mary Anne Leigh: "I could not get rid of her." Had Maria commissioned Mary Anne to distract her tiresome lover? Or was Mary Anne taking advantage of Maria's neglect of him? Later, Maria—cynically?—accused Dickens of carrying on a flirtation with Mary Anne.

The *Clari* production took place on April 27, 1833. Two weeks later, Dickens and Maria somehow encountered one another again, for we hear of him protesting to her in person that he had never made the troublesome Mary Anne Leigh a confidante in any matter touching himself and Maria; but that he had just heard "by chance that days even weeks ago" Mary Anne had made such an outrageous claim. The day after encountering Maria, he sat down to write her an indignant letter, vigorously repeating his protest. In fact, he claimed, Mary Anne had "quite unasked volunteered the information that *you* had made her a Confidante *of all that had ever passed between us without reserve.*" Again, one wonders exactly what *had* passed between Maria and Dickens— but in writing to Maria, he had no reason to spell out what she herself knew. His wording hints at an understanding of some kind, perhaps even (in his suggestible mind) an engagement: "Situated as we have been once[,] I have . . . too often thought of our earlier correspondence, and too often looked back to happy hopes the loss of which have made me the miserable reckless wretch I am, to breathe the slightest hint to any creature living of one single circumstance that ever passed between us—much less to *her*" (that is, Mary Anne Leigh).

The Mary Anne Leigh imbroglio excited him to histrionic bluster ("I care as little for her malice as I do for her"), but it had an almost schoolgirl quality to it as well. Since he had already made his denial to Maria in person, why repeat it in writing the next day? Most likely because Mary Anne's alleged duplicity offered a happy pretext for again writing to Maria and trying to coax a response from her. He was desperate to stay in touch, to prevent her from slipping away from him. He writes, he explains, to ask her permission to send Mary Anne "a violent note" of protest at her "interference." In fact, he admits, he has already written such a note and simply seeks Maria's consent to post it. "I need hardly say that if it be sent at all it should be at once and I therefore hope to receive your decision tomorrow." The hoped-for letter conveying Maria's permission was certainly of greater interest than his protest to Mary Anne Leigh. "I have once again to beg your immediate answer," his letter to Maria concludes. It was smuggled to her by his trusty ally Kolle, who as Anne Beadnell's fiancé was a welcome visitor to 2 Lombard Street—as Dickens at this point was not.

As he hoped, Maria replied promptly, and after waiting anxiously for the postman's knock he indited a reply at once, neglecting any salutation: "I cannot forbear replying to your note this moment received Miss Beadnell." Her note had evidently been quarrelsome and accusatory—which for his purposes was good enough, providing an excuse to respond and a subject for expostulation. His principal subject was, again, the useful Mary Anne Leigh.

In all of Dickens's usually well-turned correspondence, there is scarcely a more vehement and galloping effusion than this letter, cluttered with dashes and underscoring, lacking in coherence, clarity, and punctuation: "It is quite a mistake on your part but knowing (and there cannot be a stronger proof of my disliking her) what she was knowing her admirable qualifications for a Confidante and recollecting what had passed between ourselves I was more than hurt more than annoyed at the bare idea of confiding to *her* of all people living." The triviality of the dispute is overwhelmed by the rush and clatter of the rhetoric. As he knew, sparks thrown off by conflict might ignite amatory feelings, and even hostility was preferable to indifference.

Amidst her latest complaints and accusations, Maria had asked to see Dickens's letter of rebuke to Mary Anne Leigh before she would sanction its posting. He was happy to oblige; submitting the letter for her approval would involve another exchange of letters. He paused long enough in his tirade to discuss practical arrangements, again making use of the obliging Kolle: "To return to the question of what is best to be done"—actually, this question had not been raised—"I go to Kolle's at 10 oClock tomorrow Evening and I will inclose to you and give to him then a copy of the note which if I send any I *will* send to Marianne Leigh." After this business-like interruption, he returned to complaint and self-pity. If worship and gloves would not win Maria, perhaps anger, or feigned anger, would stir her. Beyond the torrent of rhetoric, his goal was simply to revive her interest. Concluding, he gave up all bellicose pretense: "Towards *you* I never had and never can have an angry feeling."

His letter to Mary Anne Leigh was duly conveyed to Maria for her inspection and approval, along with a brief covering note to Maria herself, encouraging her to respond. In his aggressive previous letter, he had haughtily declared that "I do not ask your *advice*. All I ask is whether you see any reason to *object*." Now he humbly invited her comments and correction: "Of course you will at least on this point (I mean Marianne Leigh's note) say what you think without reserve and any course you may propose or any alteration you may suggest shall on my word and honor be instantly adopted." To keep the correspondence with Maria alive, he sought permission to reply to her reply, if she should condescend to make one: "Should anything you may say (in returning her note) to *me* make me anxious to return any answer, may I have your permission to forward it to you?" That he needed permission to write to her shows how desperate his chances with Maria had become—for even had her parents forbidden her to correspond with young "Dickin," Maria felt free to disobey when so inclined. But her whims had first to be consulted.

She graciously and perhaps maliciously granted him permission to post his insulting note to her good friend Mary Anne Leigh. Better yet, she signified that he might write to her, Maria, again. That she wanted to hear anything he had to say about himself is doubtful, but she was naturally curious to hear what Mary Anne Leigh might say about her. Dickens's hopes rose; the Mary Anne Leigh controversy, a mere bubble, had effected something far more important, a renewed correspondence with Maria. At the same time, he worried about the logistics of this correspondence, for Kolle, "my only means of communicating with you," was about to wed Maria's sister Anne. When Kolle's daily calls at 2 Lombard Street ended, Dickens's conduit to Maria would disappear. Panicked that the Beadnells' door was about to be bolted against him, he seized on her permission to write and immediately drafted yet another letter.

This letter, he told Kolle, was "a very conciliatory note sans pride, sans reserve sans anything but an evident wish to be reconciled." The time for controversy was past: it would be a poor bargain to win the argument and lose the girl. The rights and wrongs of the Mary Anne Leigh issue were in any event unimportant, and he had no heart for further mock battles with Maria. The contretemps had created an opportunity; now was the moment to seize it: "I am most desirous of forwarding a note which had I received such permission earlier, I can assure you you would have received 'ere this." He abandoned the political complexities and acerbic tone of his earlier polemics:

> I will allow no feeling of pride no haughty dislike to making
> a conciliation to prevent my expressing it without reserve.—
> I will advert to nothing that has passed; I will not again
> seek to excuse any part I have acted or to justify it by any
> course you have ever pursued, I will revert to nothing that
> has ever passed between us.

And there follows the avowal that Dickens had wished to make all along: "I never have loved and I never can love any human creature breathing but yourself. . . . the Love I now tender you is as pure, and as lasting as at any period of our former correspondence."

He would not complicate matters by arguing, pleading, or justifying: "I could say much for myself, and I could entreat a favourable consideration in my own behalf but I purposely abstain from doing so because it would be only a repetition of an oft told tale." His object was simple: "There is nothing I have more at heart, nothing I more sincerely and earnestly desire than to be reconciled to you." In years to come, Dickens's letters would exhibit a uniformly robust self-assurance and assertive will. At twenty-one—passionately in love, and desperate—he was humble and pleading: "I am sure nothing I could say would have the effect of influencing your decision in any degree whatever. Need I say that to me it is a matter of vital import and the most intense anxiety?" With Anne Beadnell's wedding to Kolle just a few days off, he feared that Maria would not find the time to reply "within anything like the time which my impatience would name."

And so, dispatching this missive—a last throw of the dice—to his beloved Maria, he waited anxiously: "Let me entreat you to consider your determination well whatever it may be and let me implore you to communicate it to me as early as possible."

What was a question of the greatest anxiety to Dickens was of little urgency to Maria. Three days later, Kolle married her sister Anne. Maria certainly attended the wedding, as did Dickens as Kolle's best man. Had he received Maria's response by then? Even if she had not yet replied, her demeanor at the wedding would have made plain her answer—a decisive "no." The felicitous occasion of Anne Beadnell's and Henry Kolle's wedding must have been, for Dickens, a day of gloom and despair.

And on the Kolles' wedding day, May 22, 1833, the story of his youthful romance ends. Years later, he reminded Maria that "I wrote to you for the last time of all, with a dawn upon me of some sensible idea that we were changing into man and woman, saying Would you forget our little differences and separations and let us begin again? You answered me very coldly and reproachfully,—and so I went my way."

Maria's chilly note has disappeared. The Kolles' wedding was probably the last time he saw her for at least a year, and possibly much longer.

Why did Dickens lose the girl whom he wooed so long and so ardently?

In his final letter to Maria, he mentioned "differences" and "misunderstanding": "We have had many differences. . . . I have now done all I can to remove our most unfortunate and to me most unhappy misunderstanding." But the basic problem was probably little more than Maria's waning interest: she simply did not care enough for her earnest, hard-working young suitor to desire a continuance of his attentions. He was sadly aware of the imbalance in their affections: "If you had ever felt for me one hundredth part of my feeling for you there would have been little cause of regret, little coldness little unkindness between us"; and many years later he observed "that you never had the stake in that serious game which I had." Their fatal misunderstandings, whatever they might have been, were probably factitious issues invented or exploited by Maria.

One of her concerns was perhaps Dickens's modest means, lack of worldly standing, and impecunious family; she was a pampered young woman with high matrimonial expectations. That her suitor was over a year her junior may also have displeased the young belle. In his essay "Birthday Celebrations," Dickens claimed to recall his twenty-first birthday:

> It was a beautiful party. . . . Behind a door in the crumby part of the night when wine-glasses were to be found in unexpected spots, I spoke to Her—spoke out to Her. What passed, I cannot as a man of honour reveal. She was all angelical gentleness, but a word was mentioned—a short and dreadful word of three letters, beginning with a B—which, as I remarked at the moment, "scorched my brain."

The anecdote is probably exaggerated, if not fabricated; but as it tallies with several undoubted facts—Dickens's worship of Maria, her seniority, his twenty-first birthday party, and the end of his courtship soon after—it may contain an essential truth.

Ultimately, however, Maria's feelings remain a mystery. Years later, Dickens recalled her sister Anne "writing to me once (in answer to some burst of low-spirited madness of mine), and saying, 'My dear Charles, I really cannot understand Maria, or venture to take the responsibility of saying what the state of her affections is.'" If his recollection of Anne Beadnell's letter was correct—if she had been puzzled by the feelings of a younger sister with whom she was intimately acquainted—it is unlikely that we will do any better.

In failing to gain or at any rate retain Maria's affections, he was no less successful than his competitors. In one of his final letters to her, he reproached her for playing him off against other suitors: "I think I never should . . . encourage one dangler as a useful shield for—an excellent set off against—others more fortunate and doubtless more deserving." He may have been recalling this frustration years later, when *Great Expectations'* Pip makes a similar accusation against Estella. But while Estella practices on her suitors by design, Maria was probably vain enough simply to enjoy the competitive adulation of multiple danglers.

She gave her heart to none of them, however; or if she did, the man so happily distinguished failed to reciprocate. After discarding Dickens, she did not marry for another twelve years. Perhaps at twenty-one or twenty-two she was temperamentally unready to settle on anyone, Dickens or otherwise. Other suitors, moreover, perhaps less blindly enamored, may have harbored doubts about her. We should be cautious of judging Maria on small evidence: refusing to fall in love with Dickens is no evidence of a character flaw, and she may have had some vague intuition of his unsuitability for her, and hers for him. But apart from her light girlish charms and prettiness, she apparently possessed no exceptional strength of personality or character. It is a reassuring affirmation of the unreasonableness of human affections, that a Goliath like Dickens should have been so entirely baffled and defeated by a butterfly.

Like the early disappointments of many others, however, the greatest sorrow of his youth was a fortuitous blessing. To begin, it probably saved him from an unhappy marriage. He did not match himself particularly well anyway, as it turned out, but it is easy to imagine marriage to Maria as equally if not more disastrous, and even sooner—easy to imagine because, in fact, Dickens himself imagined it for us, in the marriage of *David Copperfield*'s hero to Dora Spenlow, a young flit inspired by Maria. David's giddy infatuation is disabused when Dora's silliness, so charming in the girl, proves less delightful in the wife. In the years after losing Maria, Dickens reflected on the might-have-been of marriage to her, and conceived reservations. It is probably fortunate that he married her only in fiction, for in novels an unwanted wife can easily be erased—David Copperfield's no-longer-useful Dora is dispatched to an early grave as unhesitatingly as Maria dispatched young Dickens himself.

If losing Maria was a blessing for the would-be husband, it was a blessing too for the novelist-to-be. He later wrote that, bitter as he felt about his mother's betrayal in the blacking factory episode, yet "I know how all these things have worked together to make me what I am." Maria Beadnell was an even more fateful experience: while he suffered in the blacking factory for about a year, he was enslaved to Maria for more than three years—a long time in youth, "when four years are equal to four times four." The influence of such intense emotions—for so long, at a susceptible age, on so impressible a nature as Dickens's—was profound. Twenty years later, he still shrank from the pain: "I began to write my life . . . . But as I began to approach within sight of that part of it [Maria], I lost courage and burned the rest." He did not actually burn the rest, but the memory of losing Maria brought his memoirs to a stop, never to be resumed.

As the beneficiaries of Dickens's genius, we should be thankful that just as he was entering manhood he fell in love with so reluctant a flame as Maria, for by engrossing his attention for three ardent years she deflected him from more sterile pursuits. Love may be futile, but never fruitless. He might have become inured to the petty disputes of Doctors' Commons, for example, and slid into a career in law; he might have interested himself in the parliamentary debates he recorded and squandered his gifts on politics. But the heliocentric glow and attraction of Maria—"the most disinterested days of my life had you for their Sun"—eclipsed law and politics. It was perhaps a narrow escape, for Dickens was vulnerable to quotidian fits of political indignation. Oliver Goldsmith had jested that Edmund Burke, "born for the Universe, narrow'd his mind,/And to party gave up, what was meant for mankind" ("Retaliation"). Maria saved Dickens from any such reproach. Her father's dinner-table monologues could scarcely interest him, when she outdazzled the candles.

He owed her more than just a happy escape from a wrong calling, however. When he met Maria, he already knew himself to be bright, energetic, and capable; but his ambitions had been mundane: economic security, status, a place in the sun. Falling in love spurred him to heroic endeavor. Looking back, David Copperfield would boast that "whatever I have tried to do in life, I have tried with all my heart to do well; that whatever I have devoted myself to, I have devoted myself to completely; that in great aims and in small, I have always been thoroughly in earnest." So too Dickens: his steel resolve and inexhaustible striving owed much to Maria Beadnell. "I began to fight my way out of poverty and obscurity," he later told her, "with one perpetual idea of you."

She taught him how passionately he could love, and how hard he could work. "All that any one can do to raise himself by his own exertions and unceasing assiduity I have done, and will do," he reminded her as his hopes dimmed in 1833; and years later, he remarked that "I have positively stood amazed at myself ever since!" He would recollect his self-amazing exertions in *David Copperfield*. Aflame with love, and poor, David resolves to "take my woodman's axe in my hand, and clear my own way through the forest of difficulty, by cutting down the trees until I came to Dora." The Dickens family history of improvidence and insolvency must have worried Maria's parents; a suitor for their youngest daughter should possess both present means and good prospects. Maria herself no doubt expected the same (*David Copperfield*'s Dora dissolves in grief when David confesses his poverty). Worldly desire for money and gentility might have awakened Dickens's energy and genius, but Maria was a far more highly charged motive.

She departed; the strenuous exertion persisted. It was an ambiguous legacy. Driving himself hard, chopping his way through difficulties, he had neither leisure nor motive for reflection. Yet his love for Maria brought wisdom of a different sort. He had little formal schooling— "small Latin, and less Greek," like Shakespeare. His reader's ticket at the British Museum gave him access to Goldsmith, Joseph Addison, Shakespeare, and other classic English writers: it was his closest approach to a university education. But Maria taught him what he could never have learned at the British Museum or Oxford. For three years, when he was young and highly susceptible, his emotions swirled around a young woman, and what he learned of love—of its devotion, desire, longing, and absorption, as well as misery, unhappiness, and despair—he learned from loving and losing her. Like Sleeping Beauty, her amatory nature awakened by a prince's kiss, Dickens was launched into manhood by the charmed kiss of Maria Beadnell.

Unlike the prince's kiss, Maria's was casual and, to herself, meaningless. She fluttered off; but looking back, Dickens acknowledged her fateful impact: "Whatever of fancy, romance, energy, passion, aspiration and determination belong to me," he told her, "I never have separated and never shall separate from the hard hearted little woman—you—whom it is nothing to say I would have died for, with the greatest alacrity!" In such eager gallantry lay the origin of one of his most potent myths, the lover's self-sacrifice. A quarter century later, for example, the idea of Sydney Carton's sacrifice of himself for Lucie Manette would inspire *A Tale of Two Cities*. In Dickens's love for Maria, desire was exalted and transfigured by innocence and devotion, and he clung to this ideal.

Two years after declaring in his last desperate letter to Maria that "I never can love any human creature breathing but yourself," Dickens became engaged to another young woman, Catherine Hogarth, and married her the following year.

His successful courtship of Catherine suggests a fairly rapid recovery from Maria. Yet poor Catherine scarcely scratched, let alone erased, Maria's influence. He later blamed Maria for a permanent alteration in his sensibility:

> My entire devotion to you, and the wasted tenderness of those hard years which I have ever since half loved half dreaded to recall, made so deep an impression on me that I refer to it a habit of suppression which now belongs to me, which I know is no part of my original nature, but which makes me chary of shewing my affections, even to my children, except when they are very young.

Wounded once, he would not commit himself so wholeheartedly a second time, and the unlucky Catherine became an unknowing victim of the love he had "wasted" on Maria.

What if anything did Catherine know of the enchantress who preceded her? Dickens never told her about the blacking factory, and perhaps she knew nothing of Maria either. Did she suspect that behind his brisk, businesslike wooing of her there lurked a ghostly rival, a girl who a little earlier had "represented the whole world to me"? Catherine herself had a more modest claim on his affections. "Unresolved, apprehensive, intoxicating sexual attraction is what Dickens learned" from Maria, suggests David Parker, long-time curator of the Dickens Museum in London. Dickens's feelings about Catherine were less intense. Having burned for Maria, he was now content with, or resigned to, lukewarm romance. His letters to Catherine before their marriage reveal "only longing for companionship, contentment, tranquillity," Parker observes. "Intense, erotic passion, longing, and frustration are nowhere to be found."

With Maria, Dickens had known ecstasy and suffered despair; with Catherine, he avoided risk by lowering his expectations. Having lost Maria, he had lost "the freshest and the best, forever" (as Fitzgerald's Jay Gatsby feels after losing Daisy). There was no choice but to move on. No longer an ardent boy, by 1835 Dickens was a rising professional writer, and he wanted a comfortable, respectable home in which to enjoy his prosperity. For such a home he needed a good income and an agreeable, genteel wife—but while his income was growing, the wife was lacking. For all his genius, and despite his sentimental radicalism, his domestic expectations were entirely conventional. Catherine's family was more distinguished and cultivated than Maria's; Mr. Hogarth was a lawyer, journalist, and music critic. Within a few years Dickens would far surpass him, but at twenty-three or twenty-four he was much impressed by his prospective father-in-law, who seemed almost a stronger draw than his fiancée herself: "I have . . . fixed Saturday next, for my marriage with Miss Hogarth—the daughter of a gentleman who has recently distinguished himself by a celebrated work on Music, who was the most intimate friend and companion of Sir Walter Scott, and one of the most eminent among the Literati of Edinburgh." Catherine in her own right was an attractive, affectionate young woman—a prudent choice. But he would have disdained prudence had he not shipwrecked so badly with Maria.

Loving Maria was a rich experience; losing her was more valuable yet. Within a few years, *The Pickwick Papers* brought him profit and acclaim, and for the rest of his life he was prosperous and celebrated. But just as his memories of the blacking factory lingered as a reminder of abandonment and hopelessness, so Maria haunted him as a lost golden ideal, a proof that worldly success alone was sadly inadequate: "There was no triumph, after all, without a girl concerned" (Fitzgerald observed in "'The Sensible Thing'"). Many years later—middle-aged, busy, famous—Dickens still clung to the idea of the young Maria. In 1855, forty-three-years-old and father of nine, he confessed that he had revisited the site of her old home on Lombard Street "within these twelve months, hoping it was not ungrateful to consider whether any reputation the world can bestow, is repayment to a man for the loss of such a vision of his youth as mine." In David Copperfield's lament that "the happiness I had vaguely anticipated, once, was not the happiness I enjoyed, and there was always something wanting," we hear the whisper of Dickens's own disappointment.

"'Tis better to have loved and lost," Tennyson argued, "than never to have loved at all." For Dickens, certainly, both loving and losing were invaluable gifts. The sorrow of losing Maria would help to protect him from the shallow complacencies lurking in the worldly success to come. In the years ahead, beneath his prosperous life and the busy world of his fiction—crowded with comedy, irony, eccentricity, sentimentality, populism, melodrama, and indignation—brooded a sorrow that lay "too deep for tears."

When Dickens's letters to Maria were first published, in 1908, their editor observed that "one of the strangest features of the whole romance is that Dickens appears to have lived for years in a perpetual dream, in which he could never picture the girl he had loved in any real or imaginative situation apart from that in which he had known her in his boyhood." Dickens was not only unable to imagine Maria except as he had known her as a girl; he could imagine happiness itself only in the form of Maria at twenty. She had seized his imagination early, and for years no other woman loosened her grip. Love may be beautiful the second time around, but no later passion can be so revolutionary as the first, or so indelible.

Maria introduced Dickens to romantic love itself—exhilarating, overpowering, all-absorbing, transforming. She introduced him as well to loss and regret, and became his image of the illusory fulfillment that the fancy pursues but life denies. In his early novels, every hero gets his girl, but Dickens knew that this gratifying consummation was contrary to general experience—certainly to his own.

A quarter century after he lost Maria, Dickens wrote two endings for *Great Expectations*. In the second, a wish-fulfillment conclusion that he had been persuaded to write by a friend, he rewarded his hero Pip by bringing him together, finally (and improbably), with his long-loved Estella.

But in the original ending, Pip sees Estella only once again after he has lost her, in a random and brief encounter many years later. With this glimpse of his old flame, and with his great expectations now only a sad memory, Pip continues down the street, still alone, into a loveless future.

CHAPTER 3

So perfect a creature never breathed:
Mary Hogarth

Macheath, the rogue hero of *The Beggar's Opera*, fondly recalls his roaming days, when "My heart was so free,/It roved like the bee":

> I sipped each flower,
> I changed ev'ry hour.

Had Dickens been similarly cavalier, he might have shaken the dust of Maria Beadnell from his feet and strolled on to a new flirtation. After all, he was a rising young man with sufficient charms of appearance and manner; and there were flounces enough in London.

But he was too earnest in his nature, and too bewitched.

The year after Maria's cool farewell, he wrote some verses for a twelve-year-old girl named Ellen Beard, younger sister of a fellow reporter and close friend, Thomas Beard. Ellen had evidently asked her brother's clever colleague to contribute to her album. At first declining, Dickens eventually obliged with a tale in the manner of Aesop, in forty-eight lines of rhyming verse, gloomily titled "A Fable (Not a gay one)."

"A Fable" begins with a Mr. Pen and a Miss Paper discussing Pen's refusal to write a verse for her. Pen laments:

> Could I behold skies, streams, and flowers
> With childhood's laughing, tearless eye,
> I might write strains for a Lady's ear,
> But my thoughts are so weary grown,
> They ne'er could charm your bosom, my dear.
> They're almost too sad for my own.

Then, stepping out of his fable, Dickens turns to address young Ellen herself:

> Ellen, I've caught the Pen's disease;
> And as my hopes are quite as dim,
> I'll try the same excuse if you please
> As succeeded so well with him.
> There's this distinction betwixt the two:—
> Ye Powers above befriend me!
> While he is easily made anew,
> There is not a knife can mend me.

(The final lines allude to the worn nibs of quill pens, mended with a knife.)

"A Fable" reveals that it was no secret among Dickens's circle that he still carried a torch for Maria; even his friend Beard's little sister apparently knew about it. The verses in Ellen Beard's album are signed "Boz," a pen name he first used in print in August 1834, and she received the album as a gift on September 20 of that year. "A Fable" probably dates from late September or October 1834—well over a year after Maria jilted Dickens in the spring of 1833. There was no roving like the bee for Dickens, sipping each flower.

In retrospect, his writing career seems inevitable: Destiny anointed him a great novelist. In 1833, however, it was by no means obvious that the young shorthand reporter, grinding away at parliamentary debates and spurned by the girl he loved, would ever write anything.

It was the unwilling girl herself whom we can thank for nudging him into writing.

The first edition of Shakespeare's sonnets carried the notoriously cryptic dedication: "To the onlie begetter of these insuing sonnets Mr. W. H." The identity of Mr. W. H. and his role in begetting the sonnets remain mysteries. Not so with the chief begetter of Dickens's earliest stories—and indirectly the novels to follow—*Pickwick Papers* and *Oliver Twist*, *A Christmas Carol* and *David Copperfield*, *Bleak House* and *Great Expectations*. It would seem a heavy responsibility for a light young woman like Maria Beadnell. Yet a single champagne bottle launches a battleship.

Only a few months after Maria repulsed him, Dickens wrote his first story, "a little paper," which an obscure magazine accepted and published. Proud and encouraged—"I have had a polite and flattering communication from The Monthly people requesting more papers," he told his friend Kolle—he soon wrote another, and the rest followed.

Mundane circumstances helped to nudge him into writing. The summer parliamentary recess of 1833, extending into October, left him idle and without income. "I am always entirely unemployed during the recess," he observed in June, the month after Maria had dropped him. "I need hardly say that I have many strong inducements for wishing to be so as little as possible." With more time on his hands than money in his pocket, he thought it a good time to step beyond his shorthand reporting and attempt to augment his income. His "first effusion" in *The Monthly Magazine*, a light story titled "A Sunday Out of Town," was published anonymously and earned him nothing, however; the *Monthly* was "'rather backward in coming forward' with the needful," he told Kolle, and threatened to send future articles elsewhere. Nonetheless, he continued to submit sketches to the *Monthly*, nine over the next fifteen months, and the *Monthly* continued to publish them without payment.

Perhaps he was taking the long view, hoping that his sketches in the *Monthly* would eventually open the door to other periodicals (as they did). For the time being, authorship alone was consoling. Years later, he recalled that his eyes "dimmed with joy and pride" when, in December 1833, his first article appeared "in all the glory of print." Since the article was unsigned, however, his celebrity was limited to the small circle of his family and friends. Not until his sixth article in the *Monthly*, eight months later, were any of his contributions signed—and then only with the pen name "Boz."

All this would seem to have little to do with Maria, to whose loss Dickens was apparently resigned. He could scarcely hope to attract her notice by anonymous articles in an unknown magazine she would probably never see.

So he immediately took steps to bring his authorship to her attention. When his first sketch appeared in print, he invited himself over to the Kolles': "I intend with the gracious permission of yourself and Spouse to look in upon you some Evening this week," he wrote Kolle. "I do not write to you however for the purpose of ceremoniously making this important announcement but to beg Mrs. K's criticism of a little paper of mine (the first of a Series) in *the Monthly*. . . . I haven't a Copy to send but if the Number falls in your way, look for the Article." With a circulation of only six hundred, the *Monthly* was unlikely to fall in Kolle's way—but Dickens could ensure that it did by taking along a copy on his prospective visit.

His eagerness that Mrs. Kolle in particular read his sketch might seem puzzling, were it not that Kolle's wife was Maria's sister Anne. While Dickens may have respected Anne's literary insight, more likely he wished to get the sketch into her hands in order that it find its way into Maria's. "All that any one can do to raise himself by his own exertions and unceasing assiduity I have done," he had assured Maria six months earlier, "and will do." "A Sunday Out of Town" was proof that he was striving still. Anne Kolle probably saw Maria frequently—the Kolles lived only a mile from Lombard Street—and she could be relied on to carry along news of Maria's old beau.

His next letter to Kolle, a week later, also contained news for Maria. He had been unable to make his promised call on the Kolles; business connected with his parliamentary reporting had taken him out of town for a week. He remained eager to visit, however: "As soon as I return, be it only for a Night, however, I shall shew myself at Newington [where the Kolles lived] and must take the chance of finding you at home." Overwhelmed by his out-of-town business, "in the shape of masses of papers, plans, and prospectusses," he could not predict when he would be free to return to London. Perhaps, conveyed to Lombard Street, this description of himself immersed in weighty-sounding affairs would impress Maria.

His new writing venture was also much on his mind. He was flattered (and made sure to inform Kolle) that soon after its publication in the *Monthly*, "A Sunday Out of Town" had been pirated by another magazine, and he announced ambitious plans for more articles:

> My next paper will be "Private Theatricals" and my next "London by Night". I shall then please God commence a series of papers (the materials for which I have been noting down for some time past) called *The Parish*. Should they be successful & as publishing is hazardous, I shall cut my proposed Novel up into little Magazine Sketches.

This is the first surviving mention of a novel, though Kolle had apparently heard of the idea earlier. Were Maria to hear of these achievements and projects—and through Anne Kolle, she would—how could she not be impressed? Also intended for Maria was another remark. It was not business alone that kept him out of town, Dickens coyly noted, but also "pleasure in the shape of a very nice pair of black eyes. . . . Of course the call is imperative and must be obeyed." Anne Kolle would certainly relay this piquant item to her younger sister.

That Dickens's thoughts still hovered moth-like around Maria is evident in another remark in the same letter. By December 1833, Anne Kolle was four or five months pregnant, and he concluded with an allusion to the approaching birth:

> When there *is* a vacancy for a Godfathership either to a young lady or young gentleman,—for I am not particular,—who can afford to have one poor Godfather will you bear me in mind?—Hint this delicately to your *Missus*.

Maria would of course attend the christening of a niece or nephew; and as godfather, Dickens could insert himself into the occasion. Perhaps he was laying plans to intercept her at the baptismal font. When a son was born to the Kolles the following April, Dickens—as he had suggested—was invited to be the boy's godfather and attend the christening. Whether he saw Maria on that occasion remains a mystery. If he did, nothing came of the reunion.

Such hints of Maria that lurk in his letters to Kolle show that Dickens could not easily escape the obsession that had so long possessed him. For months, even years, she remained a sorrow, a longing, a hope, a motive. He may have stayed in touch with Kolle only because Mrs. Kolle was now Dickens's only link to Maria, otherwise out of reach behind the unwelcoming door on Lombard Street. Only gradually did his hopes expire. His last surviving letter to Kolle during this era was probably written in January 1835—by which time, having met and begun to court another young woman, he had finally resigned himself to a life without Maria. At this point, Mr. and Mrs. Kolle too dropped out of his life.

As it turned out, the timing of Maria's departure was critical. The following year, he obtained full-time employment with a well-established newspaper, *The Morning Chronicle*, giving him an augmented and steady income. No longer would his summers be idle and unremunerative. Had Maria let him dangle for a few months longer, rather than dropping him just before the parliamentary recess of 1833, he would have had less time, and perhaps less motive, to try his hand at writing sketches. And once he had become established in a busy, promising career as a professional journalist, he might never have attempted fiction at all.

Though ardent and nostalgic, he was not one to repine. Maria "had pervaded every chink and crevice" of his mind for four years, but now he was forced to accommodate himself to a world in which she was no longer the consuming motive, but only a diminished (and diminishing) hope. Rejected, he was freed—almost compelled—to redirect the creative energies he had for so long devoted to her. Writing replaced wooing; disappointed desire redirected itself into comic invention. His earliest sketches were facetious vignettes of bourgeois life.

Yet even as he moved on, Maria lingered in memory and fancy: the passion of his youth, the flame that had ignited his most intense feelings, the face of desirability, the goad to his ambitions and striving. Her image sometimes flared up vividly. Years later, he testified:

> Sometimes in the most unlikely places—in Scotland, America, Italy—on the stateliest occasions and the most unceremonious—when I have been talking to a strange face . . . I have suddenly been carried away at the rate of a thousand miles a second, and have thought "Maria Beadnell!"

Such startling moments—*"Maria Beadnell!"*—suggest the incendiary power of her memory.

"I could not," he later wrote her, "—really *could not*—at any time within this nineteen years, have been so unmindful of my old truth, and have so set my old passion aside, as to talk to you like a person in any ordinary relation towards me." The precise "nineteen years" seems to refer to a specific occasion; and as he was writing in 1855, perhaps his last meeting with Maria had been in 1836. Perhaps, however, he was referring to his marriage, in April of that year, to Catherine Hogarth.

Sometime in the late summer or early autumn of 1834, soon after he had been hired by *The Morning Chronicle*, Dickens met George Hogarth, a senior journalist who had joined the newspaper's staff at about the same time. Taking a liking to his young colleague, admiring his abilities, and perhaps mindful of his own unmarried daughters, Hogarth invited him to his home, where Dickens encountered the Hogarth girls. With almost fairy-tale plotting, he would become fatefully linked with the three elder sisters. The oldest became his wife and the mother of his ten children; the youngest became his companion, housekeeper, confidante, and (virtually) deputy wife, supplanting her older sister in all connubial roles but that of sexual partner.

But the middle of the three elder sisters, Mary Scott Hogarth, whom he knew much more briefly, became a transcendent force in his life, a sacred memory: muse, angel, even deity.

In 1834 only the eldest Hogarth sister, eighteen-year-old Catherine, was old enough for serious courting; encouraged by her parents, Dickens set about to win her. Unable to do anything halfheartedly, he wooed her with dispatch. He had finally relinquished any hope of Maria Beadnell, though he was still mourning her in the "Fable" he wrote for Ellen Beard's album in the autumn of 1834, perhaps only a month or two before he met Catherine. No doubt his unhappy experience with Maria explains his brisk, businesslike courtship of Catherine: scorched once, he would not put his hand in the fire again.

She was willing. In February 1835, he invited her to a party for his twenty-third birthday, and she "enjoyed it very much—Mr Dickens improves very much on acquaintance[;] he is very gentlemanly and pleasant." They became engaged a few months later and married the following April, just as his first novel, *The Pickwick Papers*, began appearing in monthly numbers.

Together, marriage and *Pickwick* transformed Dickens's life: 1836 was his *annus mirabilis*, both professional and personal, as the struggling young journalist was launched into both fame and family. The early numbers of *Pickwick Papers* enjoyed only modest success, but it soon became popular beyond all expectation, and "Boz" became a literary celebrity: like Lord Byron a quarter century earlier, he awoke one morning to find himself famous. His domestic life also prospered. Within days of his marriage to Catherine, she was pregnant, and early the following year, just as he was beginning a second novel, *Oliver Twist*, she gave birth to their first child, Charles Junior.

To help with the baby, Catherine's sister Mary, "a young and lovely girl," came to stay with them in their modest chambers on an upper floor of Furnival's Inn—not a hostelry, but a set of buildings which had once housed law students.

Dickens had known Mary since his earliest visits to the Hogarths in the autumn of 1834, when she was fifteen. During the following months, she served as an occasional companion and chaperone as Dickens courted her sister; and after he and Catherine married, Mary often stayed with them in their chambers in Furnival's Inn, sometimes for weeks at a time. Six weeks after the wedding, she wrote to a cousin that "I have just returned home from spending a most delightfully happy month with dearest Catherine in her own house!" Dickens grew fond of Mary, and the liking was mutual: "I am sure you would be delighted with him if you knew him he is such a nice creature and so clever he is courted and made up to by all the literary Gentleman [*sic*]." As Catherine's confinement approached, Mary stayed at Furnival's Inn often during the autumn of 1836.

Little direct evidence of her character or personality has survived, with the exception of two surviving letters she wrote to a cousin. Her voice sings out with particular charm in the earlier of them, written when she was sixteen, a letter which is mostly a rapid stream of brief newsy updates on relations and acquaintances in London—prominent among them her newly married sister Catherine and Catherine's husband, the rising young writer Charles Dickens, with whom Mary has been staying for the past month in their chambers in Furnival's Inn—"not exactly a house but a suite of rooms opening from one to another . . . they have furnished them most tastefully and elegantly." Mary includes tidbits, affectionate in tone, or at least complimentary, about such family connections as a Mr. Clay, Peter, her brothers William and James, and "my dear *Cousin* Twins," Teenie and Jane. She is especially fond of her three-year-old brother and sister: "I wish you could see my little darling pets the twins—they get more beautiful every day and so clever it is quite amusing to hear and puzzling to answer the questions they ask." Turning to "our London friends," however—whom Mary's cousin in Scotland knew from a recent visit to London—she indulges in mild satire: "Mrs Rintoul is quere [*sic*] as ever and her two sweet children as interesting," while "Mrs Lawrance and her sisters are just as pedantic and Eliza Rose as wonderful (in their eyes at least) as before." Perhaps during her stay at Furnival's Inn, Mary had acquired a touch of her brother-in-law's comic irony, just then appearing in the early chapters of *Pickwick Papers*. Though very much the effusion of a sixteen-year-old girl, Mary's letter suggests a bright, lively, warm personality, though no angel. Reading her gay, high-spirited chatter to her cousin, one can easily understand Dickens's affection.

When his son was born on Twelfth Night 1837, he spent most of the day, he fondly recalled, with Mary:

> Mary and I wandered up and down Holborn and the streets about, for hours, looking after a little table for Kate's bedroom. . . . I took her out to Brompton [where the Hogarths lived] at night as we had no place for her to sleep in; (the two mothers being with us). She came back again next

day to keep house for me, and stopped nearly the rest of the month.

Mary returned home at the end of January and wrote to her cousin about Catherine's distress at being unable to nurse her new son, along with other family news. She soon returned to Furnival's Inn, however, and over the next few months stayed there so often that looking back, Dickens remembered her as an integral and precious member of the little household, "the grace and ornament of our home for the whole time of our marriage," he wrote later. "From the day of our marriage," he told another correspondent, "the dear girl had been the grace and life of our home, our constant companion, and the sharer of all our little pleasures." Though heightened by nostalgic afterglow, his recollections make clear that he had grown very fond of Mary.

So fond that some have wondered if she had begun to steal his affections from Catherine—a suspicion enhanced by his own later assertion that his marriage had been unhappy from the start, and that "Mary . . . understood it . . . in the first months of our marriage." But this claim seems exaggerated: during those months, Mary had in fact reported that her sister and Dickens "are more devoted than ever since their Marriage if that be possible," and that he "is kindness itself to her and is constantly studying her comfort in every thing." To Dickens, Mary had become a well-loved younger sister; there is no evidence of any dangerous attraction, much less impropriety.

In March 1837, he moved his small but growing family to a larger house at 48 Doughty Street, now the Dickens House Museum. Doughty Street, gated at either end, was a good though not swank neighborhood of row houses near Mecklenburgh Square.

Here he might savor his prosperity and bright expectations in greater space and comfort. We glimpse an evening with the Dickenses in the recollection of a guest who dined at Doughty Street when they had been living there for only a month:

> Dinner in Doughty Str. I the only stranger. Mr Dickens sen [Dickens's father], Mr Hogarth [Catherine's father], Miss Dickens [Dickens's older sister Fanny], the Misses Hogarth [Mary and her younger sister Georgina]. It was a right merry entertainment; Dickens was in force, and on joining the ladies in the drawing room, Dickens sang two or three songs, one the patter song, "The Dog's Meat Man", & gave several successful imitations of the most distinguished actors of the day. Towards midnight, it was Saturday, I rose to leave, but D. stopped [me] & pressed me to take another glass of Brandy & water. This I wd. gladly have avoided, but he begged Miss Hogarth [Mary] to give it me. At the hand of the fair Hebe I did not decline it.

This reminiscence gives us a rare view of the happy days of Dickens's early prosperity. He himself (stimulated by brandy) was the fire under the bubbling pot. His conviviality; his love of popular music, even street chants; his love of the theater; and his histrionic flair emerge "in force." And the guest's particular mention of Mary Hogarth, beguiling him to accept a stirrup cup, suggests more than a long panegyric about her young feminine charms. The gaiety of this Saturday evening at 48 Doughty Street, and especially Dickens's own high spirits, helps explain his response to what soon followed.

A week later, Mary Hogarth, the fair Hebe, was dead.

On the next Saturday evening after the cheerful dinner, Dickens took Catherine and Mary to the theater. Soon after they returned to Doughty Street, Mary collapsed. "We lost no time in procuring medical assistance, or in applying every remedy that skill and anxiety could suggest," Dickens reported. "The dear girl however sank beneath the attack." The next day, she died, only seventeen years old. "You cannot conceive the misery in which this dreadful event has plunged us," he lamented.

Mary's death and Dickens's grief, known mostly from his own accounts, form a well-known chapter in Dickens's biography. Much more is known about his grief, in fact, than about Mary herself. The story of her death was simple enough, as he described it:

> On the Saturday Evening we went to the Saint James's Theatre; she went up stairs to bed at about one o'Clock in perfect health and her usual delightful spirits; was taken ill before she had undressed; and died in my arms next afternoon at 3 o'Clock.

But behind this bare statement, as matter-of-fact as a deposition in a coroner's inquest, lay the most grievous bereavement Dickens would ever know.

Mary's youth, happiness, and apparently glowing health made her death particularly stunning. "She was taken ill without an instant's warning," he wrote, and "died in such a calm and gentle sleep, that although I had held her in my arms for some time before, when she was certainly living . . . I continued to support her lifeless form, long after her soul had fled to Heaven." The circumstances seem almost designed to evoke his strongest feelings: Mary's sudden, inexplicable collapse after a happy evening together, her gentle slide into death, her murmuring his name as she died in his arms—"Thank God she died in my arms, and the very last words she whispered were of me." Dickens the novelist could scarcely have invented a more affecting scene. All his fictional deathbeds are indebted to the poignant memory of Mary quietly slipping away in his arms.

He survived her by more than three decades. During those years, death claimed many of his friends, both his parents, most of his brothers and sisters, and two of his own children; but his grief for none of them approached his desolation in May 1837. No other event in his early life resonated so potently.

He purchased a burial plot for Mary in Kensal Green Cemetery and composed an (ungrammatical) epitaph: *Young, beautiful and good, God in His mercy numbered her with his angels at the early age of seventeen.* "Her body lies in the beautiful cemetery in the Harrow Road," he wrote a month after her death:

> I saw her grave but a few days ago, and the grass around it was as green and the flowers as bright, as if nothing of the earth in which they grew could ever wither or fade. Beneath my feet there lay a silent but solemn witness that all health and beauty are but things of the hour.

In 1837, Kensal Green Cemetery was new, a fifty-four-acre expanse of greensward in "the then still rural district of Kensal Green" (according to the cemetery guide), far from the overcrowded city churchyards of London that Dickens would later deplore in *Bleak House*. Mary's grave was among Kensal Green's earliest. For Dickens, it became hallowed ground, and to stand before her gravestone today is to stand on the same spot on which he stood sorrowfully in May 1837 and many times after.

In purchasing the Kensal Green plot for Mary, he intended one day to be buried beside her, "my dear young friend and companion for whom my love and attachment will never diminish, and by whose side if it please God to leave me in possession of sense to signify my wishes, my bones, whenever or wherever I die, will one day be laid." When Mary's brother George died a few years after Mary, Dickens relinquished his Kensal Green plot only with great reluctance: "It is a great trial to me to give up Mary's grave; greater than I can express. . . . The desire to be buried next her is as strong upon me now, as it was five years ago; and I *know* (for I don't think there ever was love like that I bear her) that it will never diminish. . . . I cannot bear the thought of being excluded from her dust." His desire for post-mortem intimacy with Mary curiously anticipates Heathcliff's desire to mingle his remains with Catherine Earnshaw's in *Wuthering Heights*. When the grave was to be opened for burial of Mary's brother, Dickens intended to "drive over there, please God, on Thursday morning . . . and look at her coffin." He did not wish to be thought superstitious: "I neither think nor hope (God forbid) that our spirits would ever mingle *there*," he assured his friend John Forster; but despite this protest and despite Andrew Marvell's assurance that "The grave's a fine and private place/But none . . . do there embrace," Dickens seems to have imagined and sought a sepulchral embrace with Mary, a final, eternal union with his beloved in the grave.

After the first shock of grief, he resolved not to shrink from painful memories of Mary, instead vowing to indulge "a melancholy pleasure in recalling the times when we were all so happy—so happy that increase of fame and prosperity has only widened the gap in my affections," as he wrote several months later. His worldly fortunes were ascending, but he was already regretting happier times. "I weary now for the three rooms in Furnival's Inn, and how I miss that pleasant smile and those sweet words which, bestowed upon an evening's work in our merry banterings round the fire, were more precious to me than the applause of a whole world would be." On New Year's Day 1838, eight months after Mary's death, he noted his gratitude for "Increased reputation and means—good health and prospects," but added that "if she were with us now, the same winning, happy, amiable companion—sympathising with all my thoughts and feelings more than any one I knew ever did or will—I think I should have nothing to wish for, but a continuance of such happiness. But she is gone, and pray God I may one day through his mercy rejoin her"; and a little later, "I shall never be so happy again as in those Chambers three Stories high [in Furnival's Inn]—never if I roll in wealth and fame"—a pessimistic prediction which proved entirely accurate. Dickens's optimism did not die with Mary—his spirits were elastic—but her death struck when his life was most hopeful, and when he was most unprepared for such a loss. He would not have grieved so intensely had her death not surprised him so completely.

He dwelt on her almost obsessively. After she died, he dreamed of her "every night for many months—I think for the better part of a year—sometimes as a spirit, sometimes as a living creature. . . . I never lay down at night without a hope of the vision coming back in one shape or other. And so it did." Six months after her death, he told Mary's mother:

> I have never had her ring off my finger by day or night, except for an instant at a time to wash my hands, since she died. I have never had her sweetness and excellence absent from my mind so long. I can solemnly say that waking or sleeping I have never once lost the recollection of our hard trial and sorrow, and I feel that I never shall.

Three months later yet, he wrote to Catherine from the north of England: "Is it not extraordinary that the same dreams which have constantly visited me since poor Mary died, follow me everywhere?" And six years later, he still thought of her perpetually, testifying that "she is so much in my thoughts at all times (especially when I am successful, and have prospered in anything) that the recollection of her is an essential part of my being, and is as inseparable from my existence as the beating of my heart is." When he died, he was wearing her ring.

Dickens lost Mary Hogarth four years after he had lost Maria Beadnell. Losing these two young women when he was a young man established his idea of the feminine: a critical element of his fiction, for women became the soul of his novels.

Mary Hogarth, in fact, became his religion. His Christianity, by contrast, was pallid.

Dickens knew the King James Bible well, at least the Gospels (he disapproved of the Old Testament), and also the Anglican Prayer Book. But the Church of England bored him, much as Sunday-morning services stupefy young David Copperfield: "In time my eyes gradually shut up; and, from seeming to hear the clergyman singing a drowsy song in the heat, I hear nothing, until I fall off the seat with a crash, and am taken out, more dead than alive." At one time Dickens even joined a Unitarian congregation, admiring their social activism: "I have carried into effect an old idea of mine, and joined the Unitarians, who *would* do something for human improvement, if they could; and who practice Charity and Toleration." He soon slid back into a nominal Anglicanism, however, and his final years found him grumbling about the sermons of the local vicar. But the Church played no vital role in his life, and its doctrines and practices have little role in his novels. For fictional purposes Dickens favored a nostalgic, non-dogmatic sort of Anglicanism, especially in the reassuring form of sleepy rural churches and churchyards.

His theology was nebulous. "The mystery is not here, but far beyond the sky," he advised a correspondent in 1850, admonishing her to "be earnest," turn her attention to practical concerns, and not waste time "brooding over mysteries." After all, he reasoned, Christ himself went busily about his Father's business, which was rather in the nature of social work: "Our Saviour did not sit down in this world and muse, but labored and did good." Restless, active, and worldly, Dickens was not reflective. Heaven was out there and England was here. A supernatural presence amidst the foggy streets of London, a mysterious interpenetration of spirit and matter—no such dreamy possibilities interested him.

He thought the Gospels plain enough for practical purposes. Samuel Johnson found the New Testament "the most difficult book in the world, for which the study of a life is required," and Dickens's contemporary John Ruskin dismissed the notion of Scripture's self-evident clarity:

> The Protestant reader . . . remains entirely ignorant of, and if left to his own will, invariably destroys as injurious, the deeply meditated interpretations of Scripture which . . . have been exalted by the trained skill and inspired imagination of the noblest souls ever enclosed in mortal clay.

But Dickens had no patience for the meditations of any soul, noble or otherwise, before his own time. His lifelong disdain for "the wisdom of the past" was perhaps integral to his genius, but his philistinism cut him off from a rich legacy of reflection and insight.

His Christianity was sentimental and pragmatic; for Dickens, Graham Greene scoffed, "Christianity is a woman serving soup to the poor." An often-quoted passage narrating the death of Jo the crossing sweeper in *Bleak House*, who is coached through the "Our Father" as he is dying, followed by the narrator's exclamations of indignation against the system which neglected Jo, summarizes Dickens's Christianity: social amelioration for the living, consolation for the dying. Any religious question beyond these was beside the point. The Church itself was largely beside the point—clergy, liturgy, ritual, sacraments, the whole thing; above all, theology and dogma. He could enter into the feelings of a lonely child, an angry woman, a hunted murderer— but he could not understand a sensibility that regarded religious truths as an urgent concern. "It is fatal to let people suppose that Christianity is only a mode of feeling; . . . it is first and foremost a rational explanation of the universe," Dorothy Sayers would argue. "It is hopeless to offer Christianity as a vaguely idealistic aspiration of a simple and consoling kind; it is, on the contrary, a hard, tough, exacting, and complex doctrine, steeped in a drastic and uncompromising realism." But nothing could have appealed less to Dickens than "hard, tough, exacting, and complex doctrine."

Like furniture, he felt, religion should be useful and comfortable. "What people don't realize is how much religion costs," Flannery O'Connor wrote. "They think faith is a big electric blanket, when of course it is the cross." Dickens's religion was of the electric-blanket variety, however. His Christ was motherly and compassionate: "No one ever lived, who was so good, so kind, so gentle, and so sorry for all people who did wrong, or were in any way ill or miserable, as he was," he explained to his children. The disruptive, prophetic Christ— "Suppose ye that I am come to give peace on earth? I tell you, Nay;

but rather division"—does not figure in Dickens's Christology. His creed was what Protestant theologian H. Richard Niebuhr would later define as the theology of romantic liberalism: "A God without wrath brought men without sin into a kingdom without judgment through the ministrations of a Christ without a cross." Dickens was a novelist rather than a theologian, however, and for his novels, Tiny Tim's "God bless us, every one!" was sufficient theology. Whether it sufficed for Dickens himself is a different question.

A perceptive Victorian reviewer observed that Dickens had the idea that "Christianity is a scheme to make things pleasant; and this notion runs throughout all his books. . . . That it should satisfy a man of a vigorous mind shows that this mind is only concerned with the superficialities of things." But the religion of uplifting sentiments did *not* satisfy the vigorous mind of Dickens, even in his sunniest years. His sentimental, demystified Christianity was too poor a thing, emotionally and imaginatively, to engage his senses, his fancy, his ardor, or his idealism. William Makepeace Thackeray, his fellow novelist and sometime friend, "used to say of Dickens that emotion ran through him as deeply and fully as blood." Passionate and romantic, Dickens needed a God who was more than just the estimable manager of a universal soup kitchen; he needed, rather, a deity to love with intensity and warmth—as ardently as he had loved Maria Beadnell.

The voice of T. S. Eliot's "Preludes" is moved by "the notion of some infinitely gentle/Infinitely suffering thing." Dickens cherished a similar idea of divinity. His God required, humanly speaking, a woman's nature (though not that of a coquette like Maria).

With Mary Hogarth's death, Dickens found the human face of his strongest religious feelings.

Her death elicited a hidden stream of reverence and adoration in his nature. His grief softened with time, and grass grew over her grave in Kensal Green, but her spirit remained a vivid presence. Like most people, Dickens expressed his deepest religious feelings not in theological terms but in images and devotions and loyalties. "The gentlest and purest creature that ever shed a light on earth," Mary became his ideal of affectionate sisterly and daughterly love, sweetness of temper, loyalty, domestic warmth, quiet moral strength, self-denial, absolute purity. For Dickens, these were more than simply human virtues; they were attributes of holiness. While he was indifferent to the mysteries of Christianity, the memory of Mary awoke his capacity for worship. He could admire Christ the social worker, but he loved the spirit of Mary.

She was more even than a sacred memory and icon. In his frequent dreams of her in the months after her death, he sensed her mystical presence: "I should be sorry to lose such visions for they are very happy ones—if it be only the seeing her in one's sleep—I would fain believe too, sometimes, that her spirit may have some influence over them, but their perpetual repetition is extraordinary." In his dreams, she crossed and re-crossed the ether between human and angelic spheres: "I dreamed of her every night for many months . . . sometimes as a spirit, sometimes as a living creature, never with any of the bitterness of my real sorrow, but always with a kind of quiet happiness, which became so pleasant to me that I never lay down at night without a hope of the vision coming back in one shape or other." A few months after her death, coming across Sir Walter Scott's reflections on his wife's death, he transcribed them: "She is sentient and conscious of my emotions *somewhere*; where we cannot tell—how we cannot tell," Scott had written; "yet would I not at this moment renounce the mysterious yet certain hope that I shall see her in a better world, for all that this world can give me"—to which Dickens added, "I know but too well, how true all of this is."

Visiting Niagara Falls in 1842, he sensed Mary's presence in the mists. An even more striking appearance was a "curious dream" he dreamed in Italy in 1844, seven years after her death. From the palazzo in Genoa where he was staying, he described his dream to Forster in a long and detailed letter:

> In an indistinct place, which was quite sublime in its
> indistinctness, I was visited by a Spirit. I could not make
> out the face, nor do I recollect that I desired to do so. It
> wore a blue drapery, as the Madonna might in a picture
> by Raphael; . . . I knew it was poor Mary's spirit.

But attempting to embrace her, he was rebuffed: "I wept very much, and stretching out my arms to it called it 'Dear.' At this, I thought it recoiled; and I felt immediately, that not being of my gross nature, I ought not to have addressed it so familiarly." The spirit's recoil betrays Dickens's assumption that the spiritual was averse to flesh. Though sympathetic, Mary's spirit shunned his physical embrace, preferring to keep their relationship rarefied, spirit to spirit, like love among Milton's angels: "Easier than air with air, if Spirits embrace,/Total they mix, union of pure with pure/Desiring. . . ." Human bodies are not means but impediments to the love of angels, and of Mary.

The Genoa dream continued. Apologizing to Mary's spirit for his presumption in trying to embrace her, Dickens requested evidence of her authenticity: "Oh! give me some token that you have really visited me!"—and then, to detain her, posed a searching question. "What is the True religion?" he asked. When Mary hesitated, he prompted her, proposing his own vague ethical faith: "You think, as I do, that the Form of religion does not so greatly matter, if we try to do good?" But Mary refused to ratify this helpful suggestion, and Dickens ventured an unthinkable alternative: ". . . or perhaps the Roman Catholic is the best? perhaps it makes one think of God oftener, and believe in him more steadily?"

Mary assented: "'For *you*,' said the Spirit, full of such heavenly tenderness for me, that I felt as if my heart would break; 'for *you*, it is the best!' Then I awoke, with the tears running down my face, and myself in exactly the condition of the dream." Since Dickens when awake harbored an inveterate fear and loathing of Catholicism, Mary's advice was revolutionary indeed, hinting at a latent Catholic strain in his imagination, a suppressed awareness that her vivid presence revealed mystical realities beyond his thin gospel of progress and social amelioration. Had Dickens (like Ebenezer Scrooge) been more susceptible to midnight suggestions, his life might have taken a decisive turn.

Nonetheless, he was powerfully affected: "I was not at all afraid, but in a great delight, so that I wept very much," he told Forster. Waking in tears, feeling "as if my heart would break," he woke his sleeping wife to insist that she listen to multiple retellings of the dream, for purposes of later authentication: "I called up Kate, and repeated it three or four times over, that I might not unconsciously make it plainer or stronger afterwards." His vision of Mary was one of the few recorded times that he felt himself in the immediate presence of the divine, which for him naturally assumed the form of a young woman—Mary Hogarth, of course, but in this case Mary Hogarth conflated with the Virgin. At its most exalted and intense, his religion was a kind of Mariolatry, an idiosyncratic worship not of *the* Virgin Mary, but of his own private virgin Mary.

In the Genoese palace where he dreamed of Mary, he observed curiously that "there is a great altar in our bedroom, at which some family who once inhabited this palace had mass performed in old time; and I had observed within myself, before going to bed, that there was a mark in the wall, above the sanctuary, where a religious picture used to be; and I had wondered within myself what the subject might have been, *and what the face was like.*" What was missing over the altar was probably a crucifix or other image of Christ, but in his dream the face of Mary Hogarth replaced Christ. In an irony, Dickens's private religion found its closest parallel in devotional customs and imagery of Roman Catholicism, which by strong and fixed prejudice he detested. He would have been scandalized (if he had learned of it) by the dogma of the Immaculate Conception, enunciated by Pope Pius IX in 1854; but his own private faith in Mary Hogarth's sinless nature was similar: "I solemnly believe that so perfect a creature never breathed. . . . She had not a fault."

Mary's death gave him an image of what he most admired and desired: gentle, self-abnegating feminine love. Strong-willed, ambitious, and driven, he craved softness, tenderness, sympathy, selfless and yielding devotion, absolute love—love to the end, and beyond. Two years after Mary's death, he consoled a friend on the death of his daughter:

> The certainty of a bright and happy world beyond the Grave, which such young and untried creatures (half Angels here) *must* be called away by God to people—the thought that in that blessed region of peace and rest there is one spirit who may well be supposed to love and watch over those whom she loved so dearly when on earth—the happiness of being always able to think of her as a young and promising girl, and not as one whom years and long sorrow and suffering had changed—above all, the thought of one day joining her again where sorrow and separation are unknown—these are all sources of consolation which none but those who have suffered deep affliction can know in all their force.

His benevolent Christianity of social improvement, for all its earnestness, inspired nothing like the emotions evoked by Mary, the impassioned yearning with which he reached out to embrace her spirit, his conviction of her abiding (and intercessory) love for himself, "whom she loved so dearly when on earth." In his Genoa dream, Mary "was moved with the greatest compassion for me" and "was so full of compassion and sorrow for me . . . that it cut me to the heart." His nature required more than just good feeling and uplift; he longed for a lover who would surrender herself unstintingly; a selfless love so keen that it could "cut" him—an image strangely akin to that of St. Teresa pierced with the arrows of divine love.

After Dickens's death, his closest confidant John Forster, by no means a sentimentalist, recalled Dickens's lifelong "loving devotion to one tender memory":

With longer or shorter intervals this [memory] was with him all his days. Never from his waking thoughts was the recollection altogether absent; and though the dream would leave him for a time, it unfailingly came back. It was the feeling of his life that always had a mastery over him. . . . In the very year before he died, the influence was potently upon him. . . . Through later troubled years, whatever was worthiest in him found in this an ark of safety; and it was the nobler part of his being which had thus become also the essential. It gave to success what success by itself had no power to give; and nothing could consist with it, for any length of time, that was not of good report and pure.

Sweet are the uses of adversity. The death that wrung Dickens's heart in 1837 proved a lasting grace, a gift to him and to his fiction. Mary Hogarth became his muse, his Beatrice, a glimpse of Heaven, the divine clothed in a pure and lovely female form.

"The first burst of anguish over," he wrote a few years after her death, "I have never thought of her with pain—never. I have never connected her idea with the grave in which she lies":

I have long since learnt to separate her from all this litter of dust and ashes, and to picture her to myself with every well-remembered grace and beauty heightened by the light of Heaven and the power of that Merciful Being who would never try our earthly affections so severely but to make their objects happy, and lead our thoughts to follow them.

Dickens was temperamentally excitable and philosophically unanchored. Had Mary Hogarth not died so young and so suddenly, his fiction might have gone on, novel after novel, striking out randomly at ephemeral grievances, the day's newspaper topics. Her death gave him what he would otherwise have lacked, a moral and spiritual center.

When Mary Hogarth died, Dickens was in the midst of writing two novels, both with monthly deadlines. *Pickwick Papers* had been under way for over a year, with six numbers yet to be written; meanwhile, he had launched *Oliver Twist*, the fourth number of which had just been published. Each novel stood at a critical turn: Mr. Pickwick had just been sent to debtors' prison; young Oliver had just been introduced to Fagin's den of thieves. Dickens had also become editor of a monthly magazine, *Bentley's Miscellany*, in which *Oliver Twist* was being serialized. For almost anyone else, it would have been too much, and even Dickens sometimes felt harassed and overworked.

In the shock of Mary's death, he had to put aside all these projects. "I have been so shaken and unnerved by the loss of one whom I so dearly loved that I have been compelled to lay aside all thoughts of my usual monthly work, for once," he told a correspondent, and both *Pickwick Papers* and *Oliver Twist* failed to appear the following month—the only time until his death thirty-three years later that he failed to meet a serial deadline.

He soon returned to both novels, however. *Pickwick* concluded several months later without further interruption. *Oliver Twist* still had many months to run in *Bentley's*, and Mary's death immediately made its way into the narrative. In the first number after her death, the benevolent old gentleman Mr. Brownlow wanders through his past, recalling

> . . . faces that the grave had changed and closed upon, but which the mind, superior to its power, still dressed in their old freshness and beauty: calling back the lustre of the eyes, the brightness of the smile, the beaming of the soul through its mask of clay: and whispering of beauty beyond the tomb, changed but to be heightened, and taken from the earth only to be set up as a light, to shed a soft and gentle glow upon the path to Heaven.

Later, Brownlow laments that "The persons on whom I have bestowed my dearest love, lie deep in their graves; . . . the happiness and delight of my life lie buried there too."

Such scattered tributes to Mary Hogarth were well enough, but Dickens finally could not resist the urge to introduce Mary herself. The plot had no need for a seventeen-year-old maiden, but the narrative was flexible, almost impromptu; and in April 1838, nearly a year after her death, a thinly disguised Mary Hogarth makes her appearance.

Oliver Twist had by now reached what would be its midpoint. Several chapters earlier, Oliver had been shot during Bill Sikes's abortive burglary attempt at Chertsey. The following chapters, taking up other threads, had left Oliver's fate in suspense. Now the narrative returned to Chertsey, opening with Sikes fleeing and snarling at the barking dogs set in pursuit of him: "Wolves tear your throats! . . . I wish I was among some of you; you'd howl the hoarser for it." But then the action moves indoors, and in melodious counterpoint to Sikes's harsh growls we hear "a sweet female voice" from above, "with a footstep as soft and gentle as the voice": a voice which "quelled . . . in an instant" a tumult of "noise and commotion." As the young lady owning this voice urges the family servants to succor the wounded burglar—Oliver himself—who has turned up on the doorstep, we recognize in her the Good Samaritan of Dickens's favorite parable. "Poor fellow! Oh! treat him kindly, Giles, for my sake!" she pleads—a Good Samaritan with the added charms of feminine tenderness and beauty.

The voice belongs to Rose Maylie, a young lady "in the lovely bloom and spring-time of womanhood; at that age, when, if ever angels be for God's good purposes enthroned in mortal forms, they may be, without impiety, supposed to abide in such as hers." A passage canceled in manuscript makes plain Rose's identity with the lost Mary: "Oh! Where are the hearts which following some halting description of youth and beauty, do not recal [*sic*] a loved original that Time has sadly changed, or Death resolved to dust." Deciding on second thought that this exclamation was too personal, perhaps, Dickens deleted it, but went on to describe Rose as a girl of exactly Mary Hogarth's age:

> She was not past seventeen. Cast in so slight and exquisite a mould; so mild and gentle; so pure and beautiful; that earth seemed not her element, nor its rough creatures her fit companions. The very intelligence that shone in her deep blue eye, and was stamped upon her noble head, seemed scarcely of her age or of the world; and yet the changing expression of sweetness and good humour; the thousand lights that played about the face, and left no shadow there; above all, the smile; the cheerful, happy smile; were made for Home; for fireside peace and happiness.

As description, this is fuzzy, but as rhapsody, deeply felt: such elevated, exaggerated, indistinct rhetoric was for Dickens the language of exalted sentiment. Rose Maylie is an angel, only temporarily inhabiting—"enthroned in"—human form.

She is the first of many Dickens heroines inspired by Mary Hogarth. Literary critics often cluck censoriously about these heroines, and certainly Rose and her successors lack the keen coloring of characters like *Oliver Twist*'s brutish Bill Sikes, or Fagin: gliding "stealthily along, creeping beneath the shelter of the walls and doorways, the hideous old man seemed like some loathsome reptile, engendered in the slime and darkness through which he moved: crawling forth, by night, in search of some rich offal for a meal." Villains and eccentrics inspired Dickens to a vivid particularity lacking in the perfections of a Rose Maylie. But Rose was no fanciful invention: she was the fictional embodiment of Mary Hogarth, and Dickens's ironic fancy would not play lightly with that sacred memory.

More than simply a memorial to Mary, though, Rose Maylie also reflects Dickens's considered reflections on the hard logic of Mary's early death. It was not after all surprising, he had come to feel, that

Mary should have died so young. So perfect a creature had not properly belonged to this world at all, but to the higher sphere to which she had willingly returned after her brief sojourn on earth.

As if to relive Mary's death, he inflicted *Oliver Twist*'s Rose Maylie with a dangerous fever. "It would be little short of a miracle, if she recovered," the doctor declares. Nonetheless, Rose survives. Urgently summoned to her bedside, her foster brother and earnest suitor Harry arrives just when she is out of danger. Harry is a blandly virtuous character, but now, finding his beloved Rose alive and recovering, he speaks for Dickens himself. Dickens's epitaph for Mary had described her as "young, beautiful and good"; Harry echoes:

> We know that when the young, the beautiful, and good, are visited with sickness, their pure spirits insensibly turn towards their bright home of lasting rest; we know, Heaven help us! that the best and fairest of our kind, too often fade in blooming.

Though relieved, Harry is surprised that Rose has survived; he can understand why her pure spirit was eager to escape its mortal prison. If the guilty Satan feels the ignominy of his angelic spirit dwelling in serpent's flesh—"O foul descent! that I who erst contended/With Gods to sit the highest, am now constrained/Into a beast, and mixed with bestial slime,/This essence to incarnate and imbrute"—how much more incongruous for Rose, an unfallen angel, to be shackled to mortal flesh. Ordinary humanity shrinks from death, but pure spirits long for it; or so Harry imagines:

> "An angel," continued the young man, passionately; "a creature as fair and innocent of guile as one of God's own angels, fluttered between life and death. Oh! who could hope, when the distant world to which she was akin, half opened to her view, that she would return to the sorrow and

calamity of this! Rose, Rose, to know that you were passing away like some soft shadow, which a light from above, casts upon the earth; to have no hope that you would be spared to those who linger here; to know no reason why you should be; to feel that you belonged to that bright sphere whither so many of the fairest and the best have winged their early flight."

His quill hurrying across the page, Dickens once again held the dying Mary Hogarth in his arms, praying for her life but well understanding her soul's flight from captivity.

Dickens has been accused of indulging himself with Rose Maylie's recovery, imposing a wish-fulfillment ending on Mary Hogarth's collapse. "The godlike novelist can answer his own prayers, of course," one critic writes disapprovingly. "Poetry can indeed deliver a golden world—for the poet, anyway." But however gratifying to her lover Harry, Rose's survival is no reason for *her* to rejoice. Why would "one of God's own angels" wish to remain amidst the corruptions and sorrows of earth? Dickens enjoyed lachrymose deaths, moreover; they would become a specialty, and Rose's death might have been a powerfully affecting scene. Fictional imperatives, not self-consolation, dictated her survival: as young Oliver's beloved protectress (also his aunt, it turns out), Rose could not be dispatched to the grave without throwing a gloom over his happy progress.

Though happy for his little hero Oliver, Rose Maylie's survival was awkward for Dickens himself. Mary Hogarth had died in *his* arms; he did not like to imagine her, even in the form of her surrogate Rose, in the arms of another man, not even the super-virtuous Harry. Rose's recovery initiated what would become a recurrent dilemma for Dickens's heroines: whether to die or marry. Readers generally prefer that heroines marry; Dickens did not. Marrying, the maiden dwindles into a wife. His reluctant concession to romantic convention is visible in the tepid romance of *Oliver Twist*, ending in Rose's marriage to Harry.

The novel's cult of Mary Hogarth contrasts with its less ardent Christianity as glimpsed in Harry's priestly vocation. Abandoning his political ambitions, Harry takes holy orders—not for religious motives, but to secure a pleasant vicarage for himself and Rose, and to give himself a respectable occupation. His rural parish offers a refuge from the septic city of Fagin and Sikes: "There are smiling fields and waving trees in England's richest county; and by one village church—mine, Rose, my own—there stands a rustic dwelling which you can make me prouder of, than all the hopes I have renounced, a thousandfold." The shady vicarage plainly appeals to Harry more than the church itself, "henceforth to be the scene of the young clergyman's labours"—as, scarcely able to disguise his boredom, Dickens describes Harry's clerical duties.

Harry's lukewarm vocation should not be overanalyzed; it was mostly a convenient fictional device. He sacrifices worldly ambition for love, and that was enough; Dickens was untroubled by Harry's view of the Anglican priesthood as simply a genteel profession (probably associated with low sex drive), which came with a pleasant house attached. (Jane Austen, daughter of a clergyman, concluded *Sense and Sensibility* with exactly the same arrangement.) Dickens demanded no more Christian fervor from Harry than he felt himself.

But while the romance of Harry and Rose limps to consummation in a clerical cottage, the novel's valedictory tribute to Rose (with no mention of Harry) soars into a glowing dream of Mary Hogarth still alive:

> I would fain linger yet with a few of those among whom I have so long moved [the characters of *Oliver Twist*], and share their happiness by endeavouring to depict it. I would show Rose Maylie in all the bloom and grace of early womanhood, shedding on her secluded path in life, such soft and gentle light, as fell on all who trod it with her, and shone into their hearts. I would paint her the life and joy

of the fire-side circle and the lively summer group; I would follow her through the sultry fields at noon, and hear the low tones of her sweet voice in the moonlit evening walk; I would watch her in all her goodness and charity abroad, and the smiling untiring discharge of domestic duties at home; . . . I would recall the tones of that clear laugh, and conjure up the sympathising tear that glistened in the soft blue eye.

The passage concludes with a wish: "These, and a thousand looks and smiles, and turns of thought and speech—I would fain recall them every one." "Recall" here has a double sense, both "remember" and "summon back," and Dickens no doubt meant both. Most of us can summon the dead only in memory; he could recall his beloved Mary to the vivid imaginary world of his fiction. So long as he was immersed in that world, Mary was with him. No wonder he wished to linger among *Oliver Twist*'s shadows.

Dickens was twenty-one when he lost Maria Beadnell, twenty-five when he lost Mary Hogarth. The two young women who ignited his love as a young man could scarcely have been more different; or at any rate they affected him very differently. Maria allured and aroused; Mary pointed upward. That women are so central to Dickens's fiction, morally and emotionally, owes much to both.

Early in the next century, Henry Adams would lament that the Anglo-American imagination had lost its sensitivity to the "the force of female energy." Take for example his friend the sculptor Augustus Saint-Gaudens and the English poet and critic Matthew Arnold: "They felt a railway train as power," Adams observed; "yet they . . . constantly complained that the power embodied in a railway train could never be embodied in art. All the steam in the world could not, like the Virgin, build Chartres." Dickens himself was fascinated by the railway as a manifestation of Victorian energy, speed, and progress, and several dynamic passages in his novels celebrate trains.

But his admiration for the railway, that clanging, roaring symbol of masculine power and self-assertion, was overpowered by his fascination with the feminine—especially those sister forces the Virgin and Venus. He could thank Mary and Maria for having met them.

CHAPTER 4

Of all my books, I like this the best:
David Copperfield

Yeats's question "Does the imagination dwell the most/Upon a woman won or a woman lost?" would not have been difficult for Dickens. For years he cherished his memories of the two women he had lost. Time had soothed his anguish, but it had scarcely diminished their sway. No woman since—no experience at all, in fact—had moved him so profoundly as Maria and Mary. "My attachments are strong attachments," he once observed, "and never weaken."

There is no better evidence of Maria's and Mary's enduring sway than Dickens's favorite among his own novels, *David Copperfield*. When he began writing it, the grass had been green over Mary's grave for a dozen years; Maria had been out of his life for sixteen. Yet *David Copperfield* fondly summons up the spirits of both, not as incidental characters but as the two women most deeply loved by the novel's hero David.

Sisters as they were in Dickens's affections, however, Maria and Mary were stepsisters to each other—Venus and the Virgin. In *David Copperfield* their opposition is most sharply drawn.

David Copperfield is the central novel of Dickens's career. Seven novels came before, seven after. It was the last novel he wrote as a full-time novelist: soon after, he began editing his own weekly magazine, *Household Words*; later yet, public readings absorbed even more of his energies. *Copperfield* was the novel that most stirred his own affections and remained his "favourite child." Parts of it were a straightforward memoir of his early years: "No one can ever believe this Narrative, in the reading, more than I have believed it in the writing," he testified. He felt a strong personal attachment to its characters and a sharp sorrow in relinquishing them at the end: it was like losing his own younger self again, and the two girls he had loved as a young man. "I am in danger," he confessed in a preface, "of wearying the reader whom I love, with personal confidences, and private emotions."

In the months before he began writing *Copperfield*, his nostalgia was stirred by the loss of another woman, his older and favorite sister Fanny. She had begun to fail two years earlier. "I am deeply, deeply grieved about it," he told Forster when he learned that she had consumption, for which the prognosis was always grim (within months of Fanny's death, both Emily and Anne Brontë also died of consumption). As Fanny sank during the summer of 1848, he arranged for her to move from Manchester to a house closer to London—for more salubrious air, but also that he might visit her more frequently. Seeing her wasting away carried his thoughts back to their childhood. "His sister Fanny and himself . . . used to wander at night about a churchyard near their house, looking up at the stars," Forster recalled Dickens reminiscing; "and her early death . . . vividly reawakened all the childish associations which made her memory dear to him."

The memories awakened by Fanny's death permeate the novel he began six months later. Its predecessor, *Dombey and Son*, had been set in the present, the 1840s of the railway boom: the locomotive era to which Dickens in his progressive, dynamic moods was strongly committed. But *David Copperfield* has nothing to do with steam engines. It is set in Dickens's own pre-railway youth, and from the beginning its mood is retrospective, reflective, wistful. Returning as a young man to the neighborhood of his earliest home, David remarks that he "had naturally an interest in . . . revisiting the old familiar scenes of my childhood":

> My occupation in my solitary pilgrimages was to recall every yard of the old road as I went along it, and to haunt the old spots, of which I never tired. I haunted them, as my memory had often done, and lingered among them as my younger thoughts had lingered when I was far away.

Nothing in *David Copperfield* is more autobiographical than its hero's nostalgia, for in writing the novel, Dickens himself was traveling "the old road" of his youth. While he was always more or less in the grip of his past, *David Copperfield* was written when he was especially haunted by memories.

His two most evocative memories were Maria Beadnell and Mary Hogarth. They had roused the most intense emotions he had ever known; they remained potent spirits. At the heart of *David Copperfield* lies a wishful fantasy: the novel's hero marries one of the girls that Dickens had lost—and then marries the other.

Though more than fifty named characters and sundry subplots crowd the pages of *David Copperfield*, at its heart lie three intertwined quests: orphaned and abandoned as a boy, David must become a man of strong character; he must find a prosperous (and genteel) profession; and most important, he must marry the right woman.

Pursuing the first two quests, David encounters miseries, struggles, complications, mistakes, setbacks, grievous losses, painful lessons. But character and prosperity, while desirable, fall in the ordinary realm of ambition; with his native intelligence, determination, hard work, and helpful mentors, David achieves both.

More difficult is the third quest—for a perfect wife is rarer and more precious than rubies. For David, in fact, she is even more: the perfect wife is life's ultimate goal, a religious prize, the Grail. Dickens himself could not boast of having succeeded in this quest, but he knew the girl with whom he could have—Mary Hogarth.

As a mythic recasting of Dickens's own moral journey, *David Copperfield* converts Maria Beadnell into a stepping-stone toward his highest love, Mary Hogarth. Dearly as he had loved Maria, warmly as he cherished her memory, she could accompany the hero David only on his first two quests, spurring him to accomplishment and teaching him fortitude. She could take him no further. Descending into Hell and ascending the mount of Purgatory, Dante is led by a virtuous pagan, Virgil; but to ascend to Paradise he must follow a holier guide, his beloved Beatrice. So too Dickens. Though dearly beloved, Maria must be left behind in order that Mary Hogarth may lead him higher.

But the journey begins with Maria: Dickens could hardly imagine a young man falling in love without recalling his own early passion for Maria. As he meditated David Copperfield's amatory initiation, Maria returned to him with a rush of feeling. David enjoys several boyhood flirtations, but his introduction to the novel's Maria, Dora Spenlow, is revolutionary, blinding, drowning:

> All was over in a moment. I had fulfilled my destiny. I was a captive and a slave. I loved Dora Spenlow to distraction!
>
> She was more than human to me. She was a Fairy, a Sylph, I don't know what she was—anything that no one ever saw, and everything that every body ever wanted. I was swallowed up in an abyss of love in an instant. There was no pausing on the brink; no looking down, or looking back; I was gone, headlong, before I had sense to say a word to her.

Narrating this event years later, the mature David recalls his infatuation with fondness, humor, fancy, and hyperbole—but for all this, there is no mistaking the intensity of the experience.

Dickens did not need to fabricate the feelings of ardent youthful love; they rose unbidden from his own poignant memories. He would later confess to Maria herself:

> I fancy . . . that you may have seen in one of my books a faithful reflection of the passion I had for you, and may have thought that it was something to have been loved so well, and may have seen in little bits of "Dora" touches of your old self sometimes, and a grace here and there that may be revived in your little girls, years hence, for the bewilderment of some other young lover—though he will never be as terribly in earnest as I and David Copperfield were . . . it was true and nothing more nor less.

Though fancifully elaborated, David Copperfield's Dora is our best portrait of the slimly documented Maria.

In blending his memories of his blacking-factory ordeal into David Copperfield's life, Dickens boasted that "I really think I have done it ingeniously, and with a very complicated interweaving of truth and fiction." David's courtship of Dora no doubt contains the same interweaving. But which strands are truth, and which fiction? What "touches" of the young Maria appear in Dora?

Some resemblances are concrete. He associated Maria with blue, and Dora's signature color is blue: her eyes are blue; she wears "a straw hat and blue ribbons" and "a dress of celestial blue"; David buys her an engagement ring with blue stones. Like Maria, again, Dora is "rather diminutive altogether. So much the more precious," David dotes. Dora has a "prettily pettish manner"; she is "captivating, girlish, bright-eyed, lovely"; "she had the most delightful little voice, the gayest little laugh, the pleasantest and most fascinating little ways." All these attractions, seen through the eyes of the besotted David Copperfield, give us a snapshot of Maria. "What a form she had, what a face she had, what a graceful, variable, enchanting manner!" Dora's "dimpled chin" and "slender arms" no doubt glance at Maria, as well, and her petted spaniel Jip certainly recalls Maria's spaniel Daphne. Dora plays the guitar and trills French ballads, accomplishments that may echo the musical accomplishments of Maria, who played the harp and had studied in Paris.

When he advised the older Maria that she might catch glimpses of her youthful self in Dora, Dickens felt no need to detail resemblances; she would recognize them herself. But he may have been chary of elaborating on the similarities for another reason, too: for though charming, lovely, and loveable, Dora is also immature, spoiled, and silly. No doubt there were touches of young Maria in these latter qualities, too.

When David's guardian Aunt Betsey loses all her money, for example, and David must inform the childlike Dora, now his betrothed, that he is suddenly penniless, she can barely comprehend the notion and proves entirely unable to cope with it—first dissolving in confusion and alarm, and then sliding into inconsequence:

> "Don't talk about being poor, and working hard!" said Dora, nestling closer to me. "Oh, don't, don't!"
>
> "My dearest love," said I, "the crust well-earned—"
>
> "Oh, yes; but I don't want to hear any more about crusts!" said Dora. "And Jip must have a mutton-chop every day at twelve, or he'll die."

David is melodramatically resolved to overcome poverty, but Dora's levity itself is invincible:

> "Oh, please don't be practical!" said Dora, coaxingly. "Because it frightens me so!"

"Sweetheart!" I returned; "there is nothing to alarm you in all this. I want you to think of it quite differently. I want to make it nerve you, and inspire you, Dora!"

"Oh, but that's so shocking!" cried Dora.

"My love, no. Perseverance and strength of character will enable us to bear much worse things."

"But I haven't got any strength at all," said Dora, shaking her curls. "Have I, Jip? Oh, do kiss Jip, and be agreeable!"

And from childish frivolity she drops into hysteria.

No such exchange ever took place between Dickens and Maria, for he had no money when they met, and Maria knew it. But the imagined scene may reflect his memories of flightiness and silliness in Maria, and perhaps, too, her (and her parents') anxiety about his lack of means; for he was well aware that his own modest position and income scarcely met the Beadnells' bankerly expectations.

Though Dora, in both her irresistible (for David) charms and probably her giddiness, echoes Maria, it is less clear how closely David's courtship follows Dickens's. Dickens might indulge sweet memories of his old flame in Dora, but larger plot imperatives had to prevail. David's courtship of Dora is both triumphant and mistaken—whereas Dickens's courtship of Maria had simply failed. But despite David's happier fortunes in love, Dickens poured his own remembered agonies into David's trials. Writing later about his passion for Maria, "the occasion of so much emotion," he confessed that "no one can imagine in the most distant degree what pain the recollection gave me in *Copperfield.*"

Dora is the daughter of a proctor, a sort of solicitor, under whom David is apprenticed. Dickens had never been articled to a proctor, but David's apprenticeship allowed him to revisit his early shorthand reporting days in Doctors' Commons, the court in which proctors practiced. To someone who had known Maria's banker father, Dora's proctor father—starched, mercenary, a complacent humbug—might have been recognizable. (Dora's mother is dead; all the novel's young characters grow up with a single living parent, or none.) When David first meets Dora, she has just returned from Paris, where Maria too had been sent for schooling. Whether Mr. Beadnell had sent her abroad to separate her from Dickens is unclear; but when David's illicit correspondence with Dora is discovered, *her* father threatens to send her to Paris: "You may make it necessary, if you are foolish or obstinate, Mr. Copperfield, for me to send my daughter abroad again, for a term." Does this threat recall Mr. Beadnell admonishing young Dickens to eschew his daughter? The removal of a beloved girl for schooling long reverberated with Dickens—in *Great Expectations*, Pip's Estella would also be sent to school in Paris.

Mr. Spenlow's threat is prompted by his discovery of David Copperfield's letters to Dora, and perhaps this incident, too, recalls a crisis in Dickens's courtship of Maria. David's letters to Dora—tied up with a blue ribbon, naturally—are unearthed by Dora's hired chaperone Miss Murdstone, and though there seems to have been no such Gorgon glooming between Dickens and Maria, certainly there were confidential letters waiting to be discovered. Dickens's invaluable friend Kolle often acted as courier, apparently undetected, but the correspondence might at some point have been exposed. Some such misadventure seems a likely explanation for Dickens's cryptic references in his letters to Maria to "*existing circumstances*" and "my existing situation," and for his difficulties in seeing her. Higher authority had evidently interposed.

Another incident in *David Copperfield* hints at this crisis in Dickens's courtship of Maria. Confronted by Dora's father, David admits to his secret correspondence with Dora:

> "There is nothing I can say, sir," I returned, "except that all the blame is mine. Dora—"
> "Miss Spenlow, if you please," said her father majestically.

—leaving David to lament this "colder designation" for Dora. This compulsory retreat from "Dora" to "Miss Spenlow" echoes the plaintive salutation of a letter Dickens wrote during the unhappy *"existing circumstances"* of his own romance: "My dear Maria.—(I fear I ought to say 'Miss Beadnell' but I hope you will pardon my adhering to the manner in which I have been accustomed to address you.)" The more intimate "Maria" no doubt suggested an engagement, or at least a familiarity tending that way; the compulsory reversion to "Miss Beadnell" reveals that any such understanding between them had been detected and proscribed.

Immediately after the crisis of the letters comes a greater crisis yet in David's courtship. Dora's father dies suddenly—a grief for her but propitious for David, removing the chief obstacle between him and Dora. Nothing like this occurred during Dickens's courtship of Maria; *her* father remained obstinately alive, and with the death of Dora's father *David Copperfield* leaves behind Dickens's futile courtship of Maria Beadnell. Much later, he joked about himself and a lover named Angelica, claiming to remember when "I, turned of eighteen, went with my Angelica to a City church on account of a shower . . . and when I said to my Angelica, 'Let the blessed event, Angelica, occur at no altar but this!' and when my Angelica consented that it should occur at no other—which it certainly never did, for it never occurred anywhere." Dickens's experience with Maria had been not Dora's complaisance but Angelica's reluctance.

But even as *David Copperfield* fondly revives young Maria Beadnell and glances at Dickens's courting her, it betrays regret for another lost figure of that earlier time—Dickens himself as a young man. What he had lost with Maria's departure was not just the pretty girl with long curly locks and blue eyes, but the ardent youth who had loved her with a freshness and intensity he had never recaptured. That first overpowering passion was irretrievable. Looking back, an older David Copperfield recalls himself in love with Dora—not just "in love," but consumed, absorbed, "saturated":

I was steeped in Dora. I was not merely over head and ears in love with her, but I was saturated through and through. Enough love might have been wrung out of me, metaphorically speaking, to drown anybody in; and yet there would have remained enough within me, and all over me, to pervade my entire existence.

In David Copperfield's love for Dora, Dickens celebrated—and mourned—the fervor of his own vanished youth. "What an idle time!" David recalls his courtship of Dora:

What an insubstantial, happy, foolish time! Of all the times of mine that Time has in his grip, there is none that in one retrospect I can smile at half so much, and think of half so tenderly.

Dickens was never more involved in his characters' lives than in *David Copperfield*. "I can never open that book as I open any other book," he later confessed. Writing it, he was once again twenty years old, and in love.

When his beloved Dora dies a year or two after their marriage, David Copperfield goes on to marry again. While his marriage to Dora has been disappointing, his second marriage is superbly happy.

And yet one cannot fall in love for the first time, twice. There could be no second Dora, no repetition of the rapture she had awakened. David Copperfield's love for the girlish Dora is the earnest, thrilling love of a very young man awakening to the romance of life and the allure of the feminine: a joyous, vernal, amorous, intoxicating experience, wholly appropriate and good—for a young man. Looking back, Dickens wondered if marrying Maria Beadnell would have been a good idea after all, but he never regretted loving her so passionately. In the chapter titled "My First Dissipation," David Copperfield gets drunk for the first time; meeting Dora two chapters later, he becomes drunk again—drunk with love. Both kinds of inebriation are rites of youth.

Maria Beadnell had been a precious gift to Dickens, just as Dora despite all her wifely incompetence is a gift to David. Before her advent, David had been content to idle in a dusty corner of the law, sliding into a cozy career which his aunt has found and bought for him, and which David has done nothing to earn. His quest for Dora spurs his ambition, motivates him to work long and hard, pushes him into manhood and vocation. The need to prove himself worthy of her and able to support her stimulates him to heroic exertion. All this echoes Dickens's experience with Maria. "I began to fight my way out of poverty and obscurity," he later told her, "with one perpetual idea of you."

More importantly, Dora gives David the invaluable experience of romantic intensity and ardor. It is good to mature, to move beyond juvenile impulse and indiscretion—but not to sink into middle-aged prudence at twenty, to bypass ardent youth altogether. Dora introduces David to amorous passion, launching him onto a sea of tempestuous, exhilarating feeling. Maria had done the same for Dickens. "I have never been so good a man since," he later told her, "as I was when you made me wretchedly happy."

There would be no turbulent emotions, no wretched happiness in David's second love. With Agnes Wickfield, a placid pool in a still glade, David Copperfield never knows the headlong rush of Eros. If his love for Dora was the amorous awakening of a sensitive, romantic youth, his love for Agnes shows him entering into man's estate. Looking back, Dickens recognized that there had been a moral logic in his own progress from Maria Beadnell to Mary Hogarth. Mary represented an ascent to higher things, a religious experience—and so, too, Agnes for David Copperfield.

The lovely young Dora quickened David's masculine senses; Agnes stirs his spiritual sensibilities. Like much religious art, her portrait in the novel is largely iconic.

When as a boy David first meets Agnes, he is instantly struck by her aura of sanctity. "On her face," David recalls, "I saw immediately the placid and sweet expression of the lady [Agnes's dead mother] whose picture had looked at me downstairs. . . . Although her face was quite bright and happy, there was a tranquillity about it, and about her—a quiet, good, calm spirit—that I never have forgotten; that I never shall forget." Dickens had no interest whatever in church architecture or religious art, but to convey Agnes's moral glow he turned to stained glass:

> I cannot call to mind where or when, in my childhood, I had seen a stained glass window in a church. Nor do I recollect its subject. But I know that when I saw her turn round, in the grave light of the old staircase, and wait for us, above, I thought of that window; and I associated something of its tranquil brightness with Agnes Wickfield ever afterwards.

Like Agnes herself, the memorable stained glass window lacks descriptive particulars—location, subject, design, hues—but details hardly matter, for the essence of both window and Agnes is a spiritual radiance, an ineffable glow of holiness.

Five years after her death, Dickens called Mary Hogarth "that spirit which directs my life, and through a heavy sorrow has pointed upwards with unchanging finger." Agnes Wickfield likewise points upward for David Copperfield. When Dora dies, Agnes is watching at her bedside, and descending to break the grievous news to David, she stands silently, her "solemn hand upraised towards Heaven!" Although she points upward on no other occasion in the novel, David seizes on this pregnant gesture as her emblem. "Until I die," he later assures her, "I shall see you always before me, pointing upward!" and, at novel's end, looking beyond, David invokes Agnes to *his* deathbed: ". . . so may I, when realities are melting from me, . . . still find thee near me, pointing upward!"

Agnes remains physically indistinct. We never learn the color of her eyes, or the shade of her hair; as to her complexion, we learn only that she has "a fair hand." Dora's color is blue, but Agnes has no color at all. Ignoring mundane visual details, David Copperfield describes instead the soothing influence of her presence. She is *tranquil, placid, quiet, good, calm, staid, discreet, pleasant, modest, orderly*; he extols the "goodness, peace, and truth" of "my sweet sister . . . my counsellor and friend, the better angel of the lives of all who come within her calm, good, self-denying influence." But we *see* Agnes only vaguely, through a veil. Why did Dickens not resurrect Mary Hogarth as vividly as he had revived Maria Beadnell in Dora? Beloved as she was, Mary seems never to have awakened his sensual imagination. What he cherished, rather, was her immaculate spirit: "So perfect a creature never breathed. . . . She had not a fault."

So too *David Copperfield*'s Agnes. Far from winning admiration, however, her unalloyed saintliness has long annoyed worldly critics. She is "a major embarrassment," a "nullity," "a religious ikon, an inert figure," "passive," a "secular Madonna," and "lifeless" (according to one Dickens biographer). But George Orwell holds preeminent rank in the tradition of Agnes-denigration with a frequently quoted quip: Agnes, he asserted in a classic essay on Dickens, is "the most disagreeable of his heroines, the real legless angel of Victorian romance."

But to complain that Agnes is not vividly embodied misses the point. She was not meant to compete with *David Copperfield*'s sharply defined eccentrics, characters like Uriah Heep or David's Aunt Betsey or the histrionic Micawbers. Agnes is, rather, the novel's moral center, the sun around which the more colorful characters revolve in their erratic orbits.

God works, indeed, through human means, even (or especially) the least likely. Flannery O'Connor could imagine grace operating through Georgia crackers, con artists, and serial killers, Graham Greene through a whiskey priest or a street punk. But while Dickens's fancy was exuberant and expansive, his theology was narrow; he could see the hand of God only in exceptional virtue. In creating Agnes, he strove not for bright color or texture, but moral luminosity. Hagiography does not as a rule appeal to novel critics—but with *David Copperfield*'s Agnes, it is what the critics must swallow. They may grumble; Dickens would not have apologized.

As Dickens brooded on his memories of Maria Beadnell and Mary Hogarth, both girls were mythically transformed into something rich and strange—but not the same "something." Maria became the eternally desirable coquette of sparkling blue vivacity and irresistible allure, every young man's romantic fancy (and often shipwreck). Mary on the other hand became a Madonna without child. In Dickens's imagination they were not just two women he loved one after the other, but antithetical feminine types. One aroused amorous desire; the other awakened immortal longings.

Eros precedes Caritas, at least for David Copperfield. As a youth he admires Agnes, but the sexual sparkle of less angelic girls dazzles him. "The influence for all good, which she came to exercise over me at a later time, begins already to descend upon my breast," he remarks of his early days with Agnes, but distinguishes between her edifying influence and the more sensual appeal of his childhood sweetheart, blue-eyed and provocative Emily: "I love little Em'ly, and I don't love Agnes—no, not at all in that way." Dickens had loved Maria Beadnell very much "in that way," while his adoration for Mary Hogarth was beyond sexual motives.

It is, in fact, *because* Agnes fails to tempt him that David venerates her. She soothes him, and excites his desire for goodness, without arousing any distracting amorous feelings. The day after becoming embarrassingly drunk, for example, he pays Agnes an expiatory visit: "She put her hand—its touch was like no other hand—upon my arm for a moment; and I felt so befriended and comforted, that I could not help moving it to my lips, and gratefully kissing it." But for all its consolatory power, Agnes's touch lacks sexual electricity. Her voice

stirs David: it "seemed to touch a chord within me, answering to that
sound alone. . . . there was a thrill in it. . . ." But the thrill is reverential
rather than romantic, a thrill of earnestness "that quite subdued me."
Agnes acts not only as David's conscience, but as a sexual depressant
as well.

No surprise if she fails to arouse him, for David's love for Agnes is
Dickens's love for his beloved Mary—long in her grave, long revered
as his tutelary saint. Removed to a higher sphere, sanctified, ethereal-
ized, and adored, Mary could not decently be imagined as descending
into "the fury and the mire of human veins." Even alive she had been
above all that; now, infinitely more so. It would be improper for anyone
to love Mary or to imagine Mary herself loving anyone "in that way."
Her last embrace had been in Dickens's arms, a sacred memory, and he
could not tolerate the notion of her in the profane embrace of another
man. Similarly, David Copperfield himself has no sexual interest in
Agnes, but cherishes her jealously nonetheless.

Agnes has a determined suitor, the novel's villain Uriah Heep.
By presuming to desire Agnes "in that way," Uriah ignites David's
most violent hatred. Uriah's intentions are actually honorable. Unlike
David's dear friend Steerforth, whom David easily forgives for cor-
rupting and abandoning little Em'ly, Uriah is no rake seducer; he
wants to marry Agnes. But this respectable ambition enrages David:
"I believe I had a delirious idea of seizing the red-hot poker out of
the fire and running him through with it . . . the image of Agnes,
outraged by so much as a thought of this red-headed animal's, . . .
made me giddy." David consistently imagines Uriah as satanic and
serpentine, even phallic: "He seemed to swell and grow before my
eyes," David recalls of the evening when Uriah announces his intent
to court Agnes.

David Copperfield's loathing of Uriah perhaps betrays a recoil from
some element of his own nature, an uneasiness with a sensual demon
lurking within. Yet Agnes is David's destined wife, and he cannot
approach her with any taint of sexual desire. The defeat of Uriah's

designs suggests a purification of David himself, a necessary expulsion of libido; yet even with Uriah's threat to Agnes erased, David cannot yet claim her. One complication is that though he has by now outgrown Dora's allurements, he is still married to her. Conveniently, Dora soon dies, and with her death David's destined union with Agnes approaches yet closer. Even now, however, he is not worthy of her. He must observe a decent interval of mourning and penance, and for three years he wanders alone through Europe, ending with lofty alpine meditations in Switzerland.

Morally, his continental exile is not simply a decorous period of mourning, but is penitential, forty days in a wilderness. His undisciplined heart must be chastened by suffering. Like the protagonists of allegories like *Everyman* and *Pilgrim's Progress*, David carries a heavy burden: "I felt its whole weight now; and I drooped beneath it, and I said in my heart that it could never be lightened." He identifies his burden as grief, not sin or guilt, but even the cadence and phrasing of the Authorized Version ("and I said in my heart") suggest that his suffering is a penance for youthful folly and a test of his perseverance. David himself refers to his wanderings, random and aimless as they seem (". . . foreign towns, palaces, cathedrals, temples, pictures, castles, tombs, fantastic streets . . ."), as "a pilgrimage": a journey through a dark night of the soul, "a ruined blank and waste, lying wide around me, unbroken, to the dark horizon." The road to Agnes, which is the road to holiness, leads through the Slough of Despond.

Agnes, meanwhile, waits and waits, like *Twelfth Night*'s Viola, who "never told her love" but "sat like Patience on a monument,/ Smiling at grief. Was not this love indeed?" (2.4). One of Agnes's divine attributes, a needful grace for an erring youth like David, is her unwavering fidelity and hope; like God, she never gives up on the prodigal. Perhaps Dickens imagined the spirit of Mary Hogarth patiently awaiting him.

"Reader, I married her," David Copperfield might finally, after sixty-two chapters, echo the triumphant final chapter of *Jane Eyre* (published just before Dickens began *David Copperfield*). But David's marriage to Agnes is more than a romantic triumph; more, even, than a sacrament. It is a mystical union, uniting David to the divine, the source and end of his own being. With Agnes "clasped in my embrace," he exclaims, "I held the source of every worthy aspiration I had ever had; the centre of myself, the circle of my life, my own, my wife; my love of whom was founded on a rock!" The Gospel allusion suggests the religious meaning of David's union with Agnes; his love for Dora had been that of the foolish man who built on sand. David's marriage to Agnes re-enacts Dickens's marriage to the spirit of Mary Hogarth, that symbolic union which was his strongest incentive to what did not come easily, a chaste otherworldliness. David's progress toward Agnes echoes (in distinctly Victorian terms) St. Augustine's *Confessions*, which narrates his progress from concupiscence to chastity. Like David, Augustine was an amorous youth: "I came to Carthage, where a cauldron of illicit loves leapt and boiled about me," he recalls, and David might echo, except that David's genteel England is no Mediterranean cauldron of vice, but a flowerpot of propriety and respectability. Yet for a susceptible romantic boy, Dora is temptation enough.

Like the young Augustine, David falls into desire; for however innocent and honorable his love for Dora, it is unquestionably sexual as well. Augustine takes a mistress, but (rather as David repents of marriage to Dora) eventually abandons her and embraces chastity—a difficult struggle. Even nearing his victory over the flesh, Augustine is tempted by whispers of sensuality: "Those trifles of all trifles, and vanities of vanities, my one-time mistresses, held me back, plucking at my garment of flesh and murmuring softly: 'Are you sending us away?'" But turning away from these sirens, he meets "the austere beauty of Continence [*Continentia*], serene and indeed joyous but not evilly, honourably soliciting me to come to her and not linger, stretching forth loving hands to receive and embrace me, hands full of multitudes of good examples."

Agnes is David Copperfield's *Continentia*. She becomes his bed-mate, but only nominally; more profoundly she represents chastity, self-restraint, spiritual serenity. By wedding her, David embraces his higher vocation. Augustine had begun his *Confessions* by anticipating the end of his journey: "Thou hast made us for Thyself and our hearts are restless till they rest in Thee." At the end of *his* quest, David's restless heart has also come to rest—not in God, but in Agnes. She is David's religion, and Dickens's too.

David Copperfield was illustrated by Hablot Browne, the regular illustrator of Dickens's early novels, who signed his work "Phiz." Phiz's final illustration for *David Copperfield* shows a domestic scene ten years after David and Agnes marry. They sit before the fire in a comfortably furnished Victorian parlor. It is the children's hour, with three young children at their feet (the text implies at least one other, elsewhere) and toys strewn about; it is perhaps the last time in Dickens's fiction that multiple children connote marital felicity. Dressed for dinner, David and Agnes await the nurse who will soon take the children off to bed.

Yet even amidst the bourgeois trappings of this scene as imagined by Phiz—respectable, conventional, sedate—Agnes's moral sway is evident. The fireplace is flanked by paintings of two scenes from David's youth: on one side his boyhood home, the Rookery; on the other the Yarmouth boathouse of his old friends the Peggottys. Between them hangs a third painting, a large portrait of Dora, her hair flowing down to her shoulders in long dark ringlets. It is a pious tribute to the departed, but also a reminder of the undisciplined heart of David's youth, when he had been fatally tangled in those enticing ringlets. By contrast, Agnes's hair is pulled back and tightly bound. While David may look back on his youthful infatuation fondly, Agnes's chaste, disciplined coif reveals his mature self, no longer susceptible to a girl's flowing hair. Flanking Dora's portrait on both sides of the mantel are two statuettes of winged angels, keeping guard against her provocative ringlets. All this is Phiz's depiction of David's marriage, not Dickens's, but it captures the spirit of the novel's conclusion.

Dickens's manuscript revisions suggest the same idea. His first thought was to begin the closing passage by having David exclaim, to Agnes, "Kiss me my dear!" But this romantic invitation struck the wrong note, he reflected; perhaps he recognized, with horror, that it echoed the lusty close of Shakespeare's *Taming of the Shrew*— "Why there's a wench! Come on and kiss me, Kate" (5.2). That Agnes should be insulted as a wench! Whether or no, "Kiss me my dear!" was plainly too amorous, inconsistent with her role as David's "better angel" guarding him from sensual indulgences like kissing. Changing direction, Dickens expunged the kiss and substituted an earnest invocation, "O Agnes, O my soul, so may thy face be by me when I close my life indeed," and a final image of Agnes pointing to Heaven.

Agnes's literary kin are figures like *The Divine Comedy*'s Beatrice— heroines who inspire and guide heroes on religious quests. That she appears in a secular Victorian novel rather than an openly theological allegory often misleads literary critics not attuned to religious language. But David Copperfield is not a literary critic and does not seek an interesting or complex wife—Dora had been interesting enough. After stormy seas, David seeks a calm, safe anchorage, a spiritual haven. "I come home, now, like a tired traveller," he has told Agnes earlier, "and find such a blessed sense of rest!"

The heroine of another allegory, Edmund Spenser's *Faerie Queene*, is a princess named Una—"oneness." Holiness is One: simple, straight-forward, undivided, unambiguous, unalloyed, non-complex. In *David Copperfield*, holiness resides not in the muddled diversity of life, but in escape from it. After all, Mary Hogarth had fled life early, aban-doning its wearying distractions and confusions. In spirit Dickens reached out to Mary; in fancy he married her in the union of David Copperfield and Agnes. Simply to embrace Mary was Dickens's most transcendent idea.

His nominal religion was an anemic protestantism, but an active fancy and acute sensibility needs something imaginatively and emotionally richer—for him, a religion with a woman's face. God the Father seemed severe and judgmental; the merciful and forgiving Son was more attractive, but nonetheless male. Just before beginning *David Copperfield*, Dickens wrote a Christmas tale, *The Haunted Man*, in which a despondent protagonist, Redlaw, returns to his rooms one day to find a small homeless boy who has been sheltered by Redlaw's kindly housekeeper Milly. Disappointed to see Redlaw instead of Milly, the boy cries: "Where's the woman? . . . I want to find the woman." Dickens too wanted to find *the* woman, to recapture the girl who had slipped away into her grave, to join himself to the woman who could steer him to blessedness. As a re-creation of Mary Hogarth, Agnes embodied a might-have-been happiness.

Though she annoys critics, Agnes stirs David Copperfield's most powerful emotions, just as Dickens's highest mystical experiences, his moments of keenest awareness of the supernatural, were associated with Mary—her presence in the mists of Niagara Falls and in his Genoese dream. Reunited with Agnes after his three-year exile, David has no words for his feelings: "She was so true, she was so beautiful, she was so good,—I owed her so much gratitude, she was so dear to me, that I could find no utterance for what I felt. . . . My love and joy were dumb." His embrace of Agnes is an ecstatic moment outside time and place, an ineffable experience beyond the powers of language, even for a successful novelist like David Copperfield, or a great one like Dickens.

Dickens might imagine himself mystically married to Mary Hogarth, but when he laid down his visionary pen he descended into the dusty streets of life from which Mary was long vanished, and in which the serenity and purity of her spirit were elusive. After ten years with Mary's fictional sister Agnes, David Copperfield enjoys perfect domestic joy; but after a dozen years married to Mary's actual sister

Catherine, Dickens was fretful. The gentle spirit of Mary whispered to him still, but he was distracted by other whisperings, as well.

David Copperfield ends in tranquil triumph. David's second marriage has replaced an inadequate wife, Dora, with an ideal partner. Escaping the consequences of his youthful mistake, he has grown in character and wisdom. Wisdom had indeed condemned Dora from the start: "Blind, blind, blind," David's Aunt Betsey mutters, and David comes to agree with her, understanding his infatuation with Dora as "the first mistaken impulse of an undisciplined heart" and tacitly agreeing with her own deathbed insight that "it would have been better, if we had only loved each other as a boy and girl, and forgotten it."

Dickens himself would never achieve the moral serenity of *David Copperfield*'s conclusion. Though devoted to Mary Hogarth, his restless heart could not rest in her or anywhere else. Even as he rhapsodized over David's perfect wife and blissful marriage, Dickens was ill at ease in his own marriage and discontented with his imperfect wife. "The old unhappy feeling pervaded my life," David had brooded while married to Dora. "It was deepened, if it were changed at all; but it was as undefined as ever, and addressed me like a strain of sorrowful music faintly heard in the night. . . . The happiness I had vaguely anticipated, once, was not the happiness I enjoyed, and there was always something wanting." At novel's end, David basks in uxorious contentment; but Dickens's own life remained mid-novel, his discontents unresolved and rankling.

One symptom of discontent was the sudden resurgence of his passion for Maria Beadnell. When out of the blue she renewed their correspondence in 1855, four and a half years after the final chapters of *David Copperfield*, the old flame flared up again—indeed, leapt as high as when he had been twenty. He was so rapturously excited about her reappearance that his sober friend Forster expressed incredulity and disapproval, in the same dubious tone as that of David's skeptical Aunt Betsey clucking about Dora. Dickens in turn rebuked Forster for his unsympathetic phlegm:

I don't quite apprehend what you mean by my over-rating the strength of the feeling of five-and-twenty years ago. If you mean of my own feeling, and will only think what the desperate intensity of my nature is, and that this began when I was [eighteen]; that it excluded every other idea from my mind for four years, at a time of life when four years are equal to four times four; . . . then you are wrong. . . . And so I suffered, and so worked, and so beat and hammered away at the maddest romances that ever got into any boy's head and stayed there, that to see the mere cause of it all, now, loosens my hold upon myself.

Too much of his younger self had been invested in Maria; ghosts of that golden era now rose to tempt and torment him. "I cannot see the face . . . or hear the voice," he told Forster, "without going wandering away over the ashes of all that youth and hope in the wildest manner." Dickens had just turned forty-three when Maria wrote to him.

Half a century earlier, William Wordsworth had mourned (in "Tintern Abbey") his own lost youth—"That time is past, and all its dizzy raptures"—consoling himself, however, that "Other gifts/Have followed, for such loss, I would believe,/Abundant recompense." This abundant recompense, Wordsworth congratulated himself, was "the philosophic mind."

For David Copperfield, youthful ardor is replaced by something better than philosophy—namely, by Agnes.

There were no happy consolations for Dickens, however. He had lost the dizzy raptures of his youth, he had lost Maria Beadnell, he had lost Mary Hogarth—and he had certainly not acquired anything like a philosophic mind.

CHAPTER 5

I counted up my years . . . and found that I should soon be grey

*D*avid Copperfield was unique in its revisiting of Dickens's younger days—the blacking-factory ordeal, his shorthand reporting, his rise to prosperity; above all, in its re-creation of Maria Beadnell and Mary Hogarth. But while the novel's hero was especially susceptible to feminine influence, the prominence of women was not new to Dickens's fiction. Female characters had dominated *David Copperfield*'s immediate predecessor.

He had begun this earlier novel, *Dombey and Son*, in 1846. Though Maria Beadnell had by then been out of his life for a dozen years and Mary Hogarth had been dead for nearly a decade, they remained the only two women who had any power over his imagination. But in the two years before *Dombey and Son*, several incidents revealed an awakening interest in other women.

Two years earlier, for example, he had become infatuated with a girl named Christiana Weller. "I know that in many points I am an excitable and headstrong man," he admitted, "and ride O God what prancing hobbies!" But the flammability of his emotions was only one lesson of the Christiana Weller episode.

He had met her in early 1844, at a benefit soiree for which she performed on the piano. She was eighteen, on the edge of woman-hood—like Mary Hogarth. He was instantly enamored, composing doggerel verses for Christiana that concluded: "I love her dear name which has won me some fame,/But Great Heaven how gladly I'd change it!" Changing her name was out of the question for him, but not since Mary Hogarth's death had his feelings been so roused. He told Christiana's father that "I read such high and such unusual matter in every look and gesture of the spiritual creature who is naturally the delight of your heart and very dear to you, that she started out alone from the whole crowd the instant I saw her, and will remain there always in my sight." More earnestly yet, he told a friend that "I cannot joke about Miss Weller; for she is too good; and interest in her (spiritual young creature that she is, and destined to an early death, I fear) has become a sentiment with me. Good God what a madman I should seem, if the incredible feeling I have conceived for that girl could be made plain to anyone!" With his notion that Christiana was "a spiritual young creature," "too good" for a long life, she approached the rarefied sphere of Mary Hogarth.

As it turned out, the fragile, ethereal Christiana Weller lived another sixty-six years, outlasting Dickens himself by a full four decades, but in 1844 he despaired of her life; there was no hope, he insisted, unless she were promptly removed to Italy—to which sunny land Dickens himself, curiously enough, had already made plans to travel:

> I *would* point out, in very tenderness and sorrow for this gentle creature, who otherwise is lost to this sad world which needs another, Heaven knows, to set it right—lost in her youth, as surely as she lives—that the course to which he

[Christiana's father] is devoting her, should not be called her life but Death; for its speedy end is certain. I saw an angel's message in her face that day that smote me to the heart.

Even worse than losing her to death, however, would be an earthly separation—losing her to distance, time, and forgetfulness:

But at the worst, contemplating the chance . . . of what is so dreadful, I could say in solemn and religious earnestness that I could bear better her passing from my arms to Heaven than I could endure the thought of coldly turning off into the World again to see her no more; to have my very name forgotten in her ears; to lose the recollection of her myself but at odd times and in remorseful glances backwards; and only to have the old thoughts stirred up at last by some indifferent person saying "You recollect her? Ah! She's dead."

The idea of Christiana "passing from my arms" was an ambiguous fantasy, recalling Mary Hogarth dying in his arms, but also suggesting an idea of Christiana alive and wrapped in his embrace—for though she might be a "spiritual young creature," Dickens's feelings for her were not wholly spiritual. His impulse to idealize young maidens was strong, and he was reluctant to admit any admixture of sexual feeling in his adoration. But he plainly regretted that Christiana was inaccessible to him.

When he was in the full flush of his infatuation with Christiana, a wealthy friend named T. J. Thompson wrote with the surprising news that *he* planned to court her. Dickens threw himself into vicarious courtship: "If I . . . felt as irresistibly impelled towards her as I should if I were in your place and as you do, I would not hesitate, or do that slight to the resolution of my own heart which hesitation would imply. But would win her if I could, by God." To Christiana herself, however, he observed of his friend Thompson that were Dickens himself not "beyond the reach—the lawful reach" of Christiana, it would be "the greatest happiness and pleasure of my life to have run him through the body. In no poetical or tender sense, I assure you, but with good sharp Steel."

The erotic violence of this fantasy coexisted curiously with his adoration for Christiana as a soaring soul, angel-winged:

> Hours of hers are years in the lives of common women . . . it is in such a face and such a spirit, as part of its high nature, to do at once what less etherial creatures must be long in doing . . . as no man ever saw a soul or caught it in its flight, no man can measure it by rule and rod.

She stirred his mystical feelings: "I had as high and confident a Faith (O Heaven what a boundless Faith it is!) in Her, and that whatever she worked out would be for Good. I know, I *do* know it, as well as if I had known her from her cradle. As, in the spirit, I have." His sense of an uncanny supernatural connection with Christiana—an intimation of having known her in spirit long before meeting her in the flesh—recalls his awareness of Mary Hogarth in the mists of Niagara Falls just two years earlier.

One skeptical critic notes disapprovingly "the frantic tone of his flirtations with younger women like Christiana Weller." Frantic he may have been, but frantic was only one aspect of Dickens's response to Christiana. His feelings echoed the reverential sentiments prompted by Mary Hogarth's death, with the addition of a more plainly romantic strain. She excited desire, fervor, frustration, even pain—for the "recollection of Miss Weller . . . has its tortures too"; but also adoration and even worship. Something of this mixture of emotions appeared in his response to Thompson's announcement that he intended to court Christiana. "I swear to you," Dickens wrote, "that when I opened and read your letter this morning . . . I felt the blood go from my face to I don't know where, and my very lips turn white. I never in my life was so surprised, or had the whole current of my life so stopped, for the instant, as when I felt, at a glance, what your letter said."

Why should he have been so startled and appalled to learn that an unmarried friend—a widower the same age as he (and wealthy)—wanted to court "a very beautiful girl"? At least one reason must have been his shocked discovery that while he had adopted Christiana Weller as an object of worship (and perhaps of never-to-be-consummated desire), someone else wanted her as wife and bedmate. Better to lose one's beloved to death, as with Mary Hogarth, than to another man. Mary was forever preserved from violation; Christiana would be lost to marriage, sex, and procreation. Nothing could be so radically disenchanting as an angel's decline into a wife: Satan's plunge from heaven was hardly more precipitate.

And so it comes as no surprise that when Christiana married Thompson the following year, Dickens's worship of her quickly waned. Less than a year after the wedding (which he attended sporting a garish striped waistcoat specially tailored for the occasion), he found her ethereal perfections sadly diminished: "Mrs. Thompson disappoints me very much. She is a mere spoiled child, I think, and doesn't turn out half as well as I expected. Matrimony has improved him, and certainly has not improved her." She was even less improved by pregnancy: "She seems . . . to have a devil of a whimpering, pouting temper—but she is large in the family way, and that may have something to do with it." His disillusion was complete: whereas Christiana the young maiden had enthralled him, Mrs. T. J. Thompson the pregnant wife bored and annoyed him—much like his own often-pregnant wife.

A few months after he met Christiana Weller, another curious episode occurred.

In July 1844, he took his family to Italy for a lengthy stay, settling in Genoa. There he met Augusta de la Rue, an Englishwoman married to a Swiss banker. Madame de la Rue suffered from "convulsions,

W. P. Frith, *Dolly Varden* (1842). No good portrait of the young Maria Beadnell exists, but this portrait of *Barnaby Rudge*'s coquette Dolly Varden probably captures Dickens's idea of Maria. The original painting was so much admired that Frith painted half a dozen copies; Dickens commissioned one, which was hanging in Gad's Hill at his death. *Courtesy of the Victoria and Albert Museum.*

TOP: Thomas Shepherd, *Cornhill, and Lombard Street, from the Poultry.* Maria Beadnell lived at 2 Lombard Street, next door to Smiths Bank, which occupied the building on the far right of this 1830 engraving. In the early 1830s Dickens haunted the spot in his thoughts, and often in person.

"When we were falling off from each other, I came from the House of Commons many a night at two or three o'Clock in the morning, only to wander past the place you were asleep in" (Dickens to Maria Beadnell Winter, February 1855).

BOTTOM LEFT: Dickens at 25, by Samuel Laurence (1837). The brilliant young author as Mary Hogarth knew him. BOTTOM RIGHT: Mary Hogarth, "the gentlest and purest creature that ever shed a light on earth." *Courtesy of the Dickens House Museum.*

TOP: Thomas Allom, *A bird's-eye view of Kensal Green Cemetery* (ca. 1832–33), showing a preliminary idea for the cemetery. Kensal Green Cemetery was new in 1837, when Mary Hogarth was buried there. Her grave is against the long wall on the right, running along the Harrow Road; Dickens hoped to be buried beside her. *Courtesy of the Museum of London.*

"*Her body lies in the beautiful cemetery in the Harrow Road. I saw her grave but a few days ago, and the grass around it was as green and the flowers as bright, as if nothing of the earth in which they grew could ever wither or fade*" (Dickens, June 1837).

BOTTOM: An 1860s Currier & Ives print of Niagara Falls, where, five years after Mary Hogarth's death, Dickens felt her ghostly presence in the mists.

"*What voices spoke from out the thundering water; what faces, faded from the earth, looked out upon me from its gleaming depths. . . . What would I give if the dear girl whose ashes lie in Kensal-green, had lived to come so far along with us—but she has been here many times, I doubt not, since her sweet face faded from my earthly sight*" (Dickens to John Forster, April 1842).

An 1861 studio photograph of a trim and jaunty-looking Dickens: the vigorous wooer that Ellen Ternan knew in the early years of their affair. *Courtesy of the Dickens House Museum.*

TOP: An 1857 engraving from the *Illustrated London News*, showing Dickens as Richard Wardour, expiring heroically in the final act of *The Frozen Deep*, in a performance at Dickens's Tavistock House. BOTTOM: Lured by the two thousand seats of the Manchester Free Trade Hall, Dickens took his *Frozen Deep* amateur company there for three performances in August 1857; but thinking the vast hall "too large and difficult, and altogether too public for my girls," he decided to hire professional actresses—including, fatefully, the Ternans.

TOP: E. F. Brewtnall, *At Doncaster Races*. In September 1857, Dickens followed the Ternans to Doncaster, and took them to watch the St. Leger Stakes in a hired barouche. BOTTOM: James Pollard, *Horses Starting for the St. Leger* (1831). The start of the St. Leger Stakes at Doncaster.

> *"Why may not this day's running—of horses, to all the rest; of precious sands of life to me—be prolonged through an everlasting autumn-sunshine, without a sunset! . . . that I . . . may wait by her side for ever, to see a Great St Leger that shall never be run!"* ("A Lazy Tour of Two Idle Apprentices").

TOP: An 1857 photograph of Ellen Ternan: the young Ellen with whom Dickens became infatuated. *Courtesy of the Dickens House Museum.* BOTTOM: The Haymarket Theatre in London's West
End. Through Dickens's influence, Ellen acted at the Haymarket in the fall and winter of 1857–58,
beginning with the role of Louisa in a comedy titled *My Son Diana*. ". . . The gentlemen will never
take the least notice of *me*," Louisa-Ellen laments at one point.

Spencer Gore, *Houghton Place* (1912). Ampthill Square, as seen from 2 Houghton Place, the London house that Dickens purchased for Ellen in 1859. A half-century later, Gore looked out on much the same scene as the Ternans saw from their front windows in the 1860s. *Courtesy of Tate Images.*

distortions of the limbs, aching headaches, insomnia, and a plague of neurasthenic symptoms, including catalepsy," all caused by a Phantom, or "myriads of bloody phantoms of the most frightful aspect," which pursued her. Learning of her troubles, Dickens set about with characteristic self-confidence ("I have a perfect conviction that I could magnetize a Frying-Pan") to exorcize her Phantom through hypnotism.

He had earlier become interested in the novel science or art of mesmerism, or "Animal Magnetism," and had already practiced "magnetizing" his wife and his sister-in-law Georgina. Now he turned his magnetic attentions to Madame de la Rue, conducting mesmerizing sessions with her that became frequent and consuming and continued for almost six months. When he and she were apart for several weeks, he hypnotized her telepathically, or thought he was doing so (echoing his belief in his uncanny connections with Mary Hogarth and Christiana Weller). Once reunited, he and Madame de la Rue became virtually inseparable: "Wheresoever I travelled in Italy, she and her husband travelled with me, and every day I magnetized her; sometimes under olive trees, sometimes in Vineyards, sometimes in the travelling carriage, sometimes at wayside Inns during the mid-day halt." His mesmeric therapy sessions ended only when he returned to England.

Dickens himself is the sole source for what Madame de la Rue revealed during her hypnotic trances, and his surviving reports, generally in the form of letters to her husband, may suppress awkward details. But whatever he may or may not have learned about her buried life, his enthusiastic invasion of her psyche suggests a probing, even prurient interest in the fantasies and desires of a mature married woman. The sexual implications of the mesmerist's power over his female subject undoubtedly appealed to him. Whatever the formal probity of his conduct with Madame de la Rue, he was surely aware of the seductive possibilities. On this point, we can trust his wife's instincts. With the many intense tête-à-têtes between her husband and the fascinating Madame de la Rue, under olive trees, in vineyards, and elsewhere, Catherine not surprisingly suspected something amiss, divining that psychic intimacy might easily progress, if it had not done so already, to physical intimacy. Her jealousy, in turn, fed his growing annoyance with her; he had no patience with her reasonable wifely anxieties.

A fireside story Dickens wrote several years later, "To Be Read at Dusk," luridly illuminates the de la Rue episode. Set in Genoa and Rome—the two sites where he had most often mesmerized Madame de la Rue—the story involves a just-married young Englishwoman "haunted" in dreams by "the face of a dark, remarkable-looking man, in black, with black hair and a grey moustache . . . looking at her fixedly, out of darkness." She dreams of this face for three nights running before her marriage, though it is "not a face she ever saw, or at all like a face she ever saw." But after her marriage, the phantom face materializes in the form of a Signor Dellombra ("of the shadows") who visits the old palazzo in Genoa where the young bride and her new husband are staying. Meeting Dellombra, the beautiful Englishwoman swoons, "nearly terrified to death, and . . . wandered in her mind about her dream, all night." In the character of the sinister Dellombra, Madame de la Rue's malign Phantom and the Phantom's mesmeric antagonist—Dickens himself—converge. Eventually—seduced, abducted, or both—she is carried off by the sinister Dellombra. "To Be Read at Dusk" betrays Dickens's awareness of the mesmerist's sexual menace and his dangerous sway over a female subject. Though Dickens advertised his hypnotic influence on Madame de la Rue as benign and indeed curative, the story's mesmeric Dellombra is, to the contrary, a sinister seducer.

Though he occasionally corresponded with the de la Rues in later years, his preoccupation with Madame de la Rue, like that with Christiana Weller, soon faded. As he admitted, he was prone to "prancing hobbies." But together, the two episodes reveal not only the fitful nature of his fancies, but also new directions in his feelings. His wife was wise to worry: he was taking a fresh interest in women. His next novel, *Dombey and Son*, would betray this awakening.

More than in any other Dickens novel, women dominate *Dombey and Son*. Saintly, forceful, or fierce, they overshadow their male counterparts.

The strongest of them is the dark heroine, Edith Dombey—a revolutionary character for Dickens, and a portent. Her prominence was unplanned; Dickens himself must have been surprised. He had initially imagined her as a conventional type, a high-society husband-hunter, jaded and languid, "put through her paces, before countless marrying men, like a horse for sale," as his working notes sketched her. "Proud and weary of her degradation, but going on, for it's too late now, to try to turn back." Anyone affecting weariness and boredom offended the earnest, intense, hard-working Dickens, and Edith is condemned as "proud and weary" again when she first strolls into the novel "carrying her gossamer parasol with a proud and weary air." She had no large role in his plans; the novel's designated heroine was rather the virtuous young maiden Florence. After writing the first few chapters, he sent his friend Forster a lengthy plan of the remaining chapters. In the outline, Florence is central; Edith is not even mentioned.

But unexpectedly, she began to assume a heroine's role. Perhaps Dickens was intrigued by his own early description of her as "very handsome, very haughty, very wilful." He had never before created a beautiful woman of complexity or power. Though he had praised Phiz's first depiction of Edith (and her mother) as "admirable—the women *quite perfect*," within a few weeks he was advising Phiz to lend her greater consequence: "I should like Edith . . . to possess the reader with a more serious notion of her having a serious part to play in the story."

Small wonder if Phiz was confused, for Dickens himself was just discovering Edith's potential. The maiden heroine Florence was too mild to ignite much trouble. Edith by contrast was radioactive: sensuous, fiery, angry, mysterious. Dickens grew fascinated. "The interest and passion" of the novel, Forster recalled, "when to himself both became centred in Florence and in Edith Dombey, took stronger hold of him, and more powerfully affected him, than had been the case in any of his previous writings, I think, excepting only the close of the *Old Curiosity Shop*" [with the celebrated death of Little Nell]; and he abandoned his annual Christmas book because (as Georgina Hogarth recalled) "he found that the engrossing interest of his novel as it approached completion made it impossible for him to finish the other work in time." Edith's advent had unexpectedly charged *Dombey and Son* with erotic tension and conflict. Matched against the two leading males, the autocratic Dombey and the crafty Carker, she baffles and humiliates both. Though intending that she would die in disgrace, the relentless Dickens relented and spared her. Edith lives to the end, defeated but unrepentant.

He had divided feelings about his problematic heroine, and it is suggestive that his fascination with Edith is most eloquently expressed by the novel's archvillain Carker. Carker is stunned by Edith's beauty: "He had never thought Edith half so beautiful before. Much as he admired the graces of her face and form, and freshly as they dwelt within his sensual remembrance, he had never thought her half so beautiful." The Devil himself can admire a lovely woman, and like Milton's Satan admiring Eve—"That space the Evil One abstracted stood/From his own evil, and for the time remained/Stupidly good"—Carker's malice is momentarily overawed by Edith's beauty. Disapproving, Dickens nonetheless understood Carker's susceptibility, his "sensual remembrance."

"Beauty" and "beautiful" are used to describe Edith some sixty times, though she appears in fewer than a third of the novel's sixty-two chapters; even Dickens's abundant verbal resources were challenged to convey her loveliness as he saw it in his mind's eye. He imagined her dangerously dark, with "rich black hair," "dark eyes" and "dark lashes," "a dark smile," "a dark glance," "a frown so black," "a dark gaze," "dark and threatening beauty." Angry, she burns with "dark pride and rage." Confronting her detested husband, "she lifted her hand to the tiara of bright jewels radiant on her head, and, plucking it off with a force that dragged and strained her rich black hair with heedless cruelty, and brought it tumbling wildly on her shoulders, cast the gems upon the ground." Frequent references to her breast and bosom—thirty-three, by one count—emphasize her sensuous richness.

If heroines like Agnes Wickfield show Dickens's admiration for the quiet sway of feminine gentleness and compassion, Edith's anger reveals his uneasy interest in erotic power. Her gypsy coloring and dark moods betoken the moral twilight she inhabits. Instructing Phiz, Dickens explained that Edith is "quite a lady in appearance, with something of a proud indifference about her, suggestive of a spark of the Devil within." When she defies Carker, he demands: "What devil possesses you?"—to which she replies: "Their name is Legion." Nothing could be further from Mary Hogarth heroines like Agnes, whom Dickens regularly compares to angels.

Edith "is about thirty—not a day more," Dickens further instructed Phiz: "handsome, though haughty-looking—good figure—well dressed—showy—and desirable." Nowhere in the novel is Edith (or anyone else) described as "desirable"; the word had a sexual edge that Dickens might venture in a private letter to another man, but not in a novel to be read aloud in the parlor. In earlier novels, seductive feminine charm had been modeled on the young Maria Beadnell; Dolly Varden in *Barnaby Rudge* is a Maria-like girl, for example: pretty, coquettish, and "plump," provocative in a flirtatious, succulent way. "When and where was there ever, such a plump, roguish, comely, bright-eyed, enticing, bewitching, captivating, maddening little puss in all this world, as Dolly!" Dark, reserved, mysterious, Edith Dombey's beauty is entirely different. No one would presume to call her a "little puss."

One of the most striking images of Edith appears in a confrontation with the insidious Carker. As she turns on him angrily, we see her from his point of view:

> "Sir," returned Edith, bending her dark gaze full upon him,
> and speaking with a rising passion that inflated her proud

nostril and her swelling neck, and stirred the delicate white down upon a robe she wore, thrown loosely over shoulders that could bear its snowy neighbourhood.

Brooding bitterly, "she plucked the feathers from a pinion of some rare and beautiful bird, which hung from her wrist by a golden thread, to serve her as a fan, and rained them on the ground." In Phiz's black-and-white illustrations, Edith's rich sensuousness is only sketched; to imagine her as Dickens did, we would do better to turn to the highly colored portraits of his contemporary Dante Gabriel Rossetti, the most sensual of the Pre-Raphaelites. With thick flowing hair, voluptuous coloring, and abstracted musings, Rossetti's women radiate eroticism. His later mistress and model Jane Morris—beautiful, dark-haired, stern—might have sat for a portrait of Edith.

Why did Dickens grow fascinated by this highly charged character of his own imagining? She corresponded to no woman in his life, certainly no woman he had ever loved; Edith is as unlike Maria Beadnell as she is unlike Mary Hogarth. With her dark haughty beauty, she does not even seem the kind of woman to whom Dickens was especially attracted. Maria had been a light, even silly, coquette, Mary a virtuous and cheerful maiden, a "winning, happy, amiable companion." Edith is neither coquettish nor amiable, and certainly not saintly.

Her origins lie not in any woman Dickens loved or even knew, perhaps, so much as in the woman missing from his life. She seems a feminine counterpart to Signor Dellombra in "To Be Read at Dusk"— a dangerously erotic dream, a creation of unfulfilled desire. Beautiful, darkly sensuous, defiant, vulnerable, aloof, passionate, Edith embodies the imaginative power of Eros—enigmatic, labyrinthine, creative. As the young wife of "To Be Read at Dusk" was mesmerized by the dark Dellombra, Dickens was himself seduced by Edith.

He had for years been a proponent, virtually *the* Victorian proponent, of optimism, bonhomie, conviviality, good cheer, warm feeling, uplifting sentiment. Now he was wandering into new regions of feeling. "The Woman had once been supreme," Henry Adams observed, ". . . not merely as a sentiment but as a force." With Edith Dombey, Aphrodite stepped into Dickens's fiction as a force, and the spirit of Mary Hogarth, ever at his side, must have been surprised to observe this portent, and apprehensive too.

In 1847, when Edith arrived in *Dombey and Son*, Dickens was thirty-five, in the middle of life's journey—the age at which Dante described himself as wandering into a "selva oscura," a dark wood. Dickens was basking in the sunshine of fame, prosperity, health, energy, and self-assurance. But a decade of discontent had begun.

He remained busy during these years; indeed his life grew even busier; but something needful was lacking. In 1852 he complained of unproductive "Wandering days" when "I seem to be always looking . . . for something I have not found in life, but may possibly come to, a few thousands of years hence, in some other part of some other system," and three years later he wondered "Why is it, that as with poor David [Copperfield], a sense comes always crushing on me now, when I fall into low spirits, as of one happiness I have missed in life, and one friend and companion I have never made?" His sense of desideratum suggests his longing for a quickening feminine presence, a woman to arouse his affections. His wife was stolidly faithful and usually pregnant, "the specialist in childbearing," her biographer notes, while her younger, more active sister Georgina usurped her other wifely roles. Georgina wholly devoted herself to Dickens, efficiently managing household and nursery; he became reliant on her and repaid her with gratitude and confidence. In the early 1850s, while he signed his letters to Catherine "Ever affectionately," to Georgina he was "Ever, my dear Georgy, most affectionately yours." But his affection for Georgina was fraternal, not romantic. Though she plainly loved him deeply, she had little choice but to accept things as they were.

In 1850, soon after finishing *David Copperfield*, he founded a weekly magazine, *Household Words*, with himself as proprietor and editor. Henceforth weekly journalism made heavy demands on his time and energies. *Household Words* was a family magazine: "All social evils, and all home affections and associations, I am particularly anxious to deal with, well," he announced at its commencement. It had a reformist mission, too, and his editorial duties contributed to his absorption in public issues, as he sifted through hundreds of manuscripts on topical matters. Like the dyer's hand, he took on the tincture of the "great mass of matter" in which he was journalistically immersed.

In the first issue of *Household Words*, he issued an optimistic, progressive manifesto:

> We seek to bring into innumerable homes, from the stirring world around us, the knowledge of many social wonders, good and evil, that are not calculated to render any of us less ardently persevering in ourselves, less tolerant of one another, less faithful in the progress of mankind, less thankful for the privilege of living in this summer-dawn of time.

Despite the thrilling summer-dawn of time, however, he often gloomed in wintry discontent. His Christmas contribution to *Household Words* in 1850 was a bleak "December Vision":

> I saw a poisoned air, in which Life drooped. I saw Disease, arrayed in all its store of hideous aspects and appalling shapes, triumphant in every alley, bye-way, court, back-street, and poor abode, in every place where human beings congregated—in the proudest and most boastful places, most of all. I saw innumerable hosts fore-doomed to dark-ness, dirt, pestilence, obscenity, misery, and early death.

The Spirit of Death casts an angry eye on the dismal scene, especially on those responsible, "a small multitude of noisy fools and greedy knaves, whose harvest was in such horrors." Nor in this Christmas vision do the knaves undergo any miraculous conversion, as in *A Christmas Carol*. The Spirit of Death condemns them:

> Whoever is a consenting party to a wrong, comforting himself with the base reflection that it will last his time, shall bear his portion of that wrong throughout ALL TIME. And, in the hour when he and I stand face to face, he shall surely know it, as my name is Death!

A few weeks later, he greeted the New Year with equally sour cheer, imagining the Old Year dictating his final reflections and wishes:

> "I bequeath to my successor," said the aged gentleman, . . . "a vast inheritance of degradation and neglect in England; and I charge him, if he be wise, to get speedily through it. I do hereby give and bequeath to him, also, Ireland. And I admonish him to leave it to his successor in a better condition than he will find it. He can hardly leave it in a worse."

So much for the joys of the summer-dawn of time.

Characteristic of Dickens's mood was his hostility to the Great Exhibition of 1851, an ambitious celebration of technology, industry, and arts held in the vast Crystal Palace, nine hundred thousand square feet of glass erected in Hyde Park. In his 1851 New Year's article in *Household Words*, again speaking in the voice of the Old Year, he first praised the Exhibition:

> "I have seen," [the Old Year] presently said, "a project carried into execution for a great assemblage of the peaceful glories of the world. I have seen a wonderful structure, reared in glass, by the energy and skill of a great natural

genius, self-improved [Joseph Paxton]: worthy descendant
of my Saxon ancestors: worthy type of industry and ingenuity triumphant!"

Changing tone abruptly, however, the Old Year proceeds to dismiss the Exhibition as braggadocio: "Which of my children," he
demands, "shall behold the Princes, Prelates, Nobles, Merchants, of
England, equally united, for another Exhibition—for a great display
of England's sins and negligences?" As a self-congratulatory, unre-
flecting celebration of British "industry and ingenuity triumphant,"
the Exhibition reflected Dickens's progressive sympathies. Yet its
complacent worship of Progress and Technology offended him.
Privately, he thought it "a very Fortunatus's purse of Boredom" and
complained of the crowds it drew to London. "I have always had
an instinctive feeling against the Exhibition, of a faint, inexplicable
sort," he admitted.

Like most decades, the 1850s were both the best and worst of
times, and his pessimism had as much or more to do with private
malaise than with mid-century England. In his frantic pace of
activities he was "more like a man/Flying from something that he
dreads than one/Who sought the thing he loved." Never idle, he pushed
himself to become even busier. With fellow novelist Edward
Bulwer-Lytton he founded a charity called the Guild of Literature and Art, and set about raising funds by means of elaborate
amateur theatrical productions into which he flung himself with
manic gusto:

> The amount of business and correspondence that I have
> to attend to in connexion with the Play, is about (I should
> imagine) equal to the business of the Home Office. As the
> time approaches, it will enormously increase. . . . Carpen-
> ters, scene painters, tailors, bootmakers, musicians, all kinds
> of people, require my constant attention. . . . To crown all,

deducting Rehearsals and journies, I have but three days
in the week to myself, and, in those, I have the Household
Words to write for and think about.

Meanwhile, he dealt with a "rolling of a sea of correspondence
which always flows and never ebbs." A few years earlier, in collabo-
ration with the wealthy banking heiress Angela Burdett Coutts,
he had established a home for homeless women, Urania Cottage,
and he actively managed this enterprise, spending almost as much
time there as at home. Even his recreation—long brisk walks—
was strenuous. Warned by Miss Coutts against cold showers, he
replied: "I have quite a remarkable power of enduring fatigue for
which I believe I am very much indebted to this treatment. . . . It
is because my cut-out way in life obliges me to be so much upon
the strain, that I think it is of service to me as a Refresher—not
as a taker out, but as a putter in of energy." Yet his "cut-out way in
life" and most of its strains were self-imposed.

His ambitious theatricals, in particular, provided much that he
craved: the "assumption" of another personality in acting, busy-ness,
stirring activity, applause. "I left Liverpool at 4 o'Clock this morning,"
he wrote in 1852, following a tour with the amateur company of
friends and family that he had organized and directed, "and am so
blinded by excitement, gas, and waving hats and handkerchiefs, that
I can scarcely see to write—but I cannot go to bed without telling you
what a triumph we have had":

> I can most seriously say that all the sights of the earth turn
> pale in my eyes, before the sight of three thousand people
> with one heart among them, and no capacity in them, in
> spite of all their efforts, of sufficiently testifying to you
> how they believe you to be right and feel that they cannot
> do enough to cheer you on. . . . They rose up, when it was
> over, with a perfect fury of delight.

His audience's furious delight was no greater than his own. "I have been so happy in all this," he declared, "that I could have cried on the shortest notice any time since Tuesday."

Small wonder that he was reluctant to return home, where his portly wife was eight months pregnant with her tenth child.

From his complex but strictly regimented amateur theatricals he derived another benefit—control. He was by nature a benevolent (usually) tyrant, and liked to think his managerial energies and force of personality indispensable. Encouraging Miss Coutts to attend one of his amateur company's performances, he boasted:

> Yet I hope you will go to this Play, consoling your mind with the belief that we have on former occasions done a great deal of good by it, and that no such thing would ever be done but for me, and that there is no one else whom these men would allow to hold them together, or to whose direction they would good-humouredly and with perfect confidence yield themselves.

His management of Urania Cottage, the "Home for Homeless Women," similarly gratified his love of control. He relished the strict regimen imposed on the Home's inmates:

> They rise, both in summer and winter, at six o'clock. Morning prayers and scripture reading take place at a quarter before eight. Breakfast is had immediately afterwards. Dinner at one. Tea at six. Evening prayers are said at half-past eight. The hour of going to bed is nine. Supposing the Home to be full, ten are employed upon the household work; two in the bed-rooms; two in the general living room; two in the Superintendents' rooms; two in the kitchen (who cook); two in the scullery; three at needlework. . . .

The conduct of the girls was graded: "The mark table is divided into the nine following heads. Truthfulness, Industry, Temper, Propriety of Conduct and Conversation, Temperance, Order, Punctuality, Economy, Cleanliness. . . . A separate account for every day is kept with every girl as to each of these items," and so on, down to the last detail of how points were awarded or subtracted—there was something of the busy bureaucrat in Dickens, too. Urania Cottage and the Guild of Literature and Art were designed to aid the unfortunate; but in gratifying his "notions of order" and love of management, they benefitted him as well.

It was a mystery to him, and a severe vexation, that the rest of the world resisted his sagacity and managerial skills. He could scarcely imagine that complex public issues might be more refractory than an unruly girl at Urania Cottage or a glitch in theatrical arrangements. "I found something frightfully wrong at the Philharmonic Hall," he described preparations for the amateurs' performance in Liverpool, "and had to find (in a moment) half a dozen upholsterers, 200 yards of calico, and no end of invention in the way of contrivance." Why couldn't Parliament govern with such dispatch and efficiency? He had no patience with complexities and conflicts in questions of national policy. The persistence of social problems argued either lack of good intentions or lack of effort: the government exerted itself too little, or wrongheadedly. He was supremely self-assured, and his political indignation often reflected the simple frustration that *he* was not in charge—of everything.

Even more frustrating were vexations at home. *Household Words*, Urania Cottage, and his amateur players yielded to his rational and benignant governance; his family were rather less tractable. His sons caused particular anxiety. Charley, the eldest, "is very much grown—an excellent boy at home," Dickens told Miss Coutts (who was underwriting Charley's education at Eton). "All he wants, is a habit of perseverance." Lack of self-discipline and purpose Dickens could scarcely understand or forgive. David Copperfield's resolution might have been directed specifically to Charley's notice:

> I will only add [David says], to what I have already written
> of my perseverance at this time of my life, and of a patient
> and continuous energy which then began to be matured
> within me, and which I know to be the strong part of
> my character, if it have any strength at all, that there, on
> looking back, I find the source of my success.

Inattentive to David's example, however, Charley had "less fixed purpose and energy than I could have supposed possible in my son." Walter, the second son, showed even less promise: "I don't think he is so clever as Charley, but he is a very steady amiable boy, of a good reliable capacity," Dickens praised him, tepidly. At sixteen, Walter was sent to India, never to return.

Worse yet was Catherine's reckless fecundity: for even as Dickens labored to launch his eldest boys in careers, new sons kept arriving. His six youngest children were boys (a daughter among them died as an infant). The male preponderance was a misfortune; he much preferred girls. The fascinating young women of Urania Cottage seem in fact to have served as an alternative family. At home he had a houseful of respectable middle-class children—mostly disappointing sons—taxing his purse and his patience; across town, in less fashionable Shepherd's Bush, was a seraglio of temperamental, colorful young women supported by Miss Coutts's money. For almost a decade he spent nearly as much time with this amusing second family as with his own.

Catherine was not only prolific but disposed to nervous complaints, which became acute after the birth of her ninth child. "As her case is a nervous one and of a peculiar kind," Dickens wrote to a physician, cryptically, "I forbear to describe it . . . until I have the pleasure of seeing you." To confidants he described her symptoms as "an alarming disposition of blood to the head, attended with giddiness and dimness of sight" and "alarming confusion and nervousness at times." He sought professional counsel but characteristically preferred his own:

"After taking the most sensible advice I could get (including my own) I have resolved to carry her down to Malvern, and put her under rigorous discipline of exercise, air, and cold water"—also characteristic of Dickens was the notion of punishing illness with cold water and "rigorous discipline."

Catherine was undergoing her invigorating cold-water treatment at Malvern when, back in London (she had never been able to nurse her babies), their infant daughter Dora suddenly died. Dickens was distressed, but not overly so: "If, with a wish, I could cancel what has happened and bring the little creature back to life, I would not do it." And yet a little daughter might have been a great consolation among his quiver of sons.

In 1852 another child arrived, their tenth, Edward (nicknamed "Plorn"), a child "whom I cannot afford to receive with perfect cordiality," Dickens joked grimly, "as on the whole I could have dispensed with him." He felt himself blameless. "Mrs. Dickens and her boy are in a most blooming condition," he told a correspondent. "I am not quite clear that I particularly wanted the latter, but I have no doubt that he is good for me in some point of view or other."

After one of his theatrical tours, he lamented: "What a thing it is, that we can't be always innocently merry, and happy with those we like best, without looking out at the back windows of life!" The view from the back windows included (among other things) many mouths to feed and a stout and overly prolific wife with bad nerves.

Plorn would be their last child. Given Catherine's fertility—ten children and a miscarriage in sixteen years—and her relative youth (in 1852 she was thirty-six), it seems likely that after Plorn, their marital intimacy greatly slackened or ceased. "Repeated pregnancies were exhausting Catherine's sexual role," one biographer suggests, "and, lacking the personality to keep her in favour with Dickens, she had no other." Dickens, just forty, was trim and vigorous, still enjoying brisk twenty-mile walks; Catherine was heavy and sedentary. He blamed her lethargy for their son Charley's "indescribable lassitude of character." She was clumsy; during a rehearsal of Dickens's amateur players in 1850 she fell into a stage trap and sprained her ankle so badly that she was hobbled for weeks.

Did he recall, as the 1850s dragged on, that David Copperfield's domestic joy had been "perfect"? It would have seemed a sad irony.

In every disturbance, Alexander Dumas advised, *"cherchez la femme"*—look for the woman. But in Dickens's case, there was no woman—and that was the problem. He felt the lack keenly. He recalled the young Maria Beadnell with warm nostalgia; he revered the spirit of Mary Hogarth—but he could no longer sustain himself on the memory of two long-lost girls, however beloved. *David Copperfield* had been a wistful tribute to both, a return to the idols of his early years. His next novel, *Bleak House*, was anything but nostalgic.

Like *Dombey and Son*, *Bleak House* features contrasting heroines: a virtuous maiden and a mature, haughty beauty. The maiden, Esther, is a sunny, sociable, voluble busybody. She narrates her own history, expansively.

But *Bleak House* has a second narrator as well, an anonymous voice observing the action from above. While Esther's perspective is domestic and feminine, the second narrator is implicitly masculine: ironic, lofty, sometimes genial, sometimes indignantly prophetic. The narration alternates between them. The chatty Esther is the heroine of her own story. Her fellow narrator ignores her.

His heroine is the novel's most private and incommunicative character: Lady Dedlock, Dickens's finest tragic heroine.

Like Edith Dombey, Lady Dedlock began as a stale character type, a great lady with a guilty secret: an affair years earlier which issued in an illegitimate child. Her lover having vanished, however, and the infant having died—she thinks—she has married Sir Leicester Dedlock, a wealthy baronet, and become a celebrated figure in Society, her secret safely buried—or so she thinks.

Dickens disapproved of Lady Dedlock, not for her sexual transgression—he was forgiving of that—but for her proud and weary manner, her aristocratic aloofness: "an exhausted composure, a worn-out placidity, an equanimity of fatigue not to be ruffled by interest or satisfaction." Yet despite her languor, we are told at her first appearance, she is susceptible to fads and fashions, and can be manipulated into taking up any vogue: "Is a new dress, a new custom, a new singer, a new dancer, a new form of jewelry, a new dwarf or giant, a new chapel, a new anything, to be set up?" Many astute tradesmen "can tell you how to manage her as if she were a baby."

But this initial concept of Lady Dedlock—vain, frivolous, gullible—soon disappears. It is testimony to the improvisational, sympathetic quality of Dickens's genius that he so often altered his attitude toward his own characters. In particular, he never created a beautiful woman whom he could not pity and forgive. Lady Dedlock begins in affectation, ennui, and foppery; but in each successive appearance she grows stronger and more admirable. Like Edith Dombey, she has a tormentor, and as she battles him we pity her vulnerability and discover her courage. The mature Lady Dedlock—that is, Dickens's mature concept of her—would never betray any vulgar weakness for a new fashion, let alone the latest dwarf. Dickens needed time to understand his own creation.

Lady Dedlock's enigmatic reserve perplexed him. His views on most issues were fixed and certain; but the emotions of a strongly passionate woman carried him into unfamiliar territory. In a curious excursion outside her aristocratic haunts, for example, Lady Dedlock makes a clandestine pilgrimage to the grave of her former lover. Presumably she is moved by nostalgia and piety, a wish to pay her respects to the man she had loved; yet her harsh, abrupt manner during her pilgrimage seems neither nostalgic nor pious, and we are given no glimpse into her thoughts. Even the anonymous narrator, usually self-confident and intrusive, refrains from drawing aside her veil. By this point we are not surprised at her daring or resolution in seeking her dead lover, despite the danger of discovery: "She has a purpose in her, and can follow it." But her feelings remain inscrutable. The mystery Dickens had created, he himself could scarcely penetrate.

His fascination grew. At first he had qualified her beauty: "She has beauty still, and if it be not in its heyday, it is not yet in its autumn. She has a fine face—originally of a character that would be rather called very pretty than handsome." But her beauty grows more potent. "She was as graceful as she was beautiful; perfectly self-possessed; and had the air," Esther testifies, "of being able to attract and interest any one, if she had thought it worth her while"; she has an "air of superiority, and power, and fascination." As with Edith Dombey, "beauty" becomes Lady Dedlock's standard epithet. In *The Age of Innocence*, Newland Archer is struck by "the mysterious authority of beauty" in Countess Olenska (ch. 8). Lady Dedlock's beauty, too, exercises power and command—even over its creator.

She becomes more formidable, growing into a character of perspicacity and penetration. "You see everything," says her husband admiringly. Not overly observant himself, Sir Leicester Dedlock is enamored of his perceptive lady, but even the skeptical narrator concedes "the quickness of her observation." Her "intelligence . . . is too quick and active to be concealed by any studied impassiveness, however habitual." Even her tormentor, a lawyer named Tulkinghorn, an "oyster of the old school," admits: "This woman understands me."

Her intelligence and refinement are stiffened by courage. "My lady . . . is afraid of nothing," the housekeeper at the Dedlock manor in Lincolnshire asserts. Her most appreciative admirer is her enemy Tulkinghorn, who recognizes in her a worthy adversary, a lady of "sense and strength of character." Confronting her with his knowledge of her illegitimate child, he studies her reaction: "Anger, and fear, and shame. All three contending. . . . And he thinks, . . . 'The power and force of this woman are astonishing!'" Her fate in his hands, she braves her danger: "It is not in her nature, when envious eyes are looking on, to yield or to droop."

Edith Dombey and Lady Dedlock were Dickens's first heroines of mature intelligence, keen sensibility, and strong passions, a world apart from the maiden heroines who for all their nascent womanly qualities are comparatively girlish. While Lady Dedlock can be maternal and tender, she can be as fierce as Lady Macbeth. When her nemesis Tulkinghorn is murdered, she feels a "wicked relief," for she "has often, often, often wished him dead." We wonder if she has shot him herself, and Dickens establishes her as the primary suspect. But Tulkinghorn has actually been shot by another woman, who has vicariously enacted Lady Dedlock's wish. "What power this woman has to keep these raging passions down!" Tulkinghorn himself had earlier observed.

While the young heroine Esther is coy and loquacious, Lady Dedlock is cool and self-contained. She is a woman of strong unfulfilled desires which express themselves silently—in her reserve, her dark beauty, her boredom, her remoteness, her haughtiness, her feelings of guilt. She is consistently associated with cold, rain, shadow, darkness, loneliness, secrecy, ghosts, pursuit, death. Her reticence is a veil, both concealing and hinting at strong emotions. "The deepest feeling shows itself in silence," Marianne Moore observed: "Not in silence but restraint" ("Silence").

That Lady Dedlock acts as hostess for houseparties at the Dedlock manor and frequents fashionable entertainments in London ironically emphasizes her isolation. It is curious that she bothers to go out at all, in fact, as she seems indifferent to social intercourse. Her silence conceals deep currents of feeling, invisible beneath the shallow chatter rippling across the drawing room and ballroom. In the novel's final glance at Lady Dedlock, she is entombed in the Dedlock mausoleum in Lincolnshire, secure forever in her privacy and silence.

When the secret of her youthful liaison and love child is about to be exposed, Lady Dedlock flees the Dedlock mansion in London. The sagacious detective Mr. Bucket, accompanied by Esther (the love child herself), tracks her through the night, out of the city and far into the countryside, in a heavy snowstorm, until he deduces that Lady Dedlock, baffling pursuit, has doubled back to London. Returning in her footsteps, Bucket and Esther finally overtake her at the gate of a London graveyard, where her old lover, Esther's father, lies buried. But Lady Dedlock, now dead herself, has eluded them again.

Her veil is finally lifted. Dying, she chooses her lover's grave for her own death. "Whither thou diest, will I die," says the Old Testament's Ruth to Naomi, "and there will I be buried." Lady Dedlock similarly professes her loyalty. In her journey through the snow to a squalid London graveyard, we discover that her secret is not her sinful liaison and illegitimate child, but her persistent love for a man who fell out of her life years earlier. Since his disappearance, her most intense feelings have been suppressed but not extinguished.

In her devotion to an old lover, Lady Dedlock is Dickens himself. The cool, elegant, beautiful aristocratic lady has little else in common with the self-made dynamo from the heart of middle-class England. But he too remained emotionally bound to a lost love—two of them, in fact. No successor to Maria and Mary had loosened their hold on him. Frozen in death, Lady Dedlock reaches futilely through the iron bars of the graveyard gate, unable to pass beyond, just as she had been barred from her lover during her life—for the iron gate is death itself. Her dying journey to his grave recalls Dickens's frustrated desire to be buried next to Mary Hogarth in Kensal Green.

Though academic critics of *Bleak House* usually belabor its social and political themes, it is more profoundly a novel about love. With her elegance, beauty, and refinement, Lady Dedlock lives a world apart from the crowded graveyard of her lover, with its rats and bones and rank exhalations of decay. Yet in her love for him, beauty and wretchedness converge. Her pilgrimage to her lover's grave offers an allegory of the spirit seeking embodiment, of the soul descending into blood and sweat and bone. Human love is ambiguous, a paradoxical marriage of imperishable spirit and corruptible flesh.

"Fair and foul are near of kin," William Butler Yeats's Crazy Jane exclaims:

> "And fair need foul," I cried.
> "My friends are gone, but that's a truth
> Nor grave nor bed denied,
> Learned in bodily lowliness
> And in the heart's pride."
>
>   ("Crazy Jane Talks with the Bishop")

Bleak House has a strong satiric, indignant flavor; there was much in England that irritated Dickens, and he intended to chastise and exhort. But lured off course by Lady Dedlock, he wandered into emotions and ideas beyond the earlier good cheer of the *Christmas Carol* philosophy, or his various vehement opinions on contemporary issues, or even his adoration for Mary Hogarth.

Ten years later, in *Great Expectations*, Dickens would write one ending, discard it, and write another.

Bleak House also has two endings—side by side. As with the halcyon ending of *David Copperfield*, the final chapter of *Bleak House* jumps ahead, "full seven happy years" beyond the main action. Esther narrates this last chapter, updating us on herself and the rest of her circle. She has married a conspicuously virtuous physician and they are living with their two daughters in a rural Yorkshire village. She modestly reports herself highly esteemed by the villagers and doted on by her uxorious husband. They regularly see the novel's other virtuous characters, making for a tight little circle of virtue. It is a characteristic Dickens ending for good characters—much like the rosy ending of *Oliver Twist*, for example, fifteen years earlier.

But this concluding idyll follows a more melancholy scene in the previous chapter, which describes the broken fortunes of the Dedlocks.

Lady Dedlock herself lies in the family mausoleum at their desolate Lincolnshire estate, Chesney Wold:

> Thus Chesney Wold. With so much of itself abandoned to darkness and vacancy; with so little change under the summer shining or the wintry lowering; so sombre and motionless always—no flag flying now by day, no rows of lights sparkling by night; with no family to come and go, no visitors to be the souls of pale cold shapes of rooms, no stir of life about it;—passion and pride, even to the stranger's eye, have died away from the place in Lincolnshire, and yielded it to dull repose.

The children of storm, the passionate Lady Dedlock and her rake lover, have been succeeded by the children of calm, Esther and her contented circle. "Passion and pride" have given way to rational, complacent virtue; fire and ice to tidy domesticity. The gain seems ambiguous, but Dickens was always drawn to cozy visions of snugness and punctilious housekeeping.

But Lady Dedlock inoculated *Bleak House* with a fundamental discontent alien to his earlier novels. A detour into moral complexities was not on his agenda; he preferred straightforward preaching. But Dickens the creator knew about feelings unknown to Dickens the moralist. The novel's anonymous narrator diagnoses Lady Dedlock's icy manner as a case of benevolent natural feelings sadly inhibited, implying that a night of fearful dreams might convert her, like Ebenezer Scrooge, into a more sociable and cheerful citizen. But the lonely woman created by Dickens resists his own facile explanation of her character. No overnight change of heart will whisk away Lady Dedlock's malaise, for her deepest affections lie in the past, and in the grave.

Dickens had a reputation for moral optimism, and disapproved of regressive emotions like Lady Dedlock's. He believed in the healing power of memory—the Ghost of Christmas Past melts Scrooge's frozen heart—but Lady Dedlock's memories are less therapeutic. *Bleak House* betrays a suspicion that urgent memories and longings cannot easily be reformed. Though censuring Lady Dedlock's chilly hauteur and unsociability, he sympathized with her too. How could he censure her? Despite his public bonhomie, he too held much in reserve.

Lady Dedlock nudged his fiction for the first time into tragedy. There is a Greek quality in her fatal progress: her warm, indiscreet love as a young woman, leading her into a guilty transgression; her rise to social and fashionable heights; an impulsive betrayal of her buried feelings; pursuit by an implacable avenger who exhumes her past; and the eventual exposure of her secret, leading to her death. She never becomes a repentant sinner, like Scrooge, contrite and eager to reform. Instead, she broods on the what-ifs and might-have-beens:

> . . . still my Lady's eyes are on the fire.
> In search of what? Of any hand that is no more, of any hand that never was, of any touch that might have magically changed her life?

Far from regretting her ruinous love, she dies struggling to rejoin her lover.

"You have achieved so much, Lady Dedlock," another character compliments her. "'So much!' she repeated, slightly laughing. 'Yes!'" Her self-mocking irony reveals her awareness of the emptiness of "success" and celebrity. Her doom approaching, she remarks, "I must travel my dark road alone, and it will lead me where it will."

Did Dickens see himself beside her, traveling the same gloomy road?

Finishing *Bleak House* in 1853, he hoped to take at least a year off from novel-writing. Within months, however, he was at work on another novel, *Hard Times.* "No man but a blockhead ever wrote, except for money," Dr. Johnson observed, and Dickens too had a pragmatic attitude toward writing: it was a business, not recreational self-expression. *Hard Times* in particular originated in mundane commercial considerations, the need to boost circulation of his magazine *Household Words*, in which it appeared in weekly installments.

Hard Times is the most journalistic and tendentious of Dickens's novels, and in consequence a frequently assigned college text. His imaginative energies depleted after two years' labor on *Bleak House*—Pegasus's wings drooping, as it were—he filled *Hard Times* with topical issues: utilitarianism, education, industrialism, labor conflict, divorce law. Among the titles he considered was *Black and White*, suggesting the novel's simplistic moral oppositions. With easy classroom talking points and comparative brevity—only a quarter the length of *Bleak House*—*Hard Times* is often imposed on bemused undergraduates who no doubt emerge from the encounter thinking the "Sparkler of Albion" a pretty dull dog.

A few months before beginning *Hard Times*, Dickens wrote an article for *Household Words* defending fairy tales. "In a utilitarian age, of all other times," he argued, "it is a matter of grave importance that Fairy tales should be respected." Innocent fantasy was the nursery of "gentleness and mercy": "Forbearance, courtesy, consideration for the poor and aged, kind treatment of animals, the love of nature, abhorrence of tyranny and brute force—many good things have been first nourished in the child's heart by this powerful aid." But even as it dramatizes this same theme, the moral value of fancy and romance, *Hard Times* is ironically the least fanciful and romantic of Dickens's novels.

Two hard businessmen, Gradgrind and Bounderby, represent the evil in *Hard Times*; the redeeming influence is of course feminine, embodied in two heroines. The better to inspire, both heroines are denied romantic distractions. In love with a married man, the elder, Rachael, not only renounces any irregular intimacy with him but saves his wretched wife from accidentally poisoning herself, although her death would benefit everyone. While the husband would prefer Rachael's embrace, she gives him, instead, uplift: "As the shining stars were to the heavy candle in the window, so was Rachael, in the rugged fancy of this man, to the common experiences of his life."

The novel's other heroine, Sissy, daughter of a horse rider in a traveling circus, is young and darkly attractive—"so dark-eyed and darkhaired, that she seemed to receive a deeper and more lustrous color from the sun." But despite the sensuous warmth hinted by her rich coloring, Dickens vetoed love for Sissy as well: "Lover for Sissy?" he queried in his plans. "No. Decide on no love at all." Her role is redemptive, not romantic. "Carry on Sissy—Power of affection," Dickens noted tersely in his working memoranda. In a climactic encounter with the novel's aristocratic cad, Sissy triumphs with gentle earnestness:

> The child-like ingenuousness with which his visitor [Sissy] spoke, her modest fearlessness, her truthfulness which put all artifice aside, her entire forgetfulness of herself in her earnest quiet holding to the object with which she had come; all this, together with her reliance on his easily-given promise—which in itself shamed him—presented something in which he was so inexperienced, and against which he knew any of his usual weapons would fall so powerless; that not a word could he rally to his relief.

No scene in Dickens better illustrates the irresistible power of the feminine spirit—the moral heart of his fiction. Despite all the ideas and opinions knocking about in *Hard Times*, the example of Mary Hogarth remained his only effective answer to the world's ills.

But *Hard Times* features a third heroine as well, much unlike the two exemplary heroines. Louisa Gradgrind is a girl of strong emotions strangled by a rationalist upbringing:

> . . . struggling through the dissatisfaction of her face, there was a light with nothing to rest upon, a fire with nothing to burn, a starved imagination keeping life in itself somehow,

which brightened its expression. Not with the brightness natural to cheerful youth, but with uncertain, eager,
doubtful flashes, which had something painful in them,
analogous to the changes on a blind face groping its way.

By denying her any childhood fancy, Louisa's father has stunted her
natural feelings, and a starved imagination issues in emotional poverty.
As with Edith Dombey and Lady Dedlock, Louisa's natural warmth
has been frozen—on the surface. When her father relays a marriage
proposal from an undesirable suitor,

> . . . she sat so long looking silently towards the town, that
> he said, at length: "Are you consulting the chimneys of the
> Coketown works, Louisa?"
> "There seems to be nothing there, but languid and
> monotonous smoke. Yet when the night comes, Fire bursts
> out, father!" she answered, turning quickly.

Inevitably, her own fires erupt. Unhappily married, courted by a
suave idler, she abandons her husband—and then jilts her would-be
paramour too. (Edith Dombey had done the same.)

Early in *Bleak House,* as Lady Dedlock sits by the fire at the stately
London house of the Dedlocks, she casually glances at a handwritten affidavit lying on the table next to her chair. She starts in
surprise—impulsively asks "Who copied that?"—and then faints,
with a faintness "like the faintness of death," she murmurs. She has
recognized the handwriting of her old and, she thought, dead lover;
alive, as it turns out, but scraping out a mean living by copying legal
documents.

Her instantaneous recognition of his handwriting, years after he
has vanished, might seem a melodramatic improbability, except that
one day in February 1855, casually glancing at his own mail, Dickens

was startled to recognize the handwriting of *his* old flame, Maria Beadnell—now Mrs. Henry Winter.

> As I was reading by my fire last night [he wrote her], a handful of notes was laid down on my table. I looked them over, and, recognizing the writing of no private friend, let them lie there, and went back to my book. But I found my mind curiously disturbed, and wandering away through so many years to such early times of my life, that I was quite perplexed to account for it. . . . At last it came into my head that it must have been suggested by something in the look of one of those letters. So I turned them over again,—and suddenly the remembrance of your hand, came upon me with an influence that I cannot express to you. Three or four and twenty years vanished like a dream.

Uncannily, Lady Dedlock's recognition of an old lover's handwriting anticipated the same scene in Dickens's own life.

It was an evening in deep winter when, sitting before his fire (like Lady Dedlock), Dickens glanced at Maria's handwriting, and the shock of recognition sent him into the past with a rush of feeling. In the twelve thick volumes of his published letters, nothing matches the intoxicated excitement of the three long letters he wrote Maria that winter. It is ironic that his only surviving love letters are not to Mary Hogarth or Ellen Ternan, nor even to the pretty young Maria Beadnell, but to a middle-aged woman he hadn't seen in years and who had in the meantime grown (in her own words) "toothless, fat, old, and ugly."

But it was of course not this matron about whom Dickens felt so excited. What stirred him was the vivid memory of the young Maria Beadnell, and even more of the young Charles Dickens who had loved her so ardently:

I have always believed since, and always shall to the last, that there never was such a faithful and devoted poor fellow as I was. Whatever of fancy, romance, energy, passion, aspiration and determination belong to me, I never have separated and never shall separate from the hard-hearted little woman—you—whom it is nothing to say I would have died for, with the greatest alacrity! I never can think, and I never seem to observe, that other young people are in such desperate earnest, or set so much, so long, upon one absorbing hope. . . . The sound of it ["Maria"] has always filled me with a kind of pity and respect for the deep truth that I had, in my silly hobbledehoyhood, to bestow upon one creature who represented the whole world to me. I have never been so good a man since, as I was when you made me wretchedly happy.

Maria's letter prompted a poignant nostalgia for that long-vanished time of "fancy, romance, energy, passion." For such loss, what gain? Genius, fame, adulation, prosperity, comfort, friends, loyal wife, loving daughters and sister-in-law, a profusion of sons, good health—nothing could compensate. He hungered for a revival of passion: for someone to die for gladly, and with the greatest alacrity!—someone about whom he could feel desperately earnest. Even the intense miseries of baffled love—"wretched" happiness—were better than emptiness. Mrs. Henry Winter, formerly Maria Beadnell, had unsuspectingly reignited the torch.

The anticipation was all; the upshot was brief and deflating. Hinting that he was open to a liaison, he arranged to meet with Maria, but recoiled to discover her no longer twenty-one and lovely. The torch was instantly quenched. Rather than tragic, like Lady Dedlock's re-encounter with her past, Dickens's reunion with Maria Beadnell was simply disillusioning. But it reaffirmed his kinship with Lady Dedlock, with whom he shared not just a good eye for handwriting but, even more, a strong commitment to dead lovers.

The brief revival of his flame for Maria has often been regarded as a folly. Dickens himself fostered this view by introducing into his next novel, *Little Dorrit*, a warm-hearted but silly character, Flora, inspired by Mrs. Winter. Thus Maria Beadnell, as girl and matron, inspired two of Dickens's most endearing female characters, Dora and Flora.

Maria had been a potent force in Dickens's early life, a memory he had long and dearly cherished. In the winter of 1855, that fancy flared out forever. It was a sad disillusion—but also, perhaps, a liberation.

Soon after his reunion with Maria Beadnell, he began writing *Little Dorrit*, his eleventh novel. In the autumn he carried his family to Paris, where he continued writing monthly installments. Meanwhile, in letters to his friends John Forster and Wilkie Collins back in England, he described Paris's diversions. Forster was steady, sober, moral, responsible, self-important; Collins openly kept a mistress (and would later juggle two at the same time). Dickens's letters to Forster detailed his theatrical outings; those to Collins glanced at more louche adventures. In January 1856, for example, he told Collins that "my head really stings with the visions of the book [*Little Dorrit*], and I am going, as we French say, to disembarrass it by plunging out into some of the strange places I glide into of nights in these latitudes."

Amidst these nocturnal adventures he wrote one of the most poignant chapters in *Little Dorrit*. The young heroine Amy Dorrit tells a feeble-minded companion named Maggie a fairy tale about a princess, a tiny spinstress, and a shadow. Amy's tale is transparently allegorical. The shadow that the little spinstress—Amy herself—hides is her hopeless love for the novel's protagonist, Arthur Clennam. The princess urges the spinstress to disclose the secret of the shadow, and the spinstress explains:

It was the shadow of Some one who had gone by long before: of Some one who had gone on far away quite out of reach, never, never to come back . . . no one so good and kind had ever passed that way, . . . She said, too, that nobody missed it, that nobody was the worse for it, that Some one had gone on to those who were expecting him.

Passing by one day and noticing the cottage empty, the princess discovers that the tiny spinstress has died. She looks in the cottage "to search for the treasured shadow":

> But there was no sign of it to be found anywhere; and then she knew that the tiny woman had told her the truth, and that it would never give any body any trouble, and that it had sunk quietly into her own grave, and that she and it were at rest together.

Silently pining for Clennam, Amy Dorrit meanwhile devotes herself to her selfish father moldering in debtors' prison and humbly serves her shiftless brother and moody, self-absorbed sister, supporting all of them by drudging as a seamstress, her "heart impelled by love and self-devotion to the lowliest work in the lowliest way of life!" As if her prison-tainted family were not burden enough, she also cares "with infinite tenderness" for the simple-minded Maggie. No heroine, not even *David Copperfield*'s Agnes, better embodies the "infinitely suffering, infinitely gentle" spirit of Dickens's religion. "The least, the quietest, and weakest of Heaven's creatures," Amy Dorrit is a pattern of feminine devotion, self-abnegation, and purity; the Beatitudes incarnate. Even as Dickens's nostalgia for Maria Beadnell received a fatal jolt, Mary Hogarth inspired another fictional saint.

Amy Dorrit's moving tale of the tiny spinstress and the shadow appeared in the seventh monthly number of *Little Dorrit*, which Dickens finished in Paris in April 1856. The same week, he "paid three francs at the door of that place where we saw the wrestling," he wrote to Collins, "and went in, at 11 o-Clock, to a Ball. Much the same as our own National Argyll Rooms"—glossed by the editors of Dickens's letters as "virtually a high-class brothel." "Some pretty faces," Dickens commented of the women, "but all of two classes—wicked and coldly calculating, or haggard and wretched in their worn beauty." But one of the worn beauties fascinated him:

> . . . a woman of thirty or so, in an Indian shawl, who never stirred from a seat in a corner all the time I was there. Handsome, regardless, brooding, and yet with some nobler qualities in her forehead. I mean to walk about tonight, and look for her.

Fresh from the affecting tale of Amy Dorrit's hidden love, Dickens thus embarked on a prowl through midnight Paris, searching for an unknown woman of dubious credentials.

What exactly was he seeking? Casual sex? That would probably over-simplify the case. On the other hand, a polite wish to pay his respects to the woman's "nobler qualities" also seems unlikely. Dickens himself seems to have been unsure of his motives, citing only a vague curiosity: "I didn't speak to her there, but I have a fancy that I should like to know more about her. Never shall, I suppose." Nor did he; or at any rate, there is no further mention of her in his letters—though he is unlikely to have divulged such an adventure to any correspondent other than Collins.

Wandering through his own private "half-deserted streets . . . of insidious intent," he was evidently moved by some mix of boredom, curiosity, restlessness, and desire; but whatever prompted him, his quest for the handsome demimondaine reveals Dickens fascinated with a woman very different from the pure, gentle, self-denying Amy Dorrit with whom his working hours were occupied. In this vaguely Jekyll-and-Hyde divergence, pursuing the saintly Amy by day and the exotic courtesan by night, the devoté of Mary Hogarth adopted at dusk a more sinister muse.

From Paris, he wrote to Forster:

> However strange it is to be never at rest, and never satis-
> fied, and ever trying after something that is never reached,
> and to be always laden with plot and plan and care and
> worry, how clear it is that it must be, and that one is
> driven by an irresistible might until the journey is worked
> out! It is much better to go on and fret, than to stop and
> fret. As to repose—for some men there's no such thing in
> this life. . . . The old days—the old days! Shall I ever, I
> wonder, get the frame of mind back as it used to be then?
> Something of it perhaps—but never quite as it used to be.
> I find that the skeleton in my domestic closet is becoming
> a pretty big one.

The skeleton was his marriage.

On the same day that he wrote to Forster of his restlessness, he wrote to Collins ridiculing his wife's excitement about the new-born son of Napoleon III: "I find Mrs. Dickens flying to the window whenever a fast carriage is heard, and then pretending to be so calmly looking toward the Ave de l'Etoile, that I know her to be on the watch for something from the Tuilleries"—that is, for a carriage carrying the infant prince. "Flying" to the window was an exaggeration, however, for Catherine was too stout to take wing. Her appetite was robust. "Last Friday," he told Collins, "I took Mrs. Dickens, Georgina, and Mary and Katey [his two daughters], to dine at the Trois freres. Mrs. Dickens nearly killed herself, but the others hardly did that justice to the dinner that I had expected." One reason he emphasized Amy Dorrit's slight girlish figure was perhaps his wife's stoutness. Employed as a seamstress, Amy Dorrit each day smuggles her dinner back to her father in debtors' prison, herself going hungry. Her fasting obliquely commented on his wife's self-indulgence at table. It is hard to imagine that he still found her sexually attractive.

He too was hungry, not for the cuisine at the Trois frères but for change. At the beginning of *Little Dorrit*, Arthur Clennam has just returned from twenty years of barren, lonely exile in China. Dickens and Catherine had been married just twenty years. Parisian adventures like that of the houri with the Indian shawl failed to appease his restlessness, and he indulged more outlandish fantasies. Earlier he had considered retreating to the Alps:

> I have visions of living for half a year or so, in all sorts of inaccessible places, and opening a new book therein. A floating idea of going up above the snow-line in Switzerland, and living in some astonishing convent, hovers about me.

In Paris, he reverted to this fancy of retreating to "the top of the Great St. Bernard. . . . Two or three years hence, perhaps you'll find me living with the Monks and the Dogs a whole winter—among the blinding snows that fall about that monastery. I have a serious idea that I shall do it, if I live." But a few months later, he announced that after finishing *Little Dorrit* he might settle in Australia.

Writing of Dickens's mood in the 1850s, his friend Forster would recall that "An unsettled feeling greatly in excess of what was usual . . . became at this time almost habitual, and the satisfactions which home should have supplied, and which indeed were essential requirements of his nature, he had failed to find in his home." This delicate mention of domestic discontents, as if the gravy at Tavistock House were lumpy or the linens wrinkled, alluded rather to Dickens's growing alienation from Catherine. The solid, sensible Forster counseled patience. Writing that "I don't know in what strange place, or at what remote elevation above the level of the sea, I might fall to work next," Dickens anticipated Forster's prudent advice:

> *Restlessness*, you will say. Whatever it is, it is always driving me, and I cannot help it. I have rested nine or ten weeks,

and sometimes feel as if it had been a year—though I had the strangest nervous miseries before I stopped. If I couldn't walk fast and far, I should just explode and perish.

By 1856, Dickens gloomed and boiled by turns.

Little Dorrit's Arthur Clennam is the most wearily middle-aged of his heroes. It would be perilous to attribute Clennam's disappointments and melancholy to his author, but the resemblances are unmistakable. Dickens was forty-three when he began writing the novel; Clennam is "a grave dark man of forty" (though only a year later, in the novel's time, he claims to be five or six years older). Whatever his exact age, he *feels* old: "I counted up my years, and considered what I am, and looked back, and looked forward, and found that I should soon be grey. I found that I had climbed the hill, and passed the level ground upon the top, and was descending quickly." Falling in love with a young woman nicknamed "Pet," Clennam sees her as a last chance for rejuvenation. Marrying her, he might erase twenty lost years of exile and, nourished by her youth and vivacity, become twenty again himself. But meeting him on the banks of the Thames and handing him roses, Pet reveals that she is betrothed to a younger man. Afterwards, alone, Clennam "walked on the river's brink in the peaceful moonlight, for some half-an-hour," and then "put his hand in his breast and tenderly took out the handful of roses . . . bent down on the shore, and gently launched them on the flowing river. Pale and unreal in the moonlight, the river floated them away." In Dickens's favorite metaphor of life as a river, Clennam watches as Pet's roses—youth, beauty, love—drift downstream and out of sight.

In fact, losing Pet proves a blessing, leaving Clennam free eventually to marry Amy Dorrit. Like young David Copperfield, he has been blinded by sexual allure, for Pet (rather like Dora) is "a fair girl with rich brown hair hanging free in natural ringlets. A lovely girl . . . round and fresh and dimpled and spoilt." But Clennam's fundamental need is not amorous arousal. Erotic temptations, however innocent, distract him from his higher destiny, union not with Pet but with the true heroine, Amy Dorrit. She, like David Copperfield's Agnes, has loved our erring hero all along, waiting like a loving God for the lost soul to accept her love.

Of all Dickens's heroines, Amy Dorrit is the most childlike in appearance, the meekest, the most timid, the most retiring, the humblest. Even her tiny stature suggests an extinction of ego, great love contained in a small vessel. In his 1856 Christmas story, "The Wreck of the Golden Mary," written while he was also writing *Little Dorrit*, the sea captain hero assures his shipwrecked companions that God will greet them in death not only as they are, burdened with a lifetime of failures, but also as the innocent children they used to be:

> "We were all of us," says I, "children once; and our baby feet have strolled in green woods ashore; and our baby hands have gathered flowers in gardens, where the birds were singing. The children that we were, are not lost to the great knowledge of our Creator. Those innocent creatures will appear with us before Him, and plead for us. What we were in the best time of our generous youth will arise and go with us too. The purest part of our lives will not desert us at the pass to which all of us here present are gliding. What we were then, will be as much in existence before Him, as what we are now."

This idiosyncratic notion of the intercessory power of childhood helps explain the imaginative roots of Amy Dorrit, who combines two types that moved Dickens strongly: the innocent child and the gentle, selfless maiden.

At novel's end, Clennam and Amy marry, but their wedding is merely a postscript to the miracle of Clennam's rebirth several chapters earlier. Arrested for debt, he has been languishing in prison when Amy enters quietly, waking him from a despairing stupor:

> She came towards him; and with her hands laid on his
> breast to keep him in his chair, and with her knees upon the
> floor at his feet, and with her lips raised up to kiss him, and
> with her tears dropping on him as the rain from Heaven had
> dropped upon the flowers, Little Dorrit, a living presence,
> called him by his name.

The last phrase echoes Isaiah: "But now saith the Lord . . . Fear not: for I have redeemed thee, I have called *thee* by thy name" (Is 43:1). Like the grace of God, freely offered, Amy Dorrit offers Clennam redemption—from debtors' prison, literally, but more importantly from the prison of his loveless death-in-life. Enriched by a legacy, as she thinks, she begs him to let her pay his debts:

> "But pray, pray, pray, do not turn from your Little Dorrit,
> now, in your affliction! Pray, pray, pray, I beg you and
> implore you with all my grieving heart, my friend—my
> dear!—take all I have, and make it a Blessing to me!"

Amy Dorrit's love has awakened Clennam's own capacity for love: "To believe that all the devotion of this great nature was turned to him in his adversity, to pour out its inexhaustible wealth of goodness upon him, . . . inspired him with an inward fortitude, that rose with his love. And how dearly he loved her, now, what words can tell!" Though still imprisoned, he has been liberated. Nowhere else in Dickens's fiction does his cult of the beatific feminine so nearly echo the Christian mysteries of Grace and Redemption.

Dickens dreamed of his own prison door opening, bringing in spring-time, love, liberation, renewal. As with Clennam, the bringer would be a woman.

Had she lived, Mary Hogarth would have been that missing friend and companion, she who had sympathized "with all my thoughts and feelings more than any one I knew ever did or will." But though dearly beloved still, Mary was a memory of faded vividness, an inspiration of waning force. Since her death two decades earlier, the river of life had carried Dickens far downstream. In "The Holly-Tree," a Christmas story written concurrently with the early chapters of *Little Dorrit*, he recalled his nightly dreams of Mary in the months after her death. The story's narrator tells of dreaming every night of "a very near and dear friend" who has died, just as Dickens dreamt of Mary after her death; but the narrator's dreams, like Dickens's, had ended as soon as he disclosed them: "I lost the beloved figure of my vision in parting with the secret. My sleep has never looked upon it since, in sixteen years, but once"—this one later occasion perhaps recalling Dickens's vision of Mary in Genoa in 1844. But despite his lingering memory of those dream-hauntings, it may suggest a dulling of their power that they should be reduced to an anecdote in a potboiler Christmas story.

Yet if Mary's power had declined, no one had replaced her as his patroness—certainly not Maria Beadnell. Perhaps Maria's disappointing reappearance in 1855 turned his thoughts back to Mary: to his love for her, to her love for him—"the very last words she whispered were of me." Amy Dorrit's redemptive influence on Arthur Clennam suggests Mary's continued inspiration. Appearing to him in prison, Amy is "a living presence," who "called him by his name." As she kneels at Clennam's feet, Amy is obviously "a living presence"; the phrase is pointless with reference to her, but pregnant with suggestions of Mary as an abiding presence to Dickens.

The 1856 story "The Wreck of the Golden Mary" reverts to Mary Hogarth. Adrift with the wreck's survivors, the hero recalls the beloved girl whom *he* had lost years earlier, explaining that he is "a single man (she was too good for this world and for me, and she died six weeks before our marriage-day)." Sliding toward death after days adrift in an open lifeboat, he dreams that she returns to him: ". . . her hands—though she was dead so long—laid me down gently in the bottom of the boat, and she . . . swung me to sleep." The approach of death turns our thoughts to those we love most deeply, and just as he had held the dying Mary in his arms, Dickens happily imagined Mary, in turn, receiving him into death with a gentle embrace.

In the meantime, he could only dream that, as with *Little Dorrit*'s Arthur Clennam, someone might glide into his life, a womanly spirit to reawaken his dead feelings. "Such tricks hath strong imagination/ That if it would but apprehend some joy,/It comprehends some bringer of that joy," Duke Theseus remarks in *A Midsummer Night's Dream* (5.1). *Little Dorrit* shows Dickens wistfully imagining the bringer of a transforming joy, a second coming of Mary Hogarth.

The young woman about to revolutionize his life, however, would be quite different.

CHAPTER 6

Enter the actress, stage left

Dickens wrote the final chapters of *Little Dorrit* in May 1857.

A month later, he was startled to hear of the death of a longtime friend, Douglas Jerrold. A prominent and controversial journalist, playwright, and wit, Jerrold had been for many years a leading writer for *Punch*, the comic and satiric magazine. Dickens had known him for two decades; the week before Jerrold's death, they had made a day's outing to Greenwich together.

As Jerrold had left his widow poorly provided for, the Jerrold family would welcome financial help—or so Dickens assumed. This was not quite the case, as it happened, but without bothering to check he immediately launched a memorial fund to assist Mrs. Jerrold and her unmarried daughter. Opening an office, enlisting prominent *literati* and theatrical figures as sponsors, and organizing an ambitious program of benefit events, he happily plunged into this new project.

After his two years' steady application on *Little Dorrit*, Jerrold's death was a fortuitous boon for Dickens, the Jerrold Fund providing an outlet for his restless energies, a distraction from his discontent. Through the summer of 1857, the Fund kept him busily occupied. He had fixed two thousand pounds as its goal, to be raised by a series of benefit performances—a public lecture by William Makepeace Thackeray, for example, as well as two public readings by himself of *A Christmas Carol*. He also decided to revive a play he had produced a few months earlier with his amateur troupe, of which Jerrold had been a sometime member.

The play was *The Frozen Deep*, written to order by Wilkie Collins with much editorial intervention by Dickens himself. Several years earlier, he had begun staging home theatricals during the Christmas season, and in Dickensian fashion they grew increasingly elaborate. In the spring of 1856, he had been seized by the notion of a more ambitious production yet. Still occupied with *Little Dorrit*, he recruited Collins to write a play, a dramatized study of a troubled but noble soul, which Dickens would produce, direct, and stage-manage. Of course he would also take the leading part, for which he added an especially stirring scene. "When the Play was put into rehearsal," a member of the production recalled, "for many weeks one particular scene was omitted, and when at last Dickens introduced it (it was a scene in which he had the stage all to himself) it was a most wonderful piece of Acting. Anything more powerful, more pathetic, more enthralling, I have never seen."

The Frozen Deep is a romantic melodrama about arctic exploration. A decade earlier, an expedition commanded by the explorer Sir John Franklin had disappeared in the Canadian arctic while searching for a Northwest Passage. Nine years later, evidence turned up suggesting (to no one's surprise) that Franklin and his party had perished; shockingly, however, the evidence also suggested that in the party's losing struggle to survive, some had resorted to cannibalism. Dickens was incredulous, indignant at this slur on British fortitude and honor— he was a staunch admirer of sailors and soldiers especially—and in a series of articles in *Household Words* he defended Franklin and his men against the charge of cannibalism. *The Frozen Deep* carried this defense onto the stage, dramatizing a heroic ideal of gallant men battling adversity.

But as Dickens conceived it, *The Frozen Deep* was actually more about Dickens than about Sir John Franklin. His extensive revisions to Collins's draft suggest how closely he identified himself with the play's angry but noble hero.

The word "elaborate" is scarcely adequate to describe the preparations for the first production of *The Frozen Deep*, on Twelfth Night 1857. Using a large room in his London home, Tavistock House on Tavistock Square, Dickens had a bank of bay windows removed and an annex constructed to extend the stage, thirty feet wide, into the garden. Large backdrops were painted for each of the three acts, and two boys were employed to climb above the set and sprinkle down paper snow. The lighting effects required such a maze of gas lines and jets that an anxious inspector "reported great additional risk from Fire," and Dickens's insurance company threatened to raise his premiums. A small chamber orchestra provided an overture and "melodramatic music" specially composed for the play. A professional costumer was hired, along with a peruquier—a wigmaker. To justify so much preparation and expense, four performances were scheduled, each for an audience of ninety, by invitation only. The fortunate few comprised not only family and friends of Dickens and his cast, but (despite his democratic sympathies) numerous *illuminati* and heavyweight dignitaries like the Duke of Devonshire, the wealthy heiress Miss Coutts, the Dean of St. Paul's, the President of the Royal Academy, the Lord Chief Justice, the Chief Baron "and half the Bench"—"Judges enow to hang us all," observed Douglas Jerrold, who attended the final performance. The drama reviewers from several newspapers, including *The Times*, were invited and encouraged to write reviews—which they did. Dickens hoped that when word of the play was bruited about in courtly circles, Queen Victoria might command a private performance at Windsor—which she did not.

Why did he determine to mount such a circus spectacle for what had formerly been a festive but modest family occasion? Perhaps the lavishness and complexity of the arrangements substituted for a lack of genuine holiday spirit. More importantly, immersing himself in his self-created heroic role distracted him from the less happy role of being himself. He loved at all times to lose himself in dramatic impersonation, and now more than ever. He enjoyed making a splash, too ("It has been the talk of all London for these three weeks," he boasted); and if the splash included tears, so much the better. "Our audiences have been excellent, with a wonderful power of crying," he gloated. Certainly the stir of preparations and rehearsals, beginning two months before opening night, proved an active and sociable escape from the solitary hours spent at his desk writing *Little Dorrit*, as well as a diversion from his fitful moods. Struggling to analyze his feelings, he explained with unusual vagueness:

> As to the play itself; when it is made as good as my care can make it, I derive a strange feeling out of it, like writing a book in company. A satisfaction of a most singular kind, which has no exact parallel in my life. A something that I suppose to belong to the life of a Labourer in Art, alone, and which has to me a conviction of its being actual Truth without its pain, that I never could adequately state if I were to try never so hard.

Knocking down the sets after the final performance at Tavistock House, he more straightforwardly reported himself "in the depressed agonies of smashing the Theatre." It was now, he lamented, "a mere chaos of scaffolding, ladders, beams, canvases, paint-pots, sawdust, artificial snow, gas-pipes, and ghastliness. I have taken such pains with it for these ten weeks in all my leisure hours, that I feel, now, shipwrecked."

Happily, however, Douglas Jerrold's death five months later offered a fine opportunity to revive *The Frozen Deep*—to revisit the excitement and cheering hurly-burly of staging the play and the gratification of more weeping audiences. Within hours of hearing of Jerrold's death, Dickens announced his plans for a benefit performance of the play; charity coincided with pleasure. The Tavistock House sets had not in fact been smashed, but dismantled and preserved. They were readily available for re-use, the cast was still at hand (and presumably willing), and Dickens was eager.

For the benefit performances, he engaged a small London theater called the Gallery of Illustration. Perhaps his failure to lure the Queen to *The Frozen Deep* in January nagged at him, for, having decided to re-stage the play, he sent an invitation to Windsor and after brief negotiations the Queen agreed to attend a private performance at the Gallery. This occasion was a fine success. "The Queen and her party made a most excellent audience," Dickens's sister-in-law Georgina reported; "so far from being cold, as was expected, they cried and laughed and applauded and made as much demonstration as so small a party (they were not more than fifty) could do." Three public performances followed, also receiving laudatory reviews.

The cast for these performances in July 1857 was much the same as that of the Twelfth Night production in Tavistock House. Dickens's two daughters and two sisters-in-law played most of the female parts; Catherine, formerly a member of his troupe, was by now too stout and ponderous to participate. His sons and various friends took the male roles, with Wilkie Collins as the romantic lead. But the actual hero—Richard Wardour—was of course Dickens himself.

Jilted by a young woman, Clara, whom he has long loved, Wardour has sunk into bitter vindictiveness, swearing vengeance on the unknown man who has stolen Clara's affections, should their paths ever cross. As bad luck would have it, of course, their paths *do* cross: Wardour and Clara's betrothed, Frank Aldersley, sail together on the same arctic expedition, each unaware of the other's connection with

Clara. The expedition's ships, like Franklin's, become icebound in the Canadian arctic; and just as a small party sets out to seek help, Wardour discovers that Aldersley is Clara's betrothed, the man he has been seeking. Aldersley and Wardour disappear together into the falling snow (shaken down by the stagehands perched above), Aldersley ill and weak, the grim, vengeful Wardour carrying a loaded rifle.

A terrible suspense—for once separated from the main party, Wardour will surely shoot or otherwise dispose of the drooping Aldersley, we fear, and in the final act a ragged Wardour in fact reappears on stage sans Aldersley, rejoining the rest of the party, who have meantime been rescued and are encamped on Newfoundland awaiting return to England. With fine implausibility, the play's women including Clara have just shown up in Newfoundland as well.

Suspicion immediately falls on the unaccompanied Wardour. "Why are you here alone? Where is Frank, you villain!" demands a stalwart ship's captain (actually the rotund Mark Lemon, editor of *Punch*). "Where is Frank?"

Faint with exhaustion and starvation, Wardour staggers off—but presently returns carrying Aldersley whom, far from murdering, he has succored at the cost of his own strength. Depositing Aldersley at Clara's feet, Wardour gasps, "He's footsore and weary, Clara. But I have saved him—I have saved him for *you*!"

At which point Wardour sinks to the ground—and Dickens, who imagined so many pathetic deaths in his novels, acted out one on stage. "Nearer, Clara—I want to look my last at *you*," Wardour-Dickens exclaims as death closes in. "My sister, Clara!—Kiss me, sister, kiss me before I die!"—and Clara obligingly does so.

That *The Frozen Deep* indulges in overwrought, almost garish emotionalism is plain; reading the bare text of this sentimental play in library calm a century and half later, one can scarcely understand its *éclat* in 1857. The explanation lies partly in the Victorians' love of melodrama and their less inhibited tears, no doubt, but also in Dickens's exuberant performance as Richard Wardour. (When staged professionally at the Royal Olympic Theatre nine years later, *The Frozen Deep* failed dismally.)

In Dickens's early novel *Nicholas Nickleby*, a theatrical manager named Crummles, unimpressed by an actor playing a black man with only his face and neck blackened, fondly recalls a "first-rate tragedy man . . . who, when he played Othello, used to black himself all over. But that's feeling a part and going into it as if you meant it." A first-rate tragedy man himself, Dickens felt the part of Wardour, and meant it. "Most awful are those wild looks and gestures of the starved, crazed man," one reviewer described his performance; "that husky voice, now fiercely vehement, and now faltering into the last sorrow; that frantic cry when he recognizes Clara; that hysterical burst of joy when he brings in his former object of hatred, to prove that he is not a murderer; and that melting tenderness with which he kisses his old friend and his early love, and passes quietly away from Life." *The Times'* reviewer reflected that no "mere actor, unless under the influence of some extraordinary sympathy with the part assumed," could have portrayed Wardour with such "elaborate detail" as Dickens had done. The reviewer's intuition (or perhaps he had been coached) of Dickens's "extraordinary sympathy" with his role was accurate. He might disguise himself as an arctic explorer—donning a parka, hefting a heavy rifle and glooming through arctic snows—but in Wardour's savage mood, tempered by his higher generosity, Dickens was dramatizing himself, enacting his own malaise and his own heroic aspirations. A few months later, he would write that "all last summer I had a transitory satisfaction in rending the very heart out of my body by doing that Richard Wardour part."

For all its stagy melodrama, *The Frozen Deep* had much in common with the novel Dickens was writing at the same time. In *Little Dorrit*, a despairing man is redeemed by a woman's love; *The Frozen Deep* shows a despairing man redeemed by *his* love for a woman. Redemption from spiritual despondency was by 1857 a pervasive theme in Dickens's creative activity, both writing and acting. Neither novel nor play concerns itself with the mundane question of the hero getting the girl; the issue in each is quasi-religious, salvation through love. Far worse than not winning the woman is having no woman to love. *The Frozen Deep*'s Wardour triumphs in *losing* the girl.

For though embittered by loss of his beloved and tossing off misogynist sentiments, Wardour continues to love Clara—as a memory, a dream, a destination: "I keep her face in my mind, though I can keep nothing else," he explains, lapsing into his final delirium:

> I must wander, wander, wander—restless, sleepless, homeless—till I find her! Over the ice and over the snow, tossing on the sea, tramping over the land—awake all night, awake all day—wander, wander, wander, till I find *her*!

Were these lines written by Wilkie Collins, one wonders, or are they Dickens's addition?—for they suggest Dickens himself wandering through a personal arctic in search of the woman who would reignite his passion; the woman for whom he might happily sacrifice himself.

In Edith Wharton's *Ethan Frome*, the protagonist is similarly frozen, his loveless purgatory expressed by images of a gray frigid wife, a cold kitchen, and a wintry New England landscape as bleak as the arctic setting of *The Frozen Deep*. Ethan Frome has been cold for so long that he can scarcely recall the sensation of warmth. He had visited Florida years earlier, he remarks, "and for a good while afterward I could call up the sight of it in winter. But now it's all snowed under" (Prologue).

So too Dickens. It had been twenty years since the beautiful sorrow of Mary Hogarth's death, even longer since the wretched happiness of his love for Maria Beadnell. Since then, the snows had piled up. Maria's reappearance had proved a false spring. Like the morose Richard Wardour, Dickens was wandering, wandering, wandering over ice and snow, tossing and tramping, until he could regain the lost intensity of loving that elusive *her*!

It was Wardour's good fortune that his "*her*" appeared in time to console him in his dying moments. Dickens's savior remained notional—a memory, a dream, a wistful fantasy.

Even before *The Frozen Deep*'s first London performances in July, Dickens received invitations to stage it in Birmingham and Manchester. Taking the play on the road would be expensive, however, and he feared that the stage sets, designed for the cozy scale of a private house, would be swallowed up in a large hall: "It cannot be done in any *very large* place." Instead, he scheduled additional performances in London, in the small Gallery of Illustration, "in effect but a great Drawing Room." Even after these extra performances, however, and after an additional reading of *A Christmas Carol* in Manchester, the Jerrold Fund stood short of two thousand pounds. Urged again to take *The Frozen Deep* to Manchester and lured by the Manchester Free Trade Hall's two thousand seats, Dickens agreed to perform the play there on two consecutive nights in August. The logistical difficulties of transferring the play to a large hall could be overcome, he concluded, and after the first night's performance had covered all the expenses, the second night would be "sheer profit."

One further difficulty remained, however: the amateur actresses—his daughters, his sisters-in-law, and the wife of his *Household Words* sub-editor W. H. Wills. The large Manchester hall was "out of the question for my girls," he declared; "their action could not be seen, and their voices could not be heard." He also felt the impropriety of gentlewomen performing before an indiscriminate multitude: "The Free Trade Hall is too large and difficult, and altogether too public for my girls." For all his love of the theater, he did not wish his daughters to be mistaken for professional actresses.

Deciding that professionals must take the women's roles in Manchester, he engaged five actresses, among them Mrs. Frances Ternan and her two younger daughters.

The widow of an actor and theater manager, Mrs. Ternan was a veteran actress, and a habitual theater-goer like Dickens would have seen her on London stages. He had seen at least one and possibly all three of her daughters on stage as well, for they had been acting since they were very young; Ellen had been less than four when she made her first appearance. The Ternans were a close-knit, respectable, well-conducted theatrical family. The two younger daughters were now twenty and eighteen; Ellen, the youngest, had just begun playing adult roles.

Dickens had their parts copied out and delivered to them, and arranged to rehearse them twice in London. The Ternans were thoroughly professional; two days' drilling under his magisterial direction would sufficiently prepare them for a quick rehearsal of the climactic third act with the rest of the company before the entire troupe entrained for Manchester. There, in the Free Trade Hall, he would conduct a single full rehearsal with the entire cast and all the sets and stage machinery, before the opening performance in the evening.

Possibly Dickens had met Ellen Ternan before *The Frozen Deep*; an early biographer, citing no source, claims that several months earlier they had met backstage just after Ellen had played her first adult role, and that Dickens had found her there weeping in shame over her scanty costume. More likely, he first met her when he hired the Ternans for the Manchester performances.

In early August, Mrs. Ternan and her daughters attended the final London staging of *The Frozen Deep* at the Gallery of Illustration to see just what they had signed on for. Then a few days before the opening in Manchester, Dickens gathered the Ternans and the other actresses in the Gallery of Illustration for their first rehearsal. Of this notable occasion, probably his first extended acquaintance with the Ternans, no record exists, and so with due caution we must imagine it for ourselves.

Dickens genially puts the ladies at their ease, but after a few prefatory remarks on the heroic action of *The Frozen Deep*, he sets them to work. He is a busy and brisk man; at rehearsals "he was all business and attention—a martinet" (one of his amateur actors would testify), "and threw himself into every part in turn—either low comedian or old man." Professional actresses, the Ternans come to the rehearsal well prepared; somewhat in awe of the great man, they have conned their parts with special care. Mrs. Ternan's heart perhaps sinks when she discovers that her lines are to be delivered in Scots dialect (such as "I see you and all around you crying bluid! The stain is on you! Oh my bairn, my bairn, the stain o' that bluid is on *you*!").

Any misgivings she might feel, however, she prudently conceals. Not only Dickens's iron will and forceful personality, but also his strong proprietary feeling, would have been quite evident. Wilkie Collins might claim authorship of *The Frozen Deep*, but Dickens had assumed moral ownership of the hero's role: Richard Wardour was *his* part—Wardour was almost Dickens himself. Nonetheless, he is cheerful and encouraging with his actresses: he is always courteous to women; he is never so happy as when busy with theatricals; and the quick grasp and proficiency of intelligent professional actresses please him, for he is used to directing amateurs. He would not fail to notice that the two Ternan sisters are attractive.

But there is much to do and small leisure for ogling or idling. With all good humor, he leads his actresses through the first act, which the play's female characters have wholly to themselves. We can safely imagine him energetically drilling them in their roles, maneuvering them about the stage, coaching them on how to deliver their lines, how to react. They skip the second act, in which only the male characters are on stage; but in the final act all the characters converge. Rehearsing this act with just the women, Dickens takes on each of the male roles himself, in rapid succession, dashing about the stage with prompt book in hand, though he knows everyone else's lines as well as he knows his own. At the very end, in his own role as the dying Wardour, he gasps his poignant farewell, "Kiss me, sister, kiss me before I die!" as he looks up into the dark eyes of the heroine kneeling over him—not Ellen Ternan, but her sister Maria.

Maria Ternan, in fact, very much struck his fancy. When on the morning of the Manchester opening he held a full-cast rehearsal, she approached him apologetically. "She came to see the play beforehand at the Gallery of Illustration," he recalled, "and when we rehearsed it [in Manchester], she said, 'I am afraid, Mr. Dickens, I shall never be able to bear it; it affected me so much when I saw it, that I hope you will excuse my trembling this morning, for I am afraid of myself.'" Nothing could have pleased him more than this ingenuous remark, for he heartily approved of sympathetic tears and relished his own power to evoke them. During the final scene of the actual performances, Maria dissolved in tears—as Dickens gleefully informed his wealthy friend Miss Coutts, telling her "how much impressed I was at Manchester by the womanly tenderness of a very gentle and good little girl who acted Mary's part [the heroine's role, played in London by his daughter Mary]:

> At night when she came out of the cave and Wardour recognized her, I never saw any thing like the distress and agitation of her face—a very good little pale face, with large black eyes;—it had a natural emotion in it (though it was turned away from the audience) which was quite a study of expression. But when she had to kneel over Wardour dying, and be taken leave of, the tears streamed out of her eyes into his mouth, down his beard, all over his rags—down his arms as he held her by the hair. At the same time she sobbed as if she were breaking her heart, and was quite convulsed with grief. It was of no use for the compassionate Wardour [that is, Dickens] to whisper "My dear child, it will be over in two minutes—there is nothing the matter—don't be so distressed!" She could only sob out, "O! It's so sad, O it's so sad!" . . . By the time the Curtain fell, we were all crying together, and then her mother and sister used to come and put her in a chair and comfort her, before taking her away

to be dressed for the Farce. I told her on the last night that I was sure she had one of the most genuine and feeling hearts in the world; and I don't think I ever saw any thing more prettily simple and unaffected.

Ellen rates scarcely a mention in this luxuriant account, except as the sister who maintained her composure while grown men wept all round her.

The two scheduled Manchester performances, on Friday and Saturday nights, were so successful that Dickens added a third on the following Monday. With the additional night and a final bath of tears, the Jerrold Fund reached the goal of two thousand pounds.

This was fortunate, for Dickens's interest in the Jerrold business had evaporated, and he had acquired a new and less philanthropic enthusiasm.

Did his patroness Miss Coutts, reading his raptures about the girl with "one of the most genuine and feeling hearts in the world," detect signs of a dangerous infatuation?

However percipient, she could scarcely have guessed that his life had just altered dramatically and irreversibly. He himself could scarcely have known. When *Little Dorrit*'s Arthur Clennam was rejected by young Pet Meagles, he became "in his own eyes, as to any similar hope or prospect, a very much older man who had done with that part of life." Clennam's middle-aged despair of amorous fulfillment may have echoed Dickens's own. He was now closer to fifty than forty.

At sixty, however—older than Dickens would live to be—Yeats would defy "decrepit age," proclaiming "Never had I more/Excited, passionate, fantastical/Imagination, nor an ear and eye/That more expected the impossible" ("The Tower"). If Dickens in his bleaker moods was the gray-spirited Clennam, he was also the excited, passionate man who had once loved Maria Beadnell. The sleeping lions now awoke. Soon after Manchester his letters began to betray turbulent emotions. "The restlessness which is the penalty of an imaginative life and constitution . . . so besets me just now, that I feel as if the scaling of all the Mountains in Switzerland, or the doing of any wild thing until I dropped, would be but a slight relief," he told one correspondent. "I want to escape from myself," he told Wilkie Collins. "For, when I *do* start up and stare myself seedily in the face, as happens to be my case at present, my blankness is inconceivable— indescribable—my misery, amazing."

During his theatrical productions, and especially during *The Frozen Deep*, his spirits and energies rose to such a pitch that the abrupt return to the mundane was bound to seem a heavy drop. Yet soon it became evident that his amazing misery now was more than routine post-play deflation. The first mention of the Ternans in his surviving corre- spondence does not occur until almost two weeks after the last Man- chester performance, in the letter to Miss Coutts describing Maria Ternan's weeping. Yet his thoughts in the meantime had dwelt on the two sisters. In Manchester, his amateur company had stayed at the Royal Hotel with their own sitting room, dining room, and twenty- three bedrooms (not counting rooms for the "professional ladies," discreetly segregated from the amateurs). The bustle of preparations and rehearsals, the holiday atmosphere of the train to Manchester and of the Royal Hotel, the glare of the gaslights in the Free Trade Hall, the intense pathos of his death on stage, the applause and tears of two thousand spectators—all this excitement threw a heightened luster on the two pretty young actresses on stage when Wardour expired so heroically. In Manchester, Wilkie Collins recalled, "Dickens surpassed himself." To return to the domestic routine of Tavistock House, with his plump lethargic wife and all those children, was a death. The busy, convivial, animating, gratifying weeks of *The Frozen Deep*, above all his own stirring role, were so emotionally charged that Dickens was left exceptionally susceptible.

His letter to Miss Coutts describing Maria's tears, written two weeks later, suggests that as yet he had no reason to disguise his interest in the Ternans; for in his dealings with Miss Coutts, a lady of strict propriety, he was always on his best behavior. When did his fascination with the Ternan girls become something to conceal? And when did his interest, centered first on Maria, fix itself on Ellen?

The answers to these questions begin to emerge from an expedition he made to the north of England two weeks after *The Frozen Deep* closed in Manchester.

The trip began with an invitation to Wilkie Collins. "Partly in the grim despair and restlessness of this subsidence from excitement, and partly for the sake of Household Words," Dickens suggested a few days after Manchester, "I want to cast about whether you and I can go anywhere—take any tour—see any thing—whereon we could write something together." Meeting a day or two later, he and Collins decided on a bachelor ramble of ten or twelve days "to out-of-the way places, to do (in inns and coast-corners) a little tour in search of an article and in avoidance of railroads." He was vague about their itinerary, mentioning only "odd corners of England" and declaring that "we have not the least idea where we are going."

These evasions are the earliest surviving evidence of questionable intentions, for Dickens had firmly in mind from the start a destination: Doncaster, in Yorkshire. Their arrival there would coincide with Doncaster's well-known Race Week, but horses were not the attraction. Some time during or after Manchester, he had learned that the Ternans had an acting engagement in Doncaster during Race Week, and even as he was declaring that he and Collins would be wandering about England aimlessly and randomly, he wrote to book rooms at the Angel Hotel in Doncaster. Perhaps in mentioning their engagement in Doncaster the Ternans had casually invited him to attend; if so, he may have startled them with a prompt acceptance. Or perhaps he received no invitation, but decided to intercept them at Doncaster anyway. To a risk-taking adventurer in *David Copperfield* he had given the name

"Steerforth," and Dickens himself now resolved to steer boldly, risking the rocky coasts, even welcoming hazards.

It is difficult to know how serious he was about either of the younger Ternan sisters before Doncaster. He may have set out to see them simply as a whim, a careless flirtation. But if so, he was dry tinder flirting with a lighted match, for shortly before departing on the bachelor travels leading to Doncaster he informed Forster that his marriage to Catherine was effectively defunct. "Poor Catherine and I are not made for each other; and there is no help for it," he declared. It was "all but hopeless that we should try to struggle on. What is now befalling me I have seen steadily coming, ever since the days you remember when Mary was born." As he had been married less than two years when his daughter Mary was born, he was essentially claiming that the marriage had been doomed from the beginning. Dickens scholars generally dismiss this assertion—the editors of his letters, for example, assert that "there is no sign whatever of their incompatibility at that date [March 1838], or for long after." Yet Dickens's reference to Mary's birth suggests some specific recollection of that time. He had parted from Maria Beadnell less than three years before marrying Catherine, and perhaps the memory of Maria cast an early shadow over a marriage that was now to founder with the advent of the Ternans.

Restless, miserable, despairing of his marriage, infatuated with one or both of the Ternan sisters—in this inflammable state of mind, Dickens set off to the north with Collins, visiting Carlisle and other Cumberland towns before making their way to Doncaster. In his letters home, addressed to Georgina and signed "Ever affectionately, my dearest Georgy," he sent his love to her and the children, neglecting to mention Catherine at all.

He soon found good material for both his letters and *Household Words*. On a climbing expedition on "a gloomy old mountain" in Cumberland, he and Collins became lost; then as they descended, Collins tumbled into a rocky creek and sprained his ankle. "I don't believe he will stand for a month to come!" Dickens informed Georgina, almost gleefully, adding that "I doubt very much whether he can go on to Doncaster." Collins's misfortune was not going to keep Dickens himself from a rendezvous with the Ternans, however: "Of course I shall go to Doncaster, whether or no." His readiness to abandon his crippled friend betrays his eagerness to see the young actresses.

Collins rallied sufficiently to accompany Dickens to Doncaster, however, where they arrived for the beginning of Race Week.

Dickens arrived in Doncaster intrigued by the Ternan sisters. A week later, he was engrossed by Ellen alone and determined at all costs to pursue her. Flirtation had turned into fixation.

His week in Doncaster is well documented. He wrote several letters to confidants like Georgina and his *Household Words* sub-editor W. H. Wills, detailing his activities and hinting at his amorous adventuring. An impressionistic and colored account of Race Week that he wrote for *Household Words* gives further details. Nonetheless, to the question of "what changed Dickens's flirtatious curiosity into an obsession?"— the answer is unclear.

Race Week attracted a large and unsavory crowd, filling the streets with "horse jockeys, bettors, drunkards, and other blackguards, from morning to night—and all night." With Collins hobbled by his ankle sprain, Dickens was free to roam. On their fourth day in Doncaster, he informed Wills that Collins "can't walk out, but can limp about the room and has had two Doncaster rides in a carriage." A vigorous and indefatigable walker and eager to see as much of the Ternans as possible, Dickens hardly intended to loiter in his hotel nursing an invalid, or to confine his outings to a few carriage rides.

On his very first evening in Doncaster, in fact, he went to a play at the Theatre Royal, alone and, he thought, unrecognized:

I was at the Theatre, where I had been behaving excessively ill in the way of gaping and rubbing my head wearily, from 7 to 11, without the slightest idea that anybody knew me;

and I was slouching out at the fall of the Curtain, with my hands in my pockets and a general expression upon me of total want of dignity, when the Pit suddenly got up without the slightest warning, and cried out "Three cheers for Charles Dickens Esquire!"

The Ternan sisters were not acting this night, accounting for his slouching indifference. The next day, a Tuesday, the races began, but he avoided the track and instead took what he described as a solitary walk through town and out into the countryside. In his *Household Words* account, he calls himself, ironically, "Mr. Goodchild" and describes his stroll as a whimsical vagary: "A walk in the wrong direction may be a better thing for Mr Goodchild today than the Course, so he walks in the wrong direction." The curious insistence on "wrong direction" suggests that far from walking alone, he had companions, some or all of the Ternans, and that the allure of one of them, at least, was leading him astray.

During the course of this walk in the wrong direction, or some other time that day, he invited the Ternans to attend the next day's races with him in his rented carriage. Next morning he wrote to Mrs. Ternan to settle the details: "We will be with you at quarter past one to day," he promised, and was at pains to place himself entirely at her disposal: "We will come away from the course at whatever time suits you best; and pray do me the favor to have no ceremony with me, but [be] quite sure that your convenience is mine." Such solicitude was perhaps motivated by something other than pure chivalry. Impressed by the attentions of the famous man, Mrs. Ternan saved this brief note—apparently the only letter he wrote to her that survives. She was certainly astute enough to recognize that she herself was not the attraction, but was evidently willing to overlook the impropriety of the great man's flirting with one or both of her younger daughters.

Dickens himself was not only conscious of the impropriety, but flaunted it. To Georgina, he described his routine with Collins in

Doncaster: "We breakfast at half-past eight, and fall to work for H. W. [*Household Words*] afterwards. Then I go out, and—hem! look for subjects." That Georgina was expected to understand this coy jest reveals that she was from the outset a confidante in the Ternan affair—and we may be surprised to find that he so freely announced his incipient infidelity to his wife's sister, a young unmarried woman, only thirty, who herself loved him deeply.

To Wills, too, he was both coy and candid about his Doncaster misbehavior. "But Lord bless you," he wrote, "the strongest parts of your present correspondent's heart are made up of weaknesses. And he just come to be here at all (if you knew it) along of his Richard Wardour! Guess *that* riddle, Mr. Wills!" Wills in responding must have mentioned the "riddle," for in his next note Dickens reverted to this code word: "I am going to take the little—riddle—into the country this morning," and "So let the riddle and the riddler go their own wild way, and no harm come of it!"—in a curious mixture of schoolgirl giddiness and manly knowingness. As his involvement with Ellen Ternan progressed from flirtation to intrigue, he would grow more circumspect.

In the meantime, his galloping infatuation is evident in the alteration of his plans for Race Week. Originally he contemplated only a brief stay in Doncaster, perhaps just a day or two. Writing (in third person) to book rooms at the Angel Hotel, he was "not certain that he may remain all through race week." In the event, not only did he remain through Race Week; he stayed beyond. Still in Doncaster on Sunday, two days after the last race, he wrote Wills that "I *think* I shall leave here on Tuesday, but I can't positively say. . . . I did intend to return home tomorrow, but have no idea now of doing that." Already he was reluctant to leave Ellen.

In the travel journal on which he and Collins were collaborating for *Household Words,* Dickens reflected on his own impetuosity. In a dialogue between himself in the person of Goodchild and his companion Thomas Idle (that is, Collins), Idle complains:

". . . to me you are an absolutely terrible fellow. You do nothing like another man. Where another fellow would fall into a footbath of action or emotion, you fall into a mine. Where any other fellow would be a painted butterfly, you are a fiery dragon. Where another man would stake a sixpence, you stake your existence. If you were to go up in a balloon, you would make for Heaven; and if you were to dive into the depths of the earth, nothing short of the other place would content you. What a fellow you are, Francis!"

The cheerful Goodchild laughed.

"It's all very well to laugh, but I wonder you don't feel it to be serious," said Idle. "A man who can do nothing by halves appears to me to be a fearful man."

Perhaps this dialogue echoed an actual exchange with Collins; whether or no, it shows that Dickens knew himself to be a man of extremes, and that his feelings about Ellen were likely to carry him to either heaven or hell, perhaps both. For a man not given to self-analysis it was an accurate insight which events would confirm. He had traveled to Doncaster for sixpence of flirtation, and departed totally invested in a young woman.

Why, despite his Manchester admiration for Maria, who had wept so piteously for Richard Wardour, did he become enamored of her sister Ellen?—for by the end of Race Week in Doncaster, Maria's affecting tears had been displaced by Ellen's less lachrymose charms.

The closest we may get to understanding Ellen's conquest is an exuberant passage Dickens wrote not for a confidant, but for the large audience of *Household Words*. The final installment of his travel journal consists of a colorful account of Doncaster during Race Week, expatiating on the degeneracy of the racing and gambling set but at one point digressing from this theme to describe Mr. Goodchild's susceptibility to a young woman:

He is suspected by Mr Idle to have fallen into a dreadful state concerning a pair of little lilac gloves and a little bonnet that he saw there. Mr Idle asserts, that he did afterwards repeat at the Angel, with an appearance of being lunatically seized, some rhapsody to the following effect: "O little lilac gloves! And O winning little bonnet, making in conjunction with her golden hair quite a Glory in the sunlight round the pretty head, why anything in the world but you and me!"

For years, he had treasured the recollection of Maria Beadnell's blue gloves; now lilac gloves dazzled him. That they belonged to a girl with golden hair shows another shift, for while Maria Beadnell probably had dark hair, Ellen was fair.

The lilac-glove rhapsody continues with Mr. Goodchild wishing that the races might never end: "Why may not this day's running—of horses, to all the rest: of precious sands of life to me—be prolonged through an everlasting autumn-sunshine, without a sunset!" The intoxicating excitement of new love: such moments of intense joy come rarely enough. But Dickens's ode to lilac gloves evinces not only a surge of boyish exuberance, but also erotic excitement. Mary Hogarth he had idealized and rarefied; Ellen is celebrated in more tangible, sensuous terms. Her halo is not of pure light, but golden hair.

He was surely attracted by more than just her golden hair, but it may have been a factor, for while the dangerously erotic women of his novels are always dark, he was fascinated by Ellen's fair hair and blue eyes. In his 1859 Christmas story, "The Haunted House," the narrator admits to a boyish infatuation with "curly light hair and blue eyes." In the novel he was writing at the same time, *A Tale of Two Cities*, Ellen's blue eyes, light hair, and expressive countenance appear in the heroine Lucie Manette, "a young lady of not more than seventeen, . . . a short, slight, pretty figure, a quantity of golden hair, a pair of blue eyes . . . with an inquiring look, and a forehead with a singular capacity (remembering how young and smooth it was) of lifting and knitting itself into an expression that was not quite one of perplexity, or wonder, or alarm, or merely of a bright fixed attention, though it included all the four expressions." Some mysterious combination of youth, vitality, alert prettiness, an innocent and ingenuous air, a willingness to please, September sunlight on golden hair—and who knows what else—operated powerfully on his eager sensibility.

Though the youngest of the Ternan sisters, moreover, Ellen was probably the most daring of them, and perhaps Dickens was drawn by hints of quiet audacity. Her eldest sister Fanny later related an anecdote of Ellen and her other sister Maria flouting railway regulations:

> They have each a little pet dog. . . . They had a coupé [a compartment for two] reserved for them on the railway and brought the dogs to St. Leonards in triumph under the very noses of the authorities. You know it is contrary to rule to have dogs in passenger carriages.

That the smuggled dogs were more likely Ellen's idea is suggested by a later compliment on her riding skills: "Ellen is a first-rate horsewoman. Mia [her sister Maria] rides well but not so well as Ellen, as she is more timid," Fanny observed. Ellen's riding master "said very solemnly one day 'Well, there's one thing I'm thankful for; she (meaning Nelly) can ride as straight to hounds as any woman in Sussex'!" Dickens would have admired such hedge-clearing mettle; perhaps he sensed Ellen's willingness to risk a perilous involvement.

Even as he was stirred amorously, however, he cherished Ellen's innocence and waxed indignant when it was insulted. Watching her act at Doncaster's Theatre Royal, he was offended by the boorish race-crowd spectators, louts exhibiting "a most odious tendency . . . to put vile constructions on sufficiently innocent phrases in the play, and then to applaud them in a Satyr-like manner." One spectator in particular, "more depraved, more foolish, more ignorant, more unable to believe in any noble or good thing of any kind, than the stupidest Bosjeman [Bushman] . . . inflames Mr Goodchild with a burning ardour to fling it into the pit." But the indignities to which the Ternan girls were subjected on stage also made him wonder, more philosophically, "whether that *is* a wholesome Art, which sets women apart on a high floor before such a thing as this"—that is, the worst of the louts. He had refused to expose his daughters even to a sober audience in Manchester; with his patronage, Ellen would soon abandon the stage.

Did Dickens, a forty-five-year-old model citizen with a faithful wife and many children, feel guilty pursuing a virginal eighteen-year-old? Soon after Doncaster, he wrote a "grim" ghost story, "a bit of Diablerie," as he described it, untitled but usually called "The Bride's Chamber," in which a young woman is hypnotically dominated and driven to her death by an insanely vengeful older man, who then commits a more violent murder yet and lives tormented by fear of discovery until, detected and condemned, he is hanged. One scholar, Harry Stone, has argued that "The Bride's Chamber," suffused with magical and fairy-tale elements, expresses self-recrimination: "The dream of felicity [with Ellen], Dickens seems to be saying to himself, is only a dream. Whether he turns to his wife or his princess or his ineffable dream, he feels thwarted, sinful, guilty, a haunted, self-convicted, self-condemned murderer . . . unable to shrive himself." Certainly Dickens *should* have felt some uneasiness in pursuing Ellen. But Stone's argument, floridly elaborated through many pages, transforms a fireside ghost tale into *Crime and Punishment*, and Dickens himself into a Raskolnikov. That the bride in "The Bride's Chamber" is named Ellen is surely no accident; there is also a character named "Dick." A conjunction of names fraught with significance? Perhaps; or perhaps just a playful allusion, comprehensible only to himself, Wilkie Collins, and the Ternans.

What did Ellen think when the renowned author traveled to Doncaster to intercept her family, and when it became evident that his attentions had focused on her? Alas, all the evidence of Race Week

comes from Dickens himself, and Ellen's feelings can only be conjectured. Dickens's daughter Katie came to know Ellen well, and years
later reflected on the young Ellen's response to her father's interest:
"Who could blame her? He had the world at his feet. She was a young
girl of eighteen, elated and proud to be noticed by him." This is likely
enough; what girl would not be flattered by the attentions of a man
of Dickens's genius and celebrity? Yet it seems unlikely that Ellen was
enamored to the same degree, if at all, and while he might discard
caution—"So let the riddle and the riddler go their own wild way"—
the riddle herself, no matter how daring, might well have hesitated
to abandon herself to *his* wild way. Where, she must have wondered,
might this excitable man's infatuation lead him, and what might be
the consequences for her?

Ellen's mother, too, must have wondered about their attentive
new friend. Ten years older than Dickens, she had been born into
a theatrical family, had acted professionally since she was two, had
married an actor, and had raised a family of actresses. She could have
been neither surprised nor scandalized by Dickens's quixotic courtship of her youngest daughter; there was a long tradition of actresses
attracting prominent admirers. Dickens was no doubt ingratiating,
too—charming, attentive, generous. As the Ternans were by no means
wealthy, Mrs. Ternan need not have been mercenary to recognize the
advantages of such an influential and affluent connection. But the
Ternan women did not indulge in casual liaisons. "Although there
are nice people on the stage," Dickens would later tell his daughter
Katie, "there are some who would make your hair stand on end." The
Ternans were among the nice. Mrs. Ternan actively superintended
her daughters, and Ellen was undoubtedly well chaperoned during
Race Week. Though anyone with eyes could have noticed Dickens's
fascination, the Ternans probably maintained the polite pretense that
he was simply a kindly family friend.

He left Doncaster in a tumult of emotions. On one hand, he was
wretched. Even six months later, "the Doncaster unhappiness remains

so strong upon me that I can't write, and (waking) can't rest, one minute." Yet he was also euphoric. Just after Doncaster, he had written of his day at the races with Ellen:

> . . . Arab drums, powerful of old to summon Genii in the desert, sound of yourselves and raise a troop for me in the desert of my heart, which shall so enchant this dusty barouche . . . that I, within it, loving the little lilac gloves, the winning little bonnet, and the dear unknown wearer with the golden hair, may wait by her side for ever, to see a Great St Leger [one of the Doncaster races] that shall never be run!"

Unhappiness and enchantment together: love flooded the desert of his heart—but love for that which was forbidden.

A quarter century earlier, Maria Beadnell had made him "wretchedly happy." Now he must have recognized the signs of that same tumult of feelings.

By 1857, the famous author was ripe for a shakeup. His restlessness of the 1850s coexisted with an unattractive complacency. Dickens was immensely self-assured.

Despite his unsolved personal discontents, he felt he could have solved England's discontents—and he was glad to share his insights. A few months before Ellen Ternan's advent, for example, he confidently informed Sir Joseph Paxton, genius of the Crystal Palace and Member of Parliament, that Parliament was incapable of governing:

> The House of Commons seems to me to be getting worse every day. I solemnly declare to you that direfully against my will, I have come to the conclusion that representative Government is a miserable failure among us. See what you are all about, down at Westminster at this moment with the wretchedest party squabble.

Perhaps Paxton was secretly gratified when with Ellen's arrival Dickens's own life swirled out of control, giving him less leisure for advising Parliament.

Just a few weeks before meeting Ellen, Dickens received a presentation copy of a book on healthful living. Acknowledging the gift, he boasted of his own healthful routine:

> As you refer to my own habits, you may be interested to learn that for the last fifteen or twenty years they have been of the most exact and punctual nature. I portion out my time methodically, take a great deal of exercise and fresh air regularly, am probably as much in all the winds that blow as any country gentleman, bathe in large quantities of cold water all the year round, and can keep a Swiss guide on his mettle during a day's journey.

Given his superabundant vigor, this strenuous regimen was evidently effective, but his self-congratulatory tone suggests the vanity of some of his more repellent fictional characters. His letters and journalism sometimes give the impression that he had figured out life much to his own satisfaction, and that everyone else would do well to heed his example. For all his vivid and ranging fancy, his moral outlook was tidy, narrow and self-righteous. Lord Melbourne is said to have remarked of Macaulay the historian, "I wish I were as sure of anything as Tom Macaulay is of everything." The same quip might have been applied to Dickens.

If his moral certitudes needed a jolt, Ellen Ternan delivered it. His orderly life, that well-regulated system of clean living, cold showers, and moral certitude, went off the rails. By the following year, he was boasting not of "exact and punctual" habits, but of violent impetuosity: "I am a man full of passion and energy," he advised a friend, "and my own wild way that I must go, is often—at the best—wild enough." This plea of irresistible compulsion was self-serving, but his certainties had nonetheless been wholesomely shaken.

The year following *The Frozen Deep* was the most troubled of his life. The well-known opening of his next novel, *A Tale of Two Cities*—"It was the best of times, it was the worst of times"—describes Dickens himself as much as pre-revolutionary France. The poor boy in the blacking factory thirty-five years earlier could scarcely have been more wretched than the great novelist: wrenching himself out of his marriage, splitting his family, alienating friends, shattering a longstanding business partnership, provoking rumor and scandal. "I have now no relief but in action," he told Forster a few weeks after Doncaster. "I am become incapable of rest. I am quite confident I should rust, break, and die, if I spared myself. Much better to die, doing. What I am in that way, nature made me first, and my way of life has of late, alas! confirmed." One night that autumn, exasperated and sleepless, he stomped out the door of his house in London and hiked to Gad's Hill in Kent, in what he described as "my celebrated feat of getting out of bed at 2 in the morning, and walking down there from Tavistock House—over 30 miles—through the dead night. I had been very much put-out; and I thought, 'After all, it would be better to be up and doing something, than lying here.' So I got up, and did that." Several months later, he lamented that "I have never known a moment's peace or content, since the last night of the Frozen Deep."

Shortly before he met Ellen, the Sepoy Mutiny broke out in India. When reports of violence, sieges, and atrocities began to arrive in England, Dickens (whose son Walter had just departed to join one of the East India Company's regiments) raged against the mutineers:

> I wish I were Commander in Chief in India. The first thing
> I would do to strike that Oriental race with amazement . . .
> should be to proclaim to them, in their language, that I
> considered my holding that appointment by the leave of
> God, to mean that I should do my utmost to exterminate

the Race upon whom the stain of the late cruelties rested; and that I begged them to do me the favor to observe that I was there for that purpose and no other, and was now proceeding, with all convenient dispatch and merciful swiftness of execution, to blot it out of mankind and raze it off the face of the earth.

A few years earlier, in the spirit of benevolent reform, he had argued against capital punishment; now he proposed genocide. As usual, his vehement rhetoric reflected personal frustrations more than any careful reflection. Mayhem and bloodshed in India mirrored his own mood, and blustering fantasies of violent revenge gratified his ferocity.

In place of cheerful seasonal uplift, Dickens's 1857 Christmas story offered more bellicosity. Inspired by reports of English courage during the Mutiny, especially that of the women, "The Perils of Certain English Prisoners" (written with Wilkie Collins) is a tale of pirates, silver, betrayal, hand-to-hand fighting, bravery, sharpshooting, and rescue, set on the coast of Central America, a region about which Dickens knew nothing. The most patriotic and martial work he ever wrote, "Perils" is essentially a boy's adventure story, a Dickensian *Treasure Island*. Its belligerence springs from his wrath at the Indian mutineers. At one point, the hero rebukes a pompous official:

> Believing that I hold my commission by the allowance of God, and not that I have received it direct from the Devil, I shall certainly use it, with all avoidance of unnecessary suffering and with all merciful swiftness of execution, to exterminate these people [the pirates] from the face of the earth.

—repeating almost verbatim Dickens's fantasy of revenge against the Sepoy mutineers, quoted above, which he wrote at the same time.

But his infatuation with Ellen also contributed to the heroic gallantry of "Perils." Amatory excitement prompted violent St. George fantasies.

> I wish I had been born in the days of Ogres and Dragon-guarded Castles. I wish an Ogre with seven heads (and no particular evidence of brains in the whole lot of them) had taken the Princess whom I adore—you have no idea how intensely I love her!—to his stronghold on the top of a high series of Mountains, and there tied her up by the hair. Nothing would suit me half so well this day, as climbing after her, sword in hand, and either winning her or being killed.

Both the Mutiny and the young actress kindled his bravado—chivalric in Ellen's case, savage in the Mutiny's.

His immense delight with "Perils," his confident predictions that it would "make a prodigious noise," suggests how far his fervor outran his judgment in the autumn of 1857. But though it is an indifferent story, its boyish ardor reveals Dickens transformed; nothing could have been less youthfully ardent than the somber novel he had finished a few months earlier, *Little Dorrit*. The romantic pathos of "Perils," springing from a soldier's lifelong love for a lady socially beyond his reach, resonated so deeply with Dickens that he was "for days and days, really unable to approach the Proofs. As often as I tried to correct them, I turned them over, looked at the last page, and was so completely overcome, that I couldn't bear to dwell upon it."

Within weeks of Doncaster, he used his theatrical connections to secure Ellen an acting engagement at the Haymarket, one of the oldest and most prosperous London theaters, specializing in comedies. Writing to convey his "cordial thanks" to the theater's manager, James Baldwin Buckstone, Dickens added that "I need hardly tell you that my interest in the young lady does not cease with the effecting of this arrangement, and that I shall always regard your taking care of her and remembering her, as an act of personal friendship to me." Along with his thanks, he enclosed a check for £50, probably to subsidize her wages.

Probably about the same time there occurred (perhaps) an awkward incident. The source is a Mrs. Whiffen, an actress whose husband had a very slight acquaintance with Dickens. Years later, she recalled that her husband had "told me that Dickens's god-daughter was one of the causes of [Mrs. Dickens's] jealousy." (Unless "god-daughter" was a polite euphemism, Mr. Whiffen was unaware of Ellen's actual relationship with Dickens.) Mrs. Dickens called at a London jeweler's shop one day (as Mrs. Whiffen recounted the story), "and the jeweler informed her that her bracelet was ready. She had ordered none. . . . It proved to be a bracelet belonging to the god-daughter, which Mr. Dickens had left to be repaired." This anecdote, often repeated, may have some truth to it, though how much is unclear. "It was pretty generally conceded that Mrs. Dickens was needlessly jealous," Mrs. Whiffen blithely observed—suggesting that she, at any rate, had no clue. Her ignorance, however, may actually enhance the story's credibility.

In May 1858, nine months after *The Frozen Deep*, Dickens separated from Catherine and exiled her from Tavistock House and her children. Her sister Georgina remained with Dickens, creating a suspicious ménage, a separated man living with his unmarried sister-in-law. Unseemly rumors circulated. Thackeray heard "all sorts of horrible stories buzzing about." In denying them, the usually adroit Dickens made matters worse, and what might have been an ephemeral gossip item among the knowing became a protracted indignity. Though vague on details, Thackeray knew there was "some row about an actress in the case, & he denies with the utmost infuriation any charge against her or himself." One of Thackeray's sources told him of an unfortunate encounter between Dickens and his eldest son.

Thackeray repeated the anecdote to his daughter Anne, who in turn relayed it to her governess: "Papa says the story is that Charley met his Father & Miss Whatsname Whatever the actress out walking on Hampstead Heath."

Dickens and his ally Georgina Hogarth vehemently denied the rumors. "I worked hard to prevent it [the separation], so long as I saw any possibility," Georgina insisted, "but latterly I have come to the conviction that there was no other way out of the domestic misery of this house. For my sister and Charles have lived unhappily for years—they were totally unsuited to each other in almost every respect." Curiously, this *apologia* was written for Maria Beadnell Winter, with whom Georgina still corresponded; learning of the separation, perhaps Maria recognized what a favor she had done both Dickens and herself by rejecting him a quarter century earlier. Georgina's explanation continued: "So, by mutual consent and for the reasons I have told you and no other, they have come to this arrangement." Unlike Thackeray, Mrs. Winter did not move in worldly circles and had very likely heard nothing about "Miss Whatsname Whatever the actress"; Georgina's fiercely underscored claim that there was *no other* reason for the Dickens separation might have struck her as strangely overinsistent. It was also, of course, quite false. In the end, the scandal injured Dickens's popularity little if at all—the reading tours on which he soon embarked attracted large friendly audiences—but he was thrown into rage and despondency. "I have been exquisitely distressed," he wrote to a friend in September 1858, lamenting that he "had unwittingly brought the foulest lies" on "the innocent and good. . . . Sometimes I *cannot* bear it. I had one of those fits yesterday, and was utterly desolate and lost." Always vexed when public affairs did not conform to his wishes, he had until now managed to command his private life, at least. Now it too boiled over.

He did not handle the stress well. "My father was like a madman when my mother left home," his daughter Katie recalled:

This affair brought out all that was worst—all that was weakest in him. He did not care a damn what happened to any of us. Nothing could surpass the misery and unhappiness of our home.

Lapsing into self-pity, he regarded himself as a victim rather than the cause of his problems: "If you could know how much I have felt within this last month, and what a sense of Wrong has been upon me, and what a strain and struggle I have lived under," he confided to a friend in June 1858, "you would see that my heart is so jagged and rent and out of shape, that it does not this day leave me hand enough to shape these words." To another he sighed that "I have been heavily wounded, but I have covered the wound up, and left it to heal."

With his separation from Catherine, he left behind more than his marriage. Petulantly and acrimoniously he broke with Bradbury and Evans, his publishers of twenty years, and for good measure swore bitter personal enmity to one of the partners, Frederick Evans. When Dickens's eldest son Charley wed Evans's daughter a few years later, Dickens stayed home. He killed off his prosperous weekly journal *Household Words*, owned jointly with Bradbury and Evans, and launched a replacement, *All the Year Round*, owned entirely by himself and (with a much smaller share) his subeditor Wills. He dropped one of his oldest friends and a leading actor in *The Frozen Deep*, Mark Lemon, because of Lemon's solicitude for Catherine, and managed to quarrel almost gratuitously with another old friend, William Makepeace Thackeray. Even his valuable association with Miss Coutts, whom he had long cultivated, lapsed, along with his involvement with their home for homeless women, Urania Cottage. Miss Coutts betrayed rather too much sympathy for Dickens's wife; perhaps, too, she had heard the rumors about a young actress—rather at odds, it must have seemed, with their joint project to reclaim fallen women.

Amidst all the turmoil generated by Ellen—where was Ellen herself?

Dickens's surviving letters say little about her, now or later. Even with twelve richly annotated volumes of letters documenting much of his life in detail, we glimpse her only occasionally.

Certainly he saw her often. He was determined to do so, and the Ternans welcomed him. Morever, he made no secret of his infatuation among his own family, if the recollection of his daughter Katie is correct: "To Mrs. Dickens, to their elder children [including Katie herself], and to Georgina Hogarth and John Forster 'all was open' regarding the affair—he concealed nothing. It was his wish that things should be that way." According to Katie, Dickens even demanded that Catherine, knowing Ellen to be "the girl with whom he had fallen in love," nonetheless call on her. Small wonder that "nothing could surpass the misery and unhappiness of our home."

Dickens himself probably spent as little time in this unhappy home as he could manage, and as much as possible with Ellen. Between novels and with no other major projects in hand in the months after Doncaster, he had more leisure than usual. With Ellen acting at the Haymarket, an easy walk from his *Household Words* offices near Covent Garden and little more than a mile from Tavistock House, he may often have strolled to watch her rehearse or perform, and perhaps escort her home afterwards. It is easy to imagine him meeting her backstage at the Haymarket after the final curtain; and though he was too well known to escort a young woman about London without causing comment, it would have been difficult for her to decline a chivalrous offer to take her home from the theater late at night, when there was less chance of recognition. On her free nights he probably spent evenings at the Ternans' house in Islington, several miles away; he was there often enough at any rate to judge it "unwholesome," and he "strongly advised Mrs. Ternan to move." No doubt he gave her not just advice but also financial help, and in September 1858, a year after Doncaster, the Ternans moved to Berners Street, closer to the theaters where both Ellen and Maria were acting—and closer to Dickens's offices, as well.

A rainy day in April 1858, eight months after *The Frozen Deep*. The "Doncaster unhappiness" still possesses him; he has been moody all winter, unhappy at home, occasionally frantic, working himself up to break free of his marriage. "Only last night, in my sleep, I was bent upon getting over a perspective of barriers, with my hands and feet bound," he described a nightmare of this time. "Pretty much what we are all about, waking, I think?" But on this wet spring day, he is visiting Hampton Court with Ellen and his spirits are much improved; he is "in the best of humours with the Palace at Hampton Court."

It is a weekday. A dozen miles up the Thames from London, newly accessible by train as well as by river, Hampton Court has by 1858 become a popular spot for Sunday outings, and for his excursion with Ellen he deliberately avoids the holiday crowds. Perhaps the wet weather, too, has kept people away, though it offers the added pleasure of sharing an umbrella with her. Was Ellen's mother or her sister Maria along to chaperone? According to Dickens, no: he and Ellen have the vast rambling palace to themselves: "There was only one other visitor (in very melancholy boots) at Hampton Court that blessed day: who soon went his long grave way . . . and was seen no more." When he and Ellen depart, Dickens's is the only umbrella in the rack at the door.

As at Doncaster, he is combining business with pleasure, for afterwards he will write an essay for *Household Words* disparaging Hampton Court. The palace is dull and dreary. In particular he dislikes the paintings, not bright enough to suit him. He has little interest in antiquities, and narrow tastes in art; surveying the paintings, he comments with broad irony, "I find the moon to be really made of green cheese; the sun to be a yellow wafer or a little round blister; the deep wild sea to be a shallow series of slate-colored festoons turned upside down; the human face Divine to be a smear; the whole material and immaterial universe to be sticky with treacle and polished up with blacking." With fine philistine confidence in his own "private judgment," he deprecates not only the paintings but also the catalog extolling their merits. "Taste" is a tyrant, he proclaims: just as he must check his umbrella at the door (the article is titled "Please to Leave Your Umbrella"), the catalog asks him to leave behind his artistic discrimination.

This may be Ellen's first visit to Hampton Court—she is not a Londoner—but Dickens has been here before and he visits this rainy spring day not with any interest in palace or grounds, but for the pleasure of an outing with her, away from the Argus eyes of London. Reclaiming his umbrella, he departs with nothing pertinent to say about the palace, except to note that with Ellen it has acquired adventitious charms. By himself he might have observed more; with her he is too preoccupied to notice anything else. In "Please to Leave Your Umbrella," he will wander from his criticisms of Hampton Court to other, unrelated grievances—judges and the House of Commons, for example, old horses he had been beating for years, surrogates for the discontent which now focused on his unhappy marriage.

Thus Hampton Court, "Taste," Parliament, the judicial system, and poor Catherine mingle as sources of annoyance. But against and overcoming this conspiracy of vexations shines Ellen. Her youth, freshness, and loveliness expose the lifeless dreariness of the palace's art, darkened by age and gloom. For that matter, how could any cold canvas compete with warm Life—that is, with Ellen? As in his rhapsody on little lilac gloves at Doncaster, again he wishes that Time might stop, making life an eternal day with her: "I wonder whether, with this little reason in my bosom"—the "little reason" being Ellen herself—"I should ever want to get out of these same interminable suites of rooms, and return to noise and bustle! It seems to me that I could stay here very well until the grisly phantom on the pale horse came at a gallop up the staircase, seeking me." Even amidst the dingy paintings, her presence creates "an encompassing universe of beauty and happiness." Together they might "keep house here [at Hampton

Court], all our lives, in perfect contentment; and when we died, our ghosts should make of this dull Palace the first building ever haunted happily!"

The conflicting moods of this excursion reveal Dickens in the springtime of his love for Ellen—frustrated by the obstacles, yet exultant. By the time of the Hampton Court visit, he had determined to separate from Catherine, and the ending of "Please to Leave Your Umbrella" looks ahead to this release. "I gave back my ticket, and got back my Umbrella," he writes, "and then I and my little reason went dreaming away under its shelter through the fast-falling spring rain, which had a sound in it that day like the rustle of the coming summer." The drought of the past decade had broken, and a summer of happiness approached—he hoped. Ellen was an escape from his loveless prison, a rebirth . . . springtime, brightness, happiness, a shared umbrella, a hidden joy.

Another glimpse of Dickens and Ellen together, six months later.

Public readings from his own works given for charity—like his readings of *A Christmas Carol* for the Jerrold Fund—had shown that such performances might generate large profits for himself as well, and in the spring of 1858 he felt pressed for funds. Educating his sons and launching them in careers were expensive. The year before, he had bought a house in the countryside, Gad's Hill in Kent, and he had begun making costly improvements. His separation from Catherine involved a generous allowance for her. He was also subsidizing the Ternans. With all these calls on his purse, he decided to begin giving readings for his own benefit.

It was a fateful decision. To his two occupations of novelist and editor he now added a third, that of performer, and for the next dozen years public readings absorbed much of his time and energies at the expense of his writing and even his health.

More immediately, the decision took him through England and Ireland on an tour of readings lasting from early August to mid-

November 1858. The tour was immensely profitable, but exhausting. He seldom had more than a day or two off in a week; often Sunday was his only free day. Whenever possible, however, he returned from the provinces for a day or two, retreating to Gad's Hill to relax and see his family, and to London to attend to business and see Ellen.

In late October, he spent a week in the midlands—Birmingham, Nottingham, Derby, Manchester—giving six readings from Monday to Saturday; on the following Monday he was booked to read in York. By now he had been touring for almost three months, and was sick: "I have a bad cold all over me, pains in my back and limbs, and a very sensitive and uncomfortable throat." Consequently he was by no means eager to rush to York early Monday morning after returning to London late Saturday night. From Derby he wrote to his daughter Mary on Friday, telling her "that if there is not a large let for York, I would rather give it up, and get Monday at Gad's Hill." With an appointment with his solicitor on Sunday "and having to start for York early on Monday, I fear I should not be able to get to Gad's Hill at all." Fortunately, ticket sales in York were weak enough to justify canceling the Monday reading, giving him an extra day off.

After seeing his solicitor in London on Sunday, and very likely Ellen as well, he took a train to Gad's Hill and spent the night there. He was back in London by late Monday, however, for he met with his sub-editor Wills in the evening, perhaps at the *Household Words* offices or perhaps for a working supper nearby.

Then, having dispatched business and editorial duties, he hurried to pay a visit to the Ternans, now on Berners Street, a ten- or fifteen-minute walk from Covent Garden.

Chances are he has made this walk before, though the Ternans have been on Berners Street for only a few weeks and he has been mostly out of town. This evening Maria and Ellen are home alone, as Dickens knows. He anticipates a pleasant, relaxing evening in the company of the two girls before catching a morning train to Hull for another week of readings. But there is no cheerful chat this evening, for Maria and Ellen have a distressing tale to recount.

On a recent night, perhaps the night before, the two girls have been stopped and questioned by a policeman on Berners Street. They may have been accosted returning home together, late, from the theater. They are of course innocent of any misdeed, but the policeman had been inquisitive, asking probing questions: Where do they live? How long have they lived there? With whom? How do they live? Actresses, were they? And so on. Exactly why he is so curious is a "mystery." Perhaps he suspected they were prostitutes. Dickens, however, forms his own dark theory: "My suspicion is, that the Policeman in question has been suborned to find out all about their domesticity by some 'Swell.'" With more glamorous acting roles than Ellen, "Maria is a good deal looked after"—that is, has attracted unwelcome admirers among stage-door idlers. With fine presence of mind, the two girls noted the impertinent policeman's badge number.

Hearing their story, Dickens grows irate. The policeman had no cause to stop the girls in the first place. Worse, the implication that they are undesirables, perhaps tarts, is intolerable.

He would be angered in any case by an insult to the Ternan girls, but there is additional cause for vexation. Mrs. Ternan is abroad with her eldest daughter, Fanny, and he has promised that in her absence he will look out for the two younger girls, living in London by themselves. Maria is twenty-one, Ellen only nineteen. "You are to understand, between you and me," he explains to Wills, "that I have sent the eldest sister to Italy, to complete a musical education—that Mrs. Ternan is gone with her, to see her comfortably established in Florence; and that our two little friends are left together, in the meanwhile, in the family lodgings." As their protector and temporary guardian, Dickens is especially sensitive to any threat or harm to them.

In the Berners Street parlor he listens with rising anger to the tale related by the distressed girls, comforts them, and promises swift and decisive action. They will not be bothered again by any policeman on the Berners Street beat, he resolves; certainly not by the officer who has harassed them already. If he has been suborned, in fact, "there can be no doubt that the man ought to be dismissed."

Returning to Tavistock House after this unhappy interview, Dickens instantly sits down and writes to Wills. "Since I left you tonight," he begins dramatically, "I have heard of a case of such extraordinary, and (apparently) dangerous and unwarrantable conduct in a Policeman, that I shall take it as a great kindness if you will go to Yardley in Scotland Yard when you know the facts for yourself, and ask him to enquire what it means." The invaluable Wills is delegated to undertake this investigation because Dickens himself must catch an early train in the morning. There is a further advantage to delegating Wills to deal with Scotland Yard, however. After the scandal of his separation from his wife a few months earlier, with accompanying rumors about a young actress, even the impetuous Dickens can see the wisdom of walking cautiously in the case of the impertinent policeman. Scotland Yard might wonder about the famous novelist's burning interest in two obscure young actresses.

Working himself up to a high pitch of indignation, he tells Wills that "I am quite sure that if the circumstances as they stand were stated in the Times, there would be a most prodigious public uproar." If this sensational possibility is meant as a threat to Scotland Yard, it is a hollow one. Any public interest in the case of the two young women would soon lead back to Dickens himself; and he is more vulnerable than Scotland Yard. On reflection, he recognizes as much. Undoubtedly he also recognizes that his fame and the notoriety of his separation have made the Ternan girls more vulnerable, too. People are inclined to make cynical assumptions about actresses, and any scandal concerning an actress will be presumed true. Dickens is uneasy about this peril, and instructs Wills to inform Scotland Yard that "you know the young ladies and can answer for them and for their being in all things most irreproachable in themselves and most respectably connected in all ways." That the Ternans are new to Berners Street might suggest, unhappily, that they are birds of passage, and he points out that "they don't live about in furnished lodgings, but have their own furniture"—a sign of gentility.

Dickens's letter directing Wills to visit Scotland Yard yields valuable clues to his relationship with Ellen as it had developed over the year since he had met her. She has become such a presence in his life that Wills has not only met her and her sister Maria, but knows them well enough (or so Dickens claims) that he "can answer for them." As a reliable and confidential factotum, Wills has likely performed other tasks relating to Ellen and her family, and may have been invited to dinner or other social occasions with Ellen.

But there is much that Wills does not know. He must be informed of the Ternans' new address on Berners Street, so he can find them the next day. He must also be informed of Mrs. Ternan's absence in Italy, encouraged and subsidized by Dickens, and of the Ternans' recent move from Islington, also encouraged and subsidized. Though Dickens makes no attempt to conceal his interest in Ellen from his trusty sub-editor, even with Wills he keeps much to himself. This reserve will become the pattern. Many of his associates and friends know about Ellen—but they don't know much. Even Wilkie Collins, his Doncaster traveling companion who himself openly keeps a mistress, is mostly in the dark. When Dickens walks out the door of the *Household Words'* offices on Wellington Street and strides toward Berners Street, or to meet Ellen elsewhere, he disappears into another life, fully known only to him and the Ternans.

One other notable point emerges. Dickens's relations with Ellen remain chaste. On this, his one documented visit to 31 Berners Street, she and Maria are home together, and this is probably standard. In any case, no chaperone is necessary. Dickens places a high value on Ellen's virtue and purity; he has stressed them repeatedly during the past year. "Upon my soul and honour," he had declared a few months earlier, "there is not on this earth a more virtuous and spotless creature than this young lady. I know her to be innocent and pure, and as good as my own dear daughters." That he has sent Ellen's mother and sister to Florence, leaving the two younger girls on their own in London, might seem suspicious, but this apparently exploitable arrangement does not suggest disreputable intentions, but rather the opposite. For all his faults—and he has a sufficiency—Dickens is no cad, or predator, or rake. In Mrs. Ternan's absence, he has assumed responsibility for Ellen and Maria as an almost sacred charge. If ever he is to take Ellen as a lover, it will not be when she is nineteen-years-old and under his guardianship.

Another glimpse of Dickens and Ellen.

During the autumn of 1858 he enjoys robust health. The separation crisis with all its scandal and acrimony has been a strain, and the reading tour that carries him all over England and Ireland week after week is taxing. Nonetheless, "the fatigue, though sometimes very great indeed, hardly tells on me at all," he reports in October. And although his readings manager and a crew of three "have given in, more or less, at times, I have never been in the least unequal to the work, though sometimes sufficiently disinclined for it." One day the week before, he has walked thirteen miles between reading sites, from Durham to Sunderland; the day after, he has walked another twelve miles, from Sunderland to Newcastle. In December, he declares "that I have been, and am, wonderfully well."

One Saturday six months later, however, he takes a train from Gad's Hill to London to consult with his physician, Frank Beard, an old friend. Requesting an appointment, he has briefly and vaguely mentioned that "My bachelor state has engendered a small malady on which I want to see you." From this cryptic allusion, Beard will have little doubt that Dickens has contracted a venereal infection.

It persists through the summer of 1859. The week after seeing Beard, he tells Wills that "I don't think I am any better today. I am rather disposed to feel it in my general health, and am languid and short of starch." A month later, he can report to Beard only that "I am very little better—really very little." The problem scarcely incapacitates him; he continues to turn out weekly installments of *A Tale of Two Cities* and one day goes rowing on the Medway, near Gad's Hill, for "20 miles at a stretch." But the malady persists. Two months after consulting Beard, he complains that "I am not quite well—can't get quite well." Sea air and salt water might help, he thinks, and he travels to Broadstairs on the Channel to try this remedy; but a bad cold keeps him out of the sea. Beard's remedies, or one of them, is silver nitrate—commonly used for cauterizing chancres.

Have he and Ellen become lovers?—and has he contracted a venereal infection from her?

The evidence again suggests the opposite—that this is *not* a glimpse of Dickens and Ellen together. He has almost certainly acquired his "small malady" from another source. The Ternans are a respectable, close-knit, well-regulated matriarchy, the mother (now back from the continent) and two younger daughters living together (the eldest, Fanny, is still taking vocal lessons in Florence). Ellen, now twenty, is very unlikely to have acquired a venereal disease to pass on to Dickens. He in turn is unlikely to risk passing on his malady to his beloved Ellen.

And the malady persists, intermittently, for another year and more. After Christmas 1859, he sends his family to Gad's Hill, but after making a brief trip to Wales he returns to London and stays there, alone, several days longer, explaining that "Unfortunately I am in the Doctor's hands for a few days, and am shut up here [in the Wellington Street offices of his new magazine, *All the Year Round*] after dark, by his orders." This tale of a nocturnal quarantine is not entirely true, for he has gone to Drury Lane Theatre just the night before, and certainly he often slips off to see Ellen as well.

These treatments in the first week of 1860 may or may not be connected with his malady, but a year later, while writing the early chapters of *Great Expectations*, he once again undergoes treatments in London after Christmas while his family stays at Gad's Hill, and this time the treatments are certainly for the same problem that has now been nagging him off and on for eighteen months. The medical regime is scarcely spartan, for "I pass my time here (I am staying here alone [in London]) in working, taking physic, and taking a Stall at a Theatre every night," he writes to a friend. At the same time he writes to Georgina, at Gad's Hill: "Now understand, both you and Mary [his daughter], that there is not the least occasion to be anxious about me. I have no kind of pain—scarcely an uneasiness—but I am not rid of the disagreeables that affected me in that hot summer [of 1859], and they *must be* put right. I have delivered myself over to be physicked, and that is the long and short of it." The euphemism ("the disagreeables") and his refusal to elaborate ("that is the long and short of it") reveal that he has not disclosed the precise nature of his ailment to his sister-in-law Georgina, and certainly not to his daughter. Scarcely an ingénue, though, Georgina must have her suspicions.

What ill-advised liaison has brought about this malady? There is no guessing with any confidence. Wellington Street, where the offices of both *Household Words* and its successor *All the Year Round* were located, is close to Covent Garden, a well-known haunt of prostitutes. In *Great Expectations*, Pip remarks in a discreet parenthesis that a club of young debauchees called the Finches of the Grove "spent their money foolishly (the Hotel we dined at was in Covent-garden)"—hinting at the Finches' whoring. Dickens frequents the West End theaters, moreover, and prostitutes notoriously circulate in and about them at night. His friendship with the Ternans now takes him to theaters more than ever, for Ellen and Maria have acting engagements at several, and meeting them there exposes him to a demi-monde rich with temptations.

A letter to Wilkie Collins at the beginning of his 1858 reading tour is suggestive. A dozen years younger, unmarried and pleasure-loving, Collins has been Dickens's companion on numerous bachelor jaunts. Now, embarking on his reading tour, Dickens has sent Collins his itinerary, with the name of the hotel where he expects to stay in each city. For several cities, however, no hotel is listed, a convenience address being given instead. Collins remarks suggestively on these omissions, and Dickens in turn responds:

> Your letter gives me great pleasure, as all letters that you write me are sure to do. But the mysterious addresses, O misconstructive one, merely refer to places where Arthur Smith [the readings manager] did not know aforehand the names of the best Hotels. As to that furtive and Don Giovanni purpose at which you hint—that may be all very well for *your* violent vigor, or that of the companions with whom you may have travelled continentally, or the Caliphs Haroon Alraschid with whom you have unbent metropolitanly; but Anchorites who read themselves red hot every night are chaste as Diana.

Among Collins's vigorous traveling companions had been Dickens himself, for they had spent time together on the continent and had probably "unbent" together in the metropolis as well. Thus, Dickens's assertion of chastity is not absolute, for Collins knows better, but an *ad hoc* regime adopted for his reading tour. It is notable that he responds to Collins's innuendo in a tone of light-hearted, facetious masculine banter, and that the exertions of the tour—and not fidelity to Ellen, let alone to his estranged wife—are adduced as the reason for his good behavior.

One reason Ellen is not cited as having a claim on Dickens's sexual fidelity is that their relationship remains chaste. Another is that Collins's world of Don-Giovanni, Arabian-Nights adventure is alien to Dickens's feelings about Ellen. Collins is part of his world of hearty masculine camaraderie and worldliness. Ellen appeals to a wholly different side of his nature; she excites desire, certainly, but she also awakes his chivalry, his protectiveness, his reverence for feminine innocence and purity, even—ironically—his strong domestic instincts. These are not feelings to be joked about with a voluptuary like Collins.

Dickens's venereal malady is a lingering result of adventuring that will be left behind with his growing loyalty to Ellen.

As an indirect consequence of the rupture in Dickens's marriage in the spring of 1858, he broke with Bradbury and Evans, the publishing firm with a half interest in his magazine *Household Words*. Shutting down *Household Words*, he inaugurated a new weekly, *All the Year Round*, the following year.

The editorial texture of the new magazine suggests Ellen's influence. Published through the 1850s, *Household Words* had been a pulpit for Dickens's opinions on almost every topic. In *All the Year Round*, by contrast, "essays of topical sociopolitical interest were almost entirely tossed out." While Ellen initially threw Dickens into near-frenzy, her effect on him was ultimately mellowing.

Rather than topical articles, *All the Year Round* featured serial fiction. To launch the new magazine, he wrote *A Tale of Two Cities*, published in weekly numbers beginning with the magazine's inaugural issue in April 1859.

The plot of *A Tale of Two Cities* was inspired by *The Frozen Deep*: in both, an unhappy hero sacrifices himself for an inaccessible woman whom he has long loved, by giving his life for her husband (or fiancé). The idea of suffering and sacrificing for a beloved woman resonated with Dickens, and *A Tale of Two Cities* echoes not only *The Frozen Deep* but also the fairy-tale fancy of saving his Princess from the seven-headed Ogre on the mountaintop. As he wrote *A Tale of Two Cities*, the idea of the lover's sacrifice took "complete possession" of him: "I have so far verified what is done and suffered in these pages, as that I have certainly done and suffered it all myself." Sydney Carton's hopeless but ultimately redemptive love for Lucie Manette re-enacted his own "wild way" of love, what he had "done and suffered" because of Ellen Ternan.

We glimpse Ellen's presence not only in Carton's sacrifice for Lucie, however, but in a more mundane detail in Dickens's correspondence.

When in 1859 an American magazine offered him a handsome sum for a single story, he hastily accepted, though busy with both *All the Year Round* and *A Tale of Two Cities*. He then wrote the story, called "Hunted Down," and dispatched it to New York. When the magazine's editor wrote to praise the story, Dickens responded that "it gives me great pleasure to receive your letter. . . . I read the story to one or two friends here, at the time of its completion, and I found that it took strong possession of them."

Ellen was certainly one of the vaguely enumerated friends to whom he read the story—perhaps the only one. In this throwaway detail, we glimpse an evening with the Ternans. It is spring 1859, probably late April. Dickens carries his just-completed story to the Ternan house, eager to read it to Ellen. Nothing gives him greater pleasure than an appreciative, demonstrative audience, and no audience at all could give him greater pleasure than Ellen. He likes his own story and reads it with strong effect. Writing stories is his greatest gift, but his flair for dramatic reading is a gift as well, and he happily lays both gifts at her feet.

"Hunted Down" is something of a gift in another way as well. Writing to Wills the same week that he has written to the American editor about reading the story to friends, he mentions that he would like to see corrected proofs for the latest installment of *A Tale of Two Cities*. "Will you send round for them [at the printers]," he instructs Wills, "and post them to Miss Ellen Ternan, 2 Houghton Place, Ampthill Square, N.W."

"Ellen," as opposed to nicknames, abbreviations, and coded references, appears rarely in surviving documents in Dickens's hand. This is one of the few instances; and, though brief, the instructions to Wills are revealing.

We learn, to begin, that the Ternans have moved yet again, for the second time since Dickens arrived in their lives less than two years earlier. Up to this point they have been renters. Now, however, Ellen's older sisters Fanny and Maria have purchased an 84-year lease on a four-story terrace house within a ten- or fifteen-minute walk from Dickens's Tavistock House. The house on Houghton Place overlooks Ampthill Square, a recently developed residential area east of Regent's Park.

It seems curious that a family of four journeyman actresses can afford to purchase a house in a pleasant residential district of London; even more curious that it should be purchased by the two older daughters rather than the head of the household, Mrs. Ternan. More curious yet—to look ahead—is that on March 3 the following year, Fanny and Maria Ternan sell the lease of 2 Houghton Place to Ellen, who at age twenty-one becomes sole owner of her own house. March 3, 1860, is in fact her twenty-first birthday when, coming of age, she can enter into legal contracts.

How did the young Ellen Ternan, who might in journalistic terms be called a "struggling" actress, come into enough money to buy a large, comfortable house in a good London neighborhood?

Undoubtedly through Dickens. He has provided the money for 2 Houghton Place and arranged the legal maneuvers by which it will come into her hands on her twenty-first birthday; no other explanation is plausible. Circumstantial details offer further evidence.

For example, in January 1859, two months before the older Ternan daughters purchase the house at 2 Houghton Place, Dickens writes a curious letter to Wills explaining an excellent idea that has occurred to him. Now that he owns a country retreat, Gad's Hill, and also maintains bachelor quarters for himself in the offices of *Household Words*, his house in London has become redundant. Why not turn Tavistock House over to the Ternans—or more precisely, why not sell them a long-term lease for eight hundred pounds? (As he is subsidizing the Ternans, much of the eight hundred pounds would be coming from his own pocket.)

Both Wills and Forster discourage the idea, strongly. In Forster's view, "such a step would most decidedly be very damaging indeed." Forster no doubt fears a rekindling of the scandal of Dickens's marital separation six months earlier; as a lawyer, moreover, Forster fears that

Dickens's letting his house to the family of a young woman in whom he is known to be interested might create a presumption of adultery, should his wife's angry Hogarth relations persuade her to sue for divorce. "With you I say," Forster admonishes him, "it is not matter of reasoning so much as of feeling." Both Forster and Wills act as prudent checks on Dickens's rashness. In a letter which does not survive, Wills writes to the same effect as Forster.

Faced with their opposition, Dickens retreats. "I will no longer doubt that you are right," he writes in acknowledging Wills's letter, "and I thank you heartily for the affectionate earnestness with which you have represented me to myself, as wrong." Perhaps his daughters Mary and Katie have also objected; in any case, he cites them as obstacles. "Will you," he directs Wills, "as early as practicable tomorrow morning, communicate to the agent, that I find my daughters so averse to the long term that I must withdraw from that proposal."

With this idea squelched, Dickens resumes his quest for better housing for the Ternans. He would like to see them comfortably established in a genteel house of their own, rather than living in cramped hired lodgings. Moreover, he wishes to endow Ellen with property. In February, he directs his bankers, Coutts & Company, to sell fifteen hundred pounds worth of bonds in his name; the following month, Maria and Fanny purchase the lease of 2 Houghton Place.

Dickens's readings the year before had been profitable, and his letters frequently talk of pounds and pence. Near the end of his reading tour, for example, he had boasted to Miss Coutts (foolishly, given her immense wealth) that "my clear profit—my own, after all deductions and expences—has been more than a Thousand Guineas a month"—for a tour of three and a half months. But as he has bought Gad's Hill just two years earlier and is pouring money into its refurbishment, and as he is meanwhile funding his wife's separate establishment, the purchase of yet another house puts a strain on his purse. In these circumstances, the American magazine's 1859 offer of one thousand pounds for a story is especially welcome. If fifteen hundred pounds has bought the house at 2 Houghton Place, "Hunted Down" has paid for almost three of its four floors.

"Hunted Down" is a melodramatic study of a smooth villain who has poisoned one of his two young nieces and is about to poison the other, when the dead niece's lover snatches the surviving niece from her peril and exposes the poisoner. Perhaps Dickens feels as if he has similarly rescued his beloved Ellen—not from death, of course, but from the scraping, precarious life of a nameless professional actress. Reading "Hunted Down" to her in the parlor of the fine house at 2 Houghton Place, he can reflect with satisfaction that the story not only allows him dramatic scope in performing, but has also helped make Ellen a young lady of property.

Accordingly, in August, just a few months after the Ternans' move to Houghton Place, Ellen makes her last appearance as a professional actress. Her theatrical career has scarcely been flourishing, but as acting has been her only means of earning a livelihood, or at least of contributing to the Ternans' collective income, abandoning the stage at twenty would seem a premature retirement—had she not acquired other means of support. Dickens's attitude toward the stage is ambivalent; while a habitué of theaters, he regards actors and actresses as a dubious class. He wants Ellen on the stage no more than he would want his daughters on it. In her acquisition of 2 Houghton Place and retirement from acting, we see a decisive transition in his role, from that of a generous friend of the Ternans to that of Ellen's acknowledged protector and patron.

Has she in turn become his mistress?

His generous subsidies to her and her family seem to create a presumption that she has granted favors to him in return. Dickens's friend William Macready kept a diary which "contained startling revelations," his granddaughter (who had read it) recalled. Excerpts were published after Macready's death; the manuscript was then burned. The published selections contain no revelations about Dickens's secret life, but expurgated entries (the granddaughter testified) revealed that Macready knew about it, and "took the Ellen Ternan affair, etc., calmly—as Dickens was not the celibate type—and the grandmother [Macready's second wife], strict though she was about such things, had been brought up in Paris at a time when such things were not unusual!"

Such things were not unknown even in moral England, and Dickens, father of ten, plainly enjoys sexual intimacy, but in 1859 his relations with Ellen probably remain chaste. Even as the Ternans settle into 2 Houghton Place and Ellen leaves the stage, he acquires the "small malady" engendered by his bachelor condition, suggesting that he has sought pleasure from other, less respectable sources. And though Ellen at twenty is well beyond the age of consent (which was then only twelve), he would hesitate to deflower a young maiden to whose spotless innocence he has more than once testified. There are Mrs. Ternan's views to consider, as well. For all Dickens's patronage and solicitude, Ellen's mother remains the governing presence in her life.

Most pertinent of all, and most uncertain, are Ellen's feelings about her famous admirer—and they are a mystery.

During this same eventful summer of 1859, Dickens contemplates a reading tour of the United States, where enormous profits allure. "I cannot help being much stirred and influenced by the golden prospects held before me," he admits. But the promoter floating these enticing prospects before Dickens's hungry eyes turns out to be a speculator offering ten thousand pounds that he doesn't actually have. "Driven into a corner, I thought of signing it," Dickens writes, "but Ouvry [his solicitor] was so strong against it, that I struck—refused—and knocked the whole thing on the head."

Beyond contractual difficulties, a more fundamental problem glooms over the American proposal. Eighty readings would take him from England for nearly half a year. "How like a winter hath my absence been/From thee, the pleasure of the fleeting year,"

Shakespeare had lamented (Sonnet 97), and Dickens dreads a similar wintry exile from Ellen. "I should be one of the most unhappy of men if I were to go," he tells Forster, without needing to elaborate. By the summer of 1859, two years after *The Frozen Deep*, she has become so indispensable that the prospect of six months' separation from her weighs heavily against ten thousand pounds. Perhaps his failure to agree with the American promoter comes as a relief.

During 1859 and the two years following, Dickens's feelings for Ellen change from excited infatuation into something deeper. She becomes the chief interest and affection of his life. Yet even as she grows in influence, documentary evidence of her presence dwindles. The diligent editors of Dickens's correspondence have ferreted out over a thousand letters from the three critical years 1859 to 1861, but turning to "Ternan" in the index of the relevant volume, one finds only three references to Ellen—two of them in the footnotes. The strongest currents in Dickens's feelings during these years flow unseen beneath the surface of his busy life.

In May 1860 he entertains American visitors, Mr. and Mrs. Fields of Boston, at Tavistock house. Mrs. Fields finds him an affable host: "Dickens talked very much and very pleasantly at dinner"—although the only conversational topic she mentions in her diary is some high-minded distress at "Catholic influence creeping into America," Dickens politely airing prejudices congenial to the properly Protestant Fieldses. But evidently impressed by the gloomy tone of the conversation, Mrs. Fields observes that "a shadow has fallen on that house, making Dickens seem rather the man of labor and of sorrowful thought than the soul of gaiety we find in all he writes" (though "gaiety" seems a strange word for Dickens's novels of the 1850s). Mrs. Fields knows about Dickens's marriage, but likely nothing of Ellen Ternan. Also at dinner are Wilkie Collins and his brother Charles, both of whom know all about Ellen, and one wonders whether an awkward restraint hovers over the table, with everyone except the two guests of honor aware of Dickens's secret life; and whether Dickens himself expatiates on grave topics like creeping Papism and "purification through pain" in order to avoid personal topics. (Later, Mrs. Fields will learn much more about Ellen.)

Dickens will not host many more dinners at Tavistock House.

He begins spending more of his time at Gad's Hill, enjoying the refurbished house, to which he continues to make improvements; the countryside around it, where he takes long walks; and the role of host and squire. He enjoys smoking a cigar after dinner and strolling about to look at the flowers. Gad's Hill's is well located—in pleasant rural surroundings, but little over an hour from London by train. Above the ground-floor editorial offices of his new magazine, *All the Year Round,* on Wellington Street, he has an apartment of "5 very good rooms" fitted up: "a sitting-room and some bedrooms . . . to be used, when there was no house in London, as occasional town quarters by himself, his daughter, and sister-in-law." With Gad's Hill in the country and with his convenient flat in London, he sells Tavistock House in 1860, explaining that "I purpose living here [at Gad's Hill] during seven months in the year and taking a small furnished house in town during the other five," to give Georgina and his daughters sociable time in London. While his family is at Gad's Hill, he spends two nights a week in London, free to occupy his evenings as he wishes—mostly with Ellen, one might guess. His quarters at *All the Year Round*'s offices are "as comfortable, cheerful, and private as anything of the kind can possibly be." Their privacy perhaps makes it possible, after business hours, to entertain her there.

He alternates identities: most of the week he is a solid family man, presiding over the dinner table at Gad's Hill; two days a week he becomes an amorous bachelor. With his family installed at Gad's Hill most of the year, he can range at will during his weekly visits to London and disappear entirely when convenient. In August 1860, for example, he writes from London to Georgina at Gad's Hill that "I *think* I shall run away tomorrow [a Wednesday], until Saturday," to gather material for an article in *All the Year Round*. His destination remains suspiciously vague; and the next article he writes for *All the Year Round*, about his childhood hometown Chatham, would scarcely require him to "run away" for four days, as Chatham is only a few miles from Gad's Hill. In all probability he has planned an out-of-town excursion with Ellen. Georgina is aware of the general nature of these disappearances, and must be content with his vagueness about particulars.

The 1861 census records all four Ternans—Ellen, her two sisters, and her mother—living together at 2 Houghton Place. If Ellen is a kept woman, she is at this point kept respectably *en famille*. Under occupation, Mrs. Ternan is described as "Annuitant," her daughters Fanny as "Vocalist," Maria as "Actress," and Ellen as—blank. ("Retired Actress" would have seemed an absurd designation for a twenty-two-year-old, and her actual means of support was no business of the census taker.) The Ternans also kept a seventeen-year-old maid-of-all-work named Jane.

By one account, Ellen recalled (much later) that Dickens visited 2 Houghton Place two or three times a week. Another recollection testified to his enjoying pleasant at-home evenings with the Ternans, probably at Houghton Place. Francesco Berger, who as a young man composed the music and conducted the orchestra for *The Frozen Deep*, reportedly claimed that he "knew the Ternan family very well, and often during the 'sixties played games of cards at their house with the mother, daughter, and Dickens, on Sunday evenings" ("daughter" should perhaps be plural). "This was generally followed after supper by Ellen and Dickens singing duets to his [Berger's] pianoforte accompaniment." Though recorded long afterward and doubted by some, this picture of a convivial Victorian evening seems eminently plausible. If true, it shows the affair of Dickens and Ellen not scarlet with scandal but benignly domestic—sedate, harmonious, wholesome.

Evening entertainment includes more than cards and music. While the Ternans are living at Houghton Place, Dickens writes both *A Tale of Two Cities* and *Great Expectations* as weekly serials for *All the Year Round*, and often brings proof sheets along when he visits the Ternans. As he reads them aloud to Ellen, a painstaking chore becomes a cheerful occasion, and his reading of the latest number of his current novel becomes a weekly ritual at Houghton Place. On occasion, he brings proofs of works by other writers. In the spring of 1861, for example, Edward Bulwer-Lytton begins a novel for *All the Year Round* and seeks reassurance from Dickens about the early chapters. Would he show them to one or two other readers for their opinion? Dickens responds: "Your first request I had already anticipated. I had read the Proofs myself to a woman whom I could implicitly trust, and in whom I have frequently observed (in the case of my own proofs) an intuitive sense and discretion that I have set great store by." Thus Ellen finds herself one of the first readers, or auditors, of Bulwer-Lytton's occult fantasy *A Strange Story*.

In addition to confirming that Dickens "frequently" reads his proofs to Ellen, his note to Bulwer-Lytton suggests why he has become so attached to her. At Doncaster he had been struck giddy by her springtime loveliness: "O little lilac gloves! And O winning little bonnet, making in conjunction with her golden hair quite a Glory in the sunlight round the pretty head." Three years later, he finds her no less lovely. But in his regard for her "sense and discretion," we see her maturing into a discriminating young woman and earning Dickens's admiration for her blossoming feminine wit.

Many years later, reminiscing to a friend named Gladys Storey, Dickens's daughter Katie recalled the young Ellen Ternan as a "small fair-haired rather pretty actress" ("of no special attraction save her youth," Storey added in her own words, presumably paraphrasing Katie); but in grudging tribute, Katie admitted that though "not a good actress," Ellen "had brains, which she used to educate herself, to bring her mind more on a level with his own." Long resentful of her father's young inamorata (exactly her own age), Katie implies that Ellen's program of self-education was artful, but it may be that with more leisure, now that she was no longer acting, Ellen simply enjoyed reading and had the wit to profit from what she read. Talking with Dickens one or two evenings every week about his novel-in-progress, or about what she has been reading on her own, or about articles or novels in *All the Year Round*, she gains an informal but unique literary education, making up for her slender formal schooling (Dickens himself had little more schooling than she).

Several months after the Ternans moved into 2 Houghton Place, Wilkie Collins's "sensation novel" *The Woman in White* began to appear weekly in *All the Year Round*. Writing to Collins in January 1860 after reading the latest proofs, Dickens praised the early chapters as "a very great advance on all your former writing, and most especially in tenderness"; but he also criticized Collins's "disposition to give an audience credit for nothing—which necessarily involves the forcing of points on their attention." With byzantine plot and multiple twists and terrors, *The Woman in White* was a great success, and Dickens no doubt read the proofs of each installment to Ellen on his visits to Houghton Place. We can imagine the two of them, afterwards, discussing not only the tortuous plot but also the merits and demerits of Collins's craftsmanship; Ellen is the first to hear Dickens's criticisms and responds with feminine flair and insight. Enjoying his role as teacher and sage, he admires her natural good sense and increasingly refined taste.

Earlier, just a few months after meeting Ellen, he had read George Eliot's just-published *Scenes of Clerical Life*, and despite the misleading pen name he immediately detected a woman's hand. "The exquisite truth and delicacy, both of the humour and pathos of those stories, I have never seen the like of," he wrote to her in admiration. ". . . I have observed what seem to me to be such womanly touches, in those moving fictions, that the assurance on the title-page is insufficient to satisfy me, even now." George Eliot, actually Marian Evans, was twenty years older than Ellen and a formidable intellectual, but Dickens's quick and admiring detection of the feminine flavor of her

stories—their "exquisite truth and delicacy" and "womanly touches"—
suggests what he may have found attractive about Ellen's response to
books and to life more generally. He spent his days in London amidst
beards and whiskers—there was no girl Friday at the offices of *All the
Year Round*. Not only Ellen's youthful charms but also her womanly
"sense and discretion" deepened his attachment.

Scattered about in his letters of these years are other hints of her
attractions. In 1860, his old friend William Macready, a sixty-seven-
year-old widower, married a woman of twenty-three. Ten years earlier,
Dickens had seemed to authorize such a January-May union in the
marriage of two characters, old Doctor Strong and his young wife
Annie in *David Copperfield*. Now he wrote to congratulate Macready:
"It is inexpressibly delightful and interesting to me, to picture you in a
new home, with new life and movement and hope and pleasure about
you." The age gap between Macready and his new wife had obvious
pertinence to Dickens himself, twenty-seven years older than Ellen,
and in celebrating Macready's domestic joy he must have thought of
his own second home at 2 Houghton Place and its warming feminine
influence. "Moreover," he wrote, remembering himself before Ellen's
advent, "I do not believe that a heart like yours, was made to hold so
large a waste-place as there has been in it. And this consideration, as
one in the eternal nature of things, I put first of all"—by implication,
giving his own love for Ellen a religious sanction.

We glimpse Ellen again in a letter of six months later. Dickens has
accepted an article for *All the Year Round* submitted by a friend, Marguerite Power, and tells her he will send a proof for her correction
the following week. "Or," he proposes, "would you like to come here
next Monday and dine with us at 1, and go over to Madame Celeste's
opening?"—that is, to a play at the Lyceum Theatre. "The charmer
is coming," he continues, "and Georgy [Georgina] will be here [in
London] all day." "The charmer" is a characteristic epithet for Ellen,
partly affectionate nickname, partly code; even as the manuscript of

the letter itself shows her effacement from the documentary record, for the editors of Dickens's letters note that the words "the charmer" are "heavily cancelled, not by CD; but sufficient tops of letters show to make 'The charmer' . . . virtually certain." (The censor was most likely Georgina, first editor of his letters; though enjoying cordial relations with Ellen after his death, she excised every reference to her in his letters.)

In this almost-obliterated reference to "the charmer," we glimpse one of many times when Dickens escorted Ellen to the theater. It was a natural outing for them. He loved the theater, and accompanied by her his pleasure would have been even greater; with her theatrical family and acting experience she would have been a perceptive and knowledgeable companion. He usually took a box at the theater, affording them relative privacy, and any stranger recognizing him might take the young woman at his side for a daughter or niece. One contemporary recalled an unhappy incident, however: "I well recollect being in a box at the theatre one evening with my mother and Mrs. Dickens; the latter burst into tears suddenly and went back into the box. Charles Dickens had come into the opposite box with some friends, and she could not bear it." Another contemporary—his daughter Katie—heard of this same incident, probably from her mother: "On one occasion, when [Mrs. Dickens] was with the Misses Frith . . . , Dickens came into the box with Ellen Ternan (the only occasion she ever saw him after the separation), when she was so overcome that she was obliged to leave the theatre."

His invitation to Marguerite Power to a theatrical evening with Ellen and Georgina reveals that he did not hesitate to bring the latter two together. Such meetings might seem an awkward mingling of the two poles of his personal life, domestic and amorous, and perhaps awkward for the two women themselves; but Dickens could be insensitive enough, and, even should his sister-in-law and young protegée feel uncomfortable together, he would have his way. Probably neither felt she had any choice but to make the best of it. His inclusion of

Georgina in this dinner-and-theater party corroborates her role as his confidante, even in the sensitive matter of his affair with Ellen. After the play at the Lyceum, Georgina would return to Gad's Hill and his daughter Mary. How much of her evening with Dickens and "the charmer," one wonders, did Georgina share with Mary?

More curious than Georgina as a confidante is the recipient of this invitation, Marguerite Power, a longtime but not intimate friend who seems to have known already who "the charmer" was, and may already have met her. Dickens's criteria for granting such a privilege are unclear. In writing to Bulwer-Lytton, another old friend, he identifies the person to whom he had read proofs of Bulwer's novel only as "a woman whom I could implicitly trust." Bulwer has certainly heard the gossip about Dickens and a young actress, and his own marriage is a notorious scandal—nonetheless, he evidently remains outside the circle of those invited to meet Ellen. Dickens seems to have been willing, even eager, to share her as freely with women he liked as with his worldly male friends. Respectable women were traditionally shielded from the women of irregular ménages; Georgina is unlikely ever to have met Wilkie Collins's mistress, Caroline Graves, for example. But with his implicit trust in feminine sympathy and tact, Dickens was drawn to women as confidantes and was tempted, in the case of Ellen, to flout the conventions.

Ultimately, letters and other scattered evidence yield only a fragmentary and superficial picture of Ellen's impact in these early years of their affair. Another source which never mentions her at all yields a richer insight into Dickens's feelings. In the autumn of 1860, three years after meeting her, he began writing *Great Expectations*. "You will find the hero to be a boy-child, like David [Copperfield]," he told Forster. "To be quite sure I had fallen into no unconscious repetitions, I read *David Copperfield* again the other day." But he scarcely needed to worry; the feelings informing *Great Expectations* would be far different from those that had flowed into *David Copperfield* a dozen years earlier.

TOP: Albert Ludovici, *The Meeting of Pip and Estella in the Inn Yard* (1903).

   "Estella, to the last hour of my life, you cannot choose but remain part of my character, part of the little good in me, part of the evil..." Pip's rhapsody in *Great Expectations* owes much to Ellen.

BOTTOM: The first illustration in *Our Mutual Friend* (1864), showing Lizzie Hexam on the river with her father.

   "To please myself, I could not be too far from that river.... I can't get away from it, I think." (Lizzie in *Our Mutual Friend*).

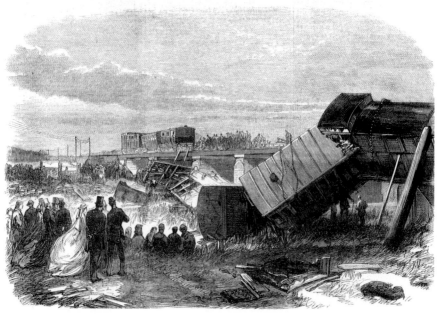

TOP: The wreck at Staplehurst, June 1865. Dickens and Ellen were in the car tilted between the embankment and the streambed at the right. *Courtesy of The Science and Society Picture Library.* LEFT: Dispatched to the scene of the fatal Staplehurst derailment the following day, an artist for *The Illustrated London News* placed the dramatically canted car carrying Dickens and the Ternans in the foreground of this 1865 engraving.

Dickens's Gad's Hill circle in an 1865 photograph, with Dickens himself "leaning against a column in a light suit and billy-cock hat, holding in his right hand a glass of wine" (F. G. Kitton). From left, standing: Katie Dickens Collins, Mary ("Mamie") Dickens, Dickens; seated: Henry Chorley (a close friend), Charles Collins, Georgina Hogarth. *Courtesy of the Dickens House Museum.*

TOP: "To off. from W [Windsor]," Dickens often noted in his 1867 pocket diary after visiting Ellen in Slough. Walking from Slough to Windsor station, he would have crossed the Thames on this bridge (as seen in an old post card). BOTTOM: G. M. Henton, *The Round Tower and the South-Western Railway Station*. Windsor station, to the left (with Windsor Castle on the hill above), as Dickens and Ellen would have seen them as they walked or rode to the station.

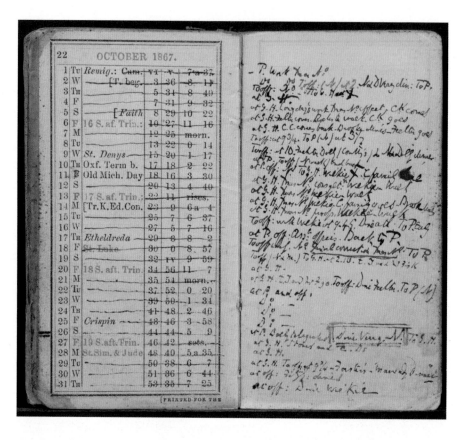

Dickens's 1867 pocket diary for October. The entry for the 26th reads: "at P. [Peckham] Dolby telegraphs Dine Verrey N. [Nelly] To G. H. [Gad's Hill]." Dolby's telegram from Boston probably vetoed Dickens's plan to take Ellen to America, and after their dinner at Verrey's he would not see her again for six months. *Courtesy of the New York Public Library.*

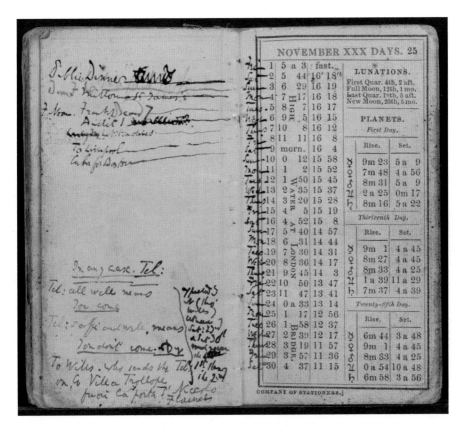

Dickens's pocket diary for November 1867, memoranda page. On the lower half is the code to summon Ellen Ternan to America—or not. *Courtesy of the New York Public Library.*

Ellen's sister Fanny Trollope, with whom Dickens was at odds over Ellen, and Fanny's husband Thomas Trollope. *Courtesy of the Firestone Library, Princeton.*
   ". . . be very strictly on your guard, if you see Tom Trollope—or his wife—or both—to make no reference to me which either can piece into anything. She is infinitely sharper than the Serpent's Tooth" (Dickens to Frances Dickinson, 1867).

Great Expectations has nothing directly to do with Ellen, and yet is very much about her—or about her impact on Dickens. Knowing that some would read the novel with gossipy curiosity, he carefully avoided details that might be applied to his own situation. The year before, casting about for a name for his new magazine, he had proposed *Household Harmony*; and when Forster discouraged the title as inapt, Dickens responded indignantly: "I am afraid we must not be too particular about the possibility of personal references and applications: otherwise it is manifest that I never can write another book." On reflection, however, he recognized that Forster was correct, and with *Great Expectations* he needed no second reminder to be circumspect.

The first biographer to unearth Dickens's affair with Ellen Ternan, a schoolmaster and prolific writer named Thomas Wright, nonetheless identified her as the model for *Great Expectations'* frigid heroine Estella. Many since have repeated the idea. Dickens would have been astonished and indignant at such a calumny; but, in suspecting Ellen's influence on *Great Expectations*, Wright was half right. Estella owes little or nothing to Ellen, but the passions and anguish of the novel's hero Pip owe much to Dickens's emotional history since meeting Ellen.

A greater error and equally common has been the insistence on reducing *Great Expectations* to a pamphlet denouncing snobbery and ingratitude. But readers who enjoy kettle-drum moralizing are likely to miss the novel's quieter tragic rhythms. It speaks sadly, wistfully, regretfully. In a penetrating essay, Graham Greene praised "the tone of Dickens's secret prose" in *Great Expectations*, "that sense of a mind speaking to itself with no one there to listen." While Dickens speaks to himself and about himself, however, he speaks obliquely. Ellen had drawn him into a swamp of perplexities. His love for her had brought him an emotional reawakening, even rebirth, but at the same time it had led him to act with cruelty to people who deserved better. No fantasies of self-justification, at which he was adept, could excuse the selfishness of his "wild way" and his "madman" behavior to his family, above all to his wife. At the end of the 1859 story "The Haunted House," the middle-aged narrator is haunted by "the ghost of my own childhood, the ghost of my own innocence, the ghost of my own airy belief." The same ghostly disillusions and regrets wander through *Great Expectations*.

But also infusing *Great Expectations* are his passion for Ellen and the frustrating impasse of his love for her. He would happily have married her, but marriage was impossible; Catherine was healthy and divorce out of the question. If he could not marry Ellen, what could he offer her? He could pour out gifts of money, jewelry, and a house—but he could not give her the respectability of "Mrs.," or a home and family. Some other man might do so; was Dickens stealing her youth, and dooming her to a lonely spinsterhood after his death? Another woman, Georgina, had already forsworn marriage for him: "She would make the best wife in the world," he wrote of Georgina, but "I doubt if she will ever marry. I don't know whether to be glad of it or sorry for it—finding the subject perplexing."

Ellen's future was even more perplexing. Two or three incidents illuminate the troubled feelings that infused *Great Expectations*. In the spring of 1860, his daughter Katie became engaged to Wilkie Collins's younger brother Charles, an artist and writer in fragile health. Katie, "although she respected him and considered him the kindest and most sweet-tempered of men, was not in the least in love with him," but saw in the marriage "an escape from 'an unhappy home.'" Dickens too was unexcited: "I do not doubt that the young lady might have done much better." Celebrated at Gad's Hill in July, the wedding "went off with the greatest success from first to last, and had no drawback whatever," he wrote with characteristic bravado—neglecting to mention a startling footnote:

> After the last of the guests not staying in the house had departed, Mamie [his daughter Mary] went up to her sister's bedroom. Opening the door, she beheld her father upon

his knees with his head buried in Katie's wedding-gown, sobbing. She stood for some moments before he became aware of her presence; when at last he got up and saw her, he said in a broken voice:

"But for me, Katey [Katie] would not have left home," and walked out of the room.

Ellen Ternan and his daughter Katie were the two women Dickens loved most, yet in a tragic irony his love for one had driven the other away from home and into an unhappy marriage: Charles Collins was a chronic invalid, and impotent ("never . . . a husband to her in the full meaning of the word," Katie's friend Gladys Storey revealed, "but of this subject she never spoke").

A few weeks after Katie's wedding there was another ceremony at Gad's Hill. "Yesterday I burnt, in the field at Gad's Hill, the accumulated letters and papers of twenty years," he jested darkly: "As it was an exquisite day when I began, and rained very heavily when I finished, I suspect my correspondence of having overcast the face of the Heavens." These were all the letters he had packed up at Tavistock House when it had been sold a few weeks earlier. Much of his past went up in the smoke: not only letters from the notable and notorious, but a many-voiced record of the three decades since Maria Beadnell. More than just housecleaning, more even than a means to prevent private correspondence from falling into wrong hands, the bonfire was a defiance. The world might gape and gossip and wonder, but he would cling to Ellen, maintain silence, and leave no evidence to haunt her. "Would to God every letter I had ever written was on that pile," he remarked as the last letters were tossed into the flames. Thereafter he burned every personal letter he received. The vast majority had nothing at all to do with Ellen, but no matter: all were sacrificed to his privacy, and hers.

His love for her inspired the most impassioned rhapsody in his fiction, the narrator Pip's declaration of love for Estella. "You will get me out of your thoughts in a week," Estella tells him as she announces her engagement to the awful Drummle. "Out of my thoughts!" Pip exclaims:

> You are part of my existence, part of myself. You have been in every line I have ever read, since I first came here. . . . You have been in every prospect I have ever seen since—on the river, on the sails of the ships, on the marshes, in the clouds, in the light, in the darkness, in the wind, in the woods, in the sea, in the streets. You have been the embodiment of every graceful fancy that my mind has ever become acquainted with. The stones of which the strongest London buildings are made, are not more real, or more impossible to be displaced by your hands, than your presence and influence have been to me, there and everywhere, and will be. Estella, to the last hour of my life, you cannot choose but remain part of my character, part of the little good in me, part of the evil.

The fervor, the absorption, the compulsion—all spring from Dickens's feelings for Ellen, as does Pip's recognition of Estella's influence on him for both good and evil.

For we hear the secret voice of Dickens, too, in Pip's brooding, his somber reflections as, for example, when walking through the summer countryside to his old village for the funeral of the sister who raised him harshly, he is moved to forgiveness: "For now, the very breath of the beans and clover whispered to my heart that the day must come when it would be well for my memory that others walking in the sunshine should be softened as they thought of me." Though reluctant to confess fault, Dickens recognized that "forgive us our sins, as we forgive others" might have some reference to himself. Soon after his separation from Catherine, his brother-in-law Henry Burnett, widowed a decade earlier on the death of Dickens's sister Fanny, had written him about a rumor that Dickens disapproved of his remarrying. Replying, Dickens denied "the least unkindness or ill will": "God knows, it is not in me—We must all go poor Fanny's way, and we shall all want sorely the gentle construction that we cannot do better than give." His moral complacency had been shaken, and from his weakness sprang much of *Great Expectations'* power.

For ultimately the value of *Great Expectations* is not that it preaches against the obvious evils of snobbery and ingratitude, but that from the most intense experience of Dickens's maturity it creates a dramatic meditation on the ambiguities of erotic love—its power to move and exalt, its power to deform and destroy. Pip's life shipwrecks on passion:

> The unqualified truth is, that when I loved Estella with the love of a man, I loved her simply because I found her irresistible. Once for all; I knew to my sorrow, often and often, if not always, that I loved her against reason, against promise, against peace, against hope, against happiness, against all discouragement that could be.

Love for Estella propels Pip into foolish and caddish behavior and drags him through agonies of despondency, guilt, and remorse. Meanwhile, another young woman would have made an excellent wife for Pip, his childhood friend Biddy. Biddy is as much the sensible choice as Estella is the wrong one; but for Pip it is not a matter of choice. Better to pursue the passion, even as it crucifies, than settle for the merely safe. In *Great Expectations*, Dickens handed his hero Pip a problem without easy solution. Perhaps that, too, reflected his own situation as he saw it.

Grieving for Cordelia, the daughter he has so fatally misused, King Lear weeps: "Thou'lt come no more,/Never never never never never." Repenting his own errors, Pip echoes this throbbing lamentation: "I could never, never, never, undo what I had done." (5.3) The word "never" occurs 317 times in *Great Expectations*. When Dickens began writing, he thought it would be "tragi-comic," assuring Forster that "you will not have to complain of the want of humour as in *The Tale of Two Cities*. I have made the opening . . . exceedingly droll." But the drollery of the early chapters, featuring Pip's termagant sister, her childlike husband Joe, and various village clowns, diminishes as his disastrous passion takes Pip by the throat. For Dickens, passion had brought joy as well as unhappiness, but *Great Expectations* explores only the unhappiness.

He wrote two endings for the novel. The first was terse, austere, grave—too bleak for his friend Bulwer-Lytton, who after reading the last chapter in proof urged him to lighten it. Yielding to Bulwer-Lytton's (and his own) sentimentality, Dickens wrote a second, more elaborate and romantic, conclusion, and this became the novel's published ending.

Alas that he let himself be swayed. Readers who are responsive to the tragic tolling of *Great Expectations*' unforgiving "never" are likely to prefer the spare unsentimental earlier ending, which narrates a final brief encounter between Pip and Estella, a chance meeting on a London street years after he has lost her. "In her face and in her voice, and in her touch," Pip concludes his story, "she gave me the assurance that suffering . . . had given her a heart to understand what my heart used to be." There is no strong love without suffering, but in the end there is a grace in suffering, too. *Great Expectations* owed this new understanding to Ellen Ternan.

CHAPTER 7

The crisis

Two years after finishing *Great Expectations*, Dickens began
writing his fourteenth novel, *Our Mutual Friend*.

One of the climactic incidents in this novel occurs along
the Thames, upstream from London, where the river flows through
meadows and woodlands. On a pleasant summer evening, the debo-
nair young Eugene Wrayburn loiters on the riverbank, wrestling with
confused feelings about a beautiful and virtuous but lower-class girl,
Lizzie Hexam. Since the earliest chapters, Dickens had been steering
his wayward hero toward this crisis:

> The rippling of the river seemed to cause a correspondent stir
> in his uneasy reflections. He would have laid them asleep if
> he could, but they were in movement, like the stream, and all
> tending one way with a strong current. As the ripple under
> the moon broke unexpectedly now and then, and palely
> flashed in a new shape and with a new sound, so parts of his
> thoughts started, unbidden, from the rest, and revealed their

wickedness. "Out of the question to marry her," said Eugene, "and out of the question to leave her. The crisis!"

Wrayburn's dilemma echoes Dickens's: he could not marry Ellen and he could not, or would not, relinquish her.

Wrayburn's crisis is unexpectedly resolved when, musing on the dark riverbank, he is surprised and bludgeoned by a rival suitor. Lizzie saves him from drowning, and his perplexities are swept away by her love. The crisis that sealed Dickens's commitment to Ellen Ternan was less violent. From his fascination with "little lilac gloves" and his insistence that "there is not on this earth a more virtuous and spotless creature than this young lady," he and Ellen had progressed to a dangerous intimacy, and in the spring of 1862 she became pregnant.

The following months were the most challenging of their long liaison.

The circumstances of Ellen's pregnancy are obscure.

During 1861 and the first half of 1862, Dickens remained in England. In October 1861 he launched a provincial reading tour that kept him away from London and Gad's Hill for much of the autumn. In early November he read in Hastings, where Charles Darwin's wife Emma happened to be visiting. She found the performance amusing, but Dickens himself repellent:

> I went one evening [she wrote to her son] to hear Dickens read the *Christmas Carol* & the Trial scene in *Pickwick* which last was very good fun. . . . Dickens himself is very horrid looking with a light coloured ragged beard which waggles up & down. He looks ruined & a roué which I don't believe he is however.

In 1861 Charles Darwin was clean-shaven, but Emma's revulsion went beyond beards. Dickens's "ruined" and "roué" appearance suggests that her perceptions were colored by disapproval. She was well aware of the scandal.

His provincial reading tour concluded at the end of January 1862, and he spent the next few months settled in London, renting a house near Hyde Park where he established himself with Georgina and Mary. Beginning in March, he gave a series of fourteen readings in London, one every week, lasting through June.

Ellen's whereabouts during the spring of 1862 are a mystery, but as Dickens was content to remain in London, very likely she too was there, probably living at 2 Houghton Place, Ampthill Square. In early March, she turned twenty-three, an occasion Dickens would not have overlooked. The following month, he wrote a check to Garrard, the London jeweler, for fifteen pounds, four shillings, probably as payment for a gift for Ellen, perhaps for her birthday the month before (whatever he purchased, it cost more than the annual wage of his housemaids). Meanwhile, Ellen's oldest sister Fanny was touring with an opera company while her other sister Maria had intermittent acting engagements in London until mid-April, when she joined Fanny's company, then performing at King's Lynn, Norfolk. Thus, in the last weeks of April 1862, Ellen was the only Ternan sister in London—perhaps the only Ternan there at all, if Mrs. Ternan accompanied Maria to Norfolk.

Several weeks later, Dickens's letters begin to speak of a worrisome problem.

Ostensibly it involved not Ellen, but his loyal friend and chatelaine Georgina Hogarth. References to her ill health, "some affection of the heart," first appear in his letters in June, and at the end of that month he traveled with her to France, supposedly for her health, but also for what he described as "a week's wandering in the strangest towns in France"—which does not sound like a particularly restful regime for a bad heart—"and I go back again for another adventure next week." This first week of wandering in picturesque French towns was unlikely to have been solely for Georgina's health, and there was no pretense that the second "adventure" had anything at all to do with her, for she remained behind at Gad's Hill. Some compelling business had begun drawing Dickens across the Channel.

His explanations for his second French excursion were inconsistent and misleading. To one correspondent he wrote that it had been "some years since I was last across the channel" (it had actually been two weeks), and that he was visiting France for a "holiday" and "a little tour of observation"; he informed another that he was going "on a little Tour in Belgium"; his sister Letitia, meanwhile, was told simply that he was going to Paris. Then, back from this enigmatic excursion in mid-July, he was off again the following week, "obliged to go away on a distant engagement," he explained vaguely. He disappeared again several times in August and September, on excursions visible only in such epistolary comments as "Coming home here on Saturday night from a visit at a distance," or "I shall be away from next Monday to Thursday, both inclusive, probably." To mask his movements, or sometimes to dodge invitations, he pursued a consistent policy of evasion and misinformation concerning his many trips to France, but by the evidence of his letters he visited France as many as eight times during the summer of 1862, "my French wanderings" as he termed his curious peripatetic activity. An essay he wrote the following year for *All the Year Round*, "The Calais Night Mail," gives an impressionistic rendering of his many cross-channel trips during the previous twelvemonth.

Several ideas emerge from his letters' allusions to his French travels. The vagueness, the mystery, and the evasions almost certainly conceal their connection with Ellen; either he and she were crossing back and forth to France together, or she was fixed in France and he was visiting her. Letters early in the summer mention the "wandering" nature of his journeys, as if he had no fixed base—as if, perhaps, he were searching for somewhere to establish Ellen. Later, the trips become more businesslike, as if to an established destination.

By early July, he had decided to settle in Paris for most of the autumn. He explained to an old friend that "The new cause of anxiety at which I have hinted is the sudden decline of the health and spirit of Georgina. She is labouring under degeneration of the heart. . . . My present project is, to remove to Paris early in the Autumn, for a couple of months of complete change." It is unclear why crowded, busy Paris should be thought be better for a weak heart than the rural tranquility of Gad's Hill; and if Georgina's health had declined so precipitously in June, it seems strange that the restorative sojourn in Paris should be postponed for almost four months, until mid-October. By August, Georgina was reported "much better"; but notwithstanding her improved health, Dickens pushed ahead with the Paris plans. Announcing that he would "go over the water a day or two in advance" of Georgina and his daughter Mary in October, in fact he crossed three days ahead of them. He had already made hotel arrangements in Paris, and once in France he was not overbusy preparing for their arrival, writing his assistant Wills that he had "leisure for adventure before meeting Mary and Georgina"—"adventure" probably being code for Ellen.

He now remained in Paris for more than two months, except for one or two brief visits to London. He had ample leisure. One friend later recalled dining at a "course of restaurants" with Dickens during these months, including "a wonderful dinner at the Café Voisin" with a party of six. Another friend, Arthur Sullivan, at the time a very young man who had not yet met his future collaborator W. S. Gilbert, visited Paris that November. He and Dickens had been introduced several months earlier, and in Paris they dined together one evening at the Café Brébant, afterwards taking in a show at the Opera Comique. On another evening they went together to see the celebrated singer Madame Viardot in the opera *Orphée et Eurydice*. "She was intensely emotional," Sullivan recalled: "We were so much moved by the performance . . . that the tears streamed down our faces." Dickens spoke French poorly, according to Sullivan—"quite an Englishman's French"—and "rushed about tremendously all the time."

Rushed about why? He had no particular business to conduct in Paris, and with each passing day Georgina's health became a less plausible pretext for his presence there. Editing his letters after his death, Georgina declined to explain the prolonged stay. "At the end of October in this year [1862], Charles Dickens, accompanied by his daughter and sister-in-law, went to reside for a couple of months in Paris, taking an apartment in the Rue du Faubourg St. Honore," she reported blandly, and "at the beginning of [1863], Charles Dickens was in Paris for the purpose of giving a reading at the English embassy. He remained in Paris until the beginning of February, staying with his servant 'John' at the Hotel du Helder." Georgina surely recognized that a single reading—or even the three he actually gave—scarcely required his presence in Paris for a month after Christmas, but she disdained elaborate excuse-making.

Dickens himself was equally reticent in explaining his months in France. He wrote from Paris in early November that "sundry ties and troubles confine my present oscillations to between this place and England." In December, he returned with Georgina and Mary to Gad's Hill for Christmas, with firm plans to return to Paris early in the new year, without Georgina and Mary: "There [Gad's Hill], I remain until about the 8th of January, when I return here alone for a month or six weeks," he wrote from Paris before Christmas. He had scheduled public readings in Paris during January, but when he returned to France after the Christmas holidays he did not cite these readings but explained instead that he was going "to see a sick friend concerning whom I am anxious, and from whom I shall work my way round to Paris." Every other year from 1861 to 1866, he rented a house in London for Georgina, Mary, and himself for several months in winter and spring. In 1863 he did not.

Even making full allowance for Dickens's fondness for France, one can scarcely doubt that some mysterious lodestone was drawing him across the Channel, insistently, repeatedly, and at length, during the eight months from mid-June 1862 to mid-February 1863. And despite

Georgina's ill health and low spirits, she was not the "sick friend" in France about whom he was so anxious—for she was usually left behind at Gad's Hill. The unidentified invalid could only have been Ellen; and given Dickens's almost continuous residence in Paris between October 1862 and the following February, it seems very likely that during those months she too, perhaps with her mother, was either in Paris or within easy reach, possibly on the rail line between Calais and Paris. With Ellen in France, Dickens's visits would make sense even if she had been in perfect health, but his distress and anxiety during these months suggest that all was not well with her.

About the specific sources of his distress and anxiety, he remained oblique. The first mention of them occurs in late May 1862 (before his anxiety about Georgina's heart), when he told his sister Letitia that though he had been meaning to visit her, "I have been sorely worried and distressed of late." In September, he told Wilkie Collins that "I have some rather miserable anxieties which I must impart one of these days. . . . I shall fight out of them, I dare say: being not easily beaten—but they have gathered and gathered." Recurrent references to uncertainty, sleeplessness, "cares," "troubles," and "all this unsettled fluctuating distress in my mind" appear in his letters through the latter half of 1862 and into the early weeks of the new year. Concurrent with these anxieties were his numerous visits to, and then prolonged stays in, France. The editors of Dickens's letters note that "There is no period in his life in which Dickens pays so many visits to France, generally alone: at least 10 separate visits are recorded in his letters; there were probably more." But that he was "generally alone" is very unlikely.

His "miserable anxieties" peaked early in 1863. When, in mid-January, Sir Joseph Olliffe, physician to the British embassy in Paris, inquired about his neuralgia, Dickens responded:

> I really have had no neuralgic pain worth mentioning, since
> I rubbed with your blessed mixture. But I have not been

able to sleep. Some unstringing of the nerves—coupled with an anxiety not to be mentioned here—holds sleep from me.

Two days later, he wrote to Wilkie Collins: "I had been meaning to write before now, but have been unsettled and made uncertain by 'circumstances over which' &c &c &c." Still in France two weeks later, he wrote to Forster on February 7, Dickens's fifty-first birthday: "An odd birthday, but I am as little out of heart as you would have me be—floored now and then, but coming up again at the call of Time."

All these curious facts—frequent and extended visits to France over eight months; a reluctance to commit details to writing, even to confidential friends who knew all about Ellen; and sleepless anxieties culminating early in 1863—lead irresistibly to the conclusion that Ellen was pregnant and due to give birth in late January. Her health alone might have made him anxious, particularly if she were suffering a difficult first pregnancy. But his sleepless nights might have been owing, even more, to the unhappy responsibility of having fathered an illegitimate child on an unmarried, much younger woman to whom he was deeply devoted but whom he could not marry. Ellen herself may have been depressed; nor would her mother, probably with her throughout, have been pleased at the "circumstances over which—" since Ellen's pregnancy was scarcely a matter for which Dickens had no responsibility.

A notable feature of his many trips to France during these months is that after they began abruptly, with a succession of quick dashes back and forth across the Channel, they became not only protracted but carefully scheduled, with their end foreseen well in advance. Before his initial crossing in June 1862, he had been so little drawn to France that it had been "some years since I was last across the channel." But this first trip was rapidly followed by another, "at short notice," and in the next few months by many more, an abrupt change in his habits strongly suggesting that Ellen herself had relocated to France. It is not clear why she should have done so unless for a compelling reason. For Dickens himself, the frequent trips across the Channel were time-consuming and costly: first-class round-trip fare from London to Paris cost four pounds seven shillings (at a time when a bank clerk might earn seventy-five or one hundred pounds a year, a housemaid fifteen). It could have been no light cause that sent him shuttling back and forth between London and France so often during the summer of 1862.

On the other hand, his decision to settle in Paris with Georgina and Mary for the autumn had been made more than three months earlier; by early July, if not sooner, he knew that Ellen would be staying in France at least through the end of the year. His return to Paris after Christmas was also determined well in advance. As early as September, he wrote to Thomas Headland, his readings manager, that "I should like to have a little talk with you concerning the feasibility of some Paris Readings," adding a caution: "Say nothing on the subject yet, to anyone." The readings were fixed for January of the new year: he was confident that whatever was keeping Ellen in France would continue to keep her there at least through January. In early December, he wrote that he would be returning to Paris, alone, in early January, and staying for "a month or six weeks": "I have some engagements to fulfil here [Paris] at that time, and have promised to read, at our Embassy, for a certain charitable British Society." The "engagements" were left vague, and apart from the readings at the embassy he appears to have had no weighty obligations in Paris.

Most suggestive of all is that the date of his departure from France was fixed weeks beforehand. Even before Christmas he was certain that his French sojourn would end by mid-February, but no sooner. "There is no likelihood of my going home again until, at the earliest, the middle of February," he told his sister Letitia on December 20. Georgina had been given the same timetable. "Mr. Dickens is in Paris," she told a correspondent in January. "The time of his absence is uncertain—but we do not expect him home before the middle of February." Growing weary of his enforced stay in France, he eagerly

232 | ROBERT GARNETT

anticipated his February liberation. Writing to Wilkie Collins on New Year's Day, he suggested a bachelor ramble: "Who knows but that towards the end of February, I might be open to any foreign proposal whatsoever? Distance no object, climate of no importance, change the advertiser's motive." By the end of January, however, he had dropped the notion of a foreign jaunt and emphasized the permanence of his homecoming:

> I shall be at this address [in Paris] until Wednesday in next week, inclusive. After that, I shall be travelling for from ten days to a fortnight. After that, at the office and home for good.

What is curious about these scheduling bulletins is Dickens's confident foreknowledge of when he would return to England—curious because if Ellen had simply been ill, he could not possibly have known two months in advance, with apparent certainty, that she would recover by early February, at which time he could return home "for good," even to the extent of proposing (inconsistently) an ambitious foreign outing with Collins at the same time.

 This pattern of activity—brief impromptu trips to France beginning in June 1862; extended stays beginning in October; and a final, predetermined departure in mid-February—suggests that after a flurry of activity getting Ellen settled in France, Dickens based his plans on a predictable timetable—that of pregnancy. If she had become pregnant in the spring of 1862, probably April, and became aware of it several weeks later, she might naturally have decided, on Dickens's advice or insistence, to retire to France for the duration. If so, his earliest trips to France, in June and July, would have been to locate a suitable place for her and her mother to stay, to accompany them across, to help them get settled, to arrange medical attendance, and the like—requiring multiple crossings. In October, Ellen would enter the last trimester of her pregnancy; anticipating this, Dickens made plans to relocate to France in the autumn to be close to her. His return to Paris after New Year's 1863 anticipated a confinement later in January, and the end of his stay in France, announced weeks in advance, likewise anticipated Ellen's convalescing sufficiently to return to England by mid-February.

She probably gave birth around January 20, 1863. On the seventeenth, he gave a charity reading at the British embassy in Paris which was so successful that he agreed to give two more, on the twenty-ninth and thirtieth. Before these latter readings, however, he quietly disappeared from Paris, telling Wilkie Collins on the twentieth that circumstances "serious enough . . . take me from Paris this evening, *for a week*. . . . My absence is entre nous." During this week, he dropped out of touch almost completely. There are no surviving letters for seven consecutive days, and on returning to Paris on the twenty-eighth he apologized for a tardy response to a letter by explaining vaguely that he had "been visiting in the country these six days" and had neglected to have his letters forwarded. Now back in Paris, he gave notice of his final departure the following week and embarked on a succession of social engagements, complaining to his daughter Mary that "I have to dine out, to say nothing of breakfasting—think of me breakfasting!—every intervening day." The editors of his letters observe that "having avoided almost all invitations when in Paris 18-21 Jan, he now felt bound to accept them." But more likely, he now felt not so much "bound" to accept invitations as free to do so, for earlier, with Ellen's due date approaching, he had kept his calendar clear. His mysterious disappearance from Paris on January 20 or 21 probably fixes within a few days the birth of their child, somewhere outside Paris.

During Ellen's pregnancy, Georgina's defective heart somehow repaired itself. In July 1862, Dickens had consulted several physicians about her case, one of them pronouncing (in Dickens's words) that "it is plainly a case of aneurism of the aorta, and that the swelling presses on a bronchial tube and roughens the breathing, and presses on the spinal cord and produces a slight tendency toward paralysis." Georgina's sister Mary and her brother George had both died young and suddenly, probably of aneurisms. By early November, however, Georgina was "wonderfully better" and by the following April "all but quite well now." In fact, she lived another fifty-four years, past her ninetieth birthday. Her restored vigor and subsequent longevity, with no further hint of heart problems, suggest that there had been nothing wrong with her heart in the first place. Dickens's concern for her drooping spirits in 1862 may have been genuine enough, but also conveniently masked his concern for Ellen.

Ellen's pregnancy itself may have caused Georgina's "affection of the heart." Georgina's biographer, Arthur Adrian, suggests that her 1862 illness was caused by her disappointment that Ellen had failed to make Dickens happy—had, in fact, "submitted to his advances . . . coldly and with a worried sense of guilt." Adrian surmises:

> Georgina, exempting her hero from the restrictions placed on ordinary men, had, very likely, entertained idealistic notions of his finding happiness at last in high romance— a Tristram-and-Iseult kind of love worthy of transcendent genius. In nothing less could she have found justification for accepting Ellen Ternan. Disillusionment would have dealt a shattering blow.

More likely, however, Georgina's low spirits had little to do with any disappointment of Dickens and much to do with her own. If Ellen became pregnant in April 1862, Dickens and his loyal confidante Georgina probably learned of it in May, perhaps June—just when he first reported a sudden decline in Georgina's health. Her symptoms as he described them were more emotional than physical: "All that alacrity and 'cheer of spirit' that used to distinguish her, are gone . . . she is very low about herself, almost as soon as one has ceased to speak to her, after brightening her up." On June 13, he reported that Georgina was "very far from well," but just two days earlier a visitor to Gad's Hill had enjoyed "a very long and most agreeable talk with Miss Hogarth," who gave no signs of being an invalid: "a really delightful person, plain, unassuming, totally unaffected and of singularly pleasant and easy manner."

But the thirty-five-year-old spinster who had devoted herself to a celibate "marriage" with her idol might well have wilted in despondency when the younger woman who had captivated him now enjoyed the further happiness (from Georgina's perspective) of carrying his child. In June 1862, Dickens wrote to his sister Letitia that "I have been so anxious and distressed about Georgina . . . that I have been altogether dazed." Georgina might have felt flattered by his concern—except that, on the same day, he sufficiently overcame his distress to cross the Channel "on my way to Paris"—without her. Who could blame her, his faithful companion of twenty years and loyal ally during the separation imbroglio of 1858, if she felt low-spirited? The timing, symptoms, and total disappearance of Georgina's heart problem all suggest an emotional crisis precipitated by a sudden, unhappy shock—the pregnancy of Dickens's young mistress.

Fortunately, he thrived on stress; for even as he fretted about Ellen during the summer and autumn of 1862, he was wrestling with another vexing issue. The War Between the States precluded a reading tour in America, but in June he was offered ten thousand pounds for an eight-month tour in Australia. After considering for several weeks, he rejected the offer; but when it was renewed with even better terms, he reconsidered, "constantly disturbed and dazzled by the great chances that seem to lie waiting over there." The prospect of twelve thousand pounds, "supposed to be a low estimate," was difficult to abandon, "with all the hands upon my skirts that I cannot fail to feel and see there, whenever I look round," he told Forster. However, "if I were to go it would be a penance and a misery, and I dread the thought more than I can possibly express. . . . It is a struggle of no common sort, as you will suppose, you who know the circumstances of the struggler." Weighing against the heavy demands on his purse, demands that were urging him to exile himself from England for many months, was Ellen. He "had a fancy," Forster later remarked of the Australian proposal, "that it might be possible to take his eldest daughter with him." But there was no reason in the world that his unattached daughter Mary could not have accompanied him (she had just spent two months with him in Paris), and "eldest daughter" is probably Forster's discreet substitution for Ellen Ternan (who is never mentioned in Forster's *Life of Charles Dickens*). "I cannot go now," Dickens wrote about Australia in November 1862; "I don't know that I ever *can* go." If he were to go, he noted, it would not be until the following May or June—when Ellen would be fully recovered from childbirth; perhaps he hoped that she might then accompany him.

Other remarks in his letters hint at the crisis of Ellen. On the last day of January 1863, he attended a performance of Charles Gounod's opera *Faust* in Paris. To Georgina he wrote:

> I went . . . to hear Faust last night. It is a splendid work, in which that noble and sad story is most nobly and sadly rendered, and it perfectly delighted me. . . . I could hardly bear the thing; it affected me so, and sounded in my ears so like a mournful echo of things that lie in my own heart.

Why did *Faust* move him so powerfully? The opera opens with the aging Faust moping in despair; soon Mephistopheles appears and offers him gold, glory, and power. Faust declines:

> No! I want a treasure
> Which includes them all; I want youth!
> For me, pleasures
> And young paramours!
> Mine, their caresses!
> Mine, their desires!

Mine, the urgency
Of strong feelings,
And the wild revel
Of the heart and the senses!

In response to Faust's desire for recharged erotic sensations, Mephistopheles grants him a vision of the lovely young Marguerite, for whom Faust promptly signs away his soul. In Faust's exciting rejuvenescence, Dickens must have seen himself a few years earlier, in the first hectic flush of infatuation with Ellen. Faust's subsequent seduction of Marguerite, who in a particularly sinister scene chooses his gift of jewels over a rival's gift of flowers, might also have resonated "like a mournful echo of things that lie in my own heart." What probably echoed most mournfully of all, however, was that Marguerite becomes pregnant.

Faust repents. "I fear," he says, hesitating at her doorstep, "that I bring back shame and misery here"—as Dickens himself might well have felt on Ellen's doorstep.

His confidante Georgina would need no gloss to understand why he found *Faust* so poignant. A little later, he described the same performance to the retired actor William Macready: "After Marguerite has taken the jewels placed in her way in the garden, a weird evening draws on, and the bloom fades from the flowers, and the leaves over-hang her chamber window which was innocently bright and gay at first. I couldn't bear it, and gave in completely." Dickens often wept at the theater—he had been "disfigured with crying" at *Orphée et Eurydice* two months earlier; and far from leaving him prostrate with gloom, *Faust* "perfectly delighted" him. But he felt a pointed personal application in *Faust's* theme of seduction and lost innocence and in Marguerite's illegitimate child. Small comfort that after murdering her infant in a frenzy of grief, the repentant Marguerite is drawn into heaven by a choir of angels—for her aging seducer Faust is left behind.

In the same letter telling Georgina about *Faust*, Dickens also reported on his final two readings at the British embassy. He had rather dreaded them, telling Collins before the first that "I read tonight and tomorrow—horribly against the grain, as the grain is at present": the "grain" no doubt being his worries about Ellen. But the readings went well after all, and he was as usual delighted with his own performance. "You have never heard me read yet!" he crowed to Georgina. "I have been twice goaded and lifted out of myself into a state that astonished *me* almost as much as the audience." Then, in a brief medical bulletin incongruously appended to this braggadocio, he noted that "I have a cold, but no neuralgia, and am 'as well as can be expected.'" The phrase "as well as can be expected" (according to Partridge's *Dictionary of Slang)* is "almost obligatory on husbands speaking of wives within a week of parturition," and Dickens's first published use of the phrase, in a sketch written almost thirty years earlier, had explicitly referred to pregnancy:

> We saw that the knocker was tied up in an old white kid glove; and we, in our innocence (we were in a state of bachelorship then), wondered what on earth it all meant, until we heard the eldest Miss Willis, *in propriâ personâ,* say, with great dignity, in answer to the next inquiry, "*My* compliments, and Mrs Robinson's doing as well as can be expected, and the little girl thrives wonderfully."

Already by the 1830s, then, "as well as can be expected" was a hackneyed phrase associated with pregnancy and childbirth; and in now using the phrase in reference to himself, Dickens was probably indulging in sly whimsy: given the circumstances, Georgina would grasp the allusion. Perhaps the phrase was in fact a coded bulletin on Ellen's health: he avoided mentioning her in letters, but if she were recovering from childbirth Georgina would expect news of her.

Leaving Paris in early February, he lingered in France before crossing the Channel, to "go on a little perfectly quiet tour for about ten days, touching the sea at Boulogne." Again he dropped out of sight:

"I don't want to pin myself down to any particular place during the ten days," he told Wills. After this holiday with Ellen, he planned to return to England "for good," as he told several people; "I do not come back to Paris or near it," he told another. In mid-February, as promised, he was back in London. Nothing had come of the proposed bachelor lark with Wilkie Collins; he had now decided, instead, to give public readings in London, declaring again that he had returned to England "for good." He plainly had no wish or need to cross the Channel any time soon; whatever had drawn him to France so insistently for the previous eight months drew him no longer. One can safely infer that Ellen too was back in England. In March, confident that he was fixed in England indefinitely, Dickens began a series of fourteen public readings in London, extending into June.

Yet scarcely a month after returning "for good," and less than two weeks after the first of his London readings, he told his solicitor that "on coming to town" from a weekend at Gad's Hill, he had discovered "strong reason" to think he would need to leave town in a few days: "I am very much afraid that some rather anxious business I have on hand (but it is not my own, I am happy to say), will take me across the Channel on Friday morning, and probably detain me four or five days." The urgency and mystery of the summons point to Ellen again as the "anxious business" calling him away. Absent for five days, he returned to London, then immediately departed for another three or four days. A week later, he was gone yet again, obeying "a hasty summons to attend upon a sick friend at a distance" which "threw me out on Friday and Saturday in obliging me to prepare for a rush across the Channel." He was again out of town the following week, when there are no surviving letters for six consecutive days, after which he reported to his sister Letitia that "I have been away for some days, and have only just now got your letter."

But there is no corroborating evidence that he actually crossed the Channel during these urgent out-of-town trips in March and April 1863, and he may not have left England. None of his extant letters from these weeks is dated from or makes any reference to France. Wherever these brief, hasty excursions may have taken him, however, they certainly took him to Ellen, and they hint at a second crisis: possibly the illness and death of their son, later reported by both his daughter Katie and son Henry to have died in infancy. At the end of March, Dickens commiserated with an ailing friend by remarking that "I am but in dull spirits myself just now."

His mysterious departures diminished or ceased after April. In mid-May he claimed that "I have been absent from England for some days," but this was probably a polite falsehood to excuse a slow response to a correspondent. Ellen seems still to have been out of circulation, however; in June, her sister Maria was married in London, but Ellen is not on record as attending. Later in the summer she was mobile again. In August, claiming that "I have not been anywhere for ever and ever so long, but am thinking of evaporating for a fortnight on the 18th," Dickens disappeared into France for ten days, and in November he spent another week abroad. Though he may have slipped across the Channel for other, briefer visits, these two occasions are the only times he can be placed with certainty in France during the latter half of 1863. These crossings were less urgent than those the year before, however. He made plans for the August trip some three weeks in advance, on the pretext of gathering material for *All the Year Round*—in other words, he intended simply to vanish—while he announced the November trip, the week prior, as "a short holiday."

Both excursions were most likely holidays with Ellen. His privacy in England was restricted by his fame: he had a wide circle of acquaintances and had been painted, engraved, photographed, and caricatured. He could go nowhere without the likelihood of being recognized. "I am a dangerous man to be seen with," he had told Maria Beadnell Winter in 1855, "for so many people know me." He was an even more dangerous companion in 1863, after tens of thousands had attended his public readings over the previous five years.

Across the Channel, on the other hand, he could travel with Ellen in relative anonymity. Both liked France and spoke French: Ellen well, Dickens like a tourist. In 1864, he wrote to a Swiss friend:

> My being on the Dover line [at Gad's Hill], and my being very fond of France, occasion me to cross the channel perpetually. Whenever I feel that I have worked too much, or am on the eve of over-doing it, and want a change, away I go by the Mail Train, and turn up in Paris, or anywhere else that suits my humour, next morning.

Did the friend, who even in Switzerland might have heard whispers about a young actress, pause to wonder if there were more to Dickens's frequent channel crossings than Francophilia and convenient rail connections? He surely did not go off on his holiday escapes *solus*, and his silence about his companion leaves no doubt who she was.

On one occasion, at least, he and Ellen were recognized as they crossed the Channel together:

> Charles Dickens was once by chance my fellow-traveller on the Boulogne packet; travelling with him was a lady not his wife, nor his sister-in-law, yet he strutted about the deck with the air of a man bristling with self-importance: every line of his face and every gesture of his limbs seemed haughtily to say—"Look at me; make the most of your chance. I am the great, the *only* Charles Dickens; whatever I may choose to do is justified by that fact."

This hostile but well-informed witness—widow of the editor of *The Morning Post*—plainly knew of Dickens's connection with Ellen. We might interpret his strutting less censoriously, however, by imagining that as the packet boat cleared Folkestone harbor and his responsibilities and celebrity in England dropped astern, he felt a holiday exultation at the prospect of a leisurely week or two in France with "the lady not his wife."

The serial ordeals of Ellen's pregnancy and the death of their child could scarcely fail to leave their imprint on Dickens's next novel.

He was loath to begin it. His public readings, he had discovered, earned more money, more quickly, than writing. A twenty-month serial novel, tying him to his desk for about two years, would scarcely earn as much as six or eight months of readings; his net income from his most profitable novel, *Little Dorrit*, had not reached twelve thousand pounds, the sum he had been offered for a reading tour in Australia. So long as an Australian tour seemed possible, he put off a novel. During his stay in Paris in the fall of 1862, he was "wavering between reading in Australia, and writing a book at home." But the Australian idea was abandoned around Christmas that year: "I have had ambassadors, well backed with money, from Australia," he summarized his decision. "But I couldn't make up my mind to go." The difficulty of taking Ellen along without scandal may have tipped the scale; possibly she herself was reluctant to go.

He had little choice but to turn back to novel-writing. It was a reluctant decision: had someone offered him twelve thousand pounds for six months of readings in England, he would not have hesitated.

His fiction-writing drive had declined. His letters show little evidence of the restless energy he usually felt when a new novel was fermenting. Instead, "I am always thinking of writing a long book, and am never beginning to do it" (as he told Wilkie Collins in August 1863). For the first time in his career, he hesitated before the marathon strain of a long novel in monthly numbers. He was fifty-one; for decades he had driven himself hard. When his old friend and traveling companion Augustus Egg died in the spring of 1863, Dickens catalogued the losses since he and Egg had acted together in *The Frozen Deep* six years earlier:

> Think what a great Frozen Deep lay close under those
> boards we acted on! my brother Alfred, Luard, Arthur,

Albert, Austin, Egg—even among the audience, Prince
Albert and poor Stone—all gone! . . .

However, this won't do. We must close up the ranks and
march on.

His correspondence during these years often reverts to this martial
metaphor of life as a battle with heavy casualties.

He had long believed in the moral and curative powers of hard
work. Could it be that he was finally inclined to ease up a little, to
indulge in the lotus pleasures of Ellen's company?

In the autumn of 1863, however, eight or nine months after
returning from France with her, he began to rally his energies. "I am
exceedingly anxious to begin my book. I am bent upon getting to work
at it. . . . I see my opening perfectly, with the one main line on which
the story is to turn," he told Forster in October but then admitted:
"If I don't strike while the iron (meaning myself) is hot, I shall drift
off again; and have to go through all this uneasiness once more." He
began writing in earnest after Christmas, and in mid-January of the
new year, 1864, he was "hard at work upon a new book"—*Our Mutual
Friend.*

Our Mutual Friend alternates between two plots, only slightly connected, but both concerned with concupiscence and reformation. The
primary plot, the "one main line" he mentioned to Forster, dramatizes
the lower and grosser forms of concupiscence, particularly lust for
money—the fortune-hunting of a flawed heroine, the crude greed of
a wooden-legged bounder. As addressed to an acquisitive Victorian
culture of ever more getting and spending, this plot had (and retains)
an undoubted pertinence. With its straightforward didacticism, it has
been the more popular plot among critics.

But there is little moral tension in this plot; for as it winds through
its various confusions and reverses, the rights and wrongs are never
in question. No sane person doubts (in principle) that greed, avarice,

and love of money are evil. But Dickens did not feel that such sins had much application to himself: though he enjoyed and assiduously pursued money, both to support others (including his mistress) and to indulge himself, he never thought himself corrupted by it, and saw nothing of himself in the novel's grasping characters. Like many reformers incensed at others' vices, he conveniently overlooked his own, and the novel's satire on money-love is undercut by the comfortable bourgeois fantasy of its conclusion, in which the hero recovers his avaricious father's fortune and establishes his little family in an opulent London mansion purchased with money he has not earned.

The second plot of *Our Mutual Friend* has nothing to do with money, however, and much to do with Dickens and Ellen. The theme is sexual love: its power to destroy, its power to ennoble.

This plot centers on the daughter of a rough Thames waterman who makes his living scavenging, with a specialty in recovering drowned bodies. His beautiful and virtuous daughter, Lizzie Hexam, meets and innocently captivates the genteel idler Eugene Wrayburn. While the main plot features a flawed heroine, the second focuses on a flawed hero.

As with *Faust*, which had moved Dickens to tears in Paris, the Lizzie Hexam action dramatizes emotions and conflicts knocking about in his own heart. *Faust* itself had continued to echo within him, in fact, and helped shape his feelings about Ellen into a plot. Like Faust, "sad and solitary," *Our Mutual Friend*'s Wrayburn is languishing at novel's opening, bored and purposeless; and, further like Faust, he is fired with new energy when he encounters a lovely young woman of humble station. Both heroines are warm, responsive, vulnerable, and yielding—to different degrees. While Marguerite yields herself to Faust, Lizzie flees her dangerous attraction to Wrayburn; no descendant of Mary Hogarth would actually fall into sin. But though retaining her chastity, Lizzie surrenders emotionally: "She tried hard to retain her firmness, but he saw it melting away under his eyes. In the moment of its dissolution, and of his first full knowledge of his influence upon her, she dropped, and he caught her on his arm." But from her weakness rises her strength: her unselfish love conquers the cynical Wrayburn.

It testifies to the complexity of Dickens's feelings that both the hero and the villain reflect his love for Ellen. Wrayburn's antagonist Bradley Headstone also wants Lizzie—violently. "I love you," he declares to her:

> "What other men may mean when they use that expression, I cannot tell; what *I* mean is, that I am under the influence of some tremendous attraction which I have resisted in vain, and which overmasters me."

Headstone sets out to court Lizzie "with a bent head hammering at one fixed idea"—like Dickens, himself a hard-hammering character, pursuing Ellen five years earlier. "The more you see of me," Dickens had once told his wife, "the better perhaps you may understand that the intense pursuit of any idea that takes complete possession of me, is one of the qualities that makes me different—sometimes for good; sometimes I dare say for evil—from other men." His own eagerly passionate nature appears in Headstone's desire for Lizzie, "an immoveable idea since he first set eyes upon her":

> It seemed to him as if all that he could suppress in himself he had suppressed, as if all that he could restrain in himself he had restrained, and the time had come—in a rush, in a moment—when the power of self-command had departed from him. Love at first sight is a trite expression quite sufficiently discussed; enough that in certain smouldering natures like this man's, that passion leaps into a blaze, and makes such head as fire does in a rage of wind, when other passions, but for its mastery, could be held in chains.

The mixed metaphors of the final sentence—fire and chains—suggest Headstone's loss of control, as the cool analytical rhetoric is swept aside by a "rush" of passion.

Headstone is a monitory study of abandonment to passion—of desire breaking all restraints, indifferent to consequences. Headstone is the violent Dickens, his Mr. Hyde. When Headstone mentions the idea of marrying and settling down with a respectable schoolmistress, Lizzie encourages him: "Why have you not done so? . . . Why do you not do so?" He explodes:

> "Far better that I never did! The only one grain of comfort I have had these many weeks . . . is, that I never did. For if I had, and if the same spell had come upon me for my ruin, I know I should have broken that tie asunder as if it had been a thread."

The bachelor Headstone's marital rupture is merely notional, whereas Dickens under the spell of Ellen had ruthlessly broken off an actual marriage of twenty-two years, with nine living children.

After that violent severance, however, he walked more softly. As a schoolmaster, Headstone echoes Dickens in another respect: both performed to an audience and depended on its respect. "Do you suppose that a man, in forming himself for the duties I discharge, and in watching and repressing himself daily to discharge them well, dismisses a man's nature?" Headstone demands. For both famous author and obscure schoolmaster, "a man's nature"—a cautious euphemism for erotic desire—had to be segregated from professional life. The intimately personal crisis of Ellen's pregnancy had had wider perils. "I have had stern occasion to impress upon my children that their father's name is their best possession," Dickens had written during the separation crisis of 1858, and his good name remained an essential asset for himself as much as for his children. Headstone develops a routine of teaching boys by day and stalking his rival Wrayburn by night, a schism reflecting Dickens's own two lives: the respectable, revered public figure, and the private man going his own wild way.

Headstone's passion for Lizzie destroys him. "You could draw me to fire, you could draw me to water," he raves; "you could draw me to the gallows, you could draw me to any death, you could draw me to anything I have most avoided, you could draw me to exposure and disgrace." But Dickens was too anxious for his reputation, and too solicitous for Ellen's privacy, to risk all. The Duke of Wellington is said to have defied blackmail by declaring "Publish and be damned," but a writer and performer dependent on public approbation could scarcely afford such aristocratic disdain. During the separation crisis of 1858, Dickens had made the mistake of broadcasting his private affairs, an indiscretion that taught him a needful lesson. His "wild way" could be indulged only with careful circumspection. In Bradley Headstone, he imagined the devil of unrestrained desire dragging a victim down to destruction—as could happen when "a man's nature" seized control.

That same devil had clawed Dickens too; Ellen's pregnancy was a result. A lighthearted, spoony fascination with little lilac gloves had led him (and her) into deep waters. Because he loved her dearly, he had to love her cautiously.

Love is a flame that sometimes destroys—but that can cleanse and refine as well. Its purgatorial potential emerges through another character in *Our Mutual Friend*—the heroine Lizzie herself. Ellen Ternan had acquainted Dickens with the quotidian fevers of desire— its excitements, its compulsions, its violence, its suffering—but she had also led him deeper into love's mysteries.

Lizzie Hexam's redemptive power begins, ironically, with Dickens's fascination with corpses—especially drowned corpses.

On his many visits to Paris, he relished visits to the morgue, a popular resort for French idlers and British tourists, where anonymous corpses, many of them murder victims or suicides, and more than half recovered from the Seine, were theatrically displayed for identification.

A few years earlier, he had gazed with macabre fascination at one such corpse, "a large dark man whose disfigurement by water was in a frightful manner, comic, and whose expression was that of a prize-fighter who had closed his eyelids under a heavy blow, but was going immediately to open them, shake his head, and 'come up smiling.'" Shortly before beginning *Our Mutual Friend*, he wrote an entire essay about corpses, describing (among others) the body of a drowned woman he had once come across, dragged up onto the towpath of Regent's Park Canal: "The feet were lightly crossed at the ankles, and the dark hair, all pushed back from the face, as though that had been the last action of her desperate hands, streamed over the ground." He was struck by the almost-alive quality of corpses, as if death had unexpectedly inter-rupted them in mid-gesture and they might at any second resume living. But the cold, permanent and distant deadness of the dead was also fascinating. Observing a crowd gaping at bodies in the Paris morgue, he was struck by the gazers' "one under-lying expression of *looking at something that could not return a look.*" The boundary between life and death was very narrow and at the same time infinitely wide, as vast as the universe—a paradox both comic and chilling.

London lacked a central arena like the Paris morgue for displaying unidentified bodies, but the Thames scarcely yielded to the Seine as an instrument of drowning. Dickens once spent a winter night on the Thames, first in a boat with a detachment of Thames Police, then on Waterloo Bridge. By night, the river was a gloomy underworld: "The air was black, the water was black, the barges and hulks were black, the piles were black, the buildings were black, the shadows were only a deeper shade of black upon a black ground." The officer in charge of the boat was used to it. "And after all, this looks so dismal?" he scoffs. At night it is gloomy enough, Dickens replies:

> The Seine at Paris is very gloomy too, at such a time, and
> is probably the scene of far more crime and greater wicked-
> ness; but this river looks so broad and vast, so murky and

silent, seems such an image of death in the midst of the great city's life. . . .

The river speaks in grim voices: "Uncomfortable rushes of water suggestive of gurgling and drowning, ghostly rattlings of iron chains, dismal clankings of discordant engines, formed the music that accompanied the dip of our oars and their rattling in the rullocks. Even the noises had a black sound to me—as the trumpet sounded red to the blind man." To cap Dickens's night on the Thames, the toll-taker on Waterloo Bridge chatted at length of suicides and attempted suicides launched from the bridge.

Even by day the Thames was not the sweet and silver streaming river of earlier times. "You will have read in the papers that the Thames at London is most horrible," Dickens had written to his Swiss friend a few years earlier: "I have to cross Waterloo or London Bridge to get to the Railroad when I come down there, and I can certify that the offensive smells, even in that short whiff, have been of a most head-and-stomach distracting nature." By mid-Victorian times, the Thames was a large open sewer into which "untreated sewage from 141 sewers between Battersea and London Bridge discharged 250 tons of fecal matter and other noxious substances" each day; and "because its river banks were shallow, only at the very highest of tides would the sewage be flushed out and down the river towards the sea. For the remaining twelve hours, the sewage lay in the river."

Aphrodite, goddess of love, sprang from the sea foam; Lizzie Hexam, heroine of *Our Mutual Friend*, emerges from a river of drowned bodies and sewage. Dickens's earliest heroine, *Oliver Twist*'s Rose Maylie, a straightforward portrait of Mary Hogarth, dwelt in an edenic garden setting: "The rose and honeysuckle clung to the cottage walls; the ivy crept round the trunks of the trees; and the garden-flowers perfumed the air with delicious odours." There is nothing rose-like about the bloated bodies that Lizzie helps her father recover from the Thames, rising from the sludge, scarcely perfuming the air like honeysuckle. "Pharoah's multitude, that were drowned in the Red Sea, ain't more beyond restoring to life" than their father's latest corpse, Lizzie's brother picturesquely observes. Rivers were Dickens's favorite metaphor for the unceasing current of life, steadily carrying everyone down to the sea of death, but the Thames that flows through *Our Mutual Friend* is no poetic metaphor but rather a workaday agent of decay and drowning: "Everything so vaunted the spoiling influences of water—discoloured copper, rotten wood, honey-combed stone, green dank deposit—that the after-consequences of being crushed, sucked under, and drawn down, looked as ugly to the imagination as the main event." The river of *Our Mutual Friend* represents the muddy undercurrents of life: flesh, corruption, and mortality; human kinship with the bottom slime and ooze; feces, sweat, lust, and violence.

But from this fetid river emerges the redemptive power of love. Dickens had come to understand love not just as a rarefied spirit, but as a mystery embedded in the flesh—"of the earth, earthy," as he liked to say (quoting St. Paul).

Lizzie Hexam is a daughter of the Thames, with its thick stew of mud, garbage, sewage, and corpses. "The very fire that warmed you when you were a baby, was picked out of the river alongside the coal barges," her father reminds her. "The very basket that you slept in, the tide washed ashore. The very rockers that I put it upon to make a cradle of it, I cut out of a piece of wood that drifted from some ship or another." She shrinks from the river's odor of mortality; yet, like it or not, she is of the river, rivery, and cannot escape it: "Whenever I am at Paris," Dickens had written, only partly in jest, "I am dragged by invisible force into the Morgue. I never want to go there, but am always pulled there." Lizzie too is implicated in what horrifies her. "To please myself, I could not be too far from that river," she remarks, but adds, with curious ambiguity: "I can't get away from it, I think. . . . It's no purpose of mine that I live by it still." Circumstances tie her to the river, but beyond them lurks a mysterious compulsion. The river is the blood in her veins, and she cannot evade the dark currents of her own being.

From her muddy origins comes Lizzie's rich sexuality: she is among Dickens's most erotic heroines. Unlike the fair Ellen Ternan, Lizzie is "a dark girl of nineteen or twenty" with a "rich brown cheek." Observing her through a window, Wrayburn sees "a deep rich piece of colour, with the brown flush of her cheek and the shining lustre of her hair, though sad and solitary, weeping by the rising and the falling of the fire." For Dickens, Aphrodite was dark. Lizzie's crippled friend Jenny Wren has long golden hair; loosened by Lizzie one evening, Jenny's hair "fell in a beautiful shower over the poor shoulders that were much in need of such adorning rain." But Lizzie's hair is no golden rain shower: when Jenny in turn "loosened her friend's dark hair, . . . it dropped of its own weight over her bosom in two rich masses"—two rich masses echoing her breasts, emphasizing her womanly allure.

Yet despite her erotic fascinations, Lizzie is a pattern of feminine virtue: modest, loving, self-sacrificing, "pure of heart and purpose." Dickens could assert her purity in no more emphatic terms than those in which he had defended his beloved Ellen during the separation crisis, when he had insisted that "upon my soul and honour, there is not on this earth a more virtuous and spotless creature than this young lady. I know her to be innocent and pure, and as good as my own dear daughters." He seems to relive his fervid defense of Ellen's virtue when he has Eugene Wrayburn assert (to his friend Lightwood) that "there is no better girl in all this London than Lizzie Hexam. There is no better among my people at home; no better among your people." Even Wrayburn's out-of-character reference to the women of his family, "my people," as a standard of feminine virtue echoes Dickens's reference to "my own dear daughters."

The dual nature of Lizzie, erotic and chaste, appears in her confused response to Wrayburn. Upon first seeing him, she is flustered: blushing and shrinking under his gaze, she flees the room to escape his gaze. Yet she soon adopts him as something like a scapegrace brother, an erring male in need of womanly care and support, filling the need of her own generous nature for someone to love. Speaking of herself (in the third person), she observes:

> She knows he [Wrayburn] has failings, but she thinks they have grown up through his being like one cast away, for the want of something to trust in, and care for, and think well of. And she says, . . . "Only put me in that empty place, only try how little I mind myself, only prove what a world of things I will do and bear for you, and I hope that you might even come to be so much better than you are, through me who am so much worse, and hardly worth the thinking of beside you."

Like earlier Mary Hogarth heroines, Lizzie glows with sympathy, earnestness, loyalty, devotion, self-abnegation, self-sacrifice. But her love for Wrayburn is not ethereal. She confesses that "Her heart—is given him, with all its love and truth. She would joyfully die with him, or, better than that, die for him." Dickens is not punning here on "die" in the sense of sexual climax, the *double entendre* so beloved of English poets, but he makes plain Lizzie's amorous susceptibility.

For Lizzie, however, vulnerability is strength, desire elevating. Her love for Wrayburn transforms him, but transforms her as well. It "has made a change within me, like—like the change in the grain of these hands, which were coarse, and cracked, and hard, and brown, when I rowed on the river with father, and are softened and made supple by this new work [as a seamstress], as you see them now." Yet her nature remains grounded in her riverside origins; her desire transcends the sensual, but never loses touch with it. In Lizzie, love is a richly embodied spirit. "Love's mysteries in souls do grow," John Donne wrote, "but yet the body is his book":

So soul into the soul may flow,
Though it to body first repair, . . .
So must pure lovers' souls descend
T'affections, and to faculties,
Which sense may reach and apprehend.

("The Ecstasy")

In the figure of Lizzie, Dickens's reverence for the chaste spirit of Mary Hogarth marries his sensual attraction to Ellen Ternan. Lizzie is desired *and* revered; both a siren of the river and an angel.

Her dark radiance reclaims the lost soul of Eugene Wrayburn. In *David Copperfield*, Agnes had saved David by leading him away from the allurements of the flesh; by contrast, Lizzie redeems Wrayburn by drawing him *into* desire. Their strong mutual attraction is unmistakably sexual. Paradoxically, however, erotic love leads Wrayburn upward, out of his purposeless dandyism into self-sacrificing love. He learns to love Lizzie generously, but only because he has first desired her. Heroines like Agnes are spiritual and loving in their essence, but flawed mortals like Wrayburn must struggle through fleshly desires to a higher love. When Lizzie drags him from the river after he is bludgeoned by Bradley Headstone, he emerges reborn. He must drown before he can live.

Until Ellen Ternan, Dickens had assumed an unbridgeable gulf between the ether of pure love and the thick currents of human life below. Even in *Our Mutual Friend*, created loveliness stands far removed from its Creator:

So, in the rosy evening, one might watch the ever-widening beauty of the landscape—beyond the newly-released workers wending home—beyond the silver river—beyond the deep green fields of corn, so prospering, that the loiterers in their narrow threads of pathway seemed to float immersed breast-high—beyond the hedgerows and the

clumps of trees—beyond the windmills on the ridge—away
to where the sky appeared to meet the earth, as if there were
no immensity of space between mankind and Heaven.

The concluding "as if" clause betrays Dickens's feeling that God kept
himself at a lofty and hygienic distance, aloof from the muddy sphere
of humanity. And yet in the character of Lizzie Hexam the antithesis
collapses, as Dickens's most exalted ideal of sanctity is incarnate in a
darkly sexual heroine.

Beginning doubtfully, with infatuation and scandal, his love for
Ellen Ternan had passed through its greatest crisis and emerged
stronger. When Lizzie Hexam unwillingly confesses her love, Eugene
Wrayburn exults that "so earnest a character must be very earnest in
that passion." Dickens himself was a very earnest character, and threw
himself into his love for Ellen with all of his ardor and strong will.

In *A Farewell to Arms*, old Count Greffi, regretting his own lack
of piety, reminds Frederic Henry that "you are in love. Do not forget
that is a religious feeling." Dickens would have agreed; his strongest
religious feelings were always evoked by women. Describing the first
time he saw the actor Charles Fechter on stage, he remarked: "He was
making love to a woman, and so elevated her as well as himself by the
sentiment in which he enveloped her that they trod into purer ether
and in another sphere quite lifted out of the present. . . . I never saw
two people more purely and instantly elevated by the power of love."
Our Mutual Friend's Lizzie Hexam reveals love's power to transform
and elevate—even to undrown the dead. Perhaps Dickens felt that he
too had been resuscitated, by Ellen.

CHAPTER 8

Mr. Tringham and the train crash

I n the years following Ellen Ternan's pregnancy, she and Dickens settled into a less eventful routine, though never bland domesticity. They never actually lived together, in fact. Although Ellen was paramount in his affections, he owed most of his time to his family and professional activities. He wrote less, beginning only one novel after finishing *Our Mutual Friend* in 1865, and leaving it unfinished at his death. But he was scarcely idle. "The older I get," he boasted the year before his death, "the more I do, and the harder I work."

During his last five years, however, his health and vigor declined, while Ellen herself may not have been entirely well. Most spectacularly, they nearly died together in a train wreck. But despite ills and accidents and despite his strenuous, protracted reading tours and the difficulties of spending time with her, his devotion to her never faltered; indeed, grew stronger. She was never merely the convenient mistress of a busy man, a voluptuary indulgence for his leisure hours. The most remarkable feature of his affair with Ellen Ternan was not its pyrotechnic origins, nor the complications that ensued—his wife's eviction, the gossip and scandal, the stealth, the pregnancy—but the steady progress of his love for her, as the excited infatuation of the older man for the young actress grew into a deep affection, admiration, and loyalty. If Mary Hogarth had inspired his young manhood, Ellen became the cult of his later years.

For two or three years after their return from France in early 1863, her whereabouts are difficult to ascertain. During these years, however, he remained mostly in or around London—presumptive evidence that she too was in London, or nearby. She probably continued to live with her mother at 2 Houghton Place, in the house Dickens had purchased for her. More exotic possibilities have been suggested. He is known to have stayed occasionally at a secluded house in Condette, a village near Boulogne, directly across the Channel, and some have suspected that he maintained Ellen there. But there is no evidence that she ever resided in Condette, or indeed that she ever went there at all, though she may well have visited with him. Most or all of his trips across the Channel in 1863 and the following years were made in her company, and Condette would have been a suitably private retreat for them. But he is unlikely to have been content with Ellen living across the Channel by herself, hidden away in a village inconveniently distant from London—and it is hard to imagine why he would have sequestered her in France while he was in England.

Despite the uncertainties, his letters reveal much about his routine during these years.

The center of his professional life was of course London, in particular the offices of *All the Year Round* on Wellington Street, near Covent Garden. Most of the business and editorial duties of the magazine were discharged by his capable subeditor, W. H. Wills; but Dickens spent one day a week at the office, sometimes more, to attend to magazine business and answer correspondence, much of it having nothing to do with *All the Year Round*, as well as for appointments. In 1867, for example, a visiting Methodist minister from Philadelphia, a complete stranger, wrote to ask if he could call on Dickens; and surprisingly Dickens consented, spending an hour in amiable chat with the Reverend Mr. Goldsmith Day Carrow. Dickens was limping on a gouty foot, but greeted his American visitor cheerfully and they sat down "knee to knee." Carrow could not help but deplore his host's "exceedingly poor taste in the matter of dress"—his "flowered purple velvet vest and checkered cashmere pantaloons" were too flashy for a sober Philadelphia eye. (Dickens had always favored smart clothes, but perhaps an aging man with a much younger mistress would especially cultivate a youthful appearance.) Despite his garish outfit, Dickens's "general bearing was earnest, frank, gracious and winning," Carrow was gratified to note, and the conversation flowed easily from topic to topic—Carrow's travels in Europe and his impressions of Europeans and the English; Dickens's work habits and his prowls about London; and of course his novels.

Carrow, for example, praised Dickens's female characters: "You have sometimes in a single paragraph laid open the heart of a woman as Sir Walter Scott has failed to do in his whole Waverley series."

"Why my dear sir!" Dickens exclaimed in surprise, and sprang to Sir Walter's defense, citing several of Scott's memorable female characters and "expatiating upon and eulogizing his genius."

Carrow politely demurred; Scott's only passion had been his ambition to found a family, he argued, and then confidently enunciated a critical principle: "I hold that a man must have really loved a woman if he would fully interpret the secrets of a woman's heart."

Dickens agreed: "'You are correct again, sir,' replied Mr. Dickens smiling." But did the smile mask a twist of sudden anxiety? Was the Reverend Mr. Carrow, Dickens might have wondered, slyly alluding to Ellen? Perhaps this chatty, apparently innocuous clergyman was in fact fishing for some compromising disclosure.

Carrow almost certainly knew nothing about Ellen. But Dickens was just then planning a reading tour of America, and his visitor's curious suggestion that Dickens "must have really loved a woman" might have seemed suspicious. Was this "clergyman" an imposter, some low American journalist nosing about for a scoop?

"But to what particular character in my works have you alluded?" Dickens pressed him.

"The question drew him more closely to me," Carrow recalled, "and replacing his hands on my knees, he added, 'Do me the favor to explain yourself.'"

This would seem a pointed, almost bellicose, demand, but Carrow was unaware that he was treading on dangerous ground. Dickens's smile, he considered, "was expressive of curiosity as well as of pleasure, and showed that he was saying to himself, 'I wonder if this Yankee clergyman does truly comprehend me?'"

Dickens may have been wondering precisely that.

Pondering which of his fictional women best testified to Dickens's experience of love, Carrow proposed Esther Summerson of *Bleak House*.

If Dickens had feared that his visitor was hinting at Ellen, Carrow's choice of Esther must have been a relief. *Bleak House* had been written a full five years before he had met Ellen; and the right-minded Esther was more indebted to another fictional paragon, Jane Eyre, than to any actual woman Dickens had ever known, let alone Ellen. Perhaps he suppressed a smile. To Carrow's eye, "the face of the great artist took on a pensive, tender aspect." Dickens almost hugged him. "I see you understand me! I see you understand me!" he exclaimed, according to Carrow. "And that is more precious to the author than fame or gold."

Mr. Carrow visited Wellington Street on a Friday in August. Afterward, Dickens joined Ellen in Peckham for the weekend, and perhaps they laughed together when he recounted his interview with the earnest clergyman from Philadelphia.

Most of his callers were less random, but Mr. Carrow's visit suggests the range of Dickens's days in London, from editing and business matters to social calls and distractions.

The offices on Wellington Street also served as his London lodgings. When he sold Tavistock House in 1860 and moved his family to Gad's Hill, he had a bedroom and sitting room fitted up for himself above the business offices of *All the Year Round*; his servant John Thompson remained in London to tend to the Wellington Street quarters as well as to help out in the offices below (although in 1866 he was dismissed for pilfering from the office cash box). Dickens often took dinner at Wellington Street, occasionally entertaining guests. At some point, a second bedroom was fitted up for his daughter Mary, and Georgina sometimes stayed there as well. Nonetheless, the Wellington Street rooms were essentially a bachelor retreat.

Did Ellen visit him there? After business hours, it would have been easy enough to escort her upstairs to his private apartment unobserved, and she was probably familiar with the *All the Year Round* offices and Dickens's lodgings above. But as to whether she knew them well, or knew them at all, his letters (as later censored by Georgina) are silent, and any visits were probably only occasional. Wellington Street was no secure hideaway, and he preferred seeing her in greater privacy.

The second corner of his triangular life was Gad's Hill. In summers and autumns especially, he spent much of his time at his Kentish retreat, enjoying long walks through the countryside, the amenities and comforts of the house, and the roles of local squire and genial host. His unmarried daughter Mary was nominally mistress of the household; Georgina was actually the indispensable domestic manager—as Wills was to *All the Year Round*, Georgina was to Gad's Hill. Dickens was continually making improvements to the property, from drilling an expensive new well the first year to having an expensive conservatory constructed in his last year. His friend Charles Fechter the actor presented him with a miniature two-story Swiss chalet, the pieces shipped to Gad's Hill in fifty-eight crates; a tunnel had been dug under the busy road in front of the house for easier and more private access to a wooded plot on the opposite side, and here Dickens had the chalet erected amidst trees and shrubs. In fine weather he used it for writing, sitting in the upper story with the shutters thrown open. On summer weekends there were usually guests, Dickens issuing invitations liberally, not just to close friends but also to more casual acquaintances. The wine cellar was kept well stocked, and in 1864 he installed a billiard table. The following year, one of his invitations to Gad's Hill advertised "Billiards, croquet, bowls, &c on the premises. Cool cups and good drinks. Good beds. Harmony, most evenings." The local cricket club used a field at Gad's Hill for their matches; Dickens did not play, but sometimes kept score.

Ellen seldom visited Gad's Hill; it was a family home, and the particular domain of the loyal Georgina; Dickens entertained many people there, but it would have been uncomfortable to host his mistress there often, or long. There are no contemporary references to any visits she made, but later reports attest to them. As an old woman, Dickens's daughter Katie recounted a visit of Ellen's: "Ellen Ternan came to stay [at Gad's Hill]; followed by Katie, who, when she heard of the visit of Nelly . . . and that she had taken a hand at cricket with the boys in the field, observed: 'I am afraid she did not play the game!'" (One could hardly expect a young woman brought up to the stage to be a cricket adept.) A friend of Ellen's recalled an occasion when Ellen, as an old woman, "looking at photographs of Gad's Hill, exclaimed, 'Ah, many's the time I've been *there*!', then whisked the lot away, with the reticence on the subject of Dickens that characterized her later years." Though her "many" visits to Gad's Hill may have been multiplied by memory, she no doubt visited on occasion.

In winter and spring each year, however, Dickens rented a furnished house in London—a different one each year, always near Hyde Park—to give Georgina and Mary time in the metropolis during the high social season. Every May, during the final weeks of their London stay, he groused about the multitude of dinner parties to which Georgina and Mary committed him. It seems unlikely that Ellen often appeared at such dinners, if she ever visited his rented London house at all.

It was not easy to find private time with her, in fact: his celebrity and his family both imposed obstacles. For a year or two following her pregnancy, his most frequent answer to the difficulty was France.

Both he and Ellen were fond of France, and comfortable there; he had visited many times over the years, and she had just spent seven or eight months there. France was readily accessible by way of express trains from London to the Channel and packet boats across the Channel; "tidal trains" ran according to the arrivals and departures of the boats, which were in turn dependent on high tide. From London to Paris was only about ten hours. Far from the offices of *All the Year Round*, with its flood of correspondence, decisions, deadlines, and problems, France offered a holiday escape with relative privacy and leisure.

In England Dickens was a prisoner of his fame; in France he was just another bowler-hatted Englishman. For further anonymity he probably employed a pseudonym. "You know how to address me, if need be," he reminded Georgina before leaving for France on one occasion in 1864, and since in the same note he included the name of his hotel in Boulogne, his reminder probably alluded instead to a French pseudonym. In England he was sometimes "Charles Tringham"; across the Channel perhaps he was Monsieur Tringham. Because he gave Georgina the name of his hotel during this trip, the Hôtel du Pavillon Impérial in Boulogne, it is for once possible to pin down his location after he crossed the Channel.

He made many "mysterious disappearances" in 1864 and 1865, most or all of them to France. In March 1864, for example, he disappeared for a week on "a little run." In June, "I expect to be in France on the 30th for a few days' holiday," he told one correspondent, though to another he described the same holiday as "a ten or twelve days visit to Belgium." Perhaps he visited both, but certainly France, for after telling Wills that "I have been working desperately hard to get away," he added that his next Christmas tale "might have a mixing in it of Paris and London," as "my present Mysterious Disappearance is in that direction." The June holiday took him and Ellen to Paris and perhaps Sens—"a pretty little town with a great two-towered cathedral and the rooks flying in and out of the loopholes and another tower atop of one of the towers like a sort of a stone pulpit," as he later described it in the Christmas story he had mentioned to Wills—and perhaps to other spots as well, but their itinerary is a mystery, for there is no surviving correspondence from the ten days of their absence, an unusually long gap, suggesting that wherever he took Ellen, he dropped out of touch with England almost completely.

How did they pass their time on their French holidays? Certainly they traveled about on the excellent French trains. The discomfort, bad food, and disobliging staff of refreshment rooms at British railway stations exasperated Dickens; and in an 1866 story, "Mugby Junction," he ironically contrasted them with their superior French counterparts: "What would you say to a general decoration of everythink," a British refreshment-room mistress disapprovingly describes French railway canteens, "to hangings (sometimes elegant), to easy velvet furniture, to abundance of little tables, to abundance of little seats, to brisk bright waiters, to great convenience, to a pervading cleanliness and tastefulness . . . ?" Such hospitable arrangements might be encountered "three times . . . between the coast and Paris, and not counting either: at Hazebroucke, at Arras, at Amiens." The listing of stations suggests Dickens's familiarity with the route between Boulogne and Paris, which he probably traveled many times with Ellen. On occasion they went further, "south of Paris," encountering even more impressive railway hospitality: "Fancy a guard coming round, with the train at full speed, to inquire how many for dinner," the refreshment-room mistress continues. "Fancy his telegraphing forward the number of dinners. Fancy every one expected, and the table elegantly laid for the complete party. Fancy a charming dinner, in a charming room, and the head-cook, concerned for the honour of every dish, superintending in his clean white jacket and cap. Fancy . . . travelling six hundred miles on end, very fast, and with great punctuality, yet being taught to expect all this." Six hundred miles would carry one from the English Channel all the way to the Mediterranean, and possibly one or more of Dickens's disappearances took him and Ellen as far as Provence and the French Riviera.

Once arrived at their destination, they would wander on foot or by carriage through the towns and view the local sights. Dickens was restless, curious, observant, always on the lookout for material and impressions for *All the Year Round*: "I will turn over this French ground with great care," he remarked before one trip. Ellen was young, and would welcome the adventure and novelties of traveling, especially escorted by the capable Dickens, who would make all the arrangements and ensure that they lodged comfortably and drank good wines. Even if staying in Boulogne or Condette for a few days, they probably made day trips in the vicinity.

But their French holidays would not have been frenetic sightseeing expeditions; no doubt they usually drifted, lounged, and loitered. Dickens may often have worked in the mornings on whatever writing or editing task he had in hand, before an afternoon of strolling about town, perhaps some shopping, a leisurely evening of dinner and conversation, later a play or other entertainment. In his 1864 Christmas story, "Mrs. Lirriper's Legacy," several of the story's English characters visit Sens, southeast of Paris: "Every evening at a regular time we all three sat out in the balcony of the hotel at the end of the courtyard, looking up at the golden and rosy light as it changed on the great towers, and looking at the shadows of the towers as they changed on all about us ourselves included." It is easy to believe that such particularity was indebted to mellow evenings that he and Ellen spent in Sens in the summer of 1864.

Even the "we all three" of "Mrs. Lirriper's Legacy" may reflect such evenings, for Ellen's mother certainly accompanied Dickens and Ellen on at least one trip to France, and possibly on others, but in alluding to his "disappearances" Dickens's letters never mention even Ellen, let alone her mother. Widowed and retired from the stage, Mrs. Ternan seems to have lived most of the time with Ellen; certainly mother and daughter were close. If she accompanied Dickens and Ellen abroad, one suspects that he would gladly have dispensed with the chaperonage. Though Mrs. Ternan plainly tolerated her daughter's irregular status and was perhaps a pleasant traveling companion, who would not prefer to travel *à deux* with his beloved? For Ellen's sake, Dickens made the best of it.

Their disappearances in France continued through 1865. At the beginning of February that year, he was "away for a week's run"; in writing from his London office to Georgina at Gad's Hill, he congratulated himself: "The mysterious 'arrangement' is, I hope, by no means a bad one." Though cryptic to us, the allusion would have been clear to Georgina, who was plainly well informed of his plans: a reminder of her extensive confidential knowledge of his life with Ellen. Had Georgina not plied her scissors vigorously when later editing his letters, we would know much more about his time with Ellen, and about Georgina's complicity; but in many of his surviving letters to Georgina, passages have been clipped out, in most cases probably references to Ellen. Other compromising letters Georgina probably destroyed altogether. Her role in Dickens's household—sister of his estranged wife, chatelaine of Gad's Hill, devoted domestic factotum, caretaker of his children—in fact, unofficial wife in an unconsummated marriage—was curious even on the surface; stranger yet was her role as confidante, adjutante, and co-conspirator in his life with his other "wife," Ellen.

After the mysterious "arrangement" in February 1865, he was off again in March, "away for 6 days"; and away again for a week in early April. Week-long gaps in his correspondence suggest later disappearances in April; during the same month he cited "a little uncertainty regarding my movements" as an excuse for a tardy response to a letter. "There is nothing like the sea for a change," he told a friend at the end of April, disingenuously: "I cross that Channel in all weathers, and thoroughly freshen myself with its air. (I am going over, tomorrow or next day)." Sea crossings refreshed him, to be sure—but the refreshment came less from the salty air than from his companion. Justifying this same trip as a relief from his labors on *Our Mutual Friend*, he told another friend that he was fleeing town for a week, adding: "I can throw anything off by going off myself." But he seldom or never went off by himself.

As promised, he stole away to France during the first week of May, and two weeks later disappeared yet again, explaining on his return simply that "I have been away for three days." By the end of May he was eager for another escape. "Work and worry, without exercise, would soon make an end of me. If I were not going away now, I should break down," he groaned as he reached the end of a monthly number of *Our Mutual Friend*, and at the beginning of June he was off to France for yet another restorative week. "The moment I got away, I began, thank God, to get well," he wrote home during this trip. "I hope to profit by this experience, and to make future dashes from my desk before I want them."

This dash was to end very differently from all his previous French holidays, however.

His many excursions to France in the early 1860s are visible in his letters, and random details emerge from the stories and journalistic pieces he wrote at the time, but his companion remains veiled.

When the veil lifts on rare occasions, allowing us to glimpse Ellen at his side, it is a lightning bolt at night, illuminating the landscape for a startling moment before the darkness surges back.

Such a revealing flash was the trip to France that he and Ellen made together in early June 1865.

On the first or second day of June, they left London, accompanied by Mrs. Ternan. Dickens had just put his next-to-youngest son Alfred on a ship bound for Australia, hoping the unpromising youth might succeed at sheep farming. (He would never see Alfred again.) He was nearing the end of *Our Mutual Friend*, which he had been writing in monthly numbers for almost two years. Although the French excursion was a holiday, he took the manuscript with him and wrote in the mornings—we know exactly which episodes he wrote in France, because in an epilogue to the novel he specifies them.

He and Ellen remained in France for a week. They returned on June 9, a Friday, crossing the Channel to Folkestone and there boarding the tidal express for London, occupying a private compartment in a first-class carriage near the front of the train. At a few minutes after two thirty in the afternoon, the train pulled away from Folkestone.

It never reached London. Near the village of Staplehurst in Kent, a work crew had taken up the rails while making repairs to a viaduct over the river Beult, at that time of year a small muddy stream. The foreman had mistaken the time of the train's arrival, and repairs were incomplete as the train approached at full speed, about fifty miles an hour. At the last minute the engineer saw a warning flag and braked hard—but too late. The locomotive and leading cars hurtled across the gap in the rails while most of the trailing cars dropped off the viaduct and fell into the stream and its marshy banks ten feet below. The coach carrying Dickens and the Ternans was at a hinge point. Still attached to the car ahead, which had reached the far side of the bridge, Dickens's coach ended up canted at a steep angle between bridge and streambed. "The carriage was the first class carriage which was dragged aslant, but did not go over, being caught upon the turn," as Dickens described it. "The Engine broke from it before, and the rest of the train broke from it behind and went into the stream below." Ten passengers died in the crash; forty others were injured.

Dickens was unhurt. Climbing out a window, he hailed a guard, secured a key to the carriage, enlisted a laborer to assist him, and helped the rest of the carriage's passengers, including Ellen and her mother, to safety. Then he returned to his compartment for his brandy flask, made his way down to the jumble of derailed cars in the streambed, and succored the injured, carrying water from the stream in his hat and administering swigs of brandy. By good fortune, he had brought along a second bottle of brandy, and he returned to the tilted carriage to retrieve it. "I have a—I don't know what to call it—constitutional (I suppose) presence of mind, and was not in the least fluttered at the time," he observed modestly. In its account of the disaster, the next day's *Times* mentioned Dickens's presence on the train, and later a London weekly, *The Pictorial Illustrated*, carried an artist's rendering of the wreck on its front page, showing Dickens in the foreground offering water from his hat to a swooning or dying young woman, with the caption: "Charles Dickens relieving the sufferers at the fatal railway accident, near Staplehurst."

This addition to his celebrity was all well enough; Dickens himself made no secret of his presence and relief activities at Staplehurst. But too much publicity was dangerous, for he scarcely wished to advertise the identity of his companions on the train. Were he summoned to testify at the inquest, as he feared, awkward questions might arise. That he was not asked to appear may indicate his ability to use connections and influence to cloak his private life.

But though avoiding public testimony, he mentioned his traveling companions in several private letters. One in particular provides details of the drama in his compartment as the train braked hard and went off the rails, and as his carriage dropped off the viaduct:

> Two ladies were my fellow passengers; an old one [Mrs. Ternan], and a young one [Ellen]. . . . Suddenly we were off the rail and beating the ground as the car of a half emptied balloon might. The old lady cried out "My God!" and the young one screamed. I caught hold of them both (the old lady sat opposite, and the young one on my left), and said: "We can't help ourselves, but we can be quiet and composed. Pray don't cry out." The old lady immediately answered, "Thank you. Rely upon me. Upon my soul, I will be quiet." The young lady said in a frantic way, "Let us join hands and die friends." We were then all tilted down

together in a corner of the carriage, and stopped. I said to them thereupon: "You may be sure nothing worse can happen. Our danger *must* be over. Will you remain here without stirring, while I get out of the window?" They both answered quite collectedly, "Yes," and I got out without the least notion what had happened.

This narrative offers a rare account of Ellen and Dickens together, and allows us to reconstruct the fateful afternoon . . .

The tidal train from Folkestone chugs toward London at high speed on a sunny June afternoon, Dickens and Ellen in a comfortable private compartment, side by side, suggesting their intimacy as a couple, while "the old lady" opposite, Ellen's mother, accompanies them as co-conspirator.

Suddenly, "the breaks were applied most vigorously, accompanied by that hoarse staccato note of the break whistle. . . . Within 20 seconds the train made a sudden jump, and it became instantly apparent that we were off the metals . . . the jolting and plunging of the carriage . . . was terrific." During the fearsome jolting and plunging, five or ten seconds which seem an eternity, Dickens and the frightened Ternans exchange hurried remarks. Mrs. Ternan's response to his plea for calm is commendable; she instantly conquers her alarm and replies sensibly. It is "the young lady," Ellen, who screams in panic. Twenty-six at the time, she is scarcely a girl, but in her reaction she seems distinctly youthful compared to her mother and Dickens. Her dramatic suggestion—"Let us join hands and die friends"—might reassure us of her self-command, had she not spoken it, Dickens reports, "in a frantic way." Only after their coach bumps to a stop does she manage to speak "collectedly."

It is difficult to recall a sequence of remarks spoken hurriedly in a moment of crisis and fear, and Dickens's account may be less accurate than his matter-of-fact narrative implies (he related the exchange somewhat differently in successive tellings). What we get, rather, are his impressions of the accident as it was occurring, and of his companions' reactions. Predictably, he recalls himself as calm and practical throughout. Ellen on the other hand was terrified. Perhaps her girlish fright appealed to his protective masculine feelings; perhaps there is a suggestion that her nerves were fragile.

After helping the two women clamber out of the tilted carriage and cross a plank to solid ground, Dickens led them to a shaded spot to recover their nerves while he circulated with water and brandy. Rescue trains soon arrived, bringing doctors and carrying the survivors to London. Taking one of these trains to Charing Cross, he escorted the Ternans home, then returned to his office on Wellington Street. Before leaving the site of the wreck he had remembered to retrieve the manuscript of his novel from the canting carriage in which he had been riding. Left behind in his compartment, however, were several other items.

This oversight allows a further glimpse of Dickens and Ellen. The day after the accident, he returned to Gad's Hill to reassure his worried family that he was intact. In the meantime, Ellen discovered that she was missing jewelry that she had been wearing or carrying on the train, and wrote to Dickens at Gad's Hill to tell him. Not until the Monday after the Friday accident did he report the loss to the station master at Charing Cross:

> A lady who was in the carriage with me in the terrible accident on Friday, lost, in the struggle of being got out of the carriage, a gold watch-chain with a smaller gold watch chain attached, a bundle of charms, a gold watch-key, and a gold seal engraved "Ellen".

Most, probably all, of these "trinkets" (as he deprecated them) were gifts from Dickens himself. He liked to see Ellen handsomely dressed and richly adorned; her position might be irregular, but she would face the world as a lady of status and means. Jewelry, moreover, was "portable property" (as *Great Expectations*' Wemmick would have said); all those gold trinkets would be assets after his death, to supplement the house he had given her, the trust fund established in her name, and perhaps other provisions as well.

Ellen and her mother had naturally been shaken by the crash, but initially thought themselves unhurt. A week after the accident, however, both were reported convalescing from unspecified injuries. "I took to London in the carriage that conveyed me up from the scene of the disaster, two wounded passengers," Dickens reported, "who have been lying ill ever since, and who had no notion at the time that there was much the matter with them." Ellen's injuries lingered. Dickens remained at Gad's Hill for several days, resting but also writing and dictating dozens of notes to well-wishers. He was anxious about Ellen, however, and a week after the accident returned to London for the day, for visits to Miss Coutts and his doctor, as well as for "other errands of business"—certainly including a visit to the Ternans. He went up to London again a few days later, "on my cause of anxiety" (as he told Wills with typical circumspection when writing of Ellen), and stayed for several days, probably spending much of his time with Ellen, still convalescent.

She was still on his mind when he returned to Gad's Hill, and presently he dispatched a note to his servant John Thompson, stationed at the *All the Year Round* offices in London. During the twenty years Thompson was employed as Dickens's servant, he must have received hundreds of notes from his master, most of which he discarded. Fortunately he saved this directive. "Dr. John," the note begins ("Dr." abbreviating not "Doctor" but "Dear"—Thompson did not rate the full spelling); it comprises two business-like sentences:

> Take Miss Ellen tomorrow morning, a little basket of fresh fruit, a jar of clotted cream from Tuckers, and a chicken, a pair of pigeons, or some nice little bird. Also on Wednesday morning, and on Friday morning, take her some other things of the same sort—making a little variety each day.

Of the thousands of Dickens's letters that survive, none expresses more affectionate solicitude than this brisk note dispatching his servant with a hamper of choice provisions to Ellen, a shower of delicacies serving as a metaphor for his affection, poured out generously, abundantly, richly—a cornucopia of love. (Meanwhile, he grudged every penny of his cast-off wife's allowance, even grousing about it in his will.)

More mundanely, in what it does *not* say, the note to Thompson reveals Thompson's familiarity with "Miss Ellen"—for he needed no prefatory explanations, no identification of "Miss Ellen," no instructions on where to find her. Having performed such tasks previously, he plainly knew all about her. The routine tone of Dickens's instructions suggests how often Thompson had run similar errands connected with her. He was, in his menial way, a trusted confidant. When the following year, after long and apparently faithful service, he was caught pilfering from the office cash box, Dickens was startled, and perhaps alarmed as well, to discover that someone so closely involved with his secret life had proved so dangerously unreliable.

Whatever her injuries, Ellen recuperated slowly. A month later, Dickens gave his sub-editor Wills a sanguine medical bulletin on Ellen, "Patient immensely better," but a month later yet—almost ten weeks after the accident—she was still convalescent: "Patient much better, I am thankful to say, but not yet well," and the following week, "Patient much the same." Even after her recovery, "the Patient" remained Dickens's code for Ellen in his correspondence with Wills.

But while she may have suffered chronic or recurrent health problems consequent on the Staplehurst wreck, the evidence is slight and she was certainly no invalid. Eight months later we glimpse her primping for and enjoying with feminine zest a "very pleasant" ball with her sister Fanny: "Would you like to know our dresses?" Fanny recalled the occasion. "Well we were dressed quite alike in pale green silk covered with tarlatane of the same colour and trimmed with white blonde and dew-drops. We had scarlet geraniums & white heath in our hair." Ellen took riding lessons and five years after Staplehurst was reported an excellent equestrian. She survived Dickens by many years, passing for a woman ten years younger than her actual age, marrying and bearing two healthy children, living actively.

Dickens, however, though "scarcely shaken" at the time, suffered the effects of Staplehurst until his death. A few days after the wreck, he dictated to Georgina a succession of notes to well-wishers, explaining in each that "This is not at all in my own hand, because I am too much shaken to write many notes"; and he told Wills that "I write two or three notes, and turn faint and sick." In London a week after the accident, he was rattled by the traffic: "The noise of the wheels of my Hansom, and of the London streets, was as much as I could bear. So I made all speed back here [Gad's Hill] again—by a slow train, though, for I felt that I was not up to the Express." For the rest of his life, express trains worried him. "My escape in the great Staplehurst accident of 3 years ago, is not to be obliterated from my nervous system," he lamented in 1868. "To this hour I have sudden vague rushes of terror, even when riding in a Hansom Cab. . . . My Reading-Secretary and companion knows so well when one of these odd momentary seizures comes upon me in a Railway Carriage, that he instantly produces a dram of brandy, which rallies the blood to the heart and generally prevails." As his reading tours took him on many long train rides, his brandy stock needed frequent replenishment. On one occasion, traveling from London to Edinburgh, he estimated "that the Railway travelling over such a distance involves something more than 30,000 shocks to the nerves" (apparently calculating a shock every second).

The Staplehurst wreck provides a dramatic snapshot of Dickens and Ellen together. We catch another glimpse from a less violent source: his unusual friendship with a wealthy, trouble-prone heiress.

In an age when marriages were seldom dissolved—Dickens, for example, never attempted to terminate his own marriage (simple conjugal discontent was no grounds for divorce)—his friend Frances Dickinson compiled a notable record of bad marriages. Her first, to a captain in the Light Dragoons, produced four daughters but eventually led to a scandalous suit in the Court of Arches, one of the Doctors' Commons courts in which Dickens had begun as a short-hand reporter. Frances Dickinson, at that point Mrs. Geils, sued for a judicial separation on grounds of cruelty, adultery (her husband had invited his mistress to their wedding, to escort his new bride to his home in Scotland), and "unnatural practices"; the evidence on all three counts, replete with "offensive and disgusting details," was explicit. ("I can hear no more," the judge declared. "I am disgusted. It is quite disgraceful to the Court, the public, and the profession.") The separation was granted; later Mrs. Geils, née Dickinson, obtained a full divorce from a Scottish court, dropped her married name, and became Mrs. Dickinson.

The details of her second marriage are obscure. She confided them to Dickens, who later alluded to it as "that adventure with the Doctor." The adventure may have occurred abroad—Mrs. Dickinson spent much time in Italy, and no record of the marriage has been located in England. It was an immediate failure—perhaps not a valid marriage at all: "the marriage (as no doubt he [the husband] very well knew at the time) is no marriage and is utterly void," Dickens later reported, some legal or physical impediment apparently rendering the union null—but Dickens's only source for this assertion would presumably have been Mrs. Dickinson herself. Like her first husband, the mysterious Doctor was likely attracted by her five thousand pounds per year.

Omitting the formality of a legal annulment, the lady then proceeded to marry yet again, this time taking as her husband a handsome, pro-gressive clergyman, Gilbert Elliot, Dean of Bristol. Dickens had by now known Mrs. Dickinson for several years, and happened to know Elliot as well, making it a marriage of "old friends of mine." To have recovered from the scandal of her divorce (from her first husband; the adventure with the Doctor was concealed) sufficiently to marry a distinguished clergyman was a triumph; but even before the wedding, there were troubling omens. Mrs. Dickinson confided to Dickens that the dean lacked romantic ardor. Dickens diagnosed waning libido: "Are you quite sure that what you are disposed to resent as indifference, is not the stealing apathy of advanced age?" Elliot was twenty years older than Mrs. Dickinson, and recognizing the analogous situation with himself and Ellen, Dickens hastened to assert his own unimpaired virility: "Under other circumstances—say in your humble servant, for example—it would be affronting or idiotic; but not in these, I think?" He discreetly acknowledged the importance of sexual affinity, telling Mrs. Dickinson that "I might be very moral in my admonitions and didactic remarks—but you are a woman—and I am a man—and we should both know better, even if I were." He was a man of the world, in other words, and Mrs. Dickinson no vestal; there was no point in feigning naïveté. Given the dean's amorous lethargy, Dickens advised Mrs. Dickinson to drop him. Time confirmed the wisdom of his counsel. The unconventional heiress and the progressive clergyman married—and soon parted, upon which Dickens was drawn into their wrangling as a reluctant intermediary. It would have taken great self-restraint not to remind Mrs. Dickinson of his earlier advice.

He had first met her only shortly before he met Ellen, during the 1857 production of *The Frozen Deep* for the Jerrold Fund. A friend of Wilkie Collins, Mrs. Dickinson had been recruited to take the role of Nurse Esther in the London performances, Collins recommending her because she could affect Nurse Esther's Scots accent; though Mrs. Dickinson was English, her first husband, Geils the dragoon, had been Scots and they had lived together on his estate in Scotland. On the *Frozen Deep* playbill, she is "Miss Francis." When Dickens took the play to Manchester and hired the Ternans, her role of Nurse Esther was taken by Mrs. Ternan.

His friendship with Mrs. Dickinson persisted, though when or how often they saw each other is unclear. She submitted several articles to *All the Year Round*, but the friendship was much more than a business relationship. She visited Gad's Hill and on one occasion, at least, Georgina stayed with her at her estate in Berkshire. Dickens always began his letters to her with "My Dear F"—a familiarity he accorded few. Other women, even old friends, he invariably saluted as "Mrs" rather than by their Christian name, let alone a diminutive. Among surviving letters, only those to Georgina—"My Dearest Georgy"—commence more affectionately. (Frances Dickinson's complicated marital history perhaps made it simpler, as well, to address her as just "F.")

Their friendship, so far as it can be reconstructed, was ambiguous. "My Dear F" often annoyed him. At one point, for example, when she submitted an article for *All the Year Round*, he responded with vexation:

My Dear F.

. . . I can not read it. Pretty well accustomed to messes in the way of manuscript, I never saw such a mess. I very much doubt whether my printers can print from it, or will do so without protest. . . . I have been at work on a new work of my own, all day, and am half blinded and maddened by your unintelligibility.

Even this petulant rebuke carries a note of familiarity, however, for he would not have berated a more casual friend so bluntly; he could apparently rely on Mrs. Dickinson taking his abuse in good spirit. The note closes "Ever affectionately/CD" (less intimate friends were dismissed more coolly, with some variant of "Faithfully yours"). Early in their acquaintance he characterized Mrs. Dickinson as *"prononcée,"* meaning forceful, strong-willed, and (in her case) exasperating. One friend recalled her as having "black hair done in a mass of thick plaits on the top of her head: a coiffure which, in very un-Victorian fashion, she loudly announced was a wig. 'I wear a wig,' she would say, puffing at her cigarette, 'my daughters wear wigs. Everyone should. It saves a deal of time and trouble.'" Dickens once noted that "she takes a resentful bounce now and then, which is more naturally impulsive than wise." In later life she became that *rara avis*, the intrepid Victorian female traveler, and wrote books about her wanderings.

This unconventional and unlikely friend evoked Dickens's lengthiest surviving letter about Ellen Ternan, a document both revealing and enigmatic.

Early in 1866, Mrs. Dickinson (now Mrs. Elliot, the dean's wife) invited Dickens to visit her in Bristol during a reading tour he was projecting for the spring. Evidently he had mentioned this tour in an earlier letter; now he informed her that his itinerary was uncertain, and "I have not yet decided upon going to Bristol at all." His earlier letter does not survive, however, and his response to her invitation is known only from an extract printed in a bookseller's catalog.

This is unfortunate, for the extract concludes with a tantalizing allusion to Ellen. In her letter, Mrs. Dickinson had evidently made a remark or inquiry about his "romance."

"As to my romance," Dickens now replied, "it belongs to my life and probably will only die out of the same with the proprietor."

What can we infer from this comment? Plainly, Mrs. Dickinson knew of Ellen, or at least of a mistress. She is unlikely to have learned of her from Dickens himself, but she was a friend of Wilkie Collins, who knew about Ellen; and no doubt he or some other knowing acquaintance had enlightened her. However Mrs. Dickinson had learned of Dickens's romance, her *prononcée* personality now asserted itself. Most women would have been curious; few would have ventured to quiz the famous man himself on so private a matter. In Mrs. Dickinson's boldly presuming to do so, we detect the easy assurance of her friendship with Dickens—but also her audacity and broadmindedness. With her own interesting history, she could scarcely begrudge Dickens his own irregular arrangement.

But his assurance that his romance was thriving suggests that while Mrs. Dickinson knew something about it, she did not know much. Was he still devoted to his young lady? she had apparently inquired—but no one in his inner circle of confidants would have had to ask. His response is candid but guarded. Acknowledging the romance, declaring it an integral and permanent part of his life, he nonetheless does not name Ellen or offer any details. Of course, the full letter might have disclosed more, omitted in the bookseller's extract. But Dickens worried about private letters falling into indiscreet or unscrupulous hands, and was cautious when he dipped his quill in ink.

The inquisitive Mrs. Dickinson persisted. His 1866 reading tour did not take him to Bristol, as it turned out, but he probably saw her elsewhere that year; in any event, they corresponded. The following year she again proposed to intercept him when another reading tour took him to Bath, a dozen miles from Bristol. Again, he discouraged her: "*Don't* come to Bath," he advised; he did not like the city, and accompanied by his readings entourage, he and she would have no privacy. Instead, "I think there is hardly a doubt of my coming to Clifton in the course of the trip. Then we shall do much better—you and I, I mean." His anxious concern for privacy is curious. Did he anticipate a tête-à-tête on sensitive topics? Her marriage to the Dean of Bristol had already soured. "I shall be very glad to have a line from you," he wrote, ". . . to tell me how, where, when, and why, the Times are hard, Bristolward." Between her own problems and her curiosity about Dickens's romance, conversation with Mrs. Dickinson was likely to gallop into personal matters.

When his Clifton reading was scheduled, he duly apprised her, inviting her and the Dean to "a half hour's supper with us" after his reading there. The invitation seems calculated to forestall any exchange of confidences: even if she contrived to leave the Dean at home, the supper party still included his readings manager George Dolby, while the brief time allotted would suffice to keep the conversation superficial. Further, he reminded Mrs. Dickinson that "of course I am away again the first thing next morning." He was evidently chary of the lady's penchant for personal topics. The supper in Clifton probably did not happen—to his relief, one suspects.

But he could not evade the persistent Mrs. Dickinson forever. She visited Gad's Hill a few weeks after his reading in Clifton, and in return invited him to her Berkshire estate, Farley Hill Court. Pleading deadlines, he declined, adding that among other things he was contemplating a trip to America: "Judge how much I have to do and think of just now."

Mrs. Dickinson responded immediately, complaining sharply of her husband, the Dean of Bristol, for his partiality to a daughter by his first marriage. Dickens in reply professed himself "really troubled" to hear of her grievance, and counseled patience.

But she also mentioned that she had recently talked to someone about Dickens and Ellen. In recounting what she had heard, the forthright Mrs. Dickinson touched a wound, and Dickens responded with agitation. Of all surviving documents referring to Ellen, his letter replying to Mrs. Dickinson is the most intriguing, both in what it reveals and in what it hints.

Mrs. Dickinson's remarks involved Ellen's eldest sister Frances, "Fanny" to her family. The year before, Fanny had married Thomas Trollope, the novelist Anthony's older brother. A prolific writer, Thomas Trollope lived comfortably in a villa outside Florence, grinding out dull novels (twenty, more or less), many volumes on Italian history, and reams of journalism; he sometimes contributed articles about Italy to Dickens's *All the Year Round*. Dickens had given Fanny Ternan a letter of introduction to Trollope when he had sent her to Italy for voice lessons nine years earlier. Later, when Trollope was widowed, Fanny was persuaded to return to Florence to act as governess for his young daughter, and presently the governess married the master, in *Jane Eyre* fashion—though the grizzled, deaf, bookish, and prolix Trollope little resembled the virile Rochester. Trollope was twenty-five years older than Fanny—a gap similar to that between Dickens and Ellen. Ellen and Mrs. Ternan attended the Trollopes' wedding in Paris in October 1866. Mrs. Dickinson would have known all about the Trollopes' marriage: she had good connections among the English community in Florence (a daughter by her first marriage was married to an Italian marquis) and knew both Anthony and Thomas Trollope.

In her letter to Dickens, Mrs. Dickinson referred to the Ternans as Dickens's "magic circle," including in this circle Ellen's sister Fanny, now Mrs. Thomas Trollope.

In response, Dickens bluntly assured Mrs. Dickinson that she was much mistaken if she thought his affection for Ellen extended to the rest of the Ternans. "The 'magic circle,'" he assured her, "consists of but one member." Fanny had returned to England in May 1867 to make arrangements for serializing her second novel in Dickens's *All the Year Round*, and Mrs. Dickinson may well have derived her news about Dickens and Ellen from Fanny herself. In any event, Dickens took aim in particular at Fanny. "I don't in the least care for Mrs. T. T.," he declared, referring to the new Mrs. Thomas Trollope, and added a mysterious qualifier—"except that her share in the story is (as far as *I* am concerned) a remembrance impossible to swallow."

In what "story" had Ellen's sister Fanny played so malignant a part? His letter gives no specifics. Later it mentions "the history"—apparently referring to the same events. Mrs. Dickinson had earlier inquired about his "romance"; now her restless curiosity had been rewarded by the discovery of a fascinating saga concerning Dickens and Ellen, in which Ellen's sister Fanny had behaved (in Dickens's eyes) unforgivably. Mrs. Dickinson must have had her facts straight, for he neither corrected nor supplemented her account. He would have been reluctant to divulge further details, in any event; for while her letter would go straight into the fire, his response might fall into doubtful hands. Though well-disposed, Mrs. Dickinson was perhaps unreliable.

We may never know what story she had heard. His use of terms like "history" and "remembrance" place it firmly in the past. But though Fanny's offense lay behind, Dickens's hostility lingered. Only for love of Ellen did he tolerate the objectionable Fanny: "For the magic sake, I scrupulously try to do her justice, and not to see her—out of my path—with a jaundiced vision." He did not hesitate to break friendships when he felt injured, as he had during the separation crisis of 1858. One of the chief villains of that imbroglio had been, to his mind, Helen Hogarth, his wife's younger sister. Now once again the villain was a sister; but this time he had to swallow his aversion. His tacit truce with Fanny was a tribute to Ellen's sway.

Not only was he obliged to tolerate Fanny as a virtual sister-in-law; he was publishing her novels in *All the Year Round*. Abandoning her singing career, she had begun writing. The previous year, he had serialized her short novel *Aunt Margaret's Trouble* ("Affectionately dedicated to E. L. T."—her sister Ellen) in *All the Year Round*; now, even as he denounced Fanny for her unforgivable "share in the story," he was publishing another of her novels, *Mabel's Progress*. *All the Year Round* required a steady supply of serial fiction and he couldn't always contrive to find first-rate material; nonetheless, one skeptical observer suspected other motives for his publishing such indifferent novels as Fanny Trollope's. Isa Blagden, a prominent hostess and gossip in the English community in Florence, knew the Trollopes and knew about Mrs. Trollope's sister Ellen. She once teasingly asked her close friend Robert Browning if he wondered why Dickens serialized Fanny Trollope's novels (which appeared in *All the Year Round* anonymously).

Browning had lived in Italy for many years and knew Thomas Trollope well, but now back in England he had fallen out of touch with Florentine gossip. To Isa Blagden's malicious question, "How it came to pass that D. paid such sums for such novels as Mrs T's," he was clueless: he "had no notion—but supposed there must be some reason beside the worth of the composition, if it were as poor as you assured me." When Isa gleefully enlightened him on Dickens's connection with Fanny Trollope, Browning admitted that the publication of her novels in *All the Year Round* seemed suspicious.

After enlightening Mrs. Dickinson on his feelings about Fanny, Dickens turned with a polite shudder to an idea that the ever-forward lady had floated in her letter. Having learned of Ellen's story, Mrs.

Dickinson had apparently proposed that she be introduced to Ellen as a friendly sympathizer.

Dickens flatly rejected this proposal. Such an introduction was "impossible." Mrs. Dickinson had conveyed her disclosure with kindness—after all, who was she to be censorious?—and he acknowledged her good intentions. "I feel your affectionate letter truly and deeply," he assured her, "but it would be inexpressibly painful to [Ellen] to think that you knew the history. She has no suspicion that your assertion of your friend against the opposite powers, ever brought you to the knowledge of it." Neither the friend nor the opposite powers are identified. The friend might have been Dickens himself; the opposite powers perhaps included Fanny Trollope. In any case, his friend-and-foe language suggests that he regarded the mysterious disagreement as a feud between open belligerents.

Only one secret seems adequate to explain his horror (and Ellen's, prospectively) to Mrs. Dickinson's proposal—namely, Ellen's pregnancy five years earlier. Ellen's discovery that Mrs. Dickinson had learned of her story, Dickens asserted, "would distress her for the rest of her life." It is hard to imagine what other disclosure might cause her such intense, lifelong pain.

The disturbing content of Mrs. Dickinson's letter elicited Dickens's warmest surviving homage to Ellen:

> She would not believe [he told Mrs. Dickinson] that you could see her with my eyes, or know her with my mind. Such a presentation is impossible. . . . I thank you none the less, but it is quite out of the question. If she could bear that, she could not have the pride and self-reliance which (mingled with the gentlest nature) has borne her, alone, through so much.

This tribute reveals much. One notable feature is the intensity of Ellen's shame at her secret history; any exposure outside her closest circle would mortify her, or so Dickens claims. A high regard for feminine purity, or at least the reputation of purity, was characteristic of her culture, but his emphasis on Ellen's vulnerability may hint at a particularly keen sensibility, a "chastity of honour which felt a stain like a wound."

Curious too is the remark that Ellen had suffered "alone." In literal terms, she was probably seldom alone: her mother was often with her; Dickens himself was a frequent and solicitous presence; she had two loyal sisters (though often at a distance). In his assertion that she bore her trials alone, does there lurk an implied disparagement of her family?—some of whom, Fanny in particular, may have urged her to break her connection with him. But by "alone" he may simply have meant unmarried. Though Ellen might be all in all to him, she had neither the comfort, security, nor distinction of being his wife, nor could he publicly acknowledge their connection; moreover, they were apart more than they were together. There was loneliness in being the clandestine mistress of a famous and busy man with a large family.

Such conclusions are speculative; but Dickens's affectionate admiration for Ellen—her gentleness, pride and self-reliance—is certain and striking. Ten years earlier, he had been infatuated by the freshness of the pretty eighteen-year-old girl with the little lilac gloves and little bonnet and golden hair. At twenty-eight, she was still attractive, but mature and womanly, and he had learned to appreciate more than just her girlish charms. He no longer extols her maidenly innocence, as he had in 1858, but rather her strength of character. His praise of her pride and self-reliance recalls his characterization of the heroine of *Bleak House*, Lady Dedlock—a woman also concealing the secret of an illegitimate child ("I must travel my dark road alone," she had said); while his praise of Ellen's gentle nature recalls heroines like *David Copperfield*'s Agnes Wickfield.

Despite "the opposite powers," Ellen had remained faithful for ten years; and though Dickens could not repay her with marriage, he gave her a wealth of fondness and attention. What woman would not be gratified by such devotion and homage? Two years before meeting Ellen, he had confessed a longstanding "habit of suppression" that made him "chary of shewing my affections." She had evidently dissolved that inhibition.

Dickens wrote his letter to Frances Dickinson about Ellen and her "history" on July 4, 1867.

Though Ellen was much on his mind, he did not see her that day. He spent the entire day, a Thursday, at Gad's Hill. Explaining his absence from a friend's funeral, he cited "an American appointment of unusual importance" at Gad's Hill, but there appear to have been no visitors of note. The mysterious appointment was probably a polite fiction: he dreaded funerals, and the funeral even of an admired friend would not draw him away from his holiday. The day before, the local cricket club had played a match on the grounds of Gad's Hill, Dickens relishing his role as village squire; the day after, he plunged into work on a series of children's stories commissioned by an American magazine (these stories may have been the important "American appointment"). But July 4 itself appears to have been spent quietly with Georgina. He wrote letters, perhaps took a walk with his large dogs, perhaps sat on the front lawn reading, with tiers of geraniums, his favorite flower, blooming scarlet around the house's bay windows. Though urban in orientation, he had grown to enjoy the summer amenity of rural Kent. "This country is really beautiful when the corn and hops are growing," he remarked a few days later. In a little pocket diary, he summarized the entire day with a simple note: "at G.H."

He probably kept a little diary each year for many years, but only one survives. He or his executors burned the others; but in the very last days of 1867, while in New York on a reading tour, he lost his diary for that year. "By-the-bye," he wrote Georgina a few days later, "on the last Sunday in the old year, I lost my old year's pocket-book, 'which,' as Mr. Pepys would add, 'do trouble me mightily.'" In fact it was probably stolen, for whoever gained possession of it took care to preserve it, no doubt knowing it was Dickens's (though his name appears nowhere in it). Eventually the diary made its way into the Berg Collection of the New York Public Library. Well might Dickens have felt troubled at its loss, for despite its laconic, abbreviated one-line entries for each day, the diary betrays a great deal about Ellen Ternan's central role in his life.

The entries are written in a small, bound 1867 date calendar, about two by four inches, with two blank pages for each month; opposite each blank page is a printed page giving Church feasts, astronomical data, and tides. On one blank page of each month Dickens made sporadic memoranda of upcoming engagements such as dinners and public readings; on the other blank page he jotted down an abbreviated record of his activities and locations, in a single cramped line for each day. He recorded where he began the day and where he ended it; he often noted train stations involved in his traveling; sometimes he noted without comment the names of visitors at Gad's Hill, or people whom he saw or dined with in London.

The entries are mostly mundane. He invariably recorded steam baths ("vapour baths"), an indulgence of which he had grown fond, and dinners at the Atheneum Club (some twenty-one during the ten months he was in England in 1867). The entries are also dryly factual. When a longtime and beloved friend, the painter Clarkson Stanfield, died, Dickens recorded: "Stanfield died yest:"; a few days later, after attending Stanfield's funeral and burial at Kensal Green, where Mary Hogarth also lay, he noted simply: "Stanfield's funeral." For the most fanciful of novelists, the pocket diary is almost perversely prosaic; for the most exuberant and expressive of writers, it is tightly reticent. If one thinks of a diary as a record of impressions and reflections, the 1867 date book is no diary at all. Through almost an entire year— the entries end on December 28—there is no mention of anything that anyone (including Dickens himself) said; only general reference to what anyone else did ("Forsters come . . . Forsters go"); and no more than scattered and oblique hints of what Dickens thought or felt about anything.

Nonetheless, the little pocket diary reveals his daily life with Ellen more fully than any other source. In the thousands of his letters that survive, his love for her flashes out at rare intervals; but the spare, clipped chronicle of those 362 days in 1867 shows her woven into the fabric of his life, day by day.

Ellen's name never occurs in the diary; she is always "N," for Nelly. As "N," she appears in the diary twenty-eight times. But the references to "N" tell only part of the story, for Dickens's time with her is usually coded not "N," but rather "Sl" or "P." To decipher these letters, the story must go back a year or two.

The Staplehurst crash in June 1865 had led to a major alteration in his routine with Ellen. For several years, he had found time and privacy with her in repeated trips to France. Their journeys across the Channel had begun with her pregnancy in 1862, but continued beyond that crisis. Plainly they both enjoyed their French escapes, but there were drawbacks. The visits required a prolonged block of free time, and took him away from home and business obligations for days at a time, interludes that could be undertaken only with careful planning, and infrequently—at best, every month or two. The journeying itself, with a Channel crossing each way, was burdensome; fares and lodgings were a drain on his purse. Staplehurst added another drawback to their French excursions: Dickens's new express-train phobia. Every journey to France and back took him across the fatal bridge at Staplehurst, twice, on the speeding tidal express. He may have felt a surge of panic each time; Ellen, also injured in the crash, may have felt the same. They went to France together at least once more, perhaps twice, in the months after Staplehurst, but at some point he or they together must have decided that the drawbacks of the French holidays had become too great.

Instead, they decided, they would find a retreat in England, outside London but within commuting range. Ellen would live there; Dickens would spend several days each week with her. The arrangement would regularize and domesticize their lives together; for the first time they would share a house.

There were probably other factors involved in this decision, but they remain obscure. With Ellen retired from the stage, there was little reason for her to remain near West End theaters. Perhaps it was thought better for her health that she move from the crowded, noisy, and none-too-savory metropolis to a relatively rural town where she could ride and walk on nearby country lanes and paths.

Whatever the reasons, in early 1866 she took up residence in Slough, Buckinghamshire.

Slough lies just north of the Thames, twenty miles upriver from London; nearby is Eton College and across the river are Windsor and, looming above, Windsor Castle, where Queen Victoria was often in residence. Slough was still a coherent town, but beginning to sprawl; it had acquired a train station on the Great Western line in 1840 (in 1842, Queen Victoria's first train ride had begun at Slough station), and by 1866 it was on its way to becoming an unlovely London suburb. Seventy years later, John Betjeman suggested violent demolition:

> Come, friendly bombs, and fall on Slough
> It isn't fit for humans now,
> There isn't grass to graze a cow
> Swarm over, Death!
>
> ("Slough")

In 1866, however, there was still ample grazing for cows in the fields around Slough. Its attraction for Dickens probably lay in its combination of remoteness and convenient rail service. Ellen would be well outside London, but accessible.

So it happened that early in 1866, a certain Mr. Tringham, first name variable, began to pay the rates, or taxes, on a cottage on High Street in Slough. The rate collector went door to door, recording the householder's name. Whoever happened to answer the door when he knocked provided the name for his ratebook. When the collector called at the modest High Street cottage in April 1866, he was informed that the head of the household was "John Tringham." When he or another collector called again a month later (to collect another tax), "John Tringham" had become "Charles." But this was not a case of two interchangeable brothers, as with the Cheeryble brothers in *Nicholas Nickleby*. Charles Tringham, alternately John, was in fact a single person: Charles Dickens (middle name, John).

At about the same time, the mysterious Mr. Tringham began paying the rates on a second house in Slough, on nearby Church Street. Did Dickens, for the sake of comfort or propriety, rent one small house in Slough for himself, and another for Ellen and perhaps her mother? Or was the second cottage for Mrs. Ternan? On two occasions, the collector wrote down "Turnan" rather than Tringham as the occupant of the house on Church Street. When the collector appeared at the two Tringham residences, there was often a suspicious confusion about names.

The rate books for Slough thus give limited and perplexing information. John or Charles Tringham—or sometimes a certain Turnan—paid the rates on two houses in Slough from early 1866 until the middle of 1867. The 1867 pocket diary, however, shows exactly when the slippery Tringham visited Slough that year.

The year began with Dickens at Gad's Hill, entertaining a party of family and friends as he did every year during the Christmas season. This traditional observance lasted until Twelfth Night. He slipped away to London for one day, January 3, working at his *All the Year Round* office and spending the night in his apartment there, but returned next day to Gad's Hill to rejoin the house party, carrying along yet another guest with him. But the day after Twelfth Night, he noted in the pocket diary, perhaps with relief, "All go" from Gad's Hill: he was liberated from family and hosting obligations. He himself departed with the last of the guests, or close on their heels, and sped to Ellen. The diary notes: "To Sl: at 2." After two weeks' enforced Christmas absence, he could scarcely wait to rejoin her.

He spent that night, the next day, and the next night in Slough. Returning to London the following morning, he worked at his office, dined with John Forster, and slept at the office. The next morning he returned to Slough, and again spent the night.

In the middle of January, Dickens began a series of fifty public readings in London, the provinces, Scotland, and Ireland. Except for Holy Week, he was out of town every week from mid-January to May. On Ellen's twenty-eighth birthday, March 3, he was in York, but noted in his pocket diary "H.B.D."—that is, "Her Birthday." He returned to London on the eighth and promptly visited Slough. Several days later, he wrote a check to Garrard the London jeweler for seventeen pounds, eleven shillings—in all likelihood a birthday gift, perhaps more than usually expensive to compensate for its lateness.

He somehow found Slough more easily accessible than Gad's Hill. In April, using Gad's Hill stationery, he wrote that "although I date from my Household Gods, I have not set eyes upon them since last Christmas Time, and am little likely to see them until my Fifty readings are finished. In the meanwhile I am here, there, everywhere, and (principally) nowhere." The last line was a cryptic joke: "nowhere," where he spent so much of his time, was in fact Slough, with his mistress. The jest had added savor in this case because he was writing to the wife of an Anglican bishop. During the early months of 1867, when he could never manage to find his way to Gad's Hill, he made his way to Ellen in Slough almost every week, between reading engagements. She has been compared to Tennyson's Mariana of the Moated Grange, pining in seclusion for her absent lover: "'My heart is aweary, aweary,/He cometh not,' she said." But the neglected woman was in fact Georgina, at Gad's Hill.

One of the idiosyncracies of the 1867 pocket diary is its regular logging of what would seem an incidental detail, train stations. Logging his many trips to Gad's Hill, to London, and to Slough, he frequently recorded the departure or arrival station, sometimes both. Since he always abbreviated station names, various letters in the diary—P, W, V, G^d, D—are at first sight mystifying. But almost a century later they were astutely deciphered by a distinguished English actor, Felix Aylmer (later Sir Felix), who came across the pocket diary at the New York Public Library. With Aylmer's key, Dickens's shuttling about becomes easy to track, and the diary's precise record of his railway travels reveals much about the peripatetic life that his eagerness to see Ellen compelled him to lead.

He spent hundreds of hours on trains in 1866 and 1867, shuttling among Gad's Hill, London, and Slough. With symbolic fitness, Gad's Hill and Slough were on opposite sides of London, Gad's Hill about thirty miles east, Slough twenty miles west. With the train to each taking an hour, more or less, from the London stations closest to his office near Covent Garden, he moved along an east-west axis between his family at one end and Ellen at the other, usually by way of his office in between. Like the ferryboat captain with a wife on either side of the harbor, he oscillated back and forth between the two poles of his life. Planning his days around railway schedules, he became an adept in routes and timetables. Alarmingly punctual, he would have brooked no obstruction or delay in catching his appointed train to Slough. Bare diary notes like "To Sl: at 2" or "To D [Datchet, near Slough] from W [London's Waterloo Station] at 11" are pregnant with eagerness, determination, and impatience. How often did business associates or visitors notice him glancing sharply at the office clock, as if he could hear the warning shriek of a departure whistle?

His mastery of the trains lay in more than just details of routes and schedules. He was an early railway enthusiast; his 1848 novel *Dombey and Son*—a decade before Ellen Ternan—was the first notable English novel to embrace the railway, both as fact and metaphor. Victorian railway expansion, spreading a vast iron spider web over England, benefitted Dickens as businessman, making possible the rapid distribution of his monthly novel installments and weekly magazine issues all over Britain, and greatly facilitating his public reading tours. But the railways also allowed him to maintain a comfortable separation between business, home, and mistress, to disappear from sight in a puff of locomotive smoke, to be "here, there, everywhere, and nowhere." It was a great convenience for a man with a secret life.

In the early months of 1867, his travels extended far beyond Gad's Hill and Slough, to two dozen cities in England, to Swansea in Wales, to Glasgow and Edinburgh, and across the Irish Sea, to Dublin and Belfast. Most weeks he gave three or four public readings and then returned to London—and from there, straight to Slough. The diary records his return from his readings in Ireland in March, for example:

22 at Dublin. Read Carol & Trial [*A Christmas Carol* and a scene from *Pickwick Papers*]. To boat at Kingston.
23 Boat starts at 7. To Holyhead & Town [London]. To Sl:
24 at Sl:
25 at Sl: Office.

Fleshing out this barebones outline, we see Dickens so impatient to return to Ellen that after "a very trying week" in Ireland he walks off the stage from his final evening performance in Dublin, takes a carriage directly to the quay, spends the night on a moored steamer due to get underway early in the morning, crosses the churlish Irish Sea, and immediately on landing at Holyhead embarks on the long train journey to London—all this "in the worst of hard weather."

But London is of course not his ultimate destination: from Euston Station he proceeds directly to Slough. Only after a restorative Sunday and two nights with Ellen does he make his way back to Wellington Street on Monday morning to catch up on editorial business. That evening, he returns to Slough for another night with Ellen. Meanwhile, Gad's Hill will not see him for another three weeks, during which absence from his Household Gods he will return to Slough another half dozen times in the intervals between his out-of-town readings.

The pocket diary reveals that in the three months between mid-January and mid-April 1867, he was away from London for all but thirty-three nights; and of those thirty-three nights, two thirds were spent in Slough. The other eleven, he slept at his Wellington Street office. Gad's Hill he did not visit at all. Only with the end of his reading tour and the arrival of spring weather did he find his way back to Gad's Hill, and even then he continued to spend two or three nights each week in Slough. In May, for example, he wrote to Georgina from London that "I cannot get down to Gad's between this [Wednesday] and Monday, being fairly overwhelmed by arrears of work." Nonetheless, he had found time to spend the day before at Slough, and would spend the following weekend there, too—after which, he still failed to appear at Gad's Hill. Georgina no doubt knew or at least suspected that "arrears of work" meant Ellen.

What was his life with Ellen in Slough like? The clipped notes of the pocket diary give hints. To begin, she is often accompanied by another figure, "M." In early February, for example, after giving readings in Leeds and Manchester, Dickens returned to London late at night, spent the rest of the night and the next morning at his office, and then took a train to Slough. The next day after spending the morning at Slough he returned to London at 12:45 (from Windsor station, he noted) and went to his office; he met Forster and they dined at the Atheneum Club. Then, "Back with N & M"—that is, back to Slough with Ellen and "M." Three days later, after three more nights at Slough: "To P [Paddington station] with N & M at 10:20. Then to Bath," where he gave a reading that evening. From the pocket diary's half dozen linkings of "N & M," it becomes plain that "M" was Ellen's steady companion. It has been argued that this companion was Dickens's eldest daughter Mary (usually called Mamie); alternatively, that "M" was Ellen's sister Maria.

"M" was undoubtedly Ellen's mother, however. Mrs. Ternan had temporarily come out of retirement in December 1865 to act in two plays produced by Dickens's friend Charles Fechter at the Lyceum Theatre; until her engagement ended in June the following year, she probably stayed in London, though she may have retreated to Slough on her off days. By the time of the 1867 pocket diary, however, she was re-retired and spending more time in Slough with Ellen. Almost a century later, Ellen's daughter, looking into old letters, learned that a family servant named "Jane [Wheeler] first went into the service of Mrs. Ternan (my grandmother) at Slough in 1866. Mrs. Ternan and my mother were then living there together." Mrs. Ternan also had a house in London, however, and with the house in London and Mr. Tringham's two cottages in Slough, the exact arrangements are uncertain. In any case, the two women probably spent much of their time together, either in London or Slough, when the busy Tringham was occupied or out of town.

The frequent presence of "M" in Slough suggests the connubial and domestic flavor of Dickens's life with Ellen as it had developed over ten years. It was not as if he alternated between two moral antipodes, a respectable home at Gad's Hill and a scarlet concubinage in Slough. His irregular arrangement with Ellen had a respectable family quality: along with a mistress, he had acquired a *de facto* mother-in-law and two sisters-in-law who figured prominently in Ellen's—and consequently his own—life. There were even the customary family tensions: he rubbed along on uneasy terms with her sister Fanny (who was in England and sometimes staying with Ellen during the summer of 1867). If not a case of *Love me, love my family*, it was at any rate *Love me, tolerate my family*. Ellen was no black-sheep child defying her family; she remained a good daughter and devoted sister. (Toward the end of their lives, the three Ternan sisters were once again all together, in Southsea.) The Ternans' tight family bond might have been occasionally inconvenient from Dickens's point of view, particularly as manifested in Mrs. Ternan's frequent presence—but it was a comfort to Ellen, for with his frequent absences she would otherwise have been much alone; it was only equitable, moreover, for Dickens spent much time with his own family at Gad's Hill. He may have welcomed the respectability that Mrs. Ternan lent to his Slough ménage; perhaps her matronly dignity quieted the neighbors.

Almost every week, Mr. Tringham showed up at Ellen's cottage in Slough, probably walking from Slough station or nearby Windsor or Datchet station, and stayed for a day or two. Sometimes he made a daily commute to London from Slough, taking a train to Paddington or Waterloo station; Waterloo was an easy walk to his Wellington Street office. In the evening he returned to Ellen. Even his longer stays in Slough were probably working vacations. He brought along correspondence to answer, submissions to *All the Year Round* to read, and proofs to correct, carrying his working papers to and from Slough in "a small black bag or Tourist's Knapsack." Returning from Slough on one occasion, he left this bag or knapsack in the hansom cab he hired from Paddington to Wellington Street. (It is reassuring to discover that even the relentlessly efficient Dickens suffered absent-minded lapses.) Sometimes he worked on his own current writing project in Slough. In 1867 he was between novels, but wrote a strange story called "George Silverman's Explanation" and a series of children's stories collectively titled "A Holiday Romance;" together with Wilkie Collins he also wrote a long alpine melodrama for *All the Year Round*, a story titled "No Thoroughfare." He wrote in the mornings, and after breakfast (always a rasher of broiled ham) and conversation with Ellen, he would have spent the next several hours at his desk.

Following a light luncheon, afternoons would have been for writing letters, or for recreation and relaxation. At Gad's Hill, relaxation often took the form of a long walk; in Slough, too, walks with Ellen in the nearby countryside were probably part of the routine. Beyond the pleasures of air and exercise, walking probably allowed him time with her alone, without Mrs. Ternan. Did he and Ellen also stroll the streets of Slough, or wander the two miles to Windsor, to shop, or to idle along the pavements? Possibly—although passersby might recognize the famous man and wonder about the attractive young woman at his side. One day, at any rate, he was recognized by two dogs: "When walking . . . between Slough and Windsor, he met a royal groom on horseback" accompanied by two great St. Bernards to whom Dickens had once been introduced (they were the sire and dam, in fact, of his own St. Bernard at Gad's Hill, Linda). The sagacious and friendly dogs greeted him warmly, "and it was with difficulty that the groom could get them to leave him." Was Ellen with him to witness this happy encounter—and did the dogs recognize her as well?

She herself had a lapdog, Lady Clara Vere de Vere, named for a heartless aristocratic beauty in a ranting poem of the same name by Tennyson. Dickens himself preferred large and truculent outdoor dogs (one of whom, Sultan, he reluctantly shot after it attacked a little girl), but since his daughter Mamie, like Ellen, had a small dog, "a tiny ball of white fluffy fur" named Mrs. Bouncer, he was willy-nilly greeted by a pampered lapdog at both doorsteps of his domestic life, Slough and Gad's Hill. (As Maria Beadnell had also doted on a dog, her spaniel Daphne, it was evidently Dickens's fate always to have his beloved's lapdog underfoot.)

Apart from the latest antics of Lady Clara Vere de Vere (nickname: Claro), what did Dickens and Ellen talk about in the cottage at Slough? There is little reason to suppose that their conversation rose much above the usual stuff of domestic chat: anecdotes of the day's happenings and mishaps, the mail, gossip, family. Ranging beyond these topics, they shared a keen interest in the theater and would have shared theatrical news and observations. Ellen was an ambitious reader, moreover, and they would naturally have talked about books, writing, and writers. But Dickens certainly, and Ellen probably, had little interest in more abstruse topics.

We may get a hint of their conversation in his epistolary conversations with another intimate woman friend—his surrogate wife back at Gad's Hill, Georgina. Though frequently dispatching instructions on business or household matters, his letters to Georgina are often newsy, gossipy, and humorous as well. From an 1867 letter from Leeds, for example:

> I think I mentioned to you that Mr. Harrington is now Master of the Post Office at York. I am sorry to say that he gave me—with tears—an account of E.Y.'s behaviour to him which presented the said E.Y. in a most repulsive, thankless, and odious light. Harrington is established in a very comfortable and pretty little house. I went home with him to see his wife. She is passée, with the remains upon her of a kind of beauty. But she too wears a wig; and it was rather comical to see the two wigs presiding at lunch opposite one another.

Or another, from Dublin:

> Finlay's wife is a very prepossessing little Scotch girl. Something remarkably pleasant both in her face and speech. A very natural manner. I was greatly pleased with her. He [Finlay] is very ill in Edinburgh under a Scotch surgeon. Has had two trying operations performed—is going to suffer under another—and is greatly reduced and cast down. I am afraid he is not naturally strong enough to bear so much.

A breezy, intimate tone; news of shared friends and acquaintances; candid, amusing observations—all suggest the character of his conversation with Georgina (who herself had a penchant for satire).

His feelings for Ellen were very different, of course: while his relationship with Georgina was companionate and friendly, his love for Ellen was romantic and ardent. Together they would have fallen into a comfortable private conversational pattern of their own; and yet at table or as they walked along the footpaths outside Slough, his talk perhaps had the ring of his chatty letters to Georgina. Perhaps in shuttling between Slough and Gad's Hill, in fact, he sometimes forgot which news item or anecdote he had related to which woman. Both women were well acquainted with his loud and bumptious friend John Forster, for example, and a lunch with Forster would always have been conversationally newsworthy. Did Georgina and Ellen hear the same account of each new Forsterism? And did one of them sometimes hear it twice?

Evenings in Slough would have been conversational, too, enlivened with Victorian parlor pastimes like singing, perhaps—Dickens loved old popular songs and ballads—and certainly with reading aloud. Ellen almost certainly heard him read his own current stories as proofs arrived from the printer, as well as other fiction appearing in *All the Year Round*. While they were in Slough, *All the Year Round* began serializing Fanny Trollope's novel *Mabel's Progress*. Dickens would have read aloud each installment as it arrived from Fanny in Italy and was cast in proof, and conversation would have revolved about the story's characters and development. The heroine of *Mabel's Progress* is an actress, and Ellen and the old stager Mrs. Ternan, if present, would have enjoyed detecting the novel's sources in their own theatrical experience. To indulge Ellen, Dickens would have suppressed his aversion to Fanny and been gentle with the novel's shortcomings.

Despite the likelihood of such evenings together, however, the 1867 pocket diary is silent on their activities in Slough, Dickens usually summarizing entire days there with the bald entry "at Sl:". The diary provides far more information on his train routes than on the time they spent together. Only occasionally did he record specifics. To the entry for April 19, a Friday, next to the usual notation of "To Sl:" he added, parenthetically, "Wills." A curious detail: on no other of his many trips to Slough does the diary mention any companion apart from Ellen and "M." Was the visit of his confidential subeditor merely a pleasant social occasion? Or did this rare visitor to the clandestine Slough ménage signal some problem or intrigue? As Wills often acted as agent in Dickens's personal affairs, one may wonder if there was more to his visit than simply dinner and chat with the Ternan ladies. But, after all, that may have been the sum of it. The diary's mysteriously brief note may lure us into imagining a ghost in the attic, when there is only a mouse.

Wills's visit, however, comes close to an even more unusual entry, to which his appearance at Slough may somehow be related. The diary is invariably an unannotated record of each day, free of summary remarks—with one exception. At the bottom of the page for April, Dickens drew a horizontal line under the entry for the thirtieth and below it added: "N ill: latter part of this month." Possibly Wills's visit had something to do with Ellen's ill health, though a physician might have been a more useful visitor. Nothing else in the diary gives any hint that she was indisposed in April, let alone quite ill. Yet she evidently was, so much so that turning the page on April, Dickens thought her poor health worth a special memorandum. It is a token of how critical her well-being was to him.

What ailed her? In the 1950s, Felix Aylmer in his analysis of the pocket diary made the argument that Ellen had given birth to a child on April 13, 1867, in which case her illness in the following weeks might naturally be ascribed to postpartum complications. But Aylmer's evidence quickly dissolved, eventually dwindling to the single word "Arrival" in the diary's entry for the thirteenth, a cryptic note which may simply refer to Dickens's own arrival in Slough that day, at 2:30 in the afternoon. Nothing else suggests a birth in 1867. Others have guessed that Ellen continued to suffer from Staplehurst injuries, but no concrete evidence exists for this theory either. One guess seems as good as another.

Whatever the case, a few weeks later Ellen and her mother took a train from Slough to Paddington with Dickens: Ellen was now well enough to travel to London. A few days later, back in Slough, she and Dickens took an evening walk together, while the diary entry for the following morning, "N walks," may mean that she walked with him from Slough to the train station in Windsor, two miles off. He took the train into London alone that day, but the next day Ellen attended a play with him at the Lyceum Theatre. She and her mother were in town the following day, as well, probably after spending the night in London, suggesting that Mrs. Ternan still maintained lodgings there.

Later in May, however, the pocket diary contains two curious entries. On the twenty-fourth, a Friday, Dickens recorded: "To Sl: at 10. again Bad night." As the bad night is recorded after his arrival in Slough—he had slept in London—it was probably Ellen who had suffered the bad night. His trip to Slough that morning, in fact, was probably an unscheduled call to check on her health, for he had engagements that required him to return to London in the afternoon. He dined in London that evening with Georgina. Did he anxiously discourse to her about Ellen's condition, and if so did Georgina feign sympathy for the woman who so monopolized his attentions? Later that evening he returned to Slough, remaining overnight and the next day—but "Out all day after 2. The Doctor—" These brief remarks are obscure, but the doctor must have been for Ellen, as Dickens would scarcely have traveled to Slough to consult his own doctor, whose practice was near Cavendish Square in London.

By this time, he had decided to relocate Ellen from Slough. The first hint of a move appears soon after he returned from Ireland in March, with a cryptic note "Houses." Two days later: "Meet for houses at 12½. To Peck^m" — that is, Peckham, a few miles south of London.

Why the decision to leave Slough, and why Peckham? Ellen's health may have been one reason; perhaps she had suffered other, unrecorded illnesses, causing him to regard Slough as too miasmal (as its name suggests), much as nine years earlier he had decided that the Ternans' house in Islington was unwholesome. Or perhaps Slough had simply proved too distant from London. Going back and forth left Dickens, accustomed to dictate his own schedule, dependent on railway timetables; and while he was always punctual, trains were not. Traveling between Wellington Street and Slough probably took close to two hours each way: a walk or hansom cab to the station; a wait on the platform; the train journey itself; another walk or cab. During the winter and early spring of 1867 he was continually on trains carrying him all over Britain and Ireland for his public readings; the last thing he wanted to do, back in London, was board yet another train. He was too well known, moreover, to travel on trains without being recognized. Perhaps his frequent journeys to such an out-of-the-way spot as Slough had prompted unwelcome notice and curiosity—even impertinent speculation. The pocket diary reveals that Ellen herself often went into London. Perhaps after living in London she found Slough dull and remote.

Behind such considerations perhaps lay another, more compelling motive: the notion that Ellen deserved something better than a cottage in Slough—deserved, rather, a home with spaciousness, comfort, elegance, and privacy. His daughter and sister-in-law were expensively maintained in a commodious country estate, while his mistress was consigned to a cramped house on a busy street. He could afford to do better for her. The year before he had augmented his income with a tour of readings earning fifteen hundred pounds; now in the early months of 1867 he was embarked on a tour that would earn even more, twenty-five hundred pounds. Ellen should live like a lady of means.

Peckham, like Slough, was a once-rural village being absorbed by the metropolis. Nearby is Walworth, home of the prototypical suburban commuter, Wemmick of *Great Expectations*. Beyond Peckham, however, lay relatively open land: market gardens, a commons called Peckham Rye, a large field called on one contemporary map "Ploughed Garlick Hill." Less than five miles from Charing Cross, Peckham is much closer than Slough to West-End London; there was regular horse-drawn omnibus service into the city, and Peckham Rye rail station had opened two years earlier. Better yet, perhaps, Dickens could walk out the door of his office near Covent Garden and be in

Peckham in half an hour by hansom cab. On at least one occasion he certainly did so, the pocket diary recording: "P (Hansom)." Unlike Slough in the Thames valley, moreover, Peckham lay on high ground, and perhaps Dickens had decided that like his own family at Gad's Hill, Ellen should be established on a salubrious height.

The move was made in June. On the twenty-first, Dickens traveled from Gad's Hill to London, dined at the Atheneum Club, then went on to Peckham and spent the night there, alone, to be on hand for Ellen's arrival next day. Apparently they were for the moment between houses, the lease on the Slough cottages terminating on the quarter day and the permanent house in Peckham not yet available; in the interim Ellen stayed in a house the pocket diary calls "temporary P." Next day she arrived at this house, late: "Long wait for N at house." Over the next four weeks he spent nine nights with her in the interim house, "P (tem)." Earlier in June he had begun writing a story titled "George Silverman's Explanation," narrated as the memoir of a morbidly diffident young man; he finished this gloomy tale while staying with Ellen in the temporary Peckham house. A few weeks later, they spent their first night together in the permanent house, 16 Linden Grove, in Nunhead, just beyond Peckham, on a hillside below Nunhead Cemetery.

In 1936, Thomas Wright, the biographer who first uncovered Dickens's liaison with Ellen Ternan, tracked down the house in Linden Grove. When his *Life of Charles Dickens* had been published the year before, his account of the affair had been attacked as unsubstantiated scandal—as indeed much of it was. Fortunately for Wright, the biography prompted correspondence from several people with alarmingly good memories. One of them was a Mrs. M. R. Mackie, who wrote:

> For many years (from about 1880) my mother . . . had in her
> employ a woman of integrity (Mrs Maria Goldring) who
> in her younger days had worked for Mr Charles Dickens

when he lived *sub rosa* at Linden Grove, Nunhead, S.E. As a child more than fifty years ago I was familiar with the house (Windsor Lodge, if I mistake not) standing in a large garden and always interesting because a great author had lived and worked there.

In later years I learned from my mother that the unofficial wife was reputed to be a connection of Mr Trollope,—presumably the writer. Our informant, Mrs Maria Goldring, always spoke most highly of her employer, and of his kindness to her in her domestic troubles. The name by which he was known was Tringham—or something very like it and the time the sixties, but am not able to give any exact date.

This anecdote, a distant recollection of an old servant's gossip, was the lever that pried open the secret of Dickens's clandestine hideaways. All of Mrs. Mackie's details—Linden Grove, Windsor Lodge, the connection with Trollope the novelist, the 1860s—were accurate. Most decisive was her recollection of the pseudonym "Tringham." It enabled Wright to check her information against the Peckham rate books, where he discovered that beginning in 1867 a certain Tringham was on record as paying the rates on 16 Linden Grove. Twenty years after Wright's biography appeared, the Tringham pseudonym allowed Felix Aylmer, in turn, to confirm Dickens's hideaway in Slough.

Less than five months after her letter to Wright, Mrs. Mackie died. Had she not recalled the name Tringham and sent it along to Wright, Dickens's pseudonym would have gone to the grave with her, and his hideaways with Ellen would have remained undiscovered, probably forever. The Peckham rate books which allowed Wright to corroborate her story were pulped a few years later, during the Second World War. The last-minute, almost accidental exposure of the long-buried secret was a novel-like plot that Dickens himself would have appreciated.

When the local rate collector came knocking at the door of 16 Linden Grove in July 1867, Ellen's first month in Peckham, he was informed that the householder was one "Frances Turnham." Turnham was a common misspelling of Ternan, and Frances "Turnham" seems likely to have been Ellen's mother Frances, though perhaps Ellen herself gave her mother's name in order to conceal her own. Six months later, the collector was told that the house was occupied by another "Turnham," this time Thomas. Ellen's father, long dead, had been Thomas Ternan; but there was evidently a misunderstanding, for in the rate book "Thomas Turnham" was subsequently changed to "Thomas Tringham." Mr. Tringham himself—Dickens—was in America at this point, and Ellen was in Italy; perhaps a servant answered the rate collector's knock, and had forgotten Tringham's name. As at Slough, there was often confusion when the collector called at Windsor Lodge. Six months later yet, in July 1868, "Thomas Tringham" was again the ratepayer; by now Dickens had returned to England, but there was still difficulty with the pseudonym. Not until the following January did Charles Tringham, late of Slough, emerge as the official occupant of Windsor Lodge, and the rates were thereafter paid in that name.

Windsor Lodge has vanished, and if the shades of Dickens and Ellen should revisit the neighborhood of Linden Grove, they would recognize little; perhaps nothing apart from the leafy green slopes of nearby Nunhead Cemetery. When they first arrived in 1867, there were only a dozen or so detached houses spaced out along a quarter-mile sweep of road leading up to the cemetery. Across the road from Windsor Lodge stood Linden Grove Congregational Church, which Dickens assuredly never attended. Behind the church, fields stretched down a gentle slope toward Peckham Rye Common several hundred yards off. Despite a rising tide of new houses, there were still several farms nearby. In the course of his researches into the shadowy Mr. Tringham, Thomas Wright visited Windsor Lodge, still standing in 1936, and described the setting as it would have looked in 1867: "Down the south side of Linden Grove ran a brook, called apparently

'The Braid,' which rose from the high ground in Nunhead Cemetery. . . . Facing the house occupied by Dickens was a cornfield. Indeed, the place had quite a rural aspect"—rather like Gad's Hill, in fact.

Windsor Lodge was new and up-to-date, and far more spacious than either of Tringham's cottages in Slough. It stood alone in a large garden, with a dozen rooms on four floors. There were two servants. Behind the house were stables; perhaps a horse was kept for Ellen's use. Small wonder if Dickens felt pressed for money. In May 1867, after the decision to relocate to Peckham, he groaned that his expenses were "enormous"; and Windsor Lodge no doubt contributed to his anxieties. Yet his resumption of public readings had opened a spigot of new income, and the extra expense of the new establishment must have seemed well worthwhile—with its easier access to London; its more open, wholesome setting; its greater space and comfort. As at Slough, he and Ellen could walk the rural lanes and footpaths around Linden Grove—when Dickens's gouty foot permitted. Sometimes they rode, or at least Ellen did; she was a good equestrian, and for the fresh air and her company, Dickens, a less enthusiastic horseman, may have accompanied her.

In fine weather, they could sit out in Windsor Lodge's garden. The most specific and evocative image of Ellen and Dickens together at Windsor Lodge comes from a tradition recorded by Thomas Wright. Having located Windsor Lodge, he elicited an invitation to tea from its 1936 owners, Mr. and Mrs. Marshall, who "knew all about the tradition that Dickens had lived there." Mrs. Marshall served quince preserves, and Wright and the Marshalls chatted about Dickens and Windsor Lodge. Some sliding Venetian shutters had, since his time, been removed from the back of the house, and Marshall and Wright examined the brackets, "which, as it happened, had never been removed." Why Wright regarded this hardware item as especially noteworthy is unclear. More interestingly, however, Marshall "spoke of Dickens's favourite seat which was under the shade of a sumach tree."

"A book of verses underneath the bough,/A jug of wine, a loaf of bread—and thou/Beside me singing in the wilderness . . ."—in Dickens's case, paradise was a field of rye across the road, the shady garden of Windsor Lodge, and his beloved Ellen beside him: during the summer and early autumn of 1867, between mid-July when she moved to Linden Grove, and late October, he spent thirty-two nights with her in Windsor Lodge. After finishing his work on Wellington Street, he often hurried off to Peckham—as early as possible. The pocket diary regularly records his eager departures from his office for Linden Grove, frequently as early as three in the afternoon, once at one, once "early," once at eleven in the morning. On August 2, a Friday, he was in Liverpool, and wrote to Georgina at Gad's Hill that "with the view of keeping myself and my foot quiet, I think I will not come to Gad's until Monday." But his ailing foot did not prevent him from returning promptly to London and from there directly to Windsor Lodge for two nights.

At Linden Grove, he no longer had to negotiate train schedules, train stations, and trains themselves. One long-time Linden Grover, a Mr. Buckeridge, recalled: "I employed a job-master [a livery stable proprietor] named Cox who stabled near the *King's Arms* [across the road from Peckham Rye Common]. I remember him stating that he had often driven Dickens and fetched him from and to Linden Grove." The 1867 pocket diary, which frequently detailed the stations involved in trips to and from Slough, makes no reference to train stations after the move to Peckham; rather than commuting by train, he probably hired Cox or another job-master, or took a hansom cab. In either case, the trip to Peckham was quicker and more private than the trains to and from Slough.

Few of their Linden Grove neighbors could have been deceived about Mr. Tringham and his young "wife" at Windsor Lodge, but they were tactfully uninquisitive or at least unintrusive. Arriving from London, he was delivered directly to the front door and disappeared into the privacy of his villa, or spent a lingering summer evening with Ellen in the embowered garden.

As he sits in the garden of Windsor Lodge on such an evening in August 1867, does he reflect that it has been exactly ten years since he escorted Mrs. Ternan and her two younger daughters to Manchester to act in *The Frozen Deep*? Very likely he does: he carefully observed birthdays and anniversaries, and his introduction to Ellen had been a fateful day.

Even as he recalled and perhaps drank a toast to this tenth anniversary, however, he was meditating another momentous venture. Early in August he had sent his readings manager George Dolby on a steamer across the Atlantic to investigate the prospects for a reading tour in the United States.

In September, as the sumac leaves at Windsor Lodge blazed scarlet, Dolby returned with his report.

CHAPTER 9

If *I go, my dear; if I go*

Dickens was not an adventurous traveler. As he relaxed with Ellen under the sumac tree in the garden of Windsor Lodge, the missionary explorer David Livingstone, a man his own age, was hiking through unmapped regions of remotest Africa, while Sir Richard Burton trekked through the malarial rain forests of Amazonian Brazil. These were exceptional cases, of course, but not anomalous. It was an age of intrepid British travelers.

As a young man, Dickens himself had made one ambitious journey, though nothing on the scale of Burton or Livingstone. In 1842, he had taken his wife to America for five months of touring, not only in the East but across the Alleghenies and down the Ohio River to the Mississippi, through rough, sparsely settled country. Finding the Americans boorish, he had in turn made himself a boorish guest, hectoring his hosts about a pet grievance, the lack of an international copyright agreement. Returning to England, he wrote a travel book detailing his American complaints, and then as a gratuitous insult detoured the action of his next novel, *Martin Chuzzlewit*, to America, portraying it as a literal and cultural swamp.

Since his American journey in the early years of his celebrity, he had confined his travels to safe, conventional European locations. He had made extended sojourns in Italy and Switzerland, and frequently crossed the Channel to France, in later years invariably with Ellen. He went nowhere else abroad.

Now, in 1867, fifty-five years old and in uncertain health, he contemplated the most ambitious trip of his life, a return journey across the Atlantic—this time not for adventure or discovery; not even for sightseeing. He had seen enough of America in 1842, and had no particular desire to see it again. The motive now was money.

Resuming public readings the year before, he had made two profitable tours through Britain, giving a total of eighty readings. But Britain was not an inexhaustible market; even Dickens's reputation could not fill halls in the same cities year after year. Meanwhile, his expenses were large and growing, as he complained to Wills: "my wife's income to pay—a very expensive position to hold—and my boys with a curse of limpness on them." There was no need to mention to Wills another expense, that of maintaining Ellen in Windsor Lodge. Dickens wanted to ensure that all his three unmarried women—Georgina, his daughter Mary, and Ellen—would be comfortably fixed after his death. "The greatest pressure of all," his readings manager Dolby later explained, "came from his desire to do his duty in promoting the interests of an already expensive family, and his wish to leave them after his death as free as possible from monetary cares." Dolby tactfully omitted to mention Dickens's concern to provide for Ellen as well as his family. Early in 1868, for example, when he was out of the country, Dickens directed Georgina to draw a check on his account for one thousand pounds, payable to Wills, who "has my instructions on how to invest the money"—instructions to invest it for Ellen, almost certainly, with the early January date suggesting an annual contribution to a trust fund, the payment delegated to Wills in Dickens's absence from England.

As if in specific answer to his financial anxieties, El Dorado glistened across the Atlantic. By 1867, the United States had passed Great Britain in population and was surging further ahead. The War Between the States had ended two years earlier, and from Boston to Chicago the North battened in triumph. Dickens was dazzled by the potential profits from American readings. So was George Dolby, his constant companion on his British tours. Just the year before, Dickens had rejected the idea of America, for "I really do not know that any sum of money that could be laid down would induce me to cross the Atlantic to read." Now he was reconsidering. Even before the last of his 1867 readings in England, he confided to Georgina "that I begin to feel myself drawn towards America, as Darnay in the Tale of Two Cities was drawn toward the Loadstone Rock, Paris."

The Darnay analogy was ominous, and Georgina was unexcited about the American idea, which left her with a "very miserable prospect for the coming winter." Doubtful of his health, Dickens's subeditor Wills and longtime adviser Forster were also opposed. Though professing to weigh their objections carefully, Dickens was strongly inclined to disregard them. "The prize looks so large!" he exclaimed. The figure scintillating in his imagination was ten thousand pounds. He reminded Wills that in England "it would take years to get ten thousand pounds. To get that sum in a heap so soon [in America] is an immense consideration to me." He was increasingly mindful of the ticking clock, and of mortality. The time remaining for strenuous exertion like his public readings was dwindling. To his American friend J. T. Fields, he confided that "I am really endeavouring tooth and nail to make my way personally to the American Public, and . . . no light obstacles will turn me aside now that my hand is in."

But there *was* an obstacle, and no light one—Ellen.

"The Patient [Ellen], I acknowledge to be the gigantic difficulty," he admitted to Wills (in a letter written on Ellen's monogrammed stationery). The very prospect of six months without her sank him into gloom. "I should be wretched beyond expression" in America, he told Forster. "My small powers of description cannot describe the state of mind in which I should drag on from day to day." The obvious solution was to take Ellen with him to America. It would be difficult to do so without scandal, "but you know I don't like to give in before a difficulty, if it can be beaten," he told Wills, and began scheming. One prerequisite was Ellen's willingness; had she read Dickens's account in *American Notes* of his distressing 1842 voyage across the North Atlantic, she might well have been hesitant to make the venture herself. But she promptly gave her consent, a decision which "cleared off one obstacle that stood in my way," he announced with relief. Ellen's family, on the other hand, or her sister Fanny at least, disapproved; or at any rate Dickens anticipated their disapproval. Writing to his friend Mrs. Dickinson in July 1867, he mentioned the proposed American tour, which she had evidently heard about: "If I decide to go to America, it will not be within my means to form a determination until the middle or latter end of September," he told her, and warned: "You will be strictly on your guard, if you see Tom Trollope—or his wife [Fanny]—or both—to make no reference to me which either can piece into anything." The strong-willed Fanny, "infinitely sharper than the Serpent's Tooth," was to be kept in the dark as long as possible.

In August, the trusty Dolby was dispatched to America to confer with Fields, a Boston publisher, and to reconnoiter. Sending his readings manager for an impartial assessment was setting the fox to guard the chickens, for Dolby was eager for an American tour.

One of Dolby's assignments during his reconnaissance had nothing to do with the financial prospects for readings, but involved a more personal issue: Would it be possible for Ellen to accompany Dickens? After Dolby sailed for Boston on the Cunard steamer *Java*, Dickens wrote him: "Madame sends you her regard, and hopes to meet you when you come home." (Does "Madame," rather than the "Mademoiselle" more appropriate for a young unmarried woman, hint at Ellen's wifely status?) "She is very anxious for your report, and is ready to commit herself to the Atlantic, under your care. To which I always add:—'*If* I go, my dear; *if* I go.'" Should he make the tour, Ellen would cross the Atlantic and slip into America with Dolby, several weeks in advance of Dickens himself—or so went the initial plan.

"*If* I go, my dear; *if* I go"—these come down to us as Dickens's only surviving words to Ellen, written or spoken, and it is fitting that they should include the affectionate "my dear." His cautionary note implies that she was eager to go; that he, rather, was the voice of restraint. She had not been to America. Shortly after their marriage, her parents had made an extended acting tour in America, and her eldest sister Fanny had been born in Philadelphia. Over the years, Ellen had perhaps been regaled with her mother's American recollections.

In September 1867, seven weeks after embarking on his American reconnaissance, Dolby returned to England, optimistic and eager. Dickens's American friends, led by Fields, had easily won him over. Hearty and gregarious, Dolby had been warmly greeted as Dickens's agent, but he was also an experienced promoter and brought back facts and figures. As he and Dickens did the calculations, the anticipated profit rose from the early guess of ten thousand pounds to a more precise estimate of fifteen thousand, five hundred pounds. It was more than Dickens could resist.

After the objections of the forceful, peremptory Forster were overcome (for Dickens felt obliged to obtain the sage's blessing), the great decision was announced. "I go!" he informed family and friends, and by way of the recently completed undersea cable he telegraphed Fields in Boston: "Yes. Go ahead." He made plans to sail to Boston in early November. Fields had suggested he extend his tour for as long as three years; but Dickens had no such lengthy exile in mind. "I am sorry to say that his residence in that country [America] will be but limited as he must be home here in the month of May," Dolby advised Fields. Dickens himself certainly did not want to be away longer than six months nor, it seems likely, did Ellen.

The weeks before sailing were feverish with activity. To his friend Mrs. Dickinson he elaborated on how much he had to do:

> I have to fix my disturbed mind on the Xmas story I am doing with Wilkie [Collins], and to hammer it out bit by bit as if there were nothing else in the world; while the regulation of my personal affairs, the six months' prospective management of a great periodical published every week [*All the Year Round*], the course to be taken in America, the apportionment of 100 nights of hard work—tug at my sleeve and pull at my pen, every minute in the day. . . . Add a correspondence which knows no cessation, and a public position fraught with appointments of all sorts and people of all kinds, and count my hours for a visit to a friend of mine (and a dear one) down in Berkshire!

But while too busy to visit his dear friend Mrs. Dickinson in Berkshire, he found time for frequent visits to Ellen in Peckham. In the four weeks after his decision to go to America, he spent fourteen nights at Windsor Lodge.

Unresolved was a great question, however—Ellen herself.

Scanning *The Times* on the day he decided to go to America, Dickens would have run across this notice:

> CUNARD LINE. BRITISH and NORTH AMERICAN ROYAL MAIL STEAMSHIPS, appointed by the Admiralty to sail between LIVERPOOL and NEW YORK and between LIVERPOOL and BOSTON, the Boston ships calling at Halifax to land and receive passengers and mails. . . .
>
> Passage money, including steward's fee and provisions, but without wines or liquers:—To Halifax and Boston,

chief cabin, £25; second cabin, £20. To New York, chief cabin £31; second cabin £23. Apply to J. B. Foord, 52, Old Broad-street, London.

Perhaps it was at just this moment—Dickens was not one to procrastinate—that he took out his pocket diary and jotted a memorandum on a blank page:

J. B. Foord
52 Old Broad St. City.
   In reference to Lady's State room 2 berths for'ard
   in front of machinery

While Dolby was responsible for getting himself and Dickens to America, Dickens would make arrangements for Ellen—smuggling her into the States was not, after all, a business matter. For his own crossing, Dolby reserved a berth on the Cunard steamship *China*, sailing on October 12; for Dickens he reserved a cabin on another Cunarder, *Cuba*, sailing four weeks later. When and with whom Ellen might cross remained uncertain.

After Dolby departed for Boston on his August reconnaissance, Dickens had written to assure him that "I don't worry you about our American affairs, because all I have to say or write respecting them, I have said and written." Dolby's instructions had no doubt included guidance on whether and how to introduce the question of Ellen in his negotiations with Fields. In the event, Dolby apparently did not raise the issue; perhaps it seemed indiscreet or impolitic to introduce this difficult personal question into a business calculation, when as yet Dickens had made no decision even to go to America.

Nonetheless, the eager Dickens was determined that if he went, Ellen would go too, and when he made the decision she became a foremost consideration. He and Dolby began to conspire, Dolby encouraging or at least humoring his chief on the possibility of getting

A studio photograph of Dickens in 1867 in New York, at the beginning of his American reading tour.

"But the best photograph—and also the most precious, as being the last—is the American one, taken by Ben Gurney. This likeness pleased my father better than any of his photographs" (Mary Dickens, 1890).

Annie Adams Fields, Dickens's most fervent American admirer. *Courtesy of Art Resource.*
"Then it seemed that Dickens came to speak to us . . . and in my joy at seeing him once more I did not faint but a fiery color suffused my whole face and I grew dizzy like one about to fall." (Annie Fields describes a dream, 1869).

TOP: Pen and ink drawing (based on a photograph) of the terrace at the Trollopes' Villa Ricorboli, outside Florence, where Ellen Ternan spent the winter of 1858 while Dickens was in America longing for her, and while Annie Fields doted on him. *Courtesy of the Firestone Library, Princeton.* BOTTOM: Working sketches of *The Mystery of Edwin Drood*'s two heroines—"two beautiful and young women, strikingly contrasted in appearance," Dickens explained. In Luke Fildes's drawings, Rosa appears pretty but slightly insipid; Helena fierce, exotic, and erotic.

E. W. Haslehust, *Gadshill Place from the Gardens* (1911). Gad's Hill on a bright summer day—like the June day in 1870 when Dickens laid down his pen for the last time.

TOP: An older, more sophisticated Ellen Ternan. The earrings and broach may be tokens of Dickens's fondness for giving her jewelry. *Courtesy of the Dickens House Museum.* BOTTOM: The four Ternan women, June 1870. After Dickens's funeral, the three Ternan sisters and Mrs. Ternan went to stay at the home of Maria in Oxford. From left: Maria Ternan Taylor, Ellen (in mourning, holding Lady Clara Vere de Vere), Mrs. Ternan, Fanny Ternan Trollope. *Courtesy of the Dickens House Museum.*

"This is a delightful place. I am quite charmed with it. There is a capital croquet lawn, and a flower garden, and a vegetable garden, and a paddock. Even a little vinery under glass! . . . There are some beautiful trees in which the little birds pipe away all day long, and it is altogether very pretty, peaceful and sweet. The air is full of the smell of flowers" (Fanny Trollope, June 1870).

Luke Fildes, *Dickens's Grave* (1873). *Courtesy of the Victoria and Albert Museum.*
"We went when in London to see Charles Dickens's grave. He is buried in Westminster Abbey. . . .
I was greatly affected, and so were we all" (Fanny Trollope, June 1870).

TOP LEFT: The grave of Mary Hogarth in Kensal Green Cemetery, outside London. TOP RIGHT: The grave of Maria Beadnell in Highland Road Cemetery, Portsmouth. BOTTOM: The grave of Ellen Ternan in Highland Road Cemetery, Portsmouth.

Thomas Wright of Olney in 1924. Antiquarian, schoolmaster, and biographer, Wright was the unlikely detective who stumbled onto and tracked down the mysterious Mr. Tringham of Windsor Lodge, Peckham. *Courtesy of The Cowper and Newton Museum.*

her to America. But the initial plan of sending her ahead with Dolby was abandoned, and in October Dolby embarked on *China* for Boston, alone. Ellen's American prospects remained uncertain.

But Dickens, as he reminded Wills, did not give up easily. Soon after dispatching the telegram to Fields announcing his decision to go, he wrote a longer, fuller letter. Fields and his wife Annie had invited Dickens to stay with them in Boston; in reply Dickens cited his rule of abjuring private hospitality during his reading tours— he always stayed in hotels. This rule was a professional discipline, allowing him to focus his attentions and energies on the readings; but looking ahead, he perhaps recognized another advantage of hotels. Should Ellen accompany him, hotels would allow them relative privacy, while he could not possibly take his mistress to a respectable private home like that of the Fieldses even for dinner, let alone as an overnight guest. Thanking Mrs. Fields for her letter of invitation, "like a pleasant voice coming from across the atlantic, with that domestic welcome in it which has no substitute on earth," he politely declined.

The matter of Ellen, indeed her very name, was too dangerous to entrust to the mails. He avoided writing of her in letters crossing London; far less would he take the risk in a letter crossing the Atlantic. Yankees were aggressive and many of them, certainly most journalists, coarse; an American newspaper catching wind of a female companion could cause great awkwardness. Dolby, preceding Dickens to Boston, was directed to investigate the Ellen question when he arrived, and Dickens wrote to warn Fields that "Dolby is charged with a certain delicate mission from me, which he will explain to you by word of mouth." The charge was to solicit Fields's views on whether Ellen might safely accompany Dickens, or whether the risk of scandal was too high. Though not yet a confidant, Fields was sufficiently well-informed to know of Dickens's irregular circumstances. Did Fields suspect that Dolby's mysterious mission might involve the young woman of whom he had heard?

After consulting with Fields, Dolby was to send their joint verdict on the Ellen question. Meanwhile, Dickens began making hopeful arrangements for her to cross the Atlantic, perhaps with him on the Cunarder *Cuba*, sailing from Liverpool in early November. Dolby had reserved an officer's cabin on the main deck for Dickens; in making his pocket diary note about a lady's stateroom, Dickens may have hoped to book passage for her on the same sailing. In any case, soon after Dolby sailed for Boston in October, Dickens made a curious change to his accommodations on *Cuba*. For economy's sake, he had planned to share his cabin with his servant Henry Scott. Now he wrote to Cunard's London booking agent to alter this arrangement: Scott was removed from Dickens's cabin and shuffled down to a second-class berth. Explaining the change to Dolby, Dickens cited a concern about Scott's cleanliness, but his expectation or at least hope may have been that Ellen would take Scott's place in his cabin; or that if she shared a stateroom with another woman, perhaps a maid, his own personal cabin would allow them some privacy together.

But there were more complexities than even the questions of whether, when, and how Ellen might sail to America: for as soon as Dickens made the decision to cross the Atlantic, Ellen and her mother had made plans to travel in the opposite direction—to Florence, for a visit to Ellen's sister Fanny at Villa Trollope. Fanny anticipated their arrival at the end of October. But Dickens was booked to sail from England on November 9, making it unclear whether he expected that Ellen might return from Florence in time to sail with him. Mrs. Ternan, "very far from well," may have been traveling to Florence to spend the winter in a milder climate; and perhaps Ellen was going along simply to escort her ailing mother, planning to return to England as soon as Mrs. Ternan was safely deposited at Villa Trollope. Fanny told her stepdaughter that she expected Ellen and her mother to stay in Florence "for a time," a vague phrasing suggesting that the plans were indeterminate or contingent.

Contingent, perhaps, on word from Dolby, crossing the Atlantic. Arriving in Boston on October 23, he consulted with Fields on the "delicate mission" concerning Ellen, while back in England Dickens anxiously awaited their verdict. The 1867 pocket diary preserves his anxiety in a jotted memorandum, "Expect Telegram," with a line drawn to the crucial date, October 26—two weeks before he himself was due to sail on *Cuba*.

Fretting about Dolby's momentous telegram, Dickens steeled himself for bad news. "It may be a relief to you when you get this [in Boston]," he wrote Dolby, "to know that I am quite prepared for your great Atlantic-cable-message being adverse. . . . I think it so likely that Fields may see shadows of danger which we in our hopeful encouragement of one another may have made light of," he reflected grimly, "that I think the message far more likely to be No than Yes." Only near the end of the letter, after unburdening himself on the paramount Ellen question, did he think to add a perfunctory wish that Dolby "may have had a reasonably fair passage" across the Atlantic.

Dolby's telegram arrived on schedule—on October 26, a Saturday. "Dolby telegraphs," Dickens recorded laconically in the pocket diary, a noncommittal comment concealing a dramatic moment, when a messenger or servant had handed him the telegram he had been anticipating for weeks with a mixture of eagerness, dread, hope, and pessimism. Perhaps when the telegram was finally in his hands he hesitated to read it. But he was not one to put things off. Ellen was probably with him when he received it, for he spent the day with her at Windsor Lodge, Peckham, and later they went into London together. It was an important telegram for her, too.

The message was No—or perhaps "Not now, maybe later." Fields coolly judged that Dickens and Ellen should not arrive in America together. With all the welcoming hoopla, fêtes, and publicity attending his advent, it would be impossible to conceal a young woman traveling with him. Even before *Cuba* landed, every other passenger aboard would have noticed the great novelist's attractive young companion;

rumors would be afoot before the ship was moored to the quay. Fields may have left open the possibility of Ellen following on a later ship and slipping into Boston unnoticed, after the sensation of Dickens's own arrival had slackened. Dickens at any rate seized on this consolatory notion. With Nelly at his side, the American tour would be almost a holiday; without her, wretchedness beyond expression, a dreary six months' absence from "all that I hold dear."

On the evening of the dismal telegram's arrival, he took her to his favorite London restaurant, Verrey's on Regent Street, for dinner. The pocket diary generally records events impassively; but this dinner is a striking exception, the most emotionally charged of all its entries. Boxed in with bold double lines, perhaps a mourning border, he wrote:

> Dine Verrey N.

It was the last time he would see his beloved Nelly for weeks—at the best, until she could follow him across the Atlantic; perhaps for much longer, until he returned to England in the spring. After the dinner and a melancholy parting, he took a train to Gad's Hill. Guests were expected, and he dutifully resumed his role of country squire and genial host. Ellen meanwhile left with her mother and sister Maria to join Fanny in Italy. By November 9, when Dickens sailed on *Cuba* from Liverpool, all four Ternan women were together in Florence.

There Ellen would wait for further word, for Dickens had by no means abandoned his hope of getting her to America. Pending his own arrival in the States, he had deferred to Fields's judgment; once in Boston, he would judge for himself. No one could be more determined than Dickens: if it were possible to bring Ellen to America, he would do so.

And he had a plan. As he crossed the Atlantic, landed in Boston, and assessed the situation, Ellen would remain with her mother and sisters at the picturesque Villa Trollope, enjoying the mellow Tuscan autumn—and awaiting a telegram from America announcing Dickens's arrival.

The telegram would be in cypher; perhaps he and Ellen had devised the code as they sat together at Verrey's on their last evening together. The precise wording of the message was critical, and Dickens made a careful memorandum of it in his pocket diary:

In any case. Tel:

Tel: all well means
You come

Tel: safe and well means
You don't come

The crucial telegram would be sent to Wills in London, who would forward the message to Ellen in Florence.

Before leaving, Dickens had given Wills a letter of instruction on business and personal matters to attend to during his absence, such as the conduct of *All the Year Round* (which was to make no reference to America while Dickens was there), and arrangements for his youngest son, Plorn (who was to be taught sheep-farming preparatory to emigrating to Australia). A most important item in Wills's agenda was:

NELLY
If she needs any help will come to you, or if she changes her address, you will immediately let me know if she changes. Until then it will be Villa Trollope, à Ricorboli, Firenze, Italy.

Wills received explicit directions about the important telegram:

> On the day after my arrival out I will send you a short
> Telegram at the office. Please copy its exact words, (as they
> will have a special meaning for her), and post them to her as
> above by the very next post after receiving my telegram.

Alongside the code itself, Dickens noted in a straggling, barely legible scrawl that "N" in Florence could expect to receive his message
between the twenty-third and thirtieth of November.

Should its wording be "all well," she would return to England and
sail to America—with whom, if anyone, is unclear. Wills was given no
instructions about an Atlantic crossing; Forster, also to be informed of
the telegraph's wording, was presumably charged with arrangements
for her sailing. The conspiracy was complete.

Cuba landed in Boston on November 19. "Seven thousand of the phi-
losophers of 'the Hub,' in breeches and in petticoats, awaited his arrival on
the dock," the *New York Herald* mocked, "but they lost the opportunity of
welcoming him with the usual demonstrations of toadyism, inasmuch as
he left the steamer on a tug, and directly he landed hastened to his hotel
in School street." Arriving at his hotel, the Parker House, Dickens was
greeted by "a perfect ovation" from "all the notabilities of Boston," Dolby
reported, "besides the ordinary crowd to be found in a large American
hotel in the evening. Through such a crowd as this, Mr. Dickens made his
way . . . to his apartments." This tumultuous reception might have been
gratifying and promised well for the readings, but it did not augur well
for any privacy with Ellen. As he ate supper in his hotel sitting-room that
first evening, the waiters left the door partially open so "that promenaders
in the corridor of the hotel might take a peep at him, through the crack
between the door and the doorpost, whilst he was sitting at table." No
wonder he was "very depressed in spirits" (Dolby recalled), as he became
aware that prying eyes would be fastened on him for the next five months.
His celebrity was double-edged.

He had instructed Wills to expect the telegram for Ellen the day
after he landed, but the morrow came and went with no message.

Perhaps he wanted another day to assess the situation; if the prospects seemed doubtful, moreover, he would be reluctant to cable the gloomy "No." On the second day after his arrival, he and Dolby took a walk to "discuss arrangements in the pleasant air rather than in this room [in Parker House]." This open-air discussion probably centered on Ellen, for Dickens noted that after speaking with Dolby, he would "get some letters ready for England." Among the "letters" was the fateful telegram for Ellen, as well as a letter to Wills with further instructions on staying in touch with her.

The all-important cable went off, with the apparently cheerful message: "Safe & well expect good letter full of Hope."

But "Safe & well" was a red light—Ellen was *not* to come. Dickens had apparently concluded that her presence would be too risky, or that his public schedule and the necessity of concealing her would leave them little time together—not enough to justify the long journey from Italy to England and thence across the North Atlantic to Boston. Dolby may have been discouraging. As a professional manager of public amusements, he might well have frowned on unprofessional distractions; and cherishing his close and confidential relationship with his "Chief," perhaps he did not welcome feminine competition. A year later, Dickens would exclaim, "Dolby! Your infernal caution will be your ruin one of these days!" Perhaps he was recalling their discussions about Ellen the year before.

Whatever the reasons, "safe & well" meant that Dickens had relinquished his hope of bringing Ellen over . . . maybe. Even now he did not wholly despair, it would seem. A few hours after his fresh-air conference with Dolby, he dined with Mr. and Mrs. Fields and a large company of the golden *illuminati* of New England, including Henry Wadsworth Longfellow, Ralph Waldo Emerson, and Oliver Wendell Holmes. He "bubbled over with fun," his hostess Annie Fields recorded in her journal. Could he have felt or even feigned such ebullience if only a few hours earlier he had resigned himself to a long winter without Ellen? His telegram to her had in fact been ambiguous; for while "safe & well" told her not to come *yet*, the added note, "expect good letter full of Hope," perhaps hinted that he was hopeful of summoning her soon.

The following week, he informed various English correspondents that he would be transferring his American headquarters from Boston's Parker House to the Westminster Hotel in New York City, "a more central position," he explained, "and we are likely to be much more there than here [in Boston]," adding that "I am going to set up a brougham in New York, and keep my rooms at that hotel"—that is, he would keep his suite at the Westminster for the duration of his American stay, even when traveling outside New York. But New York may have had virtues beyond its central location. Boston was his American base; he knew many people there, including his American host Fields and Fields's hospitable wife Annie. In Boston, it would be difficult to evade visitors, dinners, and other obligations; the pocket diary records lunch or dinner engagements for eleven straight days after he arrived there. "Your respected parent is immensely popular in Boston society, and its cordiality and unaffected heartiness are charming," he wrote to his daughter Mary. But so much cheery hospitality would be problematic if Ellen were with him.

In New York, on the other hand, he knew fewer people and none well; it would be easier to maintain his privacy. Keeping a suite at the Westminster Hotel would allow Ellen to remain in comfort there when he dashed off to Philadelphia, Baltimore, and Washington for readings. It seems unlikely, moreover, that he would keep a brougham in New York just for himself; he did not keep one in London. This luxury, too, was perhaps intended for Ellen.

Soon after his first American reading in Boston on December 2, moreover, he sent a mysterious telegram to Wills, for relay to Georgina, Forster, and other confidants: "Tremendous success greatest enthusiasm all well."

The message's concluding "all well" was the code for "*You come.*" Was Ellen now being summoned to join him in America?

The evidence is inconclusive.

When he admonished Wills that the precise wording of his first telegram from America would be critical, he had said nothing about a second telegram, and nothing in the surviving documents makes any reference to one. Yet the later telegram concludes with one of the two specific code phrases, and after its exuberant report "Tremendous success greatest enthusiasm," the bland "all well" would seem superfluous—unless it had a particular coded meaning. If "all well" did *not* mean "you come," it was confusing. Should Ellen interpret the message as a summons? or as simply a commonplace reassurance?

The pocket diary also reveals Dickens still scheming to get her to America. Next to its table of December's high and low tides at London Bridge, he made note of another code:

If P [written over an "M"]. N in London --------Tues 10
If R. N in Liverpool ----------------------------Wed 11

These jottings are cryptic, but evidently he had arranged for one of his English confidants, probably Forster or Wills, to cable news of Ellen's progress toward America. The coded message "R" would presumably mean that she had traveled to Liverpool to embark on a steamer for America, and with a line drawn to December 14 he jotted a memorandum: "Scotia for N York." On the fourteenth, the Cunarder *Scotia* indeed sailed from Liverpool, landing in New York on the twenty-sixth, when Dickens—surely no coincidence—happened to be there for readings. Had Ellen been aboard, she would have been a most gratifying Boxing Day gift.

But on that day she was not aboard *Scotia* or any other ship sailing to New York. She was instead still in Italy, making no progress whatever toward London or Liverpool, let alone America. For all his planning and plotting, Dickens was apparently in the dark as to *her* plans. Soon after arriving in Boston, he had directed Wills:

Will you specially observe, my dear fellow what I am going to add. After this present Mail, I shall address Nelly's letters to your care, for I do not quite know where she will be. But she will write to you and instruct you where to forward them.

While he evidently expected that Ellen would soon leave Florence, probably to return to England to await a summons to America, she herself had evidently decided to wait in Florence.

Dickens, several thousand miles away, remained confused about her location. He continued to write her in care of Wills, perhaps thinking her back in England ready to sail for America at short notice. But if the hotel suite in New York, the brougham, and the "all well" message were part of a strategy to bring her to America—nothing came of it all. Ellen remained in Florence.

The Ternans' journey to Florence had been primarily for Mrs. Ternan's health; and Maria too had been ill. "We shall have quite a hospital up here this winter," Fanny had remarked before they arrived. "However I trust it may benefit all the invalids." Ellen herself may have been unwell. When, in January, Fanny, her husband Thomas Trollope, and Maria traveled to see Vesuvius erupting, Ellen and her mother remained in Florence: "Mamma & Ellen were not strong enough to bear the journey," Fanny remarked. If Ellen was not strong enough for an excursion to Naples, she was scarcely strong enough to cross the North Atlantic in winter. In February, when Fanny and Maria went into Florence, masked, to observe Carnival festivities, Ellen and her mother again remained behind at the villa. Probably Mrs. Ternan, if not Ellen herself, was still unwell; if so, Ellen might have been reluctant to leave her mother behind in Florence. Besides, the strong-willed Fanny, perhaps hostile to Ellen's joining Dickens in America, may have pressed her to linger.

And as the weeks passed, an Atlantic crossing became less and less likely. By Christmas, when Dickens had been in America for over a month, it was probably too late to set out. Along with her mother and Maria, Ellen settled down to spend the winter in Florence—a particularly cold winter in Tuscany, as it happened, but nothing so dreary as an English winter, and incomparably milder than the severe winter in the American Northeast, where Dickens was sneezing and snuffling.

For, after exulting in the adulation and profits that greeted him in Boston and New York, he had fallen ill. Following a heavy snow in New York in mid-December, he dashed about "in a red sleigh covered with furs, and drawn by a pair of fine horses covered with bells, and tearing up 14 miles of snow an hour." Soon, however, a "dismal cold" began to wear him down. "Heavy cold, idle, & miserable," he summarized Christmas Day in his pocket diary, and echoed this cheerless report in a letter to his daughter Mary: "I had a frightful cold (English colds are nothing to those of this country), and was exceedingly depressed and miserable." Two days after Christmas, "I am so very unwell," he confessed, "that I have sent for a doctor." His cold—or "American catarrh," as he called it—persisted for months, nourished by fatigue and low spirits. It was probably no mere coincidence that he fell into the grip of a winter-long cold just as his dream of bringing Ellen to America dissolved.

For the next five months, he worked his way through seventy-six readings up and down the East Coast. From New York and Boston he traveled to Philadelphia, Baltimore, and Washington, where he had an audience with President Andrew Johnson; he read in half a dozen smaller cities in New England, and in March made a pleasure excursion to Niagara Falls, giving readings in Syracuse, Rochester, Buffalo, Albany, and Springfield along the way. In February, impeachment proceedings against the president had monopolized public attention and he canceled readings for a week, but the entire tour nonetheless reaped excellent profits and his letters to England invariably quoted the ticket sale for the latest reading. He grew increasingly exhausted, however, and his December cold lingered into spring: "Catarrh worse than ever!" he lamented in April. There were incidental consolations. In February he made a great facetious production of a twelve-mile walking race between his manager Dolby and an American assistant named Osgood, advertising it as the Great International Walking Match between the "Man of Ross" and the "Boston Bantam," drawing up elaborate rules, umpiring the match personally, and afterwards hosting a gala dinner at the Parker House for the contestants and a large company of his Boston literary circle.

But all the while he pined for Ellen. "It is a wearying life, away from all I love," he lamented in February, and two weeks later he was even wearier, and missing her even more: "I am beginning to be tired, and have been depressed all the time (except when reading), and have lost my appetite. I cannot tell you . . . how sorely I miss a dear friend." During the final month, "all his thoughts were of home and of the loved ones there," Dolby recalled, loyally dissembling, for he knew well that the loved one for whom Dickens yearned most wistfully was not at Gad's Hill and in fact not even in England at the time.

Dickens continued to write this loved one in care of Wills. None of his letters to her survives, but several of those to Wills do, in each of which he mentions an enclosure for Ellen:

"The enclosed letter to your care as usual." (3 December 1867)

"Enclosed is another letter for my dear girl to your kindest care." (6 December 1867)

"Enclosed is another letter for my dear girl, to your usual care and exactness." (10 December 1867)

"Enclosed, another letter 'as before'." (17 December 1867)

And on Christmas eve, he sent Wills yet another letter to forward to Ellen, accompanied with a sorrowful fantasy: "Enclosed, another letter as before, to your protection and dispatch. I would give £3,000 down (and think it cheap) if you could forward *me*, for four and twenty hours only, instead of the letter."

Over the next four months he enclosed at least six more letters to Ellen in packets mailed to Wills; there were likely others, too, for many of his letters to Wills have disappeared. He probably wrote Ellen weekly, more or less, depending on ships sailing for England; he wrote his last letter to her in mid-April, less than a week before sailing from New York himself.

There is one especially curious feature in Dickens's letters to Wills. In February, he remarked that "You will have seen too (I hope) my dear Patient, and will have achieved in so doing what I would joyfully give a Thousand Guineas to achieve myself at this present moment!" This ardent wish testifies to his longing for Ellen, whom he had not seen for almost four months. But it seems strange that he thought that Wills in London would have seen her recently, as she was still in Florence and would remain there for another two months.

How could Dickens have been so confused about her whereabouts? She must have written him often. She had little excuse *not* to, for she was highly literate and enjoyed abundant leisure at Villa Trollope. Moreover, his brief mentions of her in his letters to Wills scarcely suggest any unhappiness or uneasiness, as might be expected had she been out of touch. But the entire correspondence between Dickens and Ellen having disappeared, it is impossible to know just what he knew or didn't know about her while he was in America. Perhaps at some point she intended to return to England in February, but changed her plans. Letters between Florence and America were two weeks or more in transit, so he was always behind in his information.

In Florence, the Florentines complained of the cold damp winter. "I tell my sisters that they must stay until the spring sun begins to shine," Fanny Trollope wrote her stepdaughter in England, "and then they will know what an Italian day really is. Maria remembers how beautiful it was when she was here in September, and is always talking with great tenderness of the figs." As an additional discomfort, Villa Trollope was undergoing renovations: the family was eating in the drawing room and the library was accessible only by ladder. But rain, cold, illness, and hammering apart, the close-knit Ternan women probably enjoyed the chance to spend several months together.

From Fanny's letters to her stepdaughter during these months, we catch glimpses of Ellen.

We see her on a modest family outing for tea and punch, for example, and also attending a more glamorous affair, "a very large and brilliant reception . . . in honour of Admiral Farragut the officer who so distinguished himself in the recent American Civil War," at which "there were nearly four hundred persons present." We see her with Fanny and Mrs. Ternan "kindly" making flannel shirts for soldiers wounded in the Italian wars of unification. Hearing of her walks with her sisters ("The days are so short now that we seldom get our afternoon walk before dusk," Fanny notes in December), we recall that long afternoon walks were a Dickens habit too.

Here and there in Fanny Trollope's letters, we glimpse Ellen as a living personality.

Some Dickens biographers and scholars have assumed her to be the model for Dickens's later disobliging heroines—in particular, the icy Estella of *Great Expectations* and the mercenary Bella Wilfer of *Our Mutual Friend*. But the Ellen of Fanny Trollope's letters is a good-humored, generous, and likeable young woman.

One day, for example, she makes a special trip into Florence to buy sheet music for Fanny's stepdaughter Beatrice ("Bice"): "I have bought the songs you asked for (Ellen kindly went down to Ducci's on purpose) the day we received your letter," Fanny writes Bice. When Bice sends each of the Ternans a personally illustrated Christmas card, Fanny in thanking her remarks that "Ellen's robin redbreast drinking her health is particularly admired. She says it is evident that you consider her the 'jolly dog' of the party!"

We see Ellen laughing appreciatively at the un-English mannerisms of a small English girl, "little Emelina": "Ellen was very much amused by her funny little Italian gesticulations and airs." We see her chatting kindly with an insecure young guest at Villa Trollope: "A girl who was here last night . . . said such a pretty naïve thing to Nelly. She (a certain Miss King) is at school. . . . Nelly was showing her some attention, and she said 'Oh how kind Mrs. Trollope is to let me come. But I am very frightened.' 'Why?' asked Ellen. 'O, because I am not used to going out, and I don't know any of the people. I am just sixteen, and if you know I am only a school girl *though I look so big*!'"

Later, after her return to England, Ellen and her mother will pay a special visit to Bice, unhappy at school in Brighton; later yet, Fanny tells Bice that "I hear from Nelly that she has a little present to send you."

Fragmentary as they are, these mentions of Ellen in her sister's letters remain the most vivid images of her to survive. From them, we may begin to understand why Dickens pined for her during his long winter in America.

During his five months in America, another woman entered his life, and her affection for him is much better documented than Ellen's.

Earlier in 1867, Dickens had designated a Boston firm, Ticknor and Fields, as his authorized American publisher. Ticknor himself was dead, but the surviving partner, James T. Fields, already one of Dickens's closest American friends, now became his *de facto* American business agent.

Fields holds an honorable place in American publishing history. He had risen from clerking in a Boston bookshop to partnership in Ticknor and Fields (as it then became), the most prominent publisher of poetry and fiction in America. He was a shrewd businessman with a sharp eye for literary merit, but also a gregarious friend and patron of writers. He enjoyed close ties with most of the prominent New England *literati* of the time, including Longfellow, Lowell, Holmes,

Hawthorne, and Whittier; Ticknor and Fields published them all. Fields had rescued Hawthorne from obscurity by encouraging him to write his first novel, *The Scarlet Letter*, which Ticknor and Fields published in 1850. Hawthorne later told Fields: "My literary success, whatever it has been, or may be, is the result of my connection with you." Fields had also made himself the authorized American publisher of many well-known English writers, including Dickens, by the simple expedient of paying them royalties; with no international copyright agreement, English writers seldom profited from the publication of their books in America.

A fine photograph of Fields, his partner Ticknor, and Hawthorne shows them standing together sometime in the 1850s; though posed in a photographer's studio, Hawthorne and Ticknor wear overcoats and Fields a long cape, and all three are topped by tall stovepipe hats. Fields is heavily bearded, as he was his entire adult life, and plump, the willing victim of many hearty meals.

Fields and Dickens had first met in Boston twenty-five years earlier, during Dickens's first visit to America. Now, in 1867, Fields was fifty. He was married to a much younger woman, Annie Adams Fields, who at thirty-three was only five years older than Ellen. The Fieldses' age disparity may have attracted Dickens. Annie had been only twenty when she and Fields married; but she was attractive, intelligent, and vivacious, and held her own. The marriage was childless, and she threw herself into the social obligations and enjoyments of her husband's business with writers. In their comfortable Boston home on Charles Street, backing on the Charles River, she received a stream of callers and gave frequent dinner parties to the Ticknor and Fields circle, "the Parnassus of New England." She was a gracious and winning hostess:

> She dazzled no one by her wit, her conversation, or her brilliance. Always she stood in the background. She made her guests comfortable; she saw to it that she and her

house provided the perfect setting for the army of egos that marched into it. . . . She gave these prima donnas the attention they craved and by honestly thinking they were as good as they thought themselves she created a salon famous wherever the literary gathered.

Distinguished writers recalled her fondly. As a young man, Henry James was struck by Fields's "singularly graceful young wife . . . her beautiful head and hair and smile and voice." Years later, after Annie was widowed, Willa Cather visited her at 148 Charles Street and later testified to its "harmonious atmosphere . . . in which one seemed safe from everything ugly."

Annie Fields kept a diary for many years—sixty-one notebook journals survive—and from them her personality emerges distinctly. She was highly sociable, but she also enjoyed quiet and was widely read (she could read novels in French and German). An earnest New England moralist, she was not dogmatic. Visiting an Anglo-Catholic convent near Windsor Castle in 1869, she declared that "I believe in this thoroughly for some women and I am sure these particular women are doing a grand work and are very happy"—a more liberal-spirited sentiment than Dickens was likely to express. On Sundays, she walked three miles to the Unitarian church in Roxbury to arrange the flowers, but seldom stayed for the service. She was warmly appreciative of others' merits; easily impressed, especially by talkers—too easily, one suspects; and lavish with superlatives. She wrote (like her husband) indifferent poetry, "yet I am too much a woman to be always a poet," she regretted; "I cannot live for that—I cannot have 'a woodland walk' when I feel like it because somebody will lose their dinner. . . . Yet I know there is a heart of a singer hidden in me and I long sometimes to break loose—but on the whole I sincerely prefer to make others comfortable and happy as I can now do and fie! to my genius if he does not sing to me from the sauce-pan." Living a leisured and comfortable life (with three servants and a washerwoman), she had a genteel spirit of *noblesse oblige* and a pious wish to be of service. During Dickens's visit to America, she had "one deeply seated hope, that he will read for the Freed people before he leaves the country and I cannot help thinking he will" (he did not, however). Culturally and socially she was conservative. Looking into a suffragette convention in 1868, she recoiled from the "many hard faced unlovely women full of forthputting-ness. . . . My heart is wholly with the movement, but the movers alas! are often women who love to un-sex themselves and crave audience from the rostrum."

Dickens had met Annie Fields in 1859 when the Fieldses visited England. "Such kindliness as shines through that man's clay," she had rhapsodized after he paid them a call in London (a remark evincing Annie's roseate turn of mind, in view of Dickens's ruthlessness during his marital break the year before). He had recently completed his first English reading tour, and Fields encouraged him to give readings in America as well. Dickens considered the idea but decided against it for the time, and the War Between the States soon intervened. After the war, Fields renewed the invitation, and when Dickens landed in Boston in November 1867, Fields greeted him as business partner and host. Two days after landing, Dickens dined at the Fieldses' Charles Street home, the first of many visits.

His hostess that evening fell in love with him, and for the rest of his visit and beyond remained deeply enamored.

Annie Fields's diaries gush with adulation. After his first reading in Boston, she exclaimed: "How we all loved him! How we longed to tell him all kinds of confidences!"—but one wonders if the confiding "we" of this effusion was not mostly Annie herself. When he traveled to New York to give readings, she and Fields accompanied him. She was avid for Dickens's company, and when she failed to see him one day in New York, she went to bed "smothering a disappointment I could not help feeling at not seeing him again today." Dickens took long confidential walks with her husband, seven miles on average, and when Fields afterwards shared Dickens's disclosures with Annie, her fascination grew. On Christmas eve, Dickens read *A Christmas Carol* in Boston. "Ah! How beautiful it was! How everybody felt it!" she exclaimed; but no one felt his magnetism more powerfully than she herself. "We cannot help loving him as all must do who have the privilege of coming near him and seeing him as he is." He was in Washington, D.C., on his birthday, February 7. "The birthday of our friend! Dear Charles Dickens! What riches for one life to have such a friend," she exclaimed. "I have sent to Washington to have flowers on his breakfast table this morning. . . . We think of him far away, in love, and find ourselves companioned." The ambiguous "in love" may refer to Dickens, but certainly to Annie herself. When he thanked her for the flowers, she melted: "Nobody in Boston has as many blessings as I."

The Fieldses attended thirty of Dickens's seventy-six readings in America. Eudora Welty recalled that her mother used to "read Dickens in the spirit in which she would have eloped with him"; Annie Fields attended his readings with the same romantic eagerness. When not performing, Dickens spent many hours and even days with the Fieldses; with a single exception, theirs was the only private home at which he dined during his five months in America—and he dined with them often. After many of his readings, they attended supper parties he hosted at his hotel, convivial affairs enlivened by punch concocted by Dickens himself. When, after Christmas, he returned to Boston from New York with his miserable catarrh, he accepted the Fieldses' invitation to stay at 148 Charles Street for a week. "What a pleasure this will be to us!" Annie exclaimed. "We anticipate his coming with continual delight! To have him as much as we can, at morning, noon & night." His stay with the Fieldses was a unique compliment, the only time during a decade of reading tours that he violated his rule of always staying in hotels.

The Fields home in wintry Boston was a tranquil refuge. Willa Cather recalled that "there was never an hour in the day when the order and calm of the drawing-room were not such that one might have sat down to write a sonnet or a sonata. The sweeping and dusting were done very early in the morning, the flowers arranged before the guests were awake" (Annie loved flowers, but they must have been a precious commodity in January, in New England). Her home was the closest thing in America to Gad's Hill—or to Windsor Lodge, Peckham. Her doting attentiveness and worship supplied a warm feminine solicitude amidst a wilderness of bearded and self-complacent New England *literati*.

Her husband was equally hospitable, and with some justice Fields's biographer, Warren Tryon, ridicules both husband and wife for their worshipful cosseting of Dickens, "a cult of adoration by the Fieldses who were otherwise perfectly sober and sane people." But "like most great and creative artists," Tryon adds, Dickens "was filled with a sense of self-importance, of self-interest, and self-esteem. He took their attentions almost as his due and basked in the all but suffocating excesses of the Fieldses' love." Yet this charge of toadying is perhaps too cynical, at least with respect to Annie. She was no doubt flattered by the great man's notice, but her admiration went beyond vanity or celebrity-worship. She loved Dickens with a very personal, distinctly feminine warmth.

At one point, her journal hints that her feelings were simply filial: "I feel somehow like one of his daughters and as if I could not take too good care of him." More than twenty years her senior, Dickens was indeed old enough to be Annie's father. He was in poor health, moreover, suffering from his catarrh and exhaustion; he developed severe gout in one foot and at a large public farewell dinner at Delmonico's had to be helped into the banquet room, his swollen foot swaddled in black silk. Studio photographs taken in New York show him grizzled and aged—hardly a figure of Byronic allure. He looked so haggard on the platform that an upstate New York newspaper commented, bluntly, that he "cannot be expected to live very many years longer." No young woman, one might think, could love such a graybeard with other than daughterly tenderness.

Yet Annie's affection often had a distinctly more amorous than daughterly flavor. On the day he sailed for England, she lamented: "Rose at six this morning sleep being out of the question. I must confess to sitting down in my night-dress in a flood of tears . . . it seems more than I can bear." She loved Dickens, she felt, with such passion for a man as only a woman could feel. While her husband would regret Dickens's departure, she observed, he "will always have perhaps a more repose-ful connection [with Dickens] than is possible on earth between men and women." Her own feelings at Dickens's departure were anything but reposeful. The day after he sailed, she was too sunk in grief to write in her journal, but on the following day she recalled their parting: "My memory goes back again and again to the last scene, the last embrace the look of pain; the bitter bitter sobs after he had fairly gone." She often dreamed of him: "In the morning I awake dreaming that he has just come to say 'goodbye'—I see that sharp painful look dart up his brow like a lightning of grief. I feel his parting kiss on my cheek and see my arms stretched out to hold him—vanished." She mourned as if she had lost her lover to the grave: "He has gone home to his dear ones and to the splendor of England's summer," she consoled herself, but his happy return was a death to her: "It is the same when our dear ones go to Heaven—we know *they* are glad, but the darkness shuts down fearfully about ourselves."

For weeks after, her thoughts remained fixed on him. She followed him in fancy across the Atlantic, day by day, to his joyous arrival in England. She mused about his return to Gad's Hill, wishfully imagining herself there, devoting herself to him as a loving slave: "He is swift, restless, impatient, with moods of fire, but he is also and above all, tender, loving, strong for right, charitable and patient by moral force. Happy those who live, and bear, and do and suffer, and above all love him to the end—who love and labor with and for him." Annie Fields was not an excitable woman, ordinarily; she was, rather, a staunch New Englander, an Adams, a proper Bostonian; she never missed one of Ralph Waldo Emerson's many enlightening public lectures. Dickens awoke a sleeping ardor in her nature. Her love for him remained the emotional zenith, the great passion, of her life.

Despite her infatuation, she remained a loyal, solicitous wife. The amorous confessions of her journals were no surreptitious record of a forbidden passion, for she shared both her feelings and her journals with her husband. Indeed, she kept a journal not only as a personal narrative, but as an historical document: "It is for his sake [her husband's] as well as my own comfort that I make this little record that if we both live as years roll on . . . we may refer to points where memory fails us and make the links complete." When after Dickens's death Fields wrote a memoir, *Yesterdays with Authors*, a third of his long chapter on Dickens was borrowed (without attribution) from Annie's journals. For her, worship of Dickens was a family cult; and attributing her own feelings to her husband, she often included him in her rhapsodic tributes to her idol—"Even now the spell of his presence is upon us, his voice is in our ears," and so on. She and Fields together lamented that Dickens was not sufficiently idolized, wondering "that America does not rise to do him honor. It certainly shows a great lack of the noble spirit of worship that *more* feeling does not come out." But as she recognized, her husband's affectionate admiration for Dickens was only a candle to the blaze of her adoration.

Dickens's response to Annie Fields's overflowing adoration was friendly—but little more. He repaid her hospitality and idolatry with gratitude, but despite her attractiveness and her obvious infatuation, there is no evidence that he took any particular fancy to her. She was "one of the dearest little women in the world" (he told Georgina)—a compliment with perhaps a hint of condescension. One night after a reading, she and Fields visited him, and she exclaimed in her journal: "I believe I lay awake from pure pleasure after such a treat—hearing Marigold and having supper afterward with the dear great man. . . . Mr. Dickens was gentle kind and affectionate—indeed something more—so much more that I have forgotten to be afraid of him." The "something more" would seem to hint at a growing personal connection between them, but Annie seems never to have progressed much beyond this mark in his regard. The genteel Boston wife was no competition for the young actress, for whom he pined and to whom he remained faithful during his long chaste absence. He enjoyed Annie's admiration and lavish attentions, but perhaps no more than he enjoyed the companionship of her hearty, chatty husband, with whom he took long walks and conversed freely. Though he could not have doubted that Fields relayed all his disclosures to Annie, she herself probably never became a direct confidante of Dickens himself.

Even if she never heard a word about Ellen from him directly, however, an avid feminine curiosity gleaned details about his personal affairs, and she conjectured the rest.

How much did she learn about Ellen? Even in her journal she was reticent and discreet, making few direct references to Ellen; but those she made reveal that she knew far more than she recorded. Her primary and probably sole source was her husband, who repeated confidences dropped by Dickens during their long walks together. Between themselves the Fieldses talked about Dickens frequently and fully; to others, they remained tight-lipped. A brief entry in Annie's journal in August 1870, two months after Dickens's death, shows their discretion. "Yesterday darling J and I passed the entire day together alone. . . . Dear Dickens is seldom out of our thoughts. I see his face near mine at unexpected seasons," she wrote (whereas her husband simply thought about Dickens, Annie saw him in visions). Musing on Dickens, she went on to a more concrete item: "J told Longfellow, as was quite right, about E. L. T." The brief summary phrase "about E. L. T." betrays in a flash the Fieldses' familiarity with the whole story of Dickens and Ellen—even her middle name, or at least initial. Had Annie known less, she would have said more. Even after Dickens's death, Ellen's identity remains masked by initials in Annie's journal; and only then could the Fieldses' conspiratorial knowledge be divulged to Fields's closest friend, Henry Wadsworth Longfellow, who had also been friendly with Dickens. Together Fields and Annie had just written and published in the *Atlantic Monthly* an adulatory eulogy of Dickens, with no hint of "E. L. T." or his double life.

Her journals reveal that Annie had a due regard for the proprieties and could judge severely. Nonetheless, she was willing to allow Dickens his mistress. In addition to being a charming friend and guest, he was "perhaps the greatest genius of our time"—and one had to make allowances for genius. Moreover, he evoked her pity. He was unhappy in his sons, she learned; he had been unhappily married. He seemed "often troubled by the lack of energy his children show and has even allowed J. to see how deep his unhappiness is in having had so many children by a wife who was totally uncongenial." He hinted that his marriage had foundered because Catherine drank heavily: "He told J. yesterday in walking that nine out of ten of the cases of disagreement in marriage came from drink he believed. He is a man who has suffered evidently."

On one occasion, he spoke to Annie herself about his marriage, obliquely. As she recounted the marital problems of a friend, Dickens remarked on "how much wrong on both sides there had been in that case as in many & most others—speaking somehow with a consciousness of his own position underlying the words yet with a firm & even eager manner." Embarrassed by this plunge into personal matters, Annie looked down shyly; raising her eyes, "I saw a look of suffering about his face which showed as neither his voice nor words had done how painful the subject was upon which he had found himself launched." One need not doubt Dickens's sincerity even as one notes that the role of suffering victim was the perfect key to unlock Annie's sympathies. She melted at the unhappiness of this great man; and his sorrows trumped any sisterly compassion she might have felt for the discarded "uncongenial" wife.

Annie's uneasiness with Dickens's glancing allusion to his marriage may suggest why he avoided speaking with her on the delicate issue of Ellen. Nonetheless, with the information her husband shared with her she could form her own conclusions. She did not doubt Dickens's transgressions. "May his mistakes be expiated," she once pleaded, and after his death she confided to her journal that "I love to think of our beloved [Dickens] beyond the reach of life's turmoil and folded in life's rest . . . and forget his failures & the dark side of his strange experience." Once she enigmatically petitioned, "May God keep him from temptations which are too great—and all of us." Beyond Ellen, what temptations did she have in mind? And in the tacked-on "all of us," was Annie glancing at her own susceptibilities? However chaste in fact, her passion for Dickens may have prompted vivid fancies.

Eight months after he departed Boston, she dreamed of him yet again. He had in the meantime begun a final reading tour in Britain and (as she knew) had added to his repertory Bill Sikes's bludgeoning murder of Nancy in *Oliver Twist*. Annie decided to refresh her memory of the scene: "Read last night the murder scene from Oliver Twist before going to bed and dreamed of it and of Dickens all night." Her dream strangely conflated her beloved Dickens with the brutal Sikes:

> I was seized firmly by the wrists, in my fancy, and led to where the body lay, & I turned my head away and would not look, but the grasp grew tighter and tighter until I gave one quick glance at the livid flaccid[?] mask of that wretched face upturned in the morning light and fled shuddering away. Then it seemed that Dickens came to speak to us, for J was always near, and in my joy at seeing him once more I did not faint but a fiery color suffused my whole face and I grew dizzy like one about to fall.

What did "J" think when he read his wife's account of this violently erotic fantasy, in which he himself stands by passively while she is seized and gripped by an overmastering strength (earlier Annie had admired Dickens's "strong strong hands"); and in which her idol

Dickens, mysteriously appearing, brings a flush of desire to her face, and sends her into an ecstatic swoon?

Dreaming such dreams, Annie was naturally interested in Dickens's actual lover, Ellen Ternan.

While her journals seldom mention Ellen, they often glance at her presence in Dickens's life.

Annie probably knew little enough about Ellen when he arrived in Boston in November. But on Thanksgiving Day, a week after his arrival, he backed out of a dinner party, explaining that "he was overtaken by a sudden access of sadness wh. must prevent him from leaving the fire side and solitude of his own room," Annie noted. Yet he had seemed in excellent spirits the day before, and the day after, sitting with Fields for four hours, "the tide of laughter ran so high they could only lay their heads down & laugh it out." Observing these moody oscillations between gloom and hilarity, Annie grew intrigued by the private distresses and hidden griefs of this "noble spirit," outwardly so cheerful.

By the time he sailed for England in April, she knew much more, though just how much is uncertain. His disclosures to Fields during their long brisk walks were no doubt incomplete, and Fields perhaps edited them even further when passing them on to Annie. She was not straitlaced, but there were certain manly confidences a gentleman would hesitate to repeat to a lady, even were she his wife.

Annie's knowledge was certainly skewed in at least one respect. She heard much of Gad's Hill, little of Ellen. One evening at a large dinner hosted by Dickens, for example, she sat at his right hand as he discoursed on a range of topics—spiritualism; dreams; writers creating characters out of airy nothing; his impressions of America. In particular, Annie noted, "He loves to talk of Gad's Hill and stopped joyfully from other talk to tell me how his daughter Mary arranged his table with flowers. . . . 'Sometimes she will have nothing but water-lilies,' he said as if the memory were a fragrance." His poetic appreciation of Mamie's floral arrangements charmed Annie, who (he well knew) loved flowers; she was even more pleased by his strong attachment to home—to Gad's Hill and its two ladies, Georgina and Mamie. "Georgina Hogarth he always speaks of in the most affectionate terms, such as 'She has been a mother to my children' 'She keeps the list of the wine cellar. . . .'" For table companions, and perhaps especially for Annie, he stressed his domestic affections. Fields, too, faithfully relayed Dickens's expressions of fondness for his "home circle." "What a dear one it is to him can be seen whenever his thoughts turn that way," Annie commented; "and if his letters do not come punctually he is in low spirits." This journal entry celebrating Dickens's attachment to his "dear" home was written, by coincidence, on Ellen Ternan's birthday, March 3. Did Annie know, by now, that the letters he most eagerly anticipated were dated not from Gad's Hill but from Villa Trollope, Florence?

Perhaps discretion restrained her from open mention of Ellen in her journals, but as Dickens's time in America drew to a close, she was less guarded in speculating about his life in England. During his last week, he was re-afflicted with gout and feared (Annie reported) that "the papers will telegraph news of his illness to England. This seems to disturb him more than anything else." What disturbed him especially was that Ellen might hear of his affliction: "Ah!" Annie commented. "What a mystery these ties of love are—such pain—such ineffable happiness—the only happiness." But this rhapsodic observation, squeezed between lines, is a later insertion. Was Annie when she wrote the initial entry, just days before Dickens's departure, still unaware of the "ties of love" binding him to Ellen? Or was the commentary merely a later reflection on what she had known earlier?

Only two days after he sailed, Annie's journal again seems to glance at Ellen: "He goes to the English spring, to his own dear ones, to the tenderness of long tried love." But does the tenderness of long-tried love refer, rather, to Georgina? Annie was intrigued by Georgina's curious role as Dickens's surrogate wife—housekeeper, companion, confidante, but not bedmate. "It is not an easy service in this world to live near such a man, to love him, to desire to do for him," she reflected (though a service Annie herself would gladly have undertaken). Despite

Georgina's loyal attendance, he remained unhappy. "But even now," Annie mused, "he might be lonely such is his nature. When I recall his lonely couch and lonely hours I feel he has had a strange lot." His nature, presumably, yearned for sexual intimacy, and Annie's insistence on his loneliness—especially his lonely couch—is intriguing. Did she imagine that he spent all his time at Gad's Hill? and was she ignorant of his second home in Peckham, where his couch was probably less lonely?

"The lonely couch" suggests that Annie was under the impression that Dickens saw Ellen either infrequently, or chastely, or both. Was this the idea he had conveyed to Fields?—or was this how Fields recast Dickens's remarks for his wife?

In any case, comments that Annie made a few days later reveal that even if she thought Dickens saw Ellen only occasionally, she did not doubt their intimacy.

His ship, the Cunarder *Russia*, sailed from New York on April 22. Two days later, Ellen and her mother left Florence to return to London in time for his arrival. "If he could but confess to us all the rapture of his return!" Annie wished. "But I know this must not be." On May 2, she imagined him landing in Liverpool (he had actually landed the day before): "I awoke this morning," she wrote, "feeling that today was *his* day of joy. It rains here!!" The sun was shining for Dickens, she assumed, knowing that the first woman to greet him would be Ellen—not Georgina or his daughters. Fascinated with his reunion with Ellen, Annie imagined it, tellingly, from Ellen's point of view:

> I cannot help rehearsing in my mind the intense joy of his beloved—It is too much to face, even in one's imagination and too sacred. Yet I know today to be *the day* and these hours, *his hours*—Surely among the most painfully & joyfully intense of his whole life.

Plainly, she assumed a highly charged encounter with "his beloved"— no "lonely couch." In imagining their reunion as "too sacred" to contemplate, she evidently anticipated a nuptial consummation, a virtual wedding night. Annie entertained a sacramental, almost mystical conception of a woman's love: "Sometimes when I reflect how true love can cause a woman to blossom and develop and bear perfect fruit not only of the body but the spirit . . . I pray God to bless all women, to make them more womanly, and to elevate only those things in their *eyes* which shall show them most truly their heavenly mission." In embracing Dickens, Ellen was fulfilling her spiritual destiny—or so Annie apparently thought, perhaps with some envy.

The next day, she learned that *Russia* had in fact landed safely in Liverpool, whence Dickens proceeded directly to London: "Yesterday as I felt sure C. D. was in London. What hours for him!! How can we be grateful enough for them!" After his joyous reunion with Ellen in London, Annie expected, he would continue straight to Gad's Hill. "*This morning* therefore dear C. D. is at Gad's Hill," she wrote on May 5, a Tuesday.

Actually Dickens was still in London—or more likely in nearby Peckham, enjoying Ellen's company and in no evident hurry to return to Gad's Hill. On his first evening in London, he had taken a box at the Adelphi Theatre, no doubt with Ellen, to watch a dramatization of *No Thoroughfare*, the alpine melodrama he had written the year before with Wilkie Collins. There was much business to catch up on, too; his factotum and *All the Year Round* subeditor Wills had knocked his head in a riding accident several weeks earlier and was still convalescing. But Dickens's reluctance to leave London had more to do with Ellen than with Wills. After six months apart, he was avid for her company; his dear home and the green tranquility of rural Kent could wait. He lingered with her for a full week before finding his way back to Gad's Hill and the patient Georgina.

He soon resumed the triangular life he had left behind six months earlier, shuttling among Ellen in Peckham, his family at Gad's Hill, and his *All the Year Round* office in London.

Gad's Hill was his retreat and sanctuary. All his sons except the youngest, Plorn, were now gone, mostly at sea or overseas, and Plorn himself was soon dispatched to Australia (where his older brother Alfred had earlier emigrated). With Plorn's departure, Dickens had effectively cleared his home of other males, leaving himself surrounded with loyal women: Georgina, Mary, and Katie, who though married and living in London frequently stayed at Gad's Hill. Despite his fondness for masculine camaraderie and bonhomie, Dickens's closest male friendships had dwindled: he had lost many friends to death, and drifted apart from others, like Forster, who had married and grown pompous and dull, and Wilkie Collins, who resented Dickens's want of sympathy for his brother Charles, Katie's invalid husband. At the end of the day, Dickens preferred the companionship and care of younger women (even "Aunty"—Georgina—was fifteen years younger than he). His novels' partiality for young women expressed his own personal preferences exactly.

Gad's Hill itself he made more comfortable and gracious, hiring a new head gardener (making a total of four gardeners) and adding a new (and expensive) glass conservatory wing, his own little Crystal Palace. He continued to enjoy playing the squire: buying up neighboring fields, hosting the local cricket club, entertaining weekend guests. To write, he retreated in fair weather to his miniature chalet amidst the shrubs and trees across the road from Gad's Hill; but on his return from America in 1868 he had no major writing project in hand.

He was harassed by business affairs. "You may imagine what six months of arrear are to dispose of," he complained; "added to this, Wills has received a concussion of the brain . . . and is sent away by the doctors. . . . Consequently, all the business and money details of All the Year Round devolve upon me. And I have to get them up, for I have never had experience of them." At length, it became evident that Wills would never be able to resume his duties at *All the Year Round*. Making the best of Wills's retirement and looking ahead to his own, Dickens installed his oldest son, Charles Junior, as his new sub-editor.

Meanwhile, what of Ellen?

After the pocket diary's day-to-day record of Dickens and "N" in Slough, Peckham, and London in 1867, his life with her after his return from America again fades into twilight.

But occasional flashes of evidence show that she remained his cynosure, and his chief destination away from home and office. He continued to spend time with her every week.

Thursday in particular became an inviolable evening with Ellen, a routine beginning immediately upon his return. After their week-long reunion, he had spent two or three days at Gad's Hill and then returned to London. That Thursday, he sent a quick note to Georgina informing her that "Tomorrow I will come to Gad's by some train from New Cross"—the station on the South Eastern line closest to Peckham. He no doubt spent the night with Ellen at Windsor Lodge, and then a leisurely morning afterwards: "I will come . . . either by the train that leaves London about mid-day, or by afternoon train."

His readings manager Dolby described Dickens's routine that summer: "The early days of the week were devoted to business pur-poses; Mr. Dickens, on these days, taking up his residence at the office in London, returning to 'Gad's' with his guests, as a rule, on Friday, and remaining there until the following Monday, when all returned to London together in a saloon carriage." But Dolby tactfully omitted mention of Dickens's regular interlude between his business in London and weekend house parties at Gad's Hill. Thursday was his regular day at *All the Year Round*; afterwards he invariably retreated to Windsor Lodge. His correspondence during the summer of 1868 is sprinkled with excuses for avoiding other engagements on Thursday:

> "I have a particular engagement at half past 5 to day [Thursday], but I pledge myself beforehand to any appoint-ment you may make for tomorrow afternoon." (June 25)
>
> "Unfortunately, although I come to town on Thursday next, I am engaged for that evening. . . ." (July 12)

"On Thursday I have people to see and matters to attend to. . . ." (July 21)

"I should have . . . 'made an effort' to come to you, but that I am engaged to dine out tomorrow [Thursday] at a semi-business dinner. . . ." (August 5)

"Unfortunately I am obliged to dine in London on Thursday. It is a business engagement in association with my journal and I am specially bound to keep it." (September 1)

That these sacrosanct Thursday evenings had nothing to do with business, however, is made clear by a note he wrote Wills that summer, dated: "P Friday Thirty First July, 1868." "P," as Wills knew, was Peckham. "I had such a hard day at the office yesterday," Dickens explained, "that I had not time to write you before I left"—and we can imagine him, after a tiring day of editorial labors, so eager to be off to Windsor Lodge on Thursday afternoon that he bolts from the Wellington Street office and takes a hansom cab straight to Linden Grove, Peckham, to enjoy the lingering July evening with his beloved Nelly, sitting together under the sumac tree in the garden, with the lindens throwing long shadows, "The Braid" purling nearby, and the ripening grain glowing in the late sun—paradise enough.

Tennyson's Ulysses, home from the Trojan War after his long odyssey, soon grows restless for further wandering:

> I cannot rest from travel. . . .
> How dull it is to pause, to make an end,
> To rust unburnished, not to shine in use!
> As though to breathe were life!
>
> ("Ulysses")

So too Dickens. Scarcely back from his exhausting readings in America, he and Dolby, who replaced Wills as his factotum and confidant, started to plan his next series of public readings, which he had decided on while still in America.

Two strong and opposing impulses moved Dickens during his final years. One was love of Ellen; the other, restlessness. Ellen focused him, centered him, restored him; but he was driven as well to keep striving and wandering. Henry Wadsworth Longfellow later claimed to recall Dickens in America as "very restless, as if driven by fate—*fato profugus*" (quoting Virgil's description of Aeneas). Perhaps the restlessness Longfellow detected was simply Dickens's eagerness to return to Ellen; but in any case, once back in England he was soon restless again.

After his exhausting months in America, Gad's Hill seemed paradisal. "What with travelling, reading night after night, and speechmaking day after day, I feel the peace of the country beyond all expression," he wrote shortly after his return, and a few weeks later, in a high-spirited letter to Annie Fields, he extolled the bucolic charms of Gad's Hill with Wordsworthian joy:

> Divers birds sing here all day, and the nightingales all night. The place is lovely, and in perfect order. I have put five mirrors in the Swiss châlet (where I write) and they reflect and refract in all kinds of ways the leaves that are quivering at the windows, and the great fields of waving corn, and the sail-dotted river. My room is up among the branches of the trees; and the birds and the butterflies fly in and out, and the green branches shoot in, at the open windows, and the lights and shadows of the clouds come and go with the rest of the company. The scent of the flowers, and indeed of everything that is growing for miles and miles, is most delicious.

Yet in the same letter he remarked that he was already planning a tour of farewell readings.

He continued to improve Gad's Hill, expensively, but spent less time there. During his final reading tour, he wrote to a Swiss friend:

> You wouldn't recognize Gads Hill now; I have so changed it, and bought land about it. And yet I often think that if Mary were to marry (which she won't), I should sell it, and go genteelly vagabondizing over the face of the earth.

His responsibilities to his daughters, to Georgina, and to his sons were a strain. To a request for financial assistance, he replied that "the train I have to drag through life has become so long and heavy" that he could not oblige. He had discarded his wife, but he could not discard the rest of his family, nor did he wish to. Yet his obligations, both domestic and financial, competed with his time with Ellen.

Novel-writing had become a secondary or even tertiary source of income, subordinate to the steady profits of *All the Year Round*, to reprints of his novels, and especially to the lucrative readings. He was eager to mine this latter vein of income while his health allowed. In October 1868, less than six months after returning from America, he began his final ("for ever and ever") tour, with 103 "Farewell Readings" planned for England, Scotland, and Ireland, to extend through May the following year.

During these months, he read in provincial cities three or four times each week, returning to London every week or two for a few days; every other Tuesday he gave a reading in London. He took extended breaks in November, during the Christmas season, in February, and during Holy Week. Otherwise, he went "tearing about the country," giving multiple readings every week. In December he journeyed to Scotland for readings, in January to Ireland, in February back to Scotland. By the end he had read in twenty-five different cities and traveled many thousands of miles by rail, even while still subject to Staplehurst anxieties on fast trains.

The public readings were forced on him by the heavy train of responsibilities he was dragging, but they were also an outlet for his restlessness. He needed the exhausting activity as much as he needed the money. "I am perpetually counting the weeks before me to be 'read' through, and am perpetually longing for the end of them," he mused during his 1868-69 reading tour; "and yet I sometimes wonder whether I shall miss something when they are over." Looking beyond the readings, he wondered if even then he would be able to rest: "I have a wild fancy that I shall sometimes try to be idle afterwards, but it is one of the many things I have never been able to do yet." He could not long relax, even at Windsor Lodge with Ellen; he must be working and moving and pushing himself. His fantasy of selling Gad's Hill and vagabondizing was probably a vision of wandering about Europe with Ellen—free of all the hard work, free of domestic obligations, perhaps free of the English proprieties forcing him to keep Ellen hidden. It was a fantasy that integrated his two conflicting motives, restlessness and Ellen.

As if his ambitious road show were not strain enough, he decided to add a new reading to his repertory, a sensational re-enactment of Bill Sikes's murder of Nancy in *Oliver Twist*. His decision to adapt this violent scene was baffling but also characteristic. From a prudential point of view, it was a gratuitous strain on his health and energies, when his existing repertory already filled the houses. "It seems as though we could fill Saint Pauls," he reported of the "astonishing houses" in London before the *Twist* reading was even introduced. The cautious Dolby and others counseled against the new reading.

But Dickens was insistent. The previous year, after hearing him read in Boston, Ralph Waldo Emerson had gravely pondered the phenomenon and concluded (he informed Annie Fields) that Dickens "has too much talent for his genius, it is a fearful locomotive to which he lies bound and can never be free from it nor set at rest. You . . . would persuade me that he is a genial creature full of sweetness and amenities and superior to his talents, but I fear he is harnessed to them." (Dickens himself liked to predict that he would die "in harness.") Emerson's ominous observation uncannily anticipated Dickens's willful enslavement to the Sikes-and-Nancy reading. Delighted with its electrifying effect, he gleefully bludgeoned his audiences with horrors, though each performance left him knocked out with exhaustion. With an ambiguous mix of facetiousness and ferocity, he often identified himself with Sikes: "I murdered the girl from Oliver Twist last night in a highly successful and bloodthirsty manner," for example, and (declining an invitation), "I have a great deal of Murdering before me yet, and social pleasure must yield to it!"

Was Ellen, like his more mundane social pleasures, sacrificed to all this Murdering? Where did she fit into all the traveling and performing of these months?

He certainly saw less of her than he otherwise would have. But amidst the whirl of his touring, she remained at the center of his affections, and he probably managed to see her weekly, or at least whenever he was in or passing through London.

In early November 1868, for example, shortly after he began his reading tour, she was one of the first to hear the new *Oliver Twist* reading, in a private performance probably at Windsor Lodge. "I . . . tried it," he wrote in a long Christmas letter to the Fieldses, "merely sitting over the fire in a chair, upon two ladies separately, one of whom was Georgina." The other was transparently Ellen, as the Fieldses would easily guess; it testifies to Dickens's caution that he avoided naming her even in writing to reliable and sympathetic friends. The two ladies, Dickens reported, "both said—'O good Gracious if you are going to do *that*, it ought to be seen; but it's awful.'" This was just the response he wished; the Sikes-and-Nancy reading seems to have been designed to thrill and appall women especially. That Georgina and Ellen should be the first witnesses of this lurid experiment suggests their role as his two closest intimates; that they should witness it separately suggests their reigns in distinctly different spheres of his life.

Despite his epistolary caution, his letters betray hints of other visits to Ellen. His last out-of-town reading before Christmas 1868, for instance, was in Edinburgh, on December 19; on the following day, he returned directly to London. But before leaving Edinburgh, he declined the offer of a theater box in London, explaining that "as I do not leave Scotland until Sunday morning [the twentieth], and have to make a visit on my way home, I cannot be in town in sufficient time to accept the box you place at my disposal." He reached London in plenty of time to see the play, however; the visit "on my way home" was certainly to Peckham. He may have taken Ellen to another theater on the same evening, for a few days later he reported that "the other night I went into the new theatre in Long Acre"—for a burlesque, "I am sorry to add." As the burlesque seems not to have been his own choice, he was perhaps indulging a whim of Ellen's.

Following the Christmas holidays, he did not see Gad's Hill for the first four months of the new year, 1869, but he managed to see Ellen often. Soon after Christmas, for example, he wrote Dolby that "We propose to change the Venue to Verrey's on Monday; and to take a snug Private Box for a pantomime." It seems unlikely that the snugness was intended for an intimate evening with Dolby himself, and likely that the "we" making plans for the evening were himself and Ellen. He had taken her to Verrey's on their last night together before he left for America, and this latter dinner at Verrey's was also a farewell, for two days later he left for Ireland. This time he was gone only ten days, but he was as eager to return to London as if he had been gone six months, excusing himself from a dinner invitation in Belfast by insisting that "I MUST BE in London on the morning of Monday the 18th"—though he seems to have had no particular engagements that day, apart from seeing Ellen.

Her thirtieth birthday on March 3, 1869, was a notable event, and he started thinking about it well beforehand. In January he wrote of an *Oliver Twist* reading that "I do not commit the murder again in London, until Tuesday, the 3rd of March"—March 3 was so much on his mind that he mistook the date of the reading, which was actually Tuesday the second of March. Three weeks before the signal birthday, he reminded Wills: "Don't forget your engagement with me to dinner on Wednesday the 3rd of March." When Georgina celebrated her birthday in January, Dickens was out of town.

During the latter years of the 1860s, his health and strength began perceptibly to wane. His response was characteristic: to push himself to the edge of collapse, and sometimes beyond; to retreat and recoup for a time; and then begin again. In 1866, for example, he admitted to Forster that "For some time I have been very unwell," diagnosing the problem as "some degeneration of some function of the heart. . . . I have noticed for some time a decided change in my buoyancy and hopefulness—in other words, in my usual 'tone.' But tonics have already brought me round"—and in the next sentence he announced that after a three-year recess he was resuming public readings.

He suffered off and on from various disorders: neuralgia, piles, a shin splint, nervous anxiety on fast trains; most frustrating for an enthusiastic walker, he was recurrently bothered by gouty symptoms, first in one foot, then the other. In America, the pain and swelling had become so severe that for a time he couldn't walk. He attributed the problem to walking with wet feet in deep snow, but the complaint outlasted the New England winter. During his farewell tour in England, he was again lamed by a painfully inflamed left foot, and in February 1869 he was forced to cancel his readings for a week because he couldn't walk out onto the platform. When he resumed, he chose with perverse overexertion to do "four Murders in one week"—his exhausting *Oliver Twist* reading. "There was something of almost willful exaggeration, of a defiance of any possible overfatigue . . . in the feverish sort of energy with which these readings were entered upon and carried out," his eldest son remembered. With Time's wingèd chariot hurrying near, Dickens was incapable of husbanding his strength.

How much of this fierce resistance to aging sprang from a troubled awareness of the age difference between himself and Ellen? When he had met her a decade earlier, he had been a vigorous forty-five-year-old man, and her own youthfulness made him feel even younger. Now in the spring of 1869 he was fifty-seven, felt his age, and looked older. When Ellen, Wills, and he (and probably Dolby) dined together on March 3 that year to celebrate her thirtieth birthday, she was an attractive young woman in her prime.

In *David Copperfield* twenty years earlier, Dickens had imagined a dottery old man, ironically named Doctor Strong, married to a much younger wife. Now he had no need to guess at the feelings of an aging man in love with a young woman.

The next month, he was struck by his most serious medical problem yet. From Blackburn, a cotton-mill city in Lancashire to which his reading tour took him in April, he wrote to his London physician in alarm: "Is it *possible* that anything in my medicine can have made me extremely uncertain of my footing (especially on the left side) and extremely indisposed to raise my hands to my head?" He found himself (he later told Forster) "extremely giddy, and extremely uncertain of my sense of touch, both in the left leg and the left hand and arms." His physician hastened to Blackburn and solicited a second opinion, and together the two doctors insisted that the readings be stopped at once and the rest of the tour canceled. Dickens did not dispute their judgment. Neither he nor they seem to have realized that he had suffered a mild stroke: "a weakness and deadness . . . all *on the left side*," as he described the symptoms; "if I don't look at anything I try to touch with my left hand, I don't know where it is." He ordinarily assumed that by hard work and strength of will he could force his way through any difficulty; now his ready concurrence with his doctors' orders to abandon his reading tour suggests how exhausted and "greatly shaken" he felt.

Ellen is unlikely often to have accompanied him on his out-of-town reading journeys. During the winter, while Dickens was usually out of town on readings, she and her mother took lodgings in Worthing, on the south coast, perhaps for Mrs. Ternan's health. But Ellen plainly attended at least one of Dickens's readings, for in June 1869, a few weeks after his tour had been truncated, the Fieldses visited England and stayed at Gad's Hill for a week, and Annie Fields recorded a curious item in her journal: "C.D. told J. [her husband] that when he was ill in his reading only Nelly observed that he staggered and his eye failed, only she dared to tell him."

With respect to Ellen, this is one of the most intriguing entries in Annie Fields's journals. It was the first time they refer to Ellen by name, but the use of Ellen's family nickname "Nelly" implies that Annie was already well familiar with her, at least by report and reputation. And the entry again shows Dickens confiding not in Annie directly, but in her husband.

But this tidbit from Annie's journals also reveals that Ellen was present at least once when Dickens betrayed troubling symptoms on the platform. Was she with him on tour in April when he was afflicted with dizziness and disorientation? There is no hard evidence that she was, and both Dickens and Dolby uniformly insisted that when on tour they were all business. It may be that Ellen went, rather, to his London readings on alternate Tuesdays and observed his unsteadiness on one of those occasions. He had read in London on April 13, four days before his seizure, and perhaps she detected ominous signs of the impending stroke at this performance. If so, his failure to mention any symptoms earlier than April 17 is puzzling, since he later described in detail the onset of his apoplexy, not only to his doctor but to several confidential correspondents including Forster and Georgina, to whom he could have indicated Ellen's observation.

Other circumstances suggest that she might actually have been with Dickens when he suffered his stroke on April 17. He had read in Leeds the evening before, a Friday. He often read on Saturdays, but this weekend he was free: he would not read again until Monday, in Blackburn. With two open days, he might have caught a late train

back to London after his Friday reading and spent the weekend at
Windsor Lodge before returning to Blackburn on Monday for his
reading that evening; he often dashed back to London when he had
a free day or two, especially on weekends. Why would he want to
spend two or three idle days with Dolby in the Midlands? But rather
than returning to London that weekend, he made an excursion to
Chester with Dolby, and with Dolby alone—according to Dolby's later
account. But the note Dickens sent Georgina from Leeds, giving his
itinerary for the next several days, has lost two or three lines at the
end, victims of Georgina's scissoring: lines excised very likely because
they referred to Ellen.

That Ellen fails to appear in Dolby's account of his and Dickens's
excursion to Chester is no evidence of anything, moreover, as Dolby,
though knowing her well, never mentions her at all in his memoir.
Describing the visit, he instead mentions the charms of Chester's "old
walls and picturesque streets," and of nearby Mold, "a small and picturesque Welsh market-town." All this quaintness would scarcely have
appealed to Dickens by himself (or with only Dolby as a companion);
but it would have made for pleasant sightseeing with Ellen. As he
and Dickens took a Sunday carriage ride through the countryside to
Mold, Dolby recalled, the April day was delicious, and Dickens was
"greatly revived by the invigorating air, and the sight of the spring
blossoms." Might his spirits have been refreshed by Ellen beside him,
even more than by the zephyrs and flowers? Following the weekend
visit to Chester, he read twice more, on Monday and Tuesday, before
his doctors intervened. If Ellen observed his apoplectic symptoms at
one or both of these readings, her testimony might have carried as
much weight with Dickens as his official medical advice.

Abandoning the reading tour, he made a show of restored health
and optimism. Refusing to acknowledge his giddiness and left-side
fogginess as anything serious, he explained them as a temporary
debility brought on by "immense exertions . . . and the constant jarring
of express trains." Several months later, he analyzed the experience:

I was engaged in a pursuit [his public readings] . . . which imposed a constant strain on the attention, memory, observation, and physical powers; and which involved an almost fabulous amount of change of place and rapid railway travelling. I had followed this pursuit through an exceptionally trying winter in an always trying climate [the American Northeast] and had resumed it in England after but a brief repose. Thus it came to be prolonged until, at length—and, as it seemed, all of a sudden—it so wore me out that I could not rely, with my usual cheerful confidence, upon myself to achieve the constantly recurring task, and began to feel (for the first time in my life) giddy, jarred, shaken, faint, uncertain of voice and sight and tread and touch, and dull of spirit.

A few weeks of rest would restore him: "Just as three days' repose on the Atlantic steamer [returning from America] made me, in my altered appearance, the amazement of the captain," he observed a few days later, "so this last week has set me up, thank God, in the most wonderful manner. The sense of exhaustion seems a dream already." His usual cheerful self-assurance was surging back.

Or so it seemed. Much of this cheer may have been feigned for family, friends, and public. His stroke had in fact brought his own mortality forcibly to his attention, and within days he sent his solicitor instructions for bringing his will up to date. A few days' rest may have set him up again, but he nonetheless determined to avoid traveling and to refuse any new commitments during the summer and autumn. Even Dickens's preternatural vitality was not inexhaustible—as he himself reluctantly acknowledged. Four months later, he would complain that "I have had some distressing indications that I am not yet as well as I hoped I was." Looking back after his death, Georgina would recall that "all who loved him" observed "that from this time forth he never regained his old vigour and elasticity."

The interruption of his reading tour was widely publicized, and he received many notes of sympathy and concern, one of particular interest. Thomas Trollope, Ellen's brother-in-law, wrote from Italy to invite him to Florence to recuperate.

As Trollope and his wife Fanny were more than aware of Dickens's connection with Fanny's sister Ellen, one wonders if their invitation to him included Ellen as well. It would have seemed strange were she to remain in England while Dickens was idling in Florence with her sister. After all, Ellen knew the Villa Trollope well, having spent a winter there a year earlier, and the door was probably open for her return at any time. The Trollopes' invitation to Dickens suggests that, condoning his affair with Ellen, they were willing not only to shelter them together, but to defy gossip among the English expatriates in Florence. Had the disapproving Fanny relented?

Of course, Trollope may have issued the invitation simply as a matter of form, expecting (and hoping) Dickens would decline. If he considered Trollope's offer at all, he must have reflected not only on steamy Florentine summers, but also on the discomfort of having Fanny as his hostess. Gad's Hill had cooler summers, while Windsor Lodge, Peckham, offered greater privacy with Ellen than the Villa Trollope. In any event, Dickens politely declined Trollope's invitation: "A thousand thanks for your kind tempting," he replied. "Through the summer and autumn I have promised to be as idle *as I can*, and to oscillate only between London and Gad's Hill. I am always to be in the air, but am to be as shy as possible of railway travelling."

As he was declining Tom Trollope's invitation, his American friends James and Annie Fields were on a ship steaming toward England. While they were still at sea, Dickens wrote to assure them of his robust health, promising that "I am good for all country pleasures with you." At the moment, they themselves were feeling far from robust—they were bad sailors and, without the promise of seeing Dickens, they would probably not have submitted themselves to ten purgatorial days of seasickness. Eager to return their hospitality of the year before, he had urged them to come, however, and a reunion with Dickens was the chief purpose of their journey—at least for Annie: "We try to hold ourselves disengaged whenever Mr. Dickens wishes to see us," she wrote during their first week in London, "because nothing and nobody else can be so interesting to us as he is." During their stay in London he took rooms at St. James's Hotel, Piccadilly, to be close at hand and to usher them about; later they would spend a busy week at Gad's Hill, enjoying country pleasures.

Sailing with the Fieldses (and also seasick) was twenty-year-old Mabel Lowell, the daughter of their friend the poet James Russell Lowell. Dickens had met her in Boston the year before and taken a flirtatious liking to her. "She is a charming little thing, and very retiring in manner and expression," he told Georgina. However retiring in expression she may have seemed, her letters home from England were often quite tart, giving a vivid glimpse of mid-Victorian England—and Dickens—through the eyes of a literate, genteel, occasionally pert American girl.

Annie Fields's journals and letters also document their weeks in England. Curious to see her idol Dickens in his domestic setting and to meet the women closest to him, she was gratified to be introduced to Georgina and Mary on her first day in London; the following day she met his daughter Katie, too. In June, the Fieldses with Mabel visited Gad's Hill for a week, and Dickens carried them around to the local sights: Rochester Castle and Cathedral; the army barracks and the trooping of the colors at Chatham; Cooling Church, out on the marshes, the setting for the opening scene of *Great Expectations*; Cobham Park, the handsome estate neighboring Gad's Hill; and Canterbury. Though enjoying all this, Annie was more interested in seeing Dickens at home and getting to know Gad's Hill's female cadre, Georgina and his two daughters.

Annie and Georgina had much in common: both were childless; both lived in a world of writers and publishing; both loved Dickens.

"I have the deepest respect for her," Annie wrote in her journal. "She has been able to do everything for C.D. in his home"—as Annie herself had tried to do for him in Boston. Her journals note various private conversations with Georgina. During a game of bowls on the lawn, "Miss Hogarth and I sat by while the game went forward"; later, "Miss Hogarth told me about the family, showed me the house, the cellar etc."; another time, "Went to Chatham Wednesday—that night talked with Miss Hogarth." Just as Dickens had adopted Fields as a confidant, Georgina began to confide in Annie. Apart from her own inclination to do so, she must have had Dickens's implicit or explicit permission, perhaps in acknowledgment of Annie's loyalty and discretion. When the Fieldses visited Gad's Hill again in October, shortly before returning to America, Annie and Georgina occupied an afternoon walk with another private talk: "C.D. & dear J went together. Miss Hogarth & I, Mabel Katie & Mamie with the rest. . . ."

As to what Georgina might have disclosed during these chats, Annie's journals are silent; but it is difficult to imagine that these two Dickens devotees did not discuss the idol they shared. And once on that subject, how could they avoid Dickens's own private cult of Ellen? While Annie's journals seldom mention Ellen, when she is mentioned it is with abbreviated familiarity—as "Nelly," as "E.L.T.," as "N.T."

One moment of reticence betrays Ellen's ghostly presence as the uncanny fifth member in a party of four. After a week at Gad's Hill, the Fieldses and Mabel Lowell returned to London by train. Dickens accompanied them. Along the way, "conversation flagged," Annie recalled, "and Jamie making a desperate attempt to revive it at one point C.D. laughed at what he called his wretched use of 'mustard' as a conversational aperient." Perhaps all were exhausted by a week of busy conviviality, but perhaps too everyone was silently pondering Dickens's impending exit—for he had announced that he was detraining early. "Dickens came in the cars with us nearly to London," Annie reported. "We separated without words in the carriage and he jumped out alone." Plainly he was not going to his Wellington Street office, for in that case he would have gone on to Charing Cross with the Fieldses. How did he explain his solitary, rather awkward departure? Or was no explanation needed? He had seen little or nothing of Ellen for a week, and no doubt left the train at New Cross station, within easy walking distance of Windsor Lodge.

Annie's tactful silence about his destination hints at a perfect awareness of where he was bound, and the sight of Dickens striding away from the station platform toward Windsor Lodge led her to melancholy reflections. "It is wonderful the fun and flow of spirits C. D. has for he is a sad man," she commented. "Sleepless nights come too often, oftener than they ever would to a free heart." Annie was very aware of Dickens's love for Ellen—may even have met her by now—and her insights, plainly stated, would be invaluable. But she remains discreet and oblique even in her journal. Presumably Dickens's sleepless nights were those spent on his "lonely couch" at Gad's Hill, yearning for the absent mistress of his captive heart. Perhaps, despite her admiration for Georgina, Annie came to see Gad's Hill as not simply a loving family home but also a prison. Whatever her analysis of Dickens's situation, however, she proffered no solution and took no sides. "The sorrows of such a nature are many," she concluded despairingly, "and must often seem more than he can bear."

Fascinated with Dickens and perhaps hearing much about the woman he loved, Annie would certainly have been glad to meet Ellen herself. Though scarcely bohemian, the Fieldses plainly condoned Dickens's relationship. Two of Annie's journal references to Ellen are sympathetic, even laudatory—her report, for example, that only Ellen noticed Dickens's stumbling on stage during a public reading and dared to tell him.

But there were problems with an introduction. Whatever the Fieldses' tolerance, Victorian gentlemen did not introduce their wives and daughters to women of irregular status. Acting *in loco parentis*, moreover, the Fieldses could scarcely expose young Mabel Lowell, daughter of a good friend, to a kept woman. Even had Annie wished to meet Ellen with Mabel somehow out of the way, Dickens might have demurred; he had flatly refused to introduce the aggressive Mrs. Dickinson two years earlier.

Nonetheless, he felt more warmly toward the Fieldses than toward Mrs. Dickinson, and might have wanted to bring together his closest American friends and his dear Nelly; they had heard much of each other. Obstacles crumbled before Dickens's strong will. Two short notes he wrote after the Fieldses arrived in London suggest that he might, after all, have brought the Fieldses and Ellen together.

The first note was to Fields, proposing a day of sightseeing:

> Suppose we give the weather a longer chance, and say Monday [24 May 1869] instead of Friday. I think we must be safer with that precaution. If Monday will suit you, I propose that we meet here [Dickens's Wellington Street office] that day,—your ladies and you and I,—and cast ourselves upon the stonyhearted streets. . . . We will dine here at six, and meet here at half past two. So IF you should want to go elsewhere after dinner, it can be done, notwithstanding.

The following day, he wrote a hasty and cryptic note to Georgina making further and overlapping plans for the same Monday:

> In case Monday next will do for you—to be taken up at 4, as last time—it will suit perfectly. I believe the Fields party dine with me at the office that day. . . . Let N know whether Monday is an engagement.

Whether or how these two engagements were related to one another is unclear. The first note seems plain enough; the second is filled with shadows. By whom is Georgina being "taken up," and where is she being taken? At four, Dickens himself will be out sightseeing with the Fieldses. Is Georgina to join them afterwards for dinner at his office apartments? Ellen's plans are somehow linked with Georgina's: is Ellen already engaged to dine with the Fields party, and is it Ellen who will pick up Georgina on her way to Wellington Street?

Even with these questions left unresolved, Dickens's note to Georgina shows Ellen at the center of his life, if not of the dinner. He has made his plans with her before inviting Georgina and without even being certain of the Fieldses: whatever the engagement, they and Georgina are contingent, Ellen primary. That Dickens can casually direct Georgina to communicate with "N" without needing to explain how to do so reveals that Ellen's address or whereabouts is well known to Georgina; it may even be that she will soon see Ellen to confirm the engagement in person. They are plainly in touch with each other, perhaps even see each other frequently when Georgina is in London.

Despite the obscurities of Dickens's laconic note to Georgina about the Monday plans, it suggests the possibility, even likelihood, that the Fieldses (with Mabel Lowell) dined that evening with Dickens and Ellen (and perhaps Georgina); the phrase "as last time" suggests that this would not even have been the first occasion. Dickens's office quarters would be a pleasantly snug location for a confidential dinner party.

Let's imagine such a dinner.

Dickens has spent the afternoon strolling through the Regent's Park Zoo with the Fieldses and Mabel. The idolatrous Fields would later gush:

> What a treat it was to go with him to the London Zoö-
> logical Gardens, a place he greatly delighted in at all times!
> . . . The delight he took in the hippopotamus family was
> most exhilarating. He entered familiarly into conversation
> with the huge, unwieldy creatures, and they seemed to
> understand him. . . . He chaffed with the monkeys, coaxed
> the tigers, and bamboozled the snakes, with a dexterity
> unapproachable.

And so on. Harassed by such strenuous joviality, the zoo animals ("unphilological inhabitants," in Fields's facetious phrase) no doubt rejoice to see Dickens depart. The Fieldses and Mabel return to their hotel to change for dinner; Dickens proceeds to his office on Wellington Street, where Georgina and Ellen await him. With Ellen is Mrs. Ternan, sixty-six years old and distinguished in appearance and manner; she has played Lady Macbeth and Desdemona, and offstage could pass for a dowager duchess. "With a fine face and figure were associated great grace and intelligence," an obituary notice would comment, "and her elocution was remarkably good." She is introduced to the Fields party as a long-time friend of Dickens whom he met when she acted with his friend the celebrated Shakespearean actor William Macready. Mrs. Ternan's visible refinement and connection to Macready recommend her. Introduced with her is Miss Ternan, her daughter, a great friend of Georgina and of Dickens's daughters. Miss Ternan's obvious familiarity with Georgina lends plausibility to this explanation. The Fieldses know how the case stands; young Mabel Lowell has no clue but thinks nothing about it; keen on good horses and old paintings, she cares not at all about old actresses and their spinster daughters. In her next letter home she will briefly mention the visit to the zoo with Mr. Dickens but ignore the dinner on Wellington Street. (In her journal, Annie Fields also passes over the dinner in silence.)

There is no cook at Wellington Street; dinner is ordered from a nearby restaurant. At home, Dickens's dinner always began with a glass of Chichester milk-punch and ended with a dish of toasted cheese. One guest at another dinner at Dickens's office recalled, however, that "we began with oysters, brought in fresh from Old 'Rule's' in Maiden Lane [near Covent Garden]. . . . The principal dish was a baked leg of mutton, the bone of which had been taken out, and the space supplied with oysters and veal stuffing." In the novel that Dickens began writing a few months after his dinner with the Fieldses, a lawyer named Grewgious orders dinner for himself and two guests in his bachelor chambers in London. Perhaps the dinner in Wellington Street followed the same lines:

> "And perhaps you wouldn't mind," said Mr. Grewgious [to his clerk], "stepping over to the hotel in Furnival's, and asking them to send in materials for laying the cloth. For dinner we'll have a tureen of the hottest and strongest soup available, and we'll have the best made-dish that can be recommended, and we'll have a joint (such as a haunch of mutton), and we'll have a goose, or a turkey, or any little stuffed thing of that sort that may happen to be in the bill of fare—in short, we'll have whatever there is on hand."

(Dickens's arrangements would have been less extemporaneous; he has no doubt ordered the dinner in advance.)

> Bazzard [the clerk] returned, accompanied by two waiters—an immoveable waiter, and a flying waiter; . . . The flying waiter, who had brought everything on his shoulders, laid the cloth with amazing rapidity and dexterity; while the immoveable waiter, who had brought nothing, found fault with him in secret nudges. The flying waiter then highly polished all the glasses he had brought, and the immoveable waiter looked through them. The flying waiter then flew across Holborn for the soup, and flew back again, and then took another flight for the made-dish, and flew back again, and then took another flight for the joint and poultry, and flew back again, and between whiles took supplementary flights for a great variety of articles, as it was discovered from time to time that the immoveable waiter had forgotten them all. . . .

Dinner conversation might flow in any of several directions: the theater; the Fieldses' sightseeing in London and their plans for touring

Europe during the next several months (Ellen and her mother have spent much time in France and Italy); Dickens's reading tours in America and more recently in Britain and Ireland; Gad's Hill, where the Fieldses and Mabel will soon visit; books and publishing; Alfred Tennyson, poet laureate, whom the Fieldses and Mabel are off to visit on the Isle of Wight the following day. There are no long silences: Dickens as host is eager to keep the party lively; the ladies are in good spirits; Fields is a great talker and storyteller.

> At the conclusion of the repast [in Grewgious's chambers], by which time the flying waiter was severely blown, the immoveable waiter gathered up the tablecloth under his arm with a grand air, and . . . looked on at the flying waiter while he set clean glasses round. . . .

The ladies rise and withdraw—although Dickens's Wellington Street apartment has no drawing room—while Dickens and Fields remain at table with brandy and cigars. But not for long: a friend recalled that when Dickens was host, "there was no sitting by the men at the dinner-table after the ladies had left"—he was always quick to rise from the table and rejoin them. This evening he has assured Fields that the early dinner will allow the Fieldses and Mabel to go elsewhere that evening, but for them Dickens himself is the chief attraction, and after a tiring day of sightseeing and visiting they may be content to return to their hotel for the night.

Did this notional dinner party actually occur? Did Annie Fields ever meet the woman so dearly loved by the man she herself worshiped?

There is no certain answer, but one ambiguous footnote, to these questions. Two and a half years later, in December 1871, Annie recalled in her journal Dickens's arrival in Boston for his reading tour, four years earlier—for her, a vanished golden age. He had been dead for a year and a half now, but she nursed her memory of him in a way that recalls Dickens's own reveries about Mary Hogarth after her death. "Dear, dear Dickens," she wrote: "as this season returns, come back not only thoughts of him but visions of his presence. I see him standing beside us. I see his eyes looking into mine."

But these visionary thoughts brought to mind a more specific news item: "I heard quite accidently to human eyes the other day of N.T. being in Rome. . . ." From Dickens, her thoughts have turned naturally to Ellen, the abbreviation "N.T." suggesting friendly familiarity. From Dickens's connection with Ellen, Annie's thoughts then moved on to her own connection with Ellen, for both women had been widowed, in a way, by his death. "I feel the bond there is between us," she wrote. "She must feel it too."

But why would Annie Fields expect Ellen to feel a bond with her, unless they were acquainted? How would Ellen know that Annie felt bereaved by Dickens's death, unless she had learned of Annie's affection for Dickens from Annie herself? If Ellen had known of Dickens's most fervent American admirer only anecdotally, she would probably never have given Annie a second thought. Annie's reflection that Ellen must feel the bond between them argues that they had met and talked together in London the year before Dickens's death.

"I wonder if we shall ever meet," Annie mused finally, wistfully, pondering the mutual sympathy between herself and Ellen. But by "ever meet," did she mean meet for a first time, or meet again, as sisters together wearing black for Dickens?

This perplexing rumination in her journal is Annie Fields's last surviving comment on Ellen Ternan.

The Fieldses departed from London on a gray day in October 1869, Dickens bidding them farewell at the station as they boarded a train for Liverpool. "I knew then," Annie later wrote in her journal, ". . . that we should never meet again and though we shed no tears, the utter dreariness of that morning was something I remember with a shudder." As the train started forward, Dickens ran a few steps along the platform to keep up with their carriage, and then "all was over—except eternity."

Fortunately, Annie's grief was soon eclipsed by the more mundane misery of seasickness. Before their first night at sea, the Fieldses and Mabel "were wretched enough all of us, dear Mabel first and worst."

Back in Boston, Annie continued to dwell on Dickens—remembering him, wondering about him, hoping for letters from him, pitying him. On the last day of 1869, "I think of him much[,] indeed we both talk of him when alone continually and after waking in the night we follow him and look in his dear suffering face and long, long for what, we hardly know."

And of course she continued to revolve Ellen's role in his life. Early in 1870 Dickens's friend Charles Fechter arrived in America, and in February he was in Boston playing Hamlet. Lunching together one day, he and the Fieldses talked of Dickens and his sorrows—Annie's leading theme in these latter days. Fechter attributed Dickens's disappointments to his children, but Annie's thoughts flew to his two women. "Poor Miss Hogarth spends her life hoping to comfort and care for him," but to no avail. "I never felt more keenly her anomalous and unnatural position in the household." Annie continued: "Not one [at the luncheon] mentioned her name; they could not dare, I suppose lest they might do her wrong." Abruptly, the "her" seems no longer to refer to the steady, devoted sister-in-law, but to the disruptive mistress: the unnameable woman must be Ellen, for no one would hesitate to mention Georgina's name (Dickens himself had talked of her frequently with the Fieldses). "Ah how sad a name it must be to those who love him best," Annie lamented. "Dear dear Dickens!" This oblique comment is the only time that Annie Fields's journals hint any disapproval of Ellen.

In the autumn of 1869, Dickens began writing his fifteenth novel, *The Mystery of Edwin Drood*.

He began reluctantly. Since finishing *Our Mutual Friend* four years earlier, he had spent almost all his creative energies on his public readings. "While so engaged," he wrote early in 1868, "I cannot write," and at that point he had no plans for a novel: "What I may do next in the way of fiction, or when I may do it, are questions, therefore, on which I cannot bind myself in any way." He was then on his American tour; within six months of his return he would embark on a tour of a hundred more readings in the British Isles, and according to Dolby he again entertained the idea of reading in Australia, where two of his sons had emigrated. So long as his health held out, he was eager to continue public readings, content to defer novel-writing. Only when compelled to abandon his reading desk in April 1869 did he resign himself to his writing desk. The four years since he had finished *Our Mutual Friend* was already the longest interval between novels since his first novel more than thirty years earlier. Uncertain that he was equal to another twenty-number serial like *Our Mutual Friend*, he planned its successor for only twelve monthly numbers. As it turned out, even that was too hopeful.

The ever-rolling stream to which Dickens liked to consign his fictional characters was bearing him along rapidly. Sending his youngest son Plorn off to Australia in September 1868, he wrote him in farewell: "I need not tell you that I love you dearly, and am very, very sorry in my heart to part with you. But this life is half made up of partings, and these pains must be borne." Putting Plorn on a train in London, he knew he was unlikely to see him again (nor did he). "It was a hard parting at the last," he told his friend Fechter. "He seemed to me to become once more my youngest and favourite little child as the day drew near, and I did not think I could have been so shaken." To Dolby, who had young children, he wrote: "When you come (if you ever do) to send your youngest child thousands of miles away for an indefinite time, and have a rush into your soul of all the many fascinations of the last little child you can ever dearly love, you will have a hard experience of this wrenching life."

When his younger brother Fred died the following month, Dickens's grief was more temperate: "a wasted life," he remarked candidly. Yet like Plorn's departure, Fred's death took away a once fondly loved child: "I am truly grateful to you, in remembrance of him," he thanked Fred's physician for his deathbed care. "How tenderly I write these words you can scarcely imagine, unless you know that he was my favorite when he was a child, and that I was his tutor when he was a boy."

To the end, Ellen remained his consolation and his passion. His love for her, he had written, "belongs to my life and probably will only die out of the same with the proprietor"—and this proved the case.

She remains only intermittently visible during the last year of his life. That almost all his letters are dated from either Gad's Hill or his office, and almost none from Peckham, conceals how much time he spent with her there. In August 1869, for instance, he assured one correspondent that "any communication from you will find me with little delay. I may not be here at the moment, but in that case shall be merely cruising about the country within a short circuit, and shall be in town every week." Woven into this disingenuous comment are the three loci of Dickens's last years: "here" was Gad's Hill; "town" was London, to attend to *All the Year Round* and other business; while "cruising about the country" took him straight to Ellen in Peckham.

His inner circle—Georgina, his two daughters, Forster, and Ellen herself—maintained their conspiracy of silence until his death and beyond, excising virtually all references to her in the letters they did not destroy. Two fellow conspirators, however, his subeditor Wills and readings manager Dolby, left behind a few letters which escaped Georgina's scissors. Though often fragmentary and coded, Dickens's occasional allusions to Ellen in these letters show how thoroughly she was woven into the fabric of his life during his last years, and how she permeated his imagination.

In the summer of 1869, for example, after much deliberation, he arrived at a title for his new novel, *The Mystery of Edwin Drood*, and to celebrate "he gave a little dinner of three," Dolby recalled, "a sort of christening party, at which we drank but one toast, 'Success to the

Mystery of Edwin Drood.'" Dolby's coy mention of a third, unnamed member of this cozy dinner party guarantees that it was Ellen.

At the end of September, Dickens traveled to Birmingham to give an address at the annual banquet of the Birmingham and Midland Institute. Several weeks before, he had written to the Institute's founder, Arthur Ryland, that "I shall not be able to profit by your kind offer of hospitality when I come to Birmingham. . . . I must come down in time for a quiet dinner at the Hotel with my 'Readings' Secretary Mr. Dolby—and must away next morning. Besides having a great deal in hand just now (the trifle of a new book among other things), I shall have visitors from abroad here at that time," and so on. Did Ryland wonder about this elaborate excuse-making? Well he might, for rather than hurrying back to London the morning after his speech, Dickens instead enjoyed a day of sightseeing with Ellen: "I have a notion, if it will suit you," he had informed Dolby, "of supplementing the speechmaking with a small N excursion next Day to Stratford, or Kenilworth, or both, or somewhere else, in a jovial way." Dolby need not plan on keeping them company, he added. As Dickens scarcely needed his readings manager to manage a single banquet speech, it seems likely that the obliging Dolby was brought to Birmingham principally to escort Ellen while Dickens himself was in public view. Did any of the Birmingham worthies assembled to hear his wisdom on the subject of "Education for the People" suspect that the attractive young woman sitting with Dolby was the great writer's mistress?

Perhaps even stronger evidence of Ellen's regular presence in Dickens's life emerges from casual allusions to her in his letters, all the more suggestive just because they are so casual. Late in 1869, for example, he wrote to Dolby from his office: "In answer to your enquiry to N—I do not *think* I shall be here until Wednesday in the ordinary course." Evidently Ellen had seen Dolby recently, and Dickens himself even more recently—both encounters being routine enough to require no comment; Dolby, moreover, expected that Ellen would be familiar with Dickens's plans for the week, or at least knew that she would see Dickens soon enough to relay his inquiry. On the Wednesday in question, he attended a play in London, probably with Ellen, then he disappeared for two days—again, probably to Peckham with Ellen.

Early in the new year, 1870, he briefly resumed his public readings, giving a dozen final performances, all in London to avoid the stress and wear of railway travel. Two of the readings were special matinées for actors and actresses unable to attend evening readings. "The patient was in attendance and missed you," he wrote to Wills after the second of these afternoon performances. "I was charged with all manner of good and kind remembrance." The following week, he reported that "I have just come back (as you may possibly have heard from Dolby) after 2 days in the country"—"the country" being code for somewhat rural Peckham. The following month, he invited Wills to "a certain small dinner of four, next Thursday the 3rd. March at Blanchard's in Regent Street at 6 sharp"—to celebrate Ellen's thirty-first birthday; Dolby probably made the fourth.

Early in May, just a month before his death, he employed one of the hoariest of his Ellen alibis: "In addition to my usual engagements, I have been (and still am), in attendance on a sick friend at some distance," and he nursed the sick friend for several more days. The following Thursday he was again at Windsor Lodge. The following week, two weeks before his death, he was "away" for three days. And just the week before his death, he apologized for his tardiness in replying to a letter by explaining that he had just returned to Gad's Hill the night before, "having come here from town circuitously, to get a little change of air on the road"—the last of his evasive alibis for visits to Ellen.

Such scattered glimpses of her, each one inconclusive by itself, together assume a distinct pattern. While her inconspicuous footprint in the documentary record may make her seem an interesting but peripheral figure in the background of Dickens's last years, she was in fact center stage—as much as he, enacting Bill Sikes bludgeoning Nancy in the glare of gaslight, was the focus of the rapt audiences at his readings. Except during his months in America, he saw her frequently and intimately, at a great cost of time, trouble, secrecy, and deception. Regularly scheming to be with her, he eagerly took time from his busy and demanding life to vanish in her company. He maintained her in comfort, and set aside generous sums in trust for her. If not a notably faithful husband, he proved a loyal and ardent lover, never swerving from his devotion to his beloved Nelly, or from his desire and determination to be with her. Near or far, she was on his mind constantly.

In action and in imagination, he doted on her. Despite the frequency of their meetings and the many days they spent together—despite their ménage in Slough and then Peckham—he never took her for granted. She remained the magic circle of one. Until his death, she was his "Nelly"—"my dear," "my dear girl," "my dear Patient," "my Darling." Georgina Hogarth might be "the best and truest friend man ever had," but "friend" reveals the limits of her influence. Ellen reigned over regions of his imagination that Georgina never visited.

Writing to the Fieldses early in 1870, Dickens hoped that they had heard about "the little touch of Radicalism I gave them at Birmingham" in a speech the week before. There is something slightly absurd about a wealthy and cosseted celebrity boasting of his Radicalism (in the same letter, he announced that "The Conservatory [at Gad's Hill] is completed, and is a brilliant success:—but an expensive one!"). A legacy of the 1830s, Dickens's Radicalism was by 1870 as dated as Mr. Pickwick's breeches, and his "radical" Birmingham speech amounted to little more than commonplace populist sentiment. Far more revolutionary than anything in his political views was his intrigue with the young woman who had accompanied him to Birmingham, clandestinely, a year earlier. Under the influence of that twelve-year fascination and devotion, Dickens had gone back to school.

His gave his last public reading in March 1870. "For some fifteen years," he said in his concluding remarks, "I have had the honour of presenting my own cherished ideas before you for your recognition;

and, in closely observing your reception of them, have enjoyed an amount of artistic delight and instruction which, perhaps, is given to few men to know." In the future, to his regret, he would have to forgo the immediacy of his audiences' tears, laughter, and applause, and confine his performances to his study. During those years of readings,

> I have been uniformly cheered by the readiest response, the most generous sympathy, and the most stimulating support. Nevertheless, I have thought it well, at the full flood-tide of your favour, to retire upon those older associations between us, which date from much further back than these, and henceforth to devote myself exclusively to that art which first brought us together.

In short, as *David Copperfield*'s Mr. Micawber would have said, it was back to writing. The end of his readings, forced upon him by poor health, could only have heightened his awareness of ebbing strength, of time's irresistible current moving him along, of the final act beginning.

And as he gave his last public reading in March 1870, the first installment of his final novel, *The Mystery of Edwin Drood*, was about to appear.

It is tempting to compare *The Mystery of Edwin Drood* with *The Tempest*, traditionally considered Shakespeare's valedictory, though Dickens could not have known that *Drood* would be his final work and scarcely intended to leave it only half-finished. But it was written with a heightened awareness of mortality and of endings. "In this brief life of ours, it is sad to do almost anything for the last time," he had said after his final public reading in Boston two years earlier; and at his last public reading ever, he concluded: ". . . from these garish lights I vanish now forever, with a heartfelt, grateful, respectful, and affectionate farewell."

There is a flavor of nostalgia in *The Mystery of Edwin Drood*: to begin, its principal setting, the cathedral town of Cloisterham, reproduces the cathedral town of Dickens's childhood, Rochester. When people who grew up in Cloisterham "come back from the outer world at long intervals . . . the striking of the Cathedral clock, and the cawing of the rooks from the Cathedral tower, are like the voices of their nursery time." Yet the chief issues in *Drood* are not memory and youth, but love and death. Death is a brooding, ominous presence, lurking in the menace of the villain John Jasper and in uncertainty about his nephew Edwin's fate. ("Dead? Or Alive?" was one title Dickens considered.) The tower of Cloisterham cathedral offers a vista of life and death juxtaposed, and of life flowing toward death, naturally and inevitably:

> . . . they look down on Cloisterham, fair to see in the moonlight: its ruined habitations and sanctuaries of the dead, at the tower's base: its moss-softened red-tiled roofs and red-brick houses of the living, clustered beyond: its river winding down from the mist on the horizon, as though that were its source, and already heaving with a restless knowledge of its approach towards the sea.

To those who grew up in Cloisterham, "it has happened in their dying hours afar off, that they have imagined their chamber floor to be strewn with the autumnal leaves fallen from the elm trees in the Close: so have the rustling sounds and fresh scents of their earliest impressions, revived, when the circle of their lives was very nearly traced, and the beginning and end were drawing close together"—an image drawn from Dickens's memory of his sister Fanny on her deathbed twenty years earlier. His recollection shortly before his own death of Fanny's dying illusions seems curiously premonitory. Perhaps *Drood* is tinged with a presentiment that "the mouth of Old Time" was soon to swallow Dickens himself. Whether or no, he wrote the final words of

Drood only an hour or two before his fatal collapse. Whatever he had to say at the end of his life we must find in *Drood* or not at all.

Most of the commentary on the fragment has focused on the unsolved crime. The mystery plot is baffling: a sinister villain with an opium addiction, murderous opium fantasies, and a suspiciously long scarf; the unaccountable disappearance of the nephew he professes to love; the witch-like proprietress of an opium den who stalks the villain; a moonlit cathedral crypt; quicklime; a telltale ring; an incognito detective; genuine and false clues on every page—all invite the reader into a blind labyrinth. Even alive, Dickens kept the secret to himself—concealing it even in his working notes—and now it lies entombed forever (perhaps like Edwin Drood himself). As an insoluble riddle, *The Mystery of Edwin Drood* rather resembles life itself.

Nonetheless, there are clear indications of where the novel was going.

Its dark elements portend violence, treachery, murder—or at least a murderous attempt. The villain Jasper is always associated with darkness: ". . . a dark man of some six-and-twenty, with thick, lustrous, well-arranged black hair and whisker," his rooms "mostly in shadow"; he is a "shadow on the sun-dial," "setting, as it were, his black mark upon the very face of day"; he is nocturnal, and his nephew Drood disappears on a stormy night. Jasper's violence is barely suppressed. In a deleted manuscript passage, Jasper in an opium fit directs his nephew Edwin to "Put those knives out at the door—both of them!"—because, he declares, they may attract lightning—though there is no sign of a storm. The two knives allude to *Macbeth*; but scarcely able to restrain himself from murdering his nephew on the spot, Jasper, unlike Macbeth, seems no half-hearted murderer.

Whether Jasper in fact murders Drood, and if so how and where, remain open questions, but one certainty is that for two pairs of characters the novel will end in marriage. In this respect, *The Mystery of Edwin Drood* more closely resembles Shakespearean comedy than it does *Macbeth*. Like *Twelfth Night*, for example, *Drood* features orphaned look-alike twins, a brother and sister of obscure origin cast up on a foreign shore, the sister much the stronger character in both play and novel. Shakespeare's comedies are usually animated by spirited, resourceful heroines, and while the next-to-last chapter of *Drood* would probably have been harrowing, the final chapter would have seen the novel's two heroines, Helena and Rosa, prevail.

As usual in Dickens's novels, it is the heroines who matter most.

The dark figure of the murderous Jasper glooms so ominously over the *Drood* fragment that it is surprising to discover that in searching for an illustrator, Dickens was apparently indifferent about the portrayal of Jasper and worried instead about that of his two heroines. His son-in-law, Katie's husband Charles Collins, was initially commissioned to illustrate *The Mystery of Edwin Drood*, and got as far as designing the wrapper cover for the monthly installments. But Collins was a sick man and could go no farther, and Dickens had to seek a replacement. At the recommendation of John Everett Millais, Dickens wrote to the young painter Luke Fildes: "I see . . . that you are an adept at drawing scamps," adding "send me some specimens of pretty ladies." Complying with this demand, Fildes submitted, in addition, a sketch he had drawn of a scene in *David Copperfield*. These samples were all very well, Dickens judged, but he still worried about Fildes's knack for drawing handsome heroines. Writing to his publisher Frederic Chapman, he complained that "there are many points of merit in the Copperfield design, but it is wanting in a sense of beauty." Lest Chapman should wonder why Fildes's sense of beauty was so critical, Dickens explained: "In the new book I have two beautiful and young women, strikingly contrasted in appearance, who will both be very prominent in the story." This declaration of the heroines' prominence is one of his few explicit statements about the novel.

One of these beautiful young heroines, Rosa, is a schoolgirl, her precise age unspecified but perhaps seventeen. Dickens stresses her diminutive cuteness and pampered immaturity. A painting of her on Jasper's walls is said to show "a blooming schoolgirl . . . her flowing brown hair tied with a blue riband, and her beauty remarkable for a quite childish, almost babyish, touch of saucy discontent, comically conscious of itself." She is "wonderfully pretty, wonderfully childish, wonderfully whimsical"; "a charming little apparition"; "an amiable, giddy, wilful, winning little creature." Her blue ribbon betrays her origins in Maria Beadnell; Rosa is the last of Dickens's many tributes to the girl who had enslaved him forty years earlier. He never lost his susceptibility to such girls.

But much the more potent of the two heroines is Rosa's counterpart, Helena Landless, a dark, tigerish character who could scarcely be less like the confectionery Rosa, or like David Copperfield's mild, fair Agnes. The deepest mystery of *The Mystery of Edwin Drood* is in fact not what has happened to Drood, but how to account for this last Dickens heroine, the darkest, fiercest, most exotic of all his heroines.

On her first appearance, Helena and her twin Neville are likened to feral animals, the clergyman Mr. Crisparkle noticing

> . . . something untamed about them both; a certain air upon them of hunter and huntress; yet withal a certain air of being the objects of the chase, rather than the followers. Slender, supple, quick of eye and limb; half shy, half defiant; fierce of look; an indefinable kind of pause coming and going on their whole expression, both of face and form, which might be equally likened to the pause before a crouch, or a bound.

A little later we hear of a childhood attempt of the twins to escape their cruel stepfather, with Helena intending to disguise herself as a boy; but "when I lost the pocket-knife with which she was to have cut her hair short," Neville recalls "how desperately she tried to tear it out, or bite it off." Two decades earlier, David Copperfield's Agnes had first appeared in a stained-glass glow of serenity, gentleness, and beatitude.

But Agnes had distinctly lacked sexual fire. Not so Helena, whose darkness and ferocity, her "wild" and "intense" qualities, betray a strong erotic nature. "An unusually handsome, lithe girl," she is "very dark, and very rich in color; . . . of almost the gipsy type." In his working notes, Dickens noted:

> Neville and Helena Landless
> Mixture of Oriental blood—or imperceptibly acquired mixture in them.
> Yes

"Oriental" here means Singhalese, the Landless twins having come from Ceylon. In Fildes's illustrations, authorized by Dickens, the Landlesses are distinctly un-English in features and shading, Helena with thick dark hair, heavy eyebrows, long eyelashes, strong aquiline nose, and keen, intense features—all of which qualities are more striking in juxtaposition with the insipid features and lighter coloring of Rosa. The darkening of Dickens's heroines over the years reveals his evolving fascination with the mysteries of erotic attraction. The domesticity, patience, mildness, and tranquility of *David Copperfield*'s Agnes had been embodied in fair coloring and stained-glass brightness; fifteen years later, *Our Mutual Friend*'s heroine Lizzie Hexam had been "a deep rich piece of colour, with the brown flush of her cheek and the shining lustre of her hair." Helena Landless is darker yet. As *Wuthering Heights*' Heathcliff embodied Emily Brontë's fascination with dark, fierce, violent male power, so Helena embodies Dickens's fascination with feminine eroticism.

Helena is not just dark and fierce, however; she is also feminine in the more usual softer sense. She possesses "womanly feeling, sense, and courage." Like most other Dickens heroines she nurtures a weak or troubled male, in Helena's case her brother Neville. She also attaches herself affectionately to the girlish Rosa. Though they are roughly the same age, Helena at once assumes an older-sister, almost maternal responsibility; already in their first private conversation Helena calls Rosa "My pretty one" and "My child!" Her "sisterly earnestness" confirms her warm feminine spirit, for both "sisterly" and "earnest" convey Dickens's strongest approbation. Rosa is a schoolgirl becoming womanly, but Helena, nominally a schoolgirl herself, is already a woman, gentle but formidable. When Rosa is overcome by Jasper's hypnotic glare and swoons in fright, Helena's nurturing qualities fuse with her ferocity:

> The lustrous gipsy-face drooped over the clinging arms and bosom, and the wild black hair fell down protectingly over the childish form. There was a slumbering gleam of fire in the intense dark eyes, though they were then softened with compassion and admiration. Let whomsoever it most concerned, look well to it!

The menacing last line promises that Helena will triumph in a climactic melodramatic confrontation with the arch-villain Jasper.

She is in fact paired with her antagonist Jasper, Dickens's most Heathcliff-like character. Jasper and Helena are both emphatically dark; they may even be kin, as one of the novel's proposed titles, "The Mystery in the Drood Family," perhaps hints. A more certain affinity than any blood tie, however, is their burning intensity. In a single early paragraph, Jasper "looks on intently" and shows "a look of intentness and intensity—a look of hungry, exacting, watchful, and yet devoted affection" for his nephew Drood, whom he regards with an "always concentrated" face. Helena yields nothing to him in intensity; in the space of a few pages, her face is "intent" on Jasper, her "masterful look was intent" upon Rosa, and we see her "intense dark eyes." They are matched against each other because they are so alike; but the sexual intensity that takes a violent turn in Jasper, in Helena is made fertile.

Unlike Helena, Ellen Ternan was golden-haired and gentle-natured, and never defied a brutish stepfather or confronted a murderous villain.

Yet the name "Helena Landless" echoes "Ellen Lawless" Ternan too closely to be accidental—perhaps Dickens and Ellen laughed at this private joke, and at the incongruity of the fierce Helena taking Ellen's name. But we may wonder if in fact the heroine is not indebted to the mistress in more than just her name.

Little is known about Ellen personally—her temperament, her manner, the flavor of her presence. What is certain, though, is that she had not only the youthful freshness and charms to captivate Dickens originally, but the intelligence and character to retain his affection beyond the first flush of his infatuation, and indeed until his death. In an 1867 letter, he had praised her "pride and self reliance which (mingled with the gentlest nature) has borne her, alone, through so much." His tribute is echoed in Mr. Crisparkle's praise of Helena:

> Every day and hour of her life since Edwin Drood's disappearance, she has faced malignity and folly . . . as only a brave nature well directed can. So it will be with her to the end. Another and weaker kind of pride might sink broken-hearted, but never such a pride as hers: which knows no shrinking, and can get no mastery of her.

As he gave these words to Helena's admirer, Mr. Crisparkle, did Dickens have Ellen's "pride and self-reliance" in mind? Very likely Helena's courage, like her name, obliquely honors Ellen.

Despite such glancing allusions, however, Helena resembles neither Ellen nor any other woman Dickens had ever known. For readers keen to identify the living originals of fictional characters, her character must prove a puzzle and an anomaly. She owes much to Ellen, certainly, but not in any straightforward likeness. Rather, like every Dickens heroine since *Oliver Twist*'s Rose Maylie three decades earlier, Helena embodies strong emotions and impulses within Dickens himself. If Rose had reflected his youthful adoration of a girl's ethereal spirit, Helena reflects his mature love of a richly embodied feminine soul—a woman.

Long after Dickens's death, his daughter Katie claimed that should his missing letters to Ellen ever turn up, they would reveal "his heart and soul burning like jewels in a dark place." In the absence of those jewel-like letters (not a single word Dickens wrote to Ellen is known to have survived), we have at any rate Helena Landless, his final and fiercest heroine, an embodiment of his own passionate love.

Helena seems destined for marriage to the robust, cheery, benevolent clergyman Mr. Crisparkle. Matched with such a worthy whiskered Victorian, could Helena have avoided tea-table respectability?—her gipsy shades blanched by his radiant virtues, her fiery passions quenched? Perhaps it was best for Helena, at least, that Dickens died before *Drood*'s final chapter married her to Crisparkle. Her unreconstructed character, dark and flaming, is a better monument to his love for Ellen Ternan.

CHAPTER 10

Four graves

On June 8, 1870, after a full day's work on *The Mystery of Edwin Drood* in the miniature chalet at Gad's Hill, Dickens returned to the house, wrote several notes, and did up his accounts in the library. At about six he sat down to dinner with Georgina. They were the only family at home. Dickens looked alarmingly strange and distraught; Georgina asked if he were ill. Rising from the table, he staggered a few steps, then dropped to the floor. He was lifted to a sofa that was brought into the dining room; doctors and family were summoned. His daughters Mary and Katie arrived from London later that night and prepared themselves and others for the end. "My dear father has had a stroke of paralysis & lies insensible," Mary briefly wrote a friend as she, Katie, and Georgina kept vigil.

Dickens disliked farewells and his sudden collapse obviated the need for any. He remained unconscious until he died the following day. "We were most thankful" that he was insensible as he lay dying, Mary remarked afterwards. "His mind would have been troubled about so many things."

Just a few days before his stroke he had ordered "four boxes of his usual cigars"—probably two hundred cigars—making provision for many more after-dinner smokes. Yet by several accounts, he had a foreboding that the end was near and had already made some fare-wells. He knew himself to be unwell, and believed strongly in uncanny presentiments.

The week before his death, he went to London for his regular day at the office of *All the Year Round*, Thursday, and had his usual Thursday lunch with George Dolby—but afterwards he said good-bye with unusual emotion. "Extending my hand to him across the table where he was writing," Dolby recalled, "I was greatly shocked at a pained expression I detected in his features. His eyes . . . were becoming suffused with tears." Dolby would never see him again.

Dickens was at the office again the next day, Friday, and when his son Charles Junior, now his sub-editor, departed in the afternoon, his father seemed strangely abstracted—too dreamy even to register Charley's departure. When Charley next saw him, he was unconscious and dying.

After his Friday at the office, Dickens returned to Gad's Hill, and the next day his daughter Katie visited. Among other things, she wanted to discuss the idea of going on stage professionally, for her chronically ill husband Charles Collins was unable to support them. On Saturday night, she and her father talked, the conversation wandering from Katie's theatrical notion (which he discouraged) to other topics. He was gloomy, retrospective, and wistful. He wished he had been "a better father—a better man." They talked through the night. When she left the next day to return to London, he was working in his chalet across the road. "My father disliked partings, so I . . . intended to go away without any farewell," she recalled, but on impulse she hurried across to the chalet to say good-bye. She found him intent on his work. "On ordinary occasions he would just have raised his cheek for my kiss, . . . but on this morning, when he saw me, he pushed his chair from the writing-table, opened his arms, and took me into them. . . ." Three days later, she was summoned to his deathbed.

And Ellen? Did he part from her too with a surge of anguish that final week—with some intimation of never-again? It would have been, perhaps, the most painful parting of all.

Despite his lame foot, he spent many days with her during the month before his death. In May, for example, he put off a prospective caller with the excuse that "I have been much inconvenienced and pained this last week by a neuralgic attack in the foot. . . . The moment I can stand after such a seizure (which in the present case is this moment of writing), I have recourse to change of air"—a holiday of four or five days, he specified, and undoubtedly in the refreshing air of Peckham.

Ordinarily, after his regular day at the office during the first week of June, he would have rejoined her at Windsor Lodge on Thursday afternoon and spent the night with her. The next day, he would have returned to London, or perhaps gone straight to Gad's Hill—so that their final parting would have been on Friday morning, June 3. And perhaps it was. But the week before his death was not routine, and on that Thursday evening he was not at Windsor Lodge enjoying the warm June dusk with Ellen.

Instead, he was on the other side of London, stage-managing a play at a large mansion, Cromwell House, in South Kensington. It was characteristic that he should be busily involved in a theatrical production in his final days.

The occasion was an invitation-only charity performance of a comic drama, *The Prima Donna*. His daughters Mamie and Katie had roles in the play, and he too would have been acting but for the gouty foot, which was tormenting him. Nonetheless, he had earlier "directed all the rehearsals with a boy's spirit," one participant testified, and on the night of the performance "he was behind the scenes as prompter and stage manager, ringing all the bells and working all the lights, and went through the whole thing with infectious enjoyment." Another friend, however, claimed to have heard that "after the play was over . . . he could not for a few moments be found, and was discovered . . . behind the scenes, seated in a corner in a dreamy state and abstracted. He thought, he said, he was at home." Rousing himself from this reverie, did he take a hackney cab to Peckham and Ellen? Or was she herself in the drawing-room audience at Cromwell House?

Much as he loved theatricals, it seems unlikely that he would have allowed *The Prima Donna* to supplant his weekly visit with her; but the last day for which there is almost certain evidence that he saw her was three days before the play and nine days before his fatal stroke. Very likely he saw her again before his death, but there is no hard evidence either way.

He had intended to be in London that final week for his usual Thursday at the office and his usual evening in Peckham, to sit with Ellen in the garden of Windsor Lodge as the shadows lengthened in the lingering June evening.

That Thursday evening, he died, however, at Gad's Hill.

After he had been stricken the day before, Ellen was invited to Gad's Hill. She probably did not arrive in time to see him alive. By one report, her grief was "terrible."

Charles Dickens has died, suddenly.

So one contemporary, *Punch* editor Shirley Brooks, headed his diary for June 10, the day after Dickens's death. With its stark message and heavily inked mourning border, it was the most dramatic of Brooks's 1870 diary entries. The night before, he had dreamed of talking "in the most affectionate manner" with a dead friend of Dickens, and the coincidence disturbed him: "I beg to assure myself . . . that I note merely a small—scarcely any 'coincidence'—and have not the faintest idea that the death (unknown to me till next day) influenced my dream." Digesting the news of Dickens's death, the usually diligent Brooks was restless and perturbed all day—"disinclined to work—unsettled."

Meanwhile, hearing the news at his office in Boston, James T. Fields jotted a quick note to Annie at home:

> A telegram has just come from England to the Associated Press . . . saying that our dear dear friend Dickens died this morning. . . . I am terribly shocked by this blow, and know not how to believe the report. God help us all if it be true. A world without Dickens!

Fields and Brooks were not alone in their shock. Dickens's death "will be felt by millions as nothing less than a personal bereavement," *The Times* of London declared. "Statesmen, men of science, philanthropists, the acknowledged benefactors of their race might pass away, and yet not leave the void which will be caused by the death of DICKENS. . . . We feel that we have lost one of the foremost Englishmen of the age."

The following week, Dickens was buried in Westminster Abbey. According to his friend and executor Forster, he would have preferred burial in a more modest location, "in the small graveyard under Rochester Castle wall, or in the little churches of Cobham or Shorne"—all near Gad's Hill. But by failing to dictate any preference in his will, Dickens had left open, perhaps intentionally, the possibility of Westminster Abbey. The family first chose Shorne churchyard for burial and then accepted an offer of interment in Rochester Cathedral before consenting to "a general and very earnest desire" that he be buried in the Abbey.

Characteristically, he had given careful thought to his funeral, and in his will he "emphatically" directed that he be buried "in an inexpensive, unostentatious, and strictly private manner" and "that no public announcement be made of the time or place of my burial." In deference to his wish for a private service, his funeral was virtually clandestine. He had also put a strict limit on the number of mourners, stipulating that "at the utmost not more than three plain mourning coaches be employed." "Our hands were . . . completely tied by the terms of the will," his eldest son, Charles Junior, explained afterwards to Dickens's "oldest friend," Thomas Beard, apologizing for Beard's omission from the funeral party. "We found it absolutely impossible, after anxious and careful consideration, to ask anyone but members of the family, and Forster, Ouvry, and your brother Frank, in their official capacities of executor, solicitor, and medical attendant."

Dickens's estranged wife Catherine was also excluded, though not for lack of room in the mourning coaches.

After the "anxious and careful consideration" of family and executors, Ellen too was apparently excluded.

Or was she?

The next day, *The Times* carried a lengthy account of the funeral. Its source should have been Forster, who—as Dickens's longtime confidant, as a close family friend, as one of two executors, and as the one who had made the arrangements for the funeral—was uniquely qualified to provide a full and accurate report. Forster had in fact arranged to give an account to a leader writer for *The Times*, William Stebbing. But Forster was in poor health, and by the day of the funeral he was exhausted by grief, by all the business connected with Dickens's death, and by the strain of the funeral itself. The day before, accompanied by Dickens's eldest son, he had called on Arthur Stanley, Dean of Westminster, to discuss interment in the Abbey. Stanley later recalled: "When they entered Mr. Forster was at first, and also during several passages of the interview, so much overcome by the violence of his grief that he could hardly speak. Indeed, I have never seen any man so overcome by sorrow as he appeared to be on that occasion." Forster was in no better shape the following day, and after the burial service he asked Wilkie Collins to talk to Stebbing of *The Times*.

Collins agreed. "I have just come from Dickens's funeral," he wrote Stebbing. "Forster is perfectly incapable of calling on you—and has asked me to call in his place." Collins feared that he might be expected to write the *Times* article himself: "Shall I supply you with the names of the persons present—and all else that is to be told? And will you have the necessary article written from the facts? I am far from well—or I would offer to do it myself." He offered instead to give Stebbing a list of the mourners and other details of the funeral by two o'clock that same afternoon.

Collins too was well qualified to report on the funeral. Though not involved in the arrangements, he had been a close friend and confidant of Dickens and knew the family well; also, his brother Charles was married to Dickens's daughter Katie. Collins had attended the funeral. And even in his distress, Forster probably briefed him on what the family thought desirable—and not desirable—to make public. Forster would also have furnished him with any needful facts outside Collins's knowledge, as well as a written list of the mourners.

With the information provided by Collins and Forster, *The Times* described both the events leading up to the funeral and the service itself. The theme throughout had been secrecy. The funeral was held "with as much privacy as could have been secured for it in any little village church in Kent, or even in Wales or Cornwall." Even as the grave was being dug below the Abbey floor, "besides the Dean and Canons, hardly a member of the Cathedral body on Monday evening [the night before the funeral] was aware of the intended arrangement." On the morning of the funeral, "almost before any one was stirring," a hearse had carried Dickens's body from Gad's Hill to the nearby train station, from which a special train had conveyed the body and a select group of mourners to Charing Cross station in London. From there the body had been carried through Westminster to the Abbey in a hearse "which was plainness itself." (The gardens along the way were bright with Dickens's favorite flower, scarlet geraniums.) As the small procession made its way down Whitehall shortly after nine o'clock that morning, "not a single person of the many scores who must have met the gloomy cavalcade as it slowly paced along was aware that the hearse was conveying to its last resting-place all that was mortal of Charles Dickens."

Apart from Dickens's desire for a private funeral, was there a further motive for conducting the funeral with the surprise and stealth of a commando operation?

The Times went on to describe the graveside service. When the small procession of coaches arrived at the Abbey, "the body was carried through the cloisters to the door of the nave, where it was met by the Dean, the two Canons in residence, . . . and three of the Minor Canons." Dean Stanley read the burial service over the grave. Then:

> The earth was cast into the grave by the Clerk of the Works; the service ended, the mourners—14 in number, with perhaps as many more strangers who accidentally chanced to be present—gathered round the grave to take a last look at the coffin which held the great novelist's remains, and to place wreaths of *immortelles* and other flowers upon the coffin-lid, and the service was at an end.

So we find fourteen mourners in the funeral party, a figure confirmed by Dean Stanley in the eulogy he delivered in the Abbey the following Sunday, when he mentioned "those fourteen mourners and the handful of other persons who were gathered a few days before in the silence and stillness of that vast empty church around the grave of the great novelist."

Just as Dickens had specified, there were three mourning coaches for the funeral party, and *The Times* listed the occupants of each, so we know who kept whom company during the procession from Charing Cross station to the Abbey.

In the first coach were Dickens's four children then in England: Charles Junior; Henry, or Harry, studying at Cambridge; Dickens's eldest daughter, Mary; and his second daughter, Katie, now Mrs. Charles Collins.

In the second coach were Georgina Hogarth; Dickens's younger sister Letitia, now widowed; Charles Junior's wife Bessie; and Forster.

In the third coach were five men: Frank Beard, his physician; Charles Collins, his son-in-law; Frederic Ouvry, his solicitor; Wilkie Collins; and Edmund Dickens, a nephew.

Thus the funeral party. But after stating that there were fourteen mourners, *The Times* had named only thirteen.

Who was the mysterious fourteenth, silently omitted?

Surely none other than Ellen Ternan. We can even guess that she rode in the second coach, in which Forster escorted three other women. In describing the funeral to *The Times*, however, Wilkie Collins, probably following a directive from Forster, suppressed Ellen's name, failing to notice the discrepancy; or perhaps recognizing that the numbers failed to tally but letting the disagreement stand, as unimportant, or even as a teasing enigma for attentive readers of *The Times* the next morning.

As Dickens had always hated elaborate funerary display, his testamentary insistence on a modest, strictly private funeral was no surprise. By excluding the public, however, he also made it possible for his beloved Nelly to attend with his family, as he no doubt thought she deserved and as he would have wished. Certainly he had her much in mind as he drafted his will, for "Miss Ellen Lawless Ternan, late of Houghton Place, Ampthill Square," was boldly listed as the first legatee. ("The will of Dickens . . . gives his friends a great deal of dissatisfaction," Wilkie Collins was said to have complained. "The first person named in it is his mistress.") Given their long and intimate relationship, it is unlikely that Ellen would in any case have stayed away from Dickens's funeral, but the privacy dictated by his will allowed her to attend inconspicuously. In his death, as in his life, she was an essential but shadowy presence.

Yet how attentively did she listen at the graveside as "the service was most impressively read by the Dean"? Thirty-one years old, she had been virtually widowed. Though provided for financially, she looked ahead to an uncertain future. Looking back on her dozen years with Dickens, reflecting on her suddenly altered situation, musing on the next chapter of her life—she had much to occupy her thoughts.

The following Sunday, to a large audience in the Abbey, Dean Stanley delivered a full-blown eulogy, his allusions to Dickens's novels suggesting that he had read none of them since *Nicholas Nickleby* thirty years earlier. "Among the congregation were several members of both Houses of Parliament, some dignitaries of the Church, and a host of literary celebrities, among whom Mr. Tennyson attracted considerable attention as he sat in the centre of the Sacrarium," *The Times* reported. Ellen was probably absent from this crowd of the curious and important, however; certainly she had nothing to learn about Dickens from Dean Stanley's pulpit eloquence.

Later, however, when the Abbey was less crowded, she visited the grave with her mother and sisters. "We went when in London to see Charles Dickens's grave," Fanny Trollope wrote to her stepdaughter Bice in Florence two weeks after the funeral. "He is buried in Westminster Abbey. The tombstone was strewn with flowers scattered there by different visitors. I was greatly affected, and so were we all." The sorrowful Fanny had once been Dickens's antagonist; but time (and his death) had evidently softened her feelings. She could not in any case be indifferent to Ellen's loss. After paying their respects at the Abbey, the Ternans carried Ellen off to stay at the green and pleasant Oxford estate of her sister Maria, married to a wealthy brewer. Windsor Lodge, Peckham, was given up.

Eventually Ellen married, and as Mrs. George Wharton Robinson she bore and raised a son and daughter. Many years later, her daughter-in-law testified that she was "a most devoted wife and mother and a charming personality." She survived Dickens by more than four decades, dying on the eve of the First World War. While his bones lie beneath the Abbey pavement, sifting into dust as sightseers shuffle by overhead, Ellen's ashes lie far off the tourist rounds, in Highland Road Cemetery in Southsea, near Portsmouth. Close in life, the Ternan sisters are close in death: Ellen's beloved sisters Maria and

Frances—"Mia" and "Fanny"—share a grave just a few yards from hers. At the end of their lives, Ellen and Fanny had lived together in Southsea. Ellen's grave is scarcely two miles from the terrace house in Portsmouth where Dickens had been born a century before her death; in the house, now a museum, is the couch on which he died at Gad's Hill.

By a curious coincidence or mysterious providence, Maria Beadnell had also moved to Southsea with her clergyman husband, and died there in 1886. She too is buried in Highland Road Cemetery; so that the first and last women Dickens loved, who never met and probably never heard of each other, now lie only a few yards apart. In a quiet provincial cemetery, the beginning and end of his amorous pilgrimage have come together.

Meanwhile, beneath a high brick wall shutting out the traffic and seediness of the Harrow Road outside London, Mary Hogarth lies in a shady corner among the thousands of other graves in Kensal Green, a crowded sea of gravestones and elaborate monuments heeling and pitching at various angles like a dense fleet of small boats tossing about in choppy waters. Mary's own weathered gravestone cants slightly, with the ungrammatical epitaph composed by Dickens now barely legible: YOUNG BEAUTIFUL AND GOOD, GOD IN HIS MERCY NUMBERED HER WITH HIS ANGELS AT THE EARLY AGE OF SEVENTEEN. He had hoped to be buried beside her, but as things fell out Mary shares her grave (and gravestone) not with Dickens, but with his detested mother-in-law.

"Yet do the worst, old Time. Despite thy wrong,/My love shall in my verse ever live young," Shakespeare had boasted (Sonnet 19). Dickens himself, rejecting "any monument, memorial, or testimonial whatever," stated in his will that "I rest my claims to the remembrance of my country upon my published works." But his novels are memorials, too, to the three women he loved well, if not always wisely—his muses and teachers in the school of love. No one taught him more; no one stirred his feelings more powerfully, or enriched his imagination more generously.

A NOTE ON SOURCES

All of Dickens's novels are available in reliable inexpensive editions; I usually quote from the Oxford World Classics editions, based on the scholarly Oxford Clarendon editions. In one or two cases involving an alteration Dickens made in manuscript or proof, I cite the Clarendon edition itself. For *Great Expectations*, however, I have used the magisterial Norton Critical Edition, edited by the inimitable Edgar Rosenberg. Sources for quotations from Dickens's other published writings—such as Christmas stories, journalism, working notes for his novels—are given in the bibliography below.

Any recent scholar studying Dickens must be grateful for the twelve meticulously edited and annotated volumes of *The Letters of Charles Dickens*, usually called the Pilgrim Edition (Oxford University Press, eds. Madeline House, Graham Storey, Kathleen Tillotson, et al., 1965-2002). *The Dickensian* publishes frequent supplements to the Pilgrim letters. In citing the letters, I follow the dating of the Pilgrim Edition, which is sometimes conjectural.

For access to unpublished material, I am grateful to:

The British Library, London

The Dickens House Museum, London
Firestone Library, Princeton University
Houghton Library, Harvard University
Huntington Library, San Marino, California
The Massachusetts Historical Society, Boston
The New York Public Library
Pierpont Morgan Library, New York
Senate House Library, University of London

SELECTIVE BIBLIOGRAPHY

The following studies or editions are cited in the text or have otherwise been especially helpful.

Ackroyd, Peter. *Dickens*. New York: HarperCollins, 1990.

Adams, Henry. *The Education of Henry Adams*. 1918; reprinted Oxford: Oxford University Press (Oxford World's Classics), 1999.

Adrian, Arthur. "Charles Dickens and Dean Stanley." *Dickensian* 52 (1956), 152-56.

——. *Georgina Hogarth and the Dickens Circle*. New York: Oxford University Press, 1957.

Allen, Michael. *Charles Dickens' Childhood*. New York: St. Martin's, 1988.

Augustine, Saint. *The Confessions of St. Augustine*. Tr. F. J. Sheed. New York, Sheed & Ward, 1942.

Aylmer, Felix. "Dickens and Ellen Ternan" [letter to the editor]. *Dickensian* 51 (1955), 85-86.

——. *Dickens Incognito*. London: Hart-Davis, 1959.

Baker, George Pierce, ed. *Charles Dickens and Maria Beadnell ("Dora"): Private Correspondence*. Saint Louis: Privately Printed for William K. Bixby, 1908.

Berger, Francesco. *Reminiscences, Impressions & Anecdotes*. London: Samson Low, Marston, 1913.

Bigelow, John. *Retrospections of an Active Life: 1867-1871*. Garden City, New York: Doubleday, Page, 1913.

Boswell, James. *The Life of Samuel Johnson*. 1791; London: Oxford University Press, 1953.

Brannan, Robert Louis. *Under the Management of Mr. Charles Dickens: His Production of "The Frozen Deep."* Ithaca, NY: Cornell University Press, 1966.

Brattin, Joel J. "'Let me Pause Once More': Dickens' Manuscript Revisions in the Retrospective Chapters of *David Copperfield*." *Dickens Studies Annual* 26 (1998), 73-90.

Butt, John, and Kathleen Tillotson. *Dickens at Work*. 1957; London: Methuen, 1982.

[Byrne, Mrs. William Pitt]. *Gossip of the Century*. 2 vols. New York: Macmillan and Co., 1892.

Carey, John. *The Violent Effigy*. London: Faber and Faber, 1973.

Carlton, William J. "Dickens's Forgotten Retreat in France." *Dickensian* 62 (Spring 1966), 69-86.

Carrow, G. D. "An Informal Call on Charles Dickens." *Dickensian* 63 (1967), 112-19.

Cather, Willa. "148 Charles Street." *Not Under Forty*. 1922; reprinted Lincoln: University of Nebraska Press, 1988.

Chittick, Kathryn. *Dickens and the 1830s*. Cambridge: Cambridge University Press, 1990.

Collins, Philip, ed. *Charles Dickens: The Critical Heritage*. London: Routledge & Kegan Paul, 1971.

———, ed. *Dickens: Interviews and Recollections*. 2 vols. London: Macmillan, 1981.

———. "W. C. Macready and Dickens: Some Family Recollections." *Dickens Annual* 2 (1966): 51-56.

Collins, Wilkie. *The Public Face of Wilkie Collins: The Collected Letters*. Ed. William Baker, Andrew Gasson, Graham Law, Paul Lewis. 4 vols. London: Pickering & Chatto, 2005.

———. *The Frozen Deep and Other Stories*. 2 vols. London: Richard Bentley & Son, 1874.

Cross, Constance. "Charles Dickens: A Memory." *New Liberal Review* 2 (1901), 392-98.

Curry, George. "Charles Dickens and Annie Fields." *Huntington Library Quarterly* 51 (Winter 1988), 1-71.

Darby, Margaret. "Dickens and Women's Stories: 1845-1848." *Dickens Quarterly* 17 (2000), 67-76,127-138.

DeTernant, Andrew. "Miss Ellen Lawless Ternan." *Notes and Queries* 165 (1933), 87-88.

DeVries, Duane. *Dickens's Apprentice Years: The Making of a Novelist*. London: Harvester Press, 1976.

Dexter, Walter, ed. *Dickens to his oldest friend: the letters of a lifetime from Charles Dickens to Thomas Beard*. New York: Putnam, 1932.

———. *The Love Romance of Charles Dickens: Told in His Letters to Maria Beadnell (Mrs. Winter)*. London: The Argonaut Press, 1936.

Dickens, Charles. *American Notes*. In *American Notes and Pictures from Italy*. London: Oxford University Press, 1974 (Oxford Illustrated Dickens).

———. *Christmas Stories*. London: Oxford University Press, 1971 (Oxford Illustrated Dickens).

———. *Dickens' Journalism*. Ed. Michael Slater. 4 vols. Columbus: Ohio State University Press, 1994-2000.

——. *Dickens' Working Notes for His Novels*. Ed. Harry Stone. Chicago: University of Chicago Press, 1987.

——. *Pictures from Italy*. In *American Notes and Pictures from Italy*. London: Oxford University Press, 1974 (Oxford Illustrated Dickens).

——. *Selected Short Fiction*. Ed. Deborah A. Thomas. Harmondsworth, Middlesex: Penguin Books, 1976.

——. *The Speeches of Charles Dickens*. Ed. K. J. Fielding. Oxford: Clarendon Press, 1960.

Dickens, Charles, Jr. "Glimpses of Charles Dickens." *North American Review* 160 (1895), 525-37, 677-84.

Dickens, Henry F. *Memories of My Father*. London: Gollancz, 1928.

Dickens, Mamie. *My Father As I Recall Him*. New York: E. P. Dutton, 1897.

Dixon, Ella Hepworth. *As I Knew Them: Sketches of People I Have Met on the Way*. London: Hutchinson, [1930].

Dolby, George. *Charles Dickens as I Knew Him: The Story of the Reading Tours in Great Britain and America (1866-1870)*. London: Unwin, 1885.

Drew, John M. L. *Dickens the Journalist*. New York: Palgrave Macmillan, 2003.

Du Cann, C. G. L. *The Love-Lives of Charles Dickens*. London: Frederick Muller, 1961.

Edmonson, John, ed. *Dickens on France: Fiction, Journalism and Travel Writing*. Northampton, Mass.: Interlink Books, 2007.

Fields, J. T. *Yesterdays with Authors*. Boston: James R. Osgood, 1871.

Fitzgerald, Percy. *Memoirs of an Author*. 2 vols. London: Richard Bentley, 1895.

Flower, Sibylla Jane. "Charles Dickens and Edward Bulwer-Lytton." *Dickensian* 69 (1973), 79-89.

Forster, John. *The Life of Charles Dickens*. 2 vols. London: J. M. Dent, 1927 (Everyman edition).

Fox, Stephen. *Transatlantic: Samuel Cunard, Isambard Brunel, and the Great Atlantic Steamships*. New York: HarperCollins, 2003.

Gollin, Rita K. *Annie Adams Fields: Woman of Letters*. Amherst: University of Massachusetts Press, 2002.

Gounod, Charles. *Faust: opera in five acts*. New York: Schirmer, nd.

Greene, Graham. *Reflections*. Ed. Judith Adamson. New York: Reinhardt Books, 1990.

——. "The Young Dickens." *Collected Essays*. Harmondsworth, Middlesex: Penguin Books, 1970.

Hanna, Robert C., ed. "Before Boz: The Juvenilia and Early Writings of Charles Dickens, 1820-1833." *Dickens Studies Annual* 40 (2009), 231-364.

Hartley, Jenny. *Charles Dickens and the House of Fallen Women*. London: Methuen, 2008.

Hawksley, Lucinda. *Katey: The Life and Loves of Dickens's Artist Daughter*. London: Doubleday, 2006.

[Hogarth, Georgina, and Mamie Dickens]. *The Letters of Charles Dickens*, Edited by His Sister-in-Law and His Eldest Daughter. 1882; revised edition London: Macmillan, 1893.

Hollingshead, John. *My Lifetime.* 2 vols. London: Samson Low, Marston, 1895.

House, Humphry. *The Dickens World.* 2nd ed. Oxford: Oxford University Press, 1942.

Howe, M. A. deWolfe. *Memories of a Hostess: A Chronicle of Eminent Friendships.* Boston: Atlantic Monthly Press, 1922.

James, Henry. "Mr. and Mrs. James T. Fields." *Atlantic Monthly* 116 (July 1915), 21-31; reprinted in *Henry James: Literary Criticism,* 160-176. New York: Library of America, 1984.

Johnson, Edgar. *Charles Dickens: His Tragedy and Triumph.* 2 vols. New York: Simon and Schuster, 1952.

Kaplan, Fred. *Dickens: A Biography.* 1988; Baltimore, Johns Hopkins University Press, 1998.

———. *Dickens and Mesmerism.* Princeton: Princeton University Press, 1975.

Kitton, Frederic G. *Charles Dickens by Pen and Pencil.* London: Frank T. Sabin & John Dexter, 1889-90.

———. *A Supplement to Charles Dickens by Pen and Pencil.* London: Frank T. Sabin & John Dexter, 1890.

Lawrence, Arthur. *Sir Arthur Sullivan: Life-Story, Letters, and Reminiscences.* London: James Bowden, 1899.

Lehmann, Rudolf. *An Artist's Reminiscences.* London: Smith, Elder, 1894.

Lehmann, R. C., ed. *Memories of Half a Century: A Record of Friendships.* London: Smith, Elder & Co., 1908.

Linton, Eliza Lynn. *My Literary Life: Reminiscences of Dickens, Thackeray, George Eliot, etc.* London: Hodder & Stoughton, 1899.

Longley, Katharine M. *A Pardoner's Tale: Charles Dickens and the Ternan Family.* Unpublished typescript, Longley Papers, Senate House Library, n.d.

———. "The Real Ellen Ternan." *Dickensian* 81 (Spring 1985), 26-44.

Loy, James D. & Kent M. *Emma Darwin: A Victorian Life.* Gainesville: University Press of Florida, 2010.

Martens, Britta. "Death as Spectacle: The Paris Morgue in Dickens and Browning." *Dickens Studies Annual* 39 (2008), 223-248.

McAleer, Edward C. *Dearest Isa: Robert Browning's letters to Isabella Blagden.* Austin: University of Texas Press, 1951.

McCombie, Frank. "Sexual Repression in *Dombey and Son.*" *Dickensian* 88 (1992), 25-38.

MacKenzie, Norman and Jeanne. *Dickens: A Life.* New York: Oxford University Press, 1979.

Meckier, Jerome. "'A World Without Dickens!': James T. to Annie Fields, 10 June 1870." *Huntington Library Quarterly* 52 (Summer 1989), 409-14.

———. "Some Household Words: Two New Accounts of Dickens's Conversation." *Dickensian* 71 (1975), 5-20.

Merivale, Herman. "The Last Days of Charles Dickens" [letter to the editor]. *The Times,* 8 Feb. 1883, 8.

Monod, Sylvère. *Dickens the Novelist*. Norman: University of Oklahoma Press, 1967.

Morley, Malcolm. "The Theatrical Ternans." Published in ten parts, *Dickensian* 54-57 (1958-1961).

Nayder, Lillian. *The Other Dickens: A Life of Catherine Dickens*. Ithaca: Cornell University Press, 2011.

Niebuhr, H. Richard. *The Kingdom of God in America*. 1937; repr. Middletown, CT: Wesleyan University Press, 1988.

Nisbet, Ada. *Dickens and Ellen Ternan*. Berkeley: University of California Press, 1952.

O'Connor, Flannery. *The Habit of Being*. Sally Fitzgerald, ed. New York: Farrar, Straus & Giroux, 1979.

Oddie, William. "Dickens and the Indian Mutiny." *Dickensian* 68 (1972), 3-15.

Orwell, George. "Charles Dickens." *Dickens, Dali & Others*. New York: Reynal and Hitchcock, 1946.

[Panton, Jane]. *Leaves from a Life*. London: George Bell and Sons, 1908.

Parker, David. *The Doughty Street Novels*. New York: AMS Press, 2002.

——, and Michael Slater. "The Gladys Storey Papers." *Dickensian* 76 (1980): 2-16.

Paroissien, David. "Charles Dickens and the Weller Family," *Dickens Studies Annual* 2 (1972), 1-38.

Patten, Robert. *Charles Dickens and His Publishers*. Oxford: Oxford University Press, 1978.

Payne, John Howard. *Clari: or, The Maid of Milan, An Opera, in Three Acts, as First Performed at the Theatre Royal, Covent Garden, on Thursday, May 8th, 1823*. New York: The Circulating Library and Dramatic Repository, 1823.

Perugini, Kate. "Edwin Drood and Charles Dickens's Last days." *Pall Mall Magazine* 37 (June 1906), 642-54.

Peters, Catherine. *The King of Inventors: A Life of Wilkie Collins*. Princeton: Princeton University Press, 1991.

Philpotts, Trey. *The Companion to* Little Dorrit. Mountfield, East Sussex: Helm Information, 2003.

Richardson, Ruth. "Charles Dickens and the Cleveland Street Workhouse." *Dickens Quarterly* 28 (2011), 99-108.

Ritchie, Anne Thackeray. *Journals and Letters*. Lillian F. Shankman, Abigail Burnham Bloom, and John Maynard, eds. Columbus: Ohio State University Press, 1994.

Rosenberg, Edgar. "Launching *Great Expectations*." In *Great Expectations*. Edgar Rosenberg, ed. New York: W. W. Norton, 1999 (Norton Critical Edition), 389-423.

Ruff, Lillian M. "How Musical was Charles Dickens?" *Dickensian* 68 (1972), 31-42.

Ruskin, John. *The Bible of Amiens*. Vol. 24, *The Complete Works of John Ruskin*. 30 vols. New York: Thomas P. Crowell, [1905].

——. *Letters of John Ruskin to Charles Eliot Norton*. 2 vols. Boston: Houghton, Mifflin, 1905.

Sayers, Dorothy. *Creed or Chaos*. New York: Harcourt, Brace, 1949.

Schlicke, Paul. *Oxford Reader's Companion to Dickens*. Oxford: Oxford University Press, 1999.

Slater, Michael. *Dickens and Women*. Stanford: Stanford University Press, 1983.

———. *Douglas Jerrold: 1803-1857*. London: Duckworth, 2002.

Spielmann, Mabel H. "Florence Dombey's Tears." *Dickensian* 21 (1925), 157.

Staples, Leslie C. "Ellen Ternan—Some Letters." *Dickensian* 61 (1965), 30-35.

———. "New Letters of Mary Hogarth and Her Sister Catherine." *Dickensian* 63 (1967), 75-80.

Stokes, M. Veronica. "Charles Dickens: A Customer of Coutts & Co." *Dickensian* 68 (1972), 17-30.

Stone, Harry. *The Night Side of Dickens: Cannibalism, Passion, Necessity*. Columbus: Ohio State University Press, 1994.

Stonehouse, John Harrison. *Green Leaves: New Chapters in the Life of Charles Dickens*. London: Piccadilly Fountain Press, 1931.

Storey, Gladys. *Dickens and Daughter*. London: Frederick Muller, [1939].

Thackeray, William Makepeace. *The Letters and Private Papers of William Makepeace Thackeray*. 4 vols. Gordon N. Ray, ed. Cambridge: Harvard University Press, 1946.

Thompson, John R. "Extracts from the Diary of John R. Thompson." *Lippincott's Monthly Magazine* 42 (1888), 697-708.

Tomalin, Claire. *The Invisible Woman*. New York: Vintage, 1992.

Tryon, Warren S. *Parnassus Corner: A Life of James T. Fields*. Boston: Houghton Mifflin, 1963.

Walder, Dennis. *Dickens and Religion*. London: Allen & Unwin, 1981.

Welty, Eudora. *One Writer's Beginnings*. Cambridge: Harvard University Press, 1984.

Whiffen, Mrs. Thomas. *Keeping Off the Shelf*. New York: E. P. Dutton, 1928.

[Wilde, Jane F.]. "The Countess of Blessington." *Dublin University Magazine* 45 (1855), 333-353.

Wilson, Edmund. "The Two Scrooges." In *Eight Essays*. Garden City: Doubleday, 1954.

Wright, Thomas. *The Life of Charles Dickens*. London: Herbert Jenkins, 1935.

———. *Thomas Wright of Olney: An Autobiography*. London: Herbert Jenkins, 1936.

NOTES

Chapter 1

Our people don't think: *Letters* 3:233 (3 May 1842).

nature's greatest altar: *American Notes,* 202.

It would be hard: *Letters* 3:210-11 (26 April 1842).

the presence and influence: *Letters* 3:35 (29 Jan. 1842).

When I felt how near: *American Notes,* 200.

What would I give: *Letters* 3:211 (26 April 1842).

peace of mind: Ibid.

a very grim place: *Letters* 12:69 (8 March 1868).

We have had two brilliant sunny days: *Letters* 12:73 (16 March 1868).

All away to the horizon: *Letters* 12:75 (16 March 1868).

What I once said: Ibid.

another letter: *Letters* 12:76 (16 March 1868).

the more truly great the man: "Trading in Death," *Journalism* 3:98.

a crazy, tumble-down old house: Forster, *Life* 1:21.

a patient and continuous energy: *David Copperfield,* ch. 42.

There never existed: Mamie Dickens, *My Father As I Recall Him,* 7 & 11-13.

so long as the room: Storey, *Dickens and Daughter,* 77.

the fondness of a savage: Arthur Locker, in Kitton, *Charles Dickens by Pen and Pencil,* 173.

liked a tidy head: Ibid.

took out a pocket-comb: Thompson, "Extracts from the Diary," 703. Similarly, a houseguest at Gad's Hill was impressed by "the particular care which his host gave to his hair, and how, while the guest would be taking an early stroll out of doors, Dickens would open his window, cheerily salute his friend, and carry on a conversation from above, all the while brushing his still flowing locks with almost savage energy, vigorously wielding a pair of brushes as if he would brush his hair off, working from the back of the head and bringing the lengthy side-locks in curls over the ears" (Kitton, *Charles Dickens by Pen and Pencil*, 175).

His punctuality: Storey, *Dickens and Daughter*, 77.

The condition of the common people: *Letters* 4:266 (11 Feb. 1845).

The country is delightful: *Letters* 4:561 (?13 or 14 June 1846).

admirably educated: *Letters* 4:574 (?28 June 1846).

taken at hazard: *Letters* 4:515 (?28 June 1846).

The Genius of Dullness: *Letters* 4:597 (5 Aug. 1846).

The absence of any accessible streets: *Letters* 4:622 (?20 Sep. 1846).

giddiness and headache: *Letters* 4:627-28 (3 Oct. 1846).

The sight of the rushing Rhone: *Letters* 4:627 (30 Sep. & 1 Oct. 1846).

The whole prospect: *Pictures from Italy*, 420-21.

beautifully clean: *David Copperfield*, ch. 3.

The Bastille!: *Tale of Two Cities*, ch. 21.

the great progress: *Letters* 6:468 (22 Aug. 1851).

be trained in the spirit: *Letters* 10:266 (4 July 1863).

horrible: *Letters* 3:482 (3 May 1843).

Dickens was a pure modernist: Ruskin, *Letters to Norton* 2:5 (19 June 1870).

chary of shewing my affections: *Letters* 7:543 (22 Feb. 1855).

intense dislike: Henry Dickens, *Memories*, 19-20.

I am breaking my heart: *Letters* 2:172 (?22 Dec. 1840).

I am slowly murdering: *Letters* 2:180 (?6 Jan. 1841).

It casts the most horrible shadow: *Letters* 2:181 (?8 Jan. 1841).

I am, for the time being: *Letters* 2:184 (14 Jan. 1841).

I resolved to try: *Letters* 2:188 (?17 Jan. 1841).

who wrote so tenderly: Linton, *My Literary Life*, 64.

You know my man Cooper?: *Letters* 7:319 (20 April 1854).

Mr. Henry Bradbury: *Letters* 9:302 (4 Sep. 1860).

to exterminate the Race: *Letters* 8:473 (23 Oct. 1857).

spoke with great vehemence: Meckier, "Some Household Words," 13.

brought about by attendant revolutions: Patten, *Dickens and His Publishers* 343.

one of the greatest geniuses: Flower, "Charles Dickens and Edward Bulwer-Lytton," 89.

found Mr. Dickens very practical: Cross, "Charles Dickens: A Memory," 396.

Dickens behaved outrageously: Patten, *Dickens and His Publishers*, 86.

I do not regard: *Letters* 11:289 (27 Dec. 1866).

I made last week: *Letters* 8:647 (2 Sep. 1858).

there was perpetual sunshine: J. T. Fields, *Yesterdays with Authors*, 241.

That man is a brute: Panton, *Leaves from a Life*, 143.

sexual love: Orwell, "Charles Dickens," *Dickens, Dali & Others*, 68.

weeps eighty-eight times: Spielmann, "Florence Dombey's Tears," 157.
legless angels: Orwell, "Charles Dickens," *Dickens, Dali & Others*, 73.
The sweet scent: Perugini, *"Edwin Drood* and the Last Days," 654.

Chapter 2

In his youth: *Little Dorrit*, ch. 1:13.
Ever since that memorable time: Ibid.
You open the way: *Letters* 7:544 (22 Feb. 1855).
shivered and broke: *Little Dorrit*, ch. 1:13.
information about Maria Beadnell: Ackroyd, *Life*,1096.
dark-haired . . . slightly plump: Ibid., 130.
blond, petite: Kaplan, *Dickens*, 51.
Both Marias—brunette and blonde: In photographs of Maria in middle age she
  appears to have dark hair; but age or the developing process might have darkened it.
there used to be a tendency: *Letters* 7:544 (22 Feb. 1855).
the place where they grant: "Doctors' Commons," *Journalism* 1:89.
their address varied: Reckoning up the Dickens family's residences during Charles's
  youth, one researcher "counted seventeen addresses before Dickens left home
  when he was 22, and thought there were probably some I'd missed" (Richardson, "Charles Dickens and the Cleveland Street Workhouse," 103).
vernacular tastes in music: "I have not the least knowledge of music," Dickens
  admitted in 1854, "I only love it" (*Letters* 7:297).
Are you going out of town: *Letters* 1:7 (30 July 1832).
Will you excuse my postponing: *Letters* 1:13 (5 Jan. 1833).
Snatches of over 200 popular songs: Ruff, "How Musical was Charles Dickens?" 40.
I am exceedingly sorry: *Letters* 1:11 (20 Dec. 1832).
pocket Venus: Stonehouse, *Green Leaves*, 39.
"light butterfly" feelings: *Letters* 1:25 (16 May 1833).
seldom dined: "The Steam Excursion," *Journalism* 1:369.
Life has no charms: Hanna, "Before Boz," 306. Maria's album is in the Dickens
  House Museum; Hanna's "Before Boz" gives reliable transcriptions of Dickens's
  contributions to the album.
He saw at a window: Hanna, "Before Boz," 308.
"The Bill of Fare": Hanna, "Before Boz," 314-26. Anne Kolle's album with Dickens's
  autograph version of "The Bill of Fare" has disappeared; three copies (in other
  hands) survive, however. I quote from Hanna's transcription of the copy in the
  Dickens House Museum.
After reporting his last debate: Annie Fields Diaries, Massachusetts Historical
  Society.
Mr. Dickin: *Letters* 7:534 (10 Feb. 1855).
many old kindnesses: *Letters* 5:626 (19 Oct. 1849).
The first of his surviving letters: *Letters* 7:777 (late 1831).

I once matched a little pair: *Letters* 7:538 (15 Feb. 1855).

the epidemic of illustrated annuals: Wilde, "Countess of Blessington," 342.

This charming spot: Hanna, "Before Boz," 312.

I should not have written it: *Letters* 1:8 (Summer 1832).

Dickens was on several occasions: Stonehouse, *Green Leaves*, 28.

Situated as we have been once: *Letters* 1:23 (14 May 1833).

recollecting what had passed: *Letters* 1:25 (16 May 1833).

How it all happened: *Letters* 7:543 (22 Feb. 1855).

Mr. Dickens senior had been summoned: *London Gazette*, 22 November 1831, 2447-48.

My existence was once: *Letters* 7:534 (10 Feb. 1855).

my cold is about as bad: *Letters* 1:12 (?1832).

With our friends the Beadnell's: *Letters* 1:14 (?Jan. 1833).

Your handwriting: *Letters* 6:659 (4 May 1852).

Do not misunderstand: *Letters* 7:777 (Late 1831).

I cannot unless: *Letters* 7:777 (Late 1831).

Surely, surely: Ibid.

When we were falling off: *Letters* 7:545 (22 Feb. 1855).

I gave a party: "Birthday Celebrations," *Journalism* 4:232.

The first of these letters: *Letters* 1:16-17 (18 March 1833).

with a blue ribbon: *Letters* 7:539 (15 Feb. 1855).

expressive of the same sentiments: *Letters* 1:25 (16 May 1833).

I know what your feelings: *Letters* 1:25 (16 May 1833).

Although unfortunately: *Letters* 1:19 (?15 April 1833).

The family are busy: *Letters* 1:19 (?15 April 1833).

A father's curse: Payne, *Clari*, 52.

Hence, hence!: Ibid., 53.

Most extensive: "Mrs Joseph Porter 'Over the Way,'" *Journalism* 1:405.

on the night of the play: *Letters* 1:24 (16 May 1833).

by chance that days: *Letters* 1:22 (14 May 1833).

I cannot forbear: *Letters* 1:24 (16 May 1833).

a very conciliatory note: *Letters* 1:29 (19 May 1833).

I am most desirous: *Letters* 1:28 (19 May 1833).

I wrote to you: *Letters* 7:543 (22 Feb. 1855).

If you had ever felt: *Letters* 1:25-26 (16 May 1833).

you never had the stake: *Letters* 7:544 (22 Feb. 1855).

It was a beautiful party: "Birthday Celebrations," *Journalism* 4:233.

writing to me once: *Letters* 7:545 (22 Feb. 1855).

I think I never should: *Letters* 1:17 (18 March 1833).

I know how all these things: Forster, *Life* 1:32.

petty disputes of Doctor's Commons: Dickens's transcriptions of his own short-hand notes for two trials in Doctor's Commons survive. Both cases (in 1830) concerned "a disturbance in the vestry-room of the venerable church of St. Bartholomew-the-Great, Smithfield. Objection had been taken by some of the parishioners to the levying of a poor rate, an altercation ensued, and proceedings were instituted against two of the aggrieved ratepayers by one of the churchwardens" (William J. Carlton, quoted in Hanna, "Before Boz," where Dickens's transcripts of the verbose judgments in both cases are printed, 293-305).

when four years: *Letters* 7:557 (?Early March 1855).

I began to write: *Letters* 7:543-44 (22 Feb. 1855).

the most disinterested: *Letters* 7:539 (15 Feb. 1855).

whatever I have tried: *David Copperfield*, ch. 42.

I began to fight: *Letters* 7:539 (15 Feb. 1855).

All that any one can do: *Letters* 1:29 (19 May 1833).

I have positively stood amazed: *Letters* 7:557 (?Early March 1855).

take my woodman's axe: *David Copperfield*, ch. 36.

Whatever of fancy: *Letters* 7:538 (15 Feb. 1855).

I never can love: *Letters* 1:29 (19 May 1833).

My entire devotion: *Letters* 7:543 (22 Feb. 1855).

represented the whole world: *Letters* 7:539 (15 Feb. 1855).

Unresolved, apprehensive: Parker, *Doughty Street Novels*, 56.

only longing for companionship: *Ibid.*, 60.

I have . . . fixed: *Letters* 1:144 (31 March 1836).

within these twelve months: *Letters* 7:545 (22 Feb. 1855).

the happiness I had vaguely: *David Copperfield*, ch. 48.

one of the strangest features: Baker, *Charles Dickens and Maria Beadnell*, xxvii-xxviii.

Chapter 3

"A Fable (Not a gay one)": MS Firestone Library, Princeton; facsimile printed in *Dickensian* 28 (1932), 2-3.

a polite and flattering communication: *Letters* 1:33 (?10 Dec. 1833).

I am always entirely unemployed: *Letters* 1:30 (6 June 1833).

rather backward: *Letters* 1:33 (?10 Dec. 1833).

dimmed with joy and pride: "Preface," *Pickwick Papers* (1850 edition).

I intend with the gracious permission: *Letters* 1:32 (3 Dec. 1833).

All that any one can do: *Letters* 1:29 (19 May 1833).

As soon as I return: *Letters* 1:34 (?10 Dec. 1833).

My next paper: *Letters* 1:33-34 (?10 Dec. 1833).

had pervaded every chink: "Birthday Celebrations," *Journalism* 4:232.

Sometimes in the most unlikely: *Letters* 7:544-45 (22 Feb. 1855).

I could not: *Letters* 7:544 (22 Feb. 1855).

the three elder sisters: A fourth sister, Helen, was only one year old when Dickens was introduced to the Hogarth family, but she too eventually inspired strong feelings. Two decades later, when Dickens and Catherine separated, Helen as

Catherine's loyal ally became his "wickedest" enemy," "whom I will never forgive alive or dead" (*Letters* 8:632 & 578).

enjoyed it very much: Staples, "New Letters," 76.

a young and lovely girl: *Letters* 1:258 (8 May 1837).

I have just returned home: Mary Hogarth to Mary Scott Hogarth [her cousin], 15 May 1836, *Letters* 1:689 (Appendix E).

a letter which is mostly: Ibid.

Mary and I wandered: "Dickens's Diary," *Letters* 1:630 (Appendix A).

the grace and ornament: *Letters* 1:258 (8 May 1837).

From the day of our marriage: *Letters* 1:263 (31 May 1837).

Mary . . . understood it: *Letters* 8:560 (9 May 1858).

are more devoted than ever: Mary Hogarth to Mary Scott Hogarth, 15 May 1836, *Letters* 1:689 (Appendix E).

kindness itself: Staples, "New Letters," 77.

Dinner in Doughty Str.: Richard Bentley, MS, New York Public Library (Berg Collection); printed in *Letters* 1:253n.

We lost no time: *Letters* 1:256-57 (8 May 1837).

You cannot conceive: *Letters* 1:257 (8 May 1837).

On the Saturday Evening: *Letters* 1:263 (31 May 1837).

She was taken ill: *Letters* 1:268 (8 June 1837).

Thank God she died in my arms: *Letters* 1:259 (17 May 1837). Dickens specified in at least eight different accounts that Mary had died in his arms —in fact, in every surviving account he wrote about her death.

Her body lies in the beautiful cemetery: *Letters* 1:268 (8 June 1837).

my dear young friend: *Letters* 1:341 (11 Dec. 1837).

It is a great trial: *Letters* 2:410 (25 Oct. 1841).

drive over there: *Letters* 2:410 (26 Oct. 1841).

I neither think nor hope: *Letters* 2:410 (25 Oct. 1841).

a melancholy pleasure: *Letters* 1:323 (26 Oct. 1837).

Increased reputation: "Dickens's Diary," in *Letters* 1:629 (Appendix A).

I shall never be so happy: Ibid., 1:630.

every night for many months: *Letters* 3:483-84 (8 May 1843).

I have never had her ring off: *Letters* 1:323 (26 Oct. 1837).

Is it not extraordinary: *Letters* 1:366 (1 Feb. 1838).

she is so much in my thoughts: *Letters* 3:484 (8 May 1843).

In time my eyes: *David Copperfield*, ch. 2.

I have carried into effect: *Letters* 3:455-56 (2 March 1843).

The mystery is not here: *Letters* 6:26 (1 Feb. 1850).

the most difficult book: Boswell, *Life of Johnson*, 952.

The Protestant reader: Ruskin, *The Bible of Amiens*, 80.

Christianity is a woman: Greene, *Reflections* 113.

It is fatal to let people: Sayers, *Creed or Chaos*, 44.

What people don't realize: O'Connor, *Habits of Being*, 354.

No one ever lived: *Life of Our Lord*, 441.
Suppose ye that I am come: Luke 12:51.
A God without wrath: Niebuhr, *Kingdom of God in America*, 193.
Christianity is a scheme: [James Fitzjames Stephen?], unsigned review of *The Uncommercial Traveler*, 1861, excerpt in Collins, *Critical Heritage*, 423.
used to say of Dickens: Paul Féval, "Charles Dickens," excerpt in Collins, *Interviews and Recollections* 2:293.
The gentlest and purest: *Letters* 1:323 (26 Oct. 1837).
I should be sorry: *Letters* 1:366 (1 Feb. 1838).
I dreamed of her: *Letters* 3:484-85 (8 May 1843).
She is sentient: "Dickens's Diary," in *Letters* 1:632 (Appendix A).
In an indistinct place: *Letters* 4:196 (?30 Sep. 1844).
Easier than air with air: *Paradise Lost* 8:626-28.
I solemnly believe: *Letters* 1:259 (17 May 1837).
The certainty of a bright: *Letters* 1:515-16 (3 March 1839).
was moved with the greatest compassion: *Letters* 4:196 (?30 Sep. 1844).
With longer or shorter: Forster, *Life* 2:402.
The first burst of anguish: *Letters* 1:516.
I have been so shaken: *Letters* 1:260.
faces that the grave had changed: *Oliver Twist*, ch. 11.
The persons on whom: *Oliver Twist*, ch. 14.
Wolves tear your throats: *Oliver Twist*, ch. 28.
a sweet female voice: Ibid.
Oh! Where are the hearts: *Oliver Twist* (Clarendon Press), 187n.
She was not past seventeen: *Oliver Twist*, ch. 29.
stealthily along: *Oliver Twist*, ch. 19.
We know that when the young: *Oliver Twist*, ch. 35.
O foul descent!: *Paradise Lost* 9:163-66.
"An angel," continued the young man: *Oliver Twist*, ch. 35.
The godlike novelist: Slater, *Dickens and Women*, 94.
There are smiling fields: *Oliver Twist*, ch. 51.
henceforth to be the scene: Ibid.
I would fain linger: *Oliver Twist*, ch. 53.
They felt a railway train: Adams, *Autobiography*, 324.

Chapter 4
My attachments: *Letters* 9:309 (14 Sep. 1860).
favourite child: *David Copperfield* (Charles Dickens edition), "Preface."
No one can ever believe: *David Copperfield* (1850 edition), "Preface."
I am in danger: Ibid.
I am deeply: *Letters* 4:669 (?30 Nov. 1846).
His sister Fanny: Forster, *Life* 2:67.
had naturally an interest: *David Copperfield*, ch.22.

All was over: *David Copperfield*, ch. 26.
I fancy: *Letters* 7:539 (15 Feb. 1855).
I really think: *Letters* 5:569 (10 July 1849).
a straw hat and blue ribbons: *David Copperfield*, ch. 26.
a dress of celestial blue: *David Copperfield*, ch. 33.
an engagement ring: *David Copperfield*, ch. 38.
rather diminutive: *David Copperfield*, ch. 26. The quotations following are taken
    from the same chapter.
Don't talk about being poor: *David Copperfield*, ch. 37.
Oh, please don't: Ibid.
the occasion: *Letters* 7:557 (?Early March 1855).
You may make it necessary: *David Copperfield*, ch. 38.
There is nothing: Ibid.
My dear Maria: *Letters* 7:777 (Late 1831).
I, turned of eighteen: "City of London Churches," *Journalism* 4:112.
I was steeped: *David Copperfield*, ch. 33.
What an idle time!: Ibid.
I can never open: *Letters* 7:557 (?Early March 1855).
I began to fight: *Letters* 7:539 (15 Feb. 1855).
I have never been so good: Ibid.
On her face: *David Copperfield*, ch. 15.
I cannot call: Ibid.
solemn hand upraised: *David Copperfield*, ch. 53.
Until I die: *David Copperfield*, ch. 60.
so may I: *David Copperfield*, ch. 64.
that spirit which directs: *Letters* 3:35 (29 Jan. 1842).
a fair hand: *David Copperfield*, ch. 35.
goodness, peace: *David Copperfield*, ch. 16.
my sweet sister: *David Copperfield*, ch. 18.
So perfect a creature: *Letters* 1:259 (17 May 1837).
a major embarrassment . . . lifeless: Slater, *Dickens and Women*, 100, 161, 251-
    53.
the real legless angel: Orwell, "Charles Dickens," 102.
The influence for all good: *David Copperfield*, ch. 16.
She put her hand: *David Copperfield*, ch. 25.
seemed to touch: Ibid.
the fury and the mire: Yeats, "Byzantium."
I believe I had: *David Copperfield*, ch. 25.
He seemed to swell: Ibid.
I felt its whole weight: *David Copperfield*, ch. 58.
foreign towns, palaces: Ibid.
a ruined blank: Ibid.
clasped in my embrace: *David Copperfield*, ch. 62.

I came to Carthage: Augustine, *Confessions* 3:1.

Those trifles: Ibid., 8:11.

Thou hast made us: Ibid., 1:1.

paintings of two scenes: The illustration's framed painting of the Peggottys' boat-house reproduces in miniature Phiz's vignette for the novel's title page, which shows the upside-down hull on the shore and Emily seated on the shingle in the foreground. With this picture within a picture of Emily, and with Agnes herself seated in the parlor and Dora's portrait over the mantel, this final illustration in *David Copperfield* includes images of the three loves of David's life: his childhood sweetheart Emily, his youthful passion Dora, and his predestined wife Agnes.

Kiss me my dear!: Dickens's manuscript revisions are reproduced in Brattin, "'Let me Pause Once More' . . .," 88.

O Agnes, O my soul: *David Copperfield*, ch. 62.

I come home: *David Copperfield*, ch. 39.

Where's the woman?: "The Haunted Man," *Christmas Stories*, 150.

She was so true: *David Copperfield*, ch. 60.

Blind, blind, blind: *David Copperfield*, ch. 35. These words are ominously echoed a little later by a blind beggar David passes in the street.

the first mistaken impulse: *David Copperfield*, ch. 48, repeating the words of Annie Strong three chapters earlier.

it would have been better: *David Copperfield*, ch. 53.

The old unhappy feeling: *David Copperfield*, ch. 48.

I don't quite apprehend: *Letters* 7:556-57 (?Early March 1855).

Chapter 5

I know that in many points: *Letters* 4:69 (11 March 1844).

She was eighteen: Christiana Weller's resemblance to Mary Hogarth was not simply a fevered notion of Dickens. Talking with Christiana one day the following year, Mary's mother Mrs. Hogarth "mentioned how the [Hogarth] family thought she was like Mary Hogarth—'and a charming compliment,'" Christiana noted in her diary, "'for she must have been an angel'" (Paroissien, "Charles Dickens and the Weller Family," 7).

I love her dear name: *Letters* 4:54n. The "dear name" that had won Dickens some fame alluded to Christiana's surname, the same as that of Sam Weller, the celebrated cockney footman of *Pickwick Papers*.

I read such high: *Letters* 4:58 (1 March 1844).

I cannot joke: *Letters* 4:55 (28 Feb. 1844).

I *would* point out: *Letters* 4:70 (11 March 1844).

But at the worst: Ibid.

If I . . . felt: Ibid.

beyond the reach: *Letters* 4:99 (8 April 1844).

Hours of hers: *Letters* 4:70 (11 March 1844).

I had as high: *Letters* 4:99-100 (8 April 1844).

the frantic tone: Darby, "Dickens and Women's Stories: 1845-1848," 67.

recollection of Miss Weller: *Letters* 4:57 (1 March 1844).

I swear to you: *Letters* 4:69 (11 March 1844).

a very beautiful girl: *Letters* 4:398 (4 Oct. 1845).

Mrs. Thompson disappoints: *Letters* 4:604 (17 Aug. 1846).

She seems . . . to have: *Letters* 4:615 (30 Aug. 1846).

convulsions, distortions: Kaplan, *Dickens and Mesmerism*, 77.

myriads of bloody phantoms: *Letters* 12:443 (24 Nov. 1869).

I have a perfect conviction: *Letters* 4.265 (10 Feb. 1845).

Wheresoever I travelled: *Letters* 12:443 (24 Nov. 1869).

"To Be Read at Dusk," reprinted in *Short Fiction*, 68-74.

put through her paces: Stone, *Working Notes*, 75.

carrying her gossamer parasol: *Dombey and Son*, ch. 21.

very handsome: Ibid.

admirable—the women *quite perfect*: *Letters* 5:35 (15 March 1847).

I should like Edith: *Letters* 5:67 (Mid-May 1847).

The interest and passion: Forster, *Life* 2:33.

the engrossing interest: "1847 Narrative," [Hogarth & Dickens], *Letters of Charles Dickens*, 162.

He had never thought: *Dombey and Son*, ch. 42.

That space the Evil One: *Paradise Lost* 9:463-65.

He imagined her dangerously dark: *Dombey and Son*, chs. 27, 37, 42, 45, 47 and 54.

she lifted her hand: *Dombey and Son*, ch. 47.

references to her breast and bosom: McCombie, "Sexual Repression in *Dombey and Son*," 34.

quite a lady: *Letters* 5:34 (10 March 1847).

What devil: *Dombey and Son*, ch. 54.

about thirty: *Letters* 5:34 (10 March 1847).

When and where: *Barnaby Rudge*, ch. 41.

"Sir," returned Edith: *Dombey and Son*, ch. 45.

winning, happy, amiable: "Dickens's Diary," *Letters* 1:629 (Appendix A).

The Woman had once: Adams, *Autobiography*, 321.

Wandering days: *Letters* 6:721 (22 July 1852).

Why is it: *Letters* 7:523 (3 & ?4 Feb. 1855).

the specialist in childbearing: Nayder, *The Other Dickens*, 152.

All social evils: *Letters* 6:41 (22 Feb. 1850).

great mass of matter: *Letters* 6:41 (22 Feb. 1850).

We seek to bring: "A Preliminary Word," *Journalism* 2:177.

I saw a poisoned air: "A December Vision," *Journalism* 2:307-8.

I bequeath to my successor: "The Last Words of the Old Year," *Journalism* 2:314-15.

I have seen: "The Last Words of the Old Year," *Journalism* 2:313.

a very Fortunatus's purse: *Letters* 6:525 (23 Oct. 1851).

I have always had: *Letters* 6:448 (27 July 1851).

more like a man: Wordsworth, "Tintern Abbey."

The amount of business: *Letters* 6:329-30 (23 March 1851).

rolling of a sea: *Letters* 6:521 (15 Oct. 1851).

I have quite: *Letters* 6:574 (13 Jan. 1852).

I left Liverpool: *Letters* 6:599-600 (15 Feb. 1852).

Yet I hope: *Letters* 6:328 (23 March 1851).

They rise: "Home for Homeless Women," *Journalism* 3:130-32.

I found something: *Letters* 6:598 (13 Feb. 1852).

is very much grown: *Letters* 6:467 (22 Aug. 1851).

I will only add: *David Copperfield*, ch. 42.

less fixed purpose: *Letters* 7:245 (14 Jan. 1854).

I don't think: *Letters* 6:467 (22 Aug. 1851).

As her case: *Letters* 6:309 (8 March 1851).

an alarming disposition: *Letters* 6:311 (9 March 1851).

After taking: *Letters* 6:314 (12 March 1851).

If, with a wish: *Letters* 6:355 (17 April 1851).

whom I cannot afford: *Letters* 6:627 (16 March 1852).

Mrs. Dickens and her boy: *Letters* 6:629 (19 March 1852).

What a thing it is: *Letters* 6:266 (24 Jan. 1851).

Repeated pregnancies: MacKenzie, *Life*, 246.

indescribable lassitude: *Letters* 7:245 (14 Jan. 1854).

an exhausted composure: *Bleak House*, ch. 2.

Is a new dress: Ibid.

She has a purpose: *Bleak House*, ch. 16.

She has beauty still: *Bleak House*, ch. 2.

She was as graceful: *Bleak House*, ch. 18.

air of superiority: Ibid.

You see everything: *Bleak House*, ch. 12.

the quickness: *Bleak House*, ch. 12.

intelligence . . . is too quick: *Bleak House*, ch. 28.

oyster of the old school: *Bleak House*, ch. 10.

This woman: *Bleak House*, ch. 48.

My lady . . . is afraid: *Bleak House*, ch. 7.

sense and strength of character: *Bleak House*, ch. 48.

Anger, and fear: *Bleak House*, ch. 41.

It is not in her nature: *Bleak House*, ch. 48.

wicked relief: *Bleak House*, ch. 55.

What power: *Bleak House*, ch. 41.

full seven happy years: *Bleak House*, ch. 67.

Thus Chesney Wold: *Bleak House*, ch. 66.

still my Lady's eyes: *Bleak House*, ch. 28.

You have achieved: *Bleak House*, ch. 18.

I must travel: *Bleak House,* ch. 36.

No man but a blockhead: Boswell, *Life of Johnson*, 731 (5 April 1776).

In a utilitarian age: "Frauds on the Fairies," *Journalism* 3:168.

As the shining stars: *Hard Times*, ch. 1:13.

so dark-eyed: *Hard Times*, ch. 1:2.

Lover for Sissy?: Stone, *Working Notes*, 257. In the novel's final chapter, a single phrase, "happy Sissy's happy children," implies that she eventually marries.

Carry on Sissy: Stone, *Working Notes*, 255.

The child-like ingenuousness: *Hard Times*, ch. 3:2.

struggling through: *Hard Times*, ch. 1:3.

she sat so long: *Hard Times*, ch. 1:15.

like the faintness of death: *Bleak House*, ch. 1:2.

As I was reading: *Letters* 7:532 (10 Feb. 1855).

toothless, fat, old, and ugly: *Letters* 7:544 (22 Feb. 1855).

I have always believed: *Letters* 7:538-39 (15 Feb. 1855).

my head really stings: *Letters* 8:40 (30 Jan. 1856).

It was the shadow: *Little Dorrit*, ch. 1:24.

impelled by love: *Little Dorrit*, ch. 1:7.

with infinite tenderness: *Little Dorrit*, ch. 1:9.

The least, the quietest: Ibid.

paid three francs: *Letters* 8:96 (22 April 1856). It seems unlikely that he would encounter the woman as he haphazardly strolled the streets of Paris; a better course would likely have been to revisit the "ball" on another evening. But the prowl itself was perhaps much of the attraction.

However strange it is: *Letters* 8:89 (13 April 1856).

I find Mrs. Dickens: *Letters* 8:87 (13 April 1856).

Last Friday: *Letters* 8:95 (22 April 1856).

I have visions: *Letters* 7:428 (?29 Sep. 1854).

the top of the Great St. Bernard: *Letters* 8:33 (20 Jan. 1856).

An unsettled feeling: Forster, *Life* 2:193.

I don't know: *Letters* 7:428-29 (?29 Sep. 1854).

a grave dark man: *Little Dorrit*, ch. 1:2. Speaking to Amy Dorrit, said to be twenty-two at novel's opening, Clennam asks rhetorically: "Why do I show you, my child, the space of years that there is between us, and recall to you that I have passed, by the amount of your whole life, the time that is present to you?" (ch. 1:32). The arithmetic of this convoluted question would make Clennam about forty-six, as Little Dorrit would now be twenty-three. But perhaps Clennam exaggerates his own age or mistakes that of the youthful-looking Amy—or perhaps Dickens himself had forgotten.

I counted up: *Little Dorrit*, ch. 1:32.

walked on the river's brink: *Little Dorrit*, ch. 1:28.

a fair girl: *Little Dorrit*, ch. 1:2.

We were all of us: "The Wreck of the Golden Mary," *Christmas Stories*, 154.

She came towards him: *Little Dorrit*, ch. 2:29.

But pray, pray, pray: Ibid.

To believe that all: Ibid.

with all my thoughts: "Dickens's Diary," *Letters* 1:629 (Appendix A).

a very near and dear friend: "The Holly-Tree," *Christmas Stories*, 106-7. Dickens's
  regular dreams of Mary Hogarth had ended about seventeen years earlier, after
  he wrote of them to his wife in February 1838.

the very last words: *Letters* 1:259 (17 May 1837).

a single man: "The Wreck of the Golden Mary," *Christmas Stories*, 134.

her hands—though she was dead: "The Wreck of the Golden Mary," *Christmas
  Stories*, 155.

Chapter 6

When the Play: Berger, *Reminiscences*, 22.

reported great additional risk: *Letters* 8:230 (3 Dec. 1856).

and half the Bench *Letters* 8:230 (3 Dec. 1856).

Judges enow to hang us all: quoted in Slater, *Douglas Jerrold*, 265.

It has been the talk: *Letters* 8:265 (19 Jan. 1857).

Our audiences: *Letters* 8:262 (14 Jan. 1857).

As to the play itself: *Letters* 8:256 (9 Jan. 1857).

in the depressed agonies: *Letters* 8:262 (16 Jan. 1857).

a mere chaos: *Letters* 8:265 (19 Jan. 1857).

The Queen and her party: Georgina Hogarth to Maria Beadnell Winter, 21 July
  1857, Dickens Family Correspondence, Huntington Library.

Why are you here: *The Frozen Deep*, act 3, in Brannan, *Under the Management*, 157.

He's footsore: Ibid., 158.

Nearer, Clara: Ibid., 160.

first-rate tragedy man: *Nicholas Nickleby*, ch. 48.

Most awful: *The Leader*, 10 January 1857, quoted in Berger, *Reminiscences*, 27-28.

no mere actor: quoted in Brannan, *Under the Management*, 81.

all last summer: *Letters* 8:488 (7 Dec. 1857).

I keep her face: quoted in Brannan, *Under the Management*, 81.

It cannot be done: *Letters* 8:358 (23 June 1857).

in effect but a great Drawing Room: *Letters* 8:388 (25 July 1857).

sheer profit: *Letters* 8:401 (3 Aug. 1857).

out of the question: *Letters* 8:397 (2 Aug. 1857).

The Free Trade Hall: *Letters* 8:401 (3 Aug. 1857).

he was all business: Herman Merivale, in Kitton, *Supplement to Charles Dickens by Pen
  and Pencil*, 30.

I see you: *The Frozen Deep*, act 1, in Brannan, *Under the Management*, 116.

Kiss me, sister: *The Frozen Deep*, act 3, in Brannan, *Under the Management*, 160.

She came to see: *Letters* 8:432 (5 Sep. 1857).

how much impressed: *Letters* 8:432-33 (5 Sep. 1857).

in his own eyes: *Little Dorrit*, ch. 1:28.

The restlessness: *Letters* 8:423 (29 Aug. 1857).

I want to escape: Ibid.

Dickens surpassed himself: Collins, *The Frozen Deep and Other Stories* 1:5.

Partly in the grim despair: *Letters* 8:423 (29 Aug. 1857).

to out-of-the way places: *Letters* 8:425 (?1 Sep. 1857).

odd corners of England: *Letters* 8:426 (2 Sep. 1857).

we have not the least idea: *Letters* 8:427 (2 Sep. 1857).

Poor Catherine and I: *Letters* 8:430 (?3 Sep. 1857).

there is no sign: *Letters* 8:430n.

a gloomy old mountain: *Letters* 8:439 (9 Sep. 1857).

I don't believe: *Letters* 8:442 (9 Sep. 1857).

horse jockeys, bettors: *Letters* 8:447 (15 Sep. 1857).

can't walk out: *Letters* 8:448 (17 Sep. 1857).

I was at the Theatre: *Letters* 8:472 (23 Oct. 1857).

A walk in the wrong direction: "A Lazy Tour of Two Idle Apprentices," *Journalism* 3:469.

We will be with you: *Letters* 12:679 (16 Sep. 1857).

We breakfast: *Letters* 8:448 (15 Sep. 1857).

But Lord bless you: *Letters* 8:449 (17 Sep. 1857).

I am going to take: *Letters* 8:450 (20 Sep. 1857).

not certain: *Letters* 8:429 (3 Sep. 1857).

I *think* I shall leave: *Letters* 8:450-51 (20 Sep. 1857).

To me you are an absolutely: "A Lazy Tour of Two Idle Apprentices," *Journalism* 3:448.

He is suspected: "A Lazy Tour of Two Idle Apprentices," *Journalism* 3:471.

Why may not: Ibid.

curly light hair: "The Haunted House," *Christmas Stories*, 246.

a young lady: *Tale of Two Cities*, ch. 1:4.

They have each: Frances Ternan Trollope to Beatrice Trollope, 16 Feb. 1866, Trollope Papers, Princeton.

Ellen is a first-rate horsewoman: Frances Ternan Trollope to Beatrice Trollope, 28 June 1870, Trollope Papers, Princeton.

a most odious tendency: "A Lazy Tour of Two Idle Apprentices," *Journalism* 3:472.

grim . . . a bit of Diablerie: *Letters* 8:458 (4 Oct. 1857).

"The Bride's Chamber": "A Lazy Tour of Two Idle Apprentices," *Journalism* 3:453-60.

The dream of felicity: Stone, *Night Side*, 323.

Who could blame her: Storey, *Dickens and Daughter*, 94.

Although there are nice people: Ibid., 133.

the Doncaster unhappiness: *Letters* 8:536 (21 March 1858).

Arab drums: "A Lazy Tour of Two Idle Apprentices," *Journalism* 3:471.

The House of Commons: *Letters* 8:292 (1 March 1857).

As you refer: *Letters* 8:386 (23 July 1857).

I am a man: *Letters* 8:717 (9 Dec. 1858).

I have now no relief: *Letters* 8:464 (?Early Oct. 1857).

my celebrated feat: *Letters* 8:489 (7 Dec. 1857).

I have never known: *Letters* 8:536 (21 March 1858).

I wish I were: *Letters* 8:459 (4 Oct. 1857).

Believing that I hold: "The Perils of Certain English Prisoners," *Christmas Stories,* 179.

I wish I had been born: *Letters* 8:488 (7 Dec. 1857).

make a prodigious noise: *Letters* 8:482 (24 Nov. 1857).

for days and days: *Letters* 8:507 (23 Jan. 1858).

I need hardly tell you: *Letters* 8:465-66 (13 Oct. 1857).

told me that Dickens's god-daughter: Whiffen, *Keeping Off the Shelf,* 53-54.

all sorts of horrible stories: Thackeray to Mrs. Carmichael-Smyth, May 1858, in
    Thackeray, *Letters and Private Papers* 4:86.

some row about an actress: Ibid.

Papa says: Ritchie, *Journals and Letters,* 58.

I worked hard to prevent it: Georgina Hogarth to Maria Beadnell Winter, 31 May
    1858, Dickens Family Correspondence, Huntington Library.

I have been exquisitely distressed: *Letters* 8:656 (10 Sep. 1858).

My father was: Storey, *Dickens and Daughter,* 94.

If you could know: *Letters* 8:581 (8 June 1858).

I have been heavily wounded: *Letters* 8:597 (7 July 1858).

To Mrs. Dickens: Storey, *Dickens and Daughter,* 96.

unwholesome: *Letters* 8:687 (25 Oct. 1858).

Only last night: *Letters* 8:531 (15 March 1858).

in the best of humours: The outing to Hampton Court is described in "Please to
    Leave Your Umbrella," *Journalism* 3:484-88.

I have a bad cold: *Letters* 8:684 (22 Oct. 1858).

if there is not a large let: *Letters* 8:684 (22 Oct. 1858).

My suspicion is: *Letters* 8:687 (25 Oct. 1858). Other quoted passages from Dickens's
    account of this incident are from the same letter.

Upon my soul: "The 'Violated' Letter," *Letters* 8:740 (Appendix F) (25 May 1858).

the fatigue: *Letters* 8:677 (10 Oct. 1858).

I have been: *Letters* 8:718 (13 Dec. 1858).

My bachelor state: *Letters* 9:84 (25 June 1859).

I don't think: *Letters* 9:87 (30 June 1859).

I am very little better: *Letters* 9:99 (29 July 1859).

20 miles: *Letters* 9:106 (16 Aug. 1859).

I am not quite well: *Letters* 9:111 (25 Aug. 1859).

Unfortunately I am in the Doctor's hands: *Letters* 9:189 (1 Jan. 1860).

I pass my time: *Letters* 9:354 (28 Dec. 1860).

Now understand: *Letters* 9:356 (28 Dec. 1860).

spent their money: *Great Expectations,* ch. 34.

Your letter gives me: *Letters* 8:623 (11 Aug. 1858).

essays of topical: Rosenberg, "Launching *Great Expectations*," in *Great Expectations* (Norton Critical Edition), 392.

I have so far verified: "Preface," *Tale of Two Cities*.

it gives me great pleasure: *Letters* 9:89 (7 July 1859).

Will you send round: *Letters* 9:87 (30 June 1859).

a curious letter to Wills: *Letters* 9:10-11 (14 Jan. 1859).

such a step: *Letters* 9:11n.

I will no longer doubt: *Letters* 9:10-11 (14 Jan. 1859).

In February: *Letters* 9:29 (17 Feb. 1859).

my clear profit: *Letters* 8:689 (27 Oct. 1858).

three of its four floors: In addition to four floors of family rooms, 2 Houghton Place had a basement kitchen and a garret.

took the Ellen Ternan affair: Collins, "W. C. Macready and Dickens," 52-3

I cannot help: *Letters* 9:92 (9 July 1859).

Driven into a corner: *Letters* 9:106 (16 Aug. 1859).

I should be one: *Letters* 9:91-92 (9 July 1859).

Dickens talked very much: Annie Fields journals, 6 May 1860, Annie Fields Papers, Massachusetts Historical Society.

5 very good rooms: *Letters* 9:289 (19 Aug. 1860).

a sitting-room: [Hogarth & Dickens], *Letters of Charles Dickens*, 490.

I purpose living: *Letters* 9:289 (19 Aug. 1860).

as comfortable, cheerful: *Letters* 9:315 (23 Sep. 1860).

I *think* I shall run: *Letters* 9:292 (21 Aug. 1860).

By one account: Wright, *Life*, 280, citing Canon Benham, a friend of Ellen Ternan after Dickens's death and her marriage.

knew the Ternan family very well: DeTernant, "Miss Ellen Lawless Ternan," 87-88. With respect to his testimony on a different matter DeTernant has been called "a compulsive liar" (Patrick Spedding, "The Many Mrs. Greys: Confusion and Lies about Elizabeth Caroline Grey, Catherine Maria Grey, Maria Georgina Grey, and Others," *Publication of the Bibliographic Society of America* 104 (2010), 327).

Your first request: *Letters* 9:415 (15 May 1861).

small fair-haired: Storey, *Dickens and Daughter*, 93-94.

a very great advance: *Letters* 9:194 (7 Jan. 1860).

The exquisite truth: *Letters* 8:506 (18 Jan. 1858).

It is inexpressibly delightful: *Letters* 9:229 (30 March 1860).

Or would you like: *Letters* 9:318 (25 Sep. 1860).

heavily cancelled: *Letters* 9:318n.

I well recollect: Panton, *Leaves from a Life*, 143.

On one occasion: Storey, draft TS, *Dickens and Daughter*, Storey Papers, Dickens House Museum.

You will find the hero: *Letters* 9:325 (Early Oct. 1860).

I am afraid: *Letters* 9:15-16 (?25 Jan. 1859).

In a provocative essay: Greene, "The Young Dickens."

the ghost of my own childhood: "The Haunted House, *Christmas Stories*, 252.
She would make: *Letters* 9:247 (3 May 1860).
although she respected: Storey, *Dickens and Daughter*, 105.
I do not doubt: *Letters* 9:246 (3 May 1860).
went off with the greatest success: *Letters* 9:273 (19 July 1860).
After the last: Storey, *Dickens and Daughter*, 106.
never . . . a husband: Storey, draft TS, *Dickens and Daughter*, Storey Papers, Dickens
    House Museum.
Yesterday I burnt: *Letters* 9:304 (4 Sep. 1860).
Would to God: Storey, *Dickens and Daughter*, 107.
You will get me: *Great Expectations*, ch. 44.
For now, the very breath: *Great Expectations*, ch. 35.
the least unkindness: *Letters* 8:665 (18 Sep. 1858).
The unqualified truth: *Great Expectations*, ch. 29.
I could never: *Great Expectations*, ch. 39.
you will not have to complain: *Letters* 9:325 (Early Oct. 1860).
In her face: The original (canceled) ending of *Great Expectations* is printed as an
    appendix in most modern editions (for example the Norton Critical Edition,
    with Edgar Rosenberger's comprehensive discussion of the endings, "Putting an
    End to *Great Expectations*," 491-527).

Chapter 7
The rippling of the river: *Our Mutual Friend*, ch 4:6.
I went one evening: Loy and Loy, *Emma Darwin: A Victorian Life*, 185.
In early April: Stokes, "Charles Dickens: A Customer of Coutts & Co.," 28.
some affection of the heart: *Letters* 10:95 (20 June 1862).
a week's wandering: *Letters* 10:102 (3 July 1862).
some years since: *Letters* 10:103 (7-8 July 1862).
on a little Tour: *Letters* 10:104 (7 July 1862).
his sister Letitia: *Letters* 10:105 (8 July 1862).
obliged to go away: *Letters* 10:108 (20 July 1862).
Coming home here: *Letters* 10:122 (1 Sep. 1862).
I shall be away: *Letters* 10:124 (9 Sep. 1862).
my French wanderings: *Letters* 10:160 (11 Nov. 1862).
"The Calais Night Mail": *Journalism* 4:211-18.
The new cause of anxiety: *Letters* 10:99-100 (2 July 1862).
much better: *Letters* 10:120 (23 Aug. 1862).
go over the water: *Letters* 10:139 (12 Oct. 1862).
leisure for adventure: *Letters* 10:147 (17 Oct. 1862).
She was intensely emotional: Lawrence, *Sir Arthur Sullivan: Life-Story, Letters, and
    Reminiscences*, 51-52.
course of restaurants: Lehmann, *Memories*, 4.
a wonderful dinner: Ibid., 78.

Another friend, Arthur Sullivan: Sullivan's reminiscences of Dickens in Paris are printed in Lawrence, *Sir Arthur Sullivan*, 51-52.

At the end of October: [Hogarth & Dickens], *Letters of Charles Dickens*, 538-39.

sundry ties and troubles: *Letters* 10:154 (4 Nov. 1862).

There, I remain: *Letters* 10:173 (7 Dec. 1862).

to see a sick friend: *Letters* 10:191 (6 Jan. 1863).

I have been sorely worried: *Letters* 10:88 (31 May 1862).

I have some rather miserable anxieties: *Letters* 10:129 (20 Sep. 1862).

There is no period: *Letters* 10:xii.

I really have had: *Letters* 10:196 (18 Jan. 1863).

I had been meaning: *Letters* 10:198 (20 Jan. 1863).

An odd birthday: *Letters* 10:212 (7 Feb. 1863).

at short notice: *Letters* 10:105 (16 July 1862).

I should like: *Letters* 10:124 (9 Sep. 1862).

I have some engagements: *Letters* 10:173 (7 Dec. 1862).

There is no likelihood: *Letters* 10:178 (20 Dec. 1862).

Mr. Dickens is in Paris: Georgina Hogarth to an unidentified recipient, 14 Jan. 1863, Pierpont Morgan.

I shall be at this address: *Letters* 10:201 (29 Jan. 1863).

Who knows but that: *Letters* 10:187 (1 Jan 1863).

serious enough: *Letters* 10:198 (20 Jan. 1863).

visiting in the country: *Letters* 10:201 (29 Jan. 1863).

I have to dine out: *Letters* 10:204 (1 Feb. 1863).

having avoided: *Letters* 10:204n.

it is plainly a case: *Letters* 10:109 (20 July 1862).

wonderfully better: Letters 10:157 (7 Nov. 1862).

all but quite well now: Letters 10:233 (13 April 1863).

submitted to his advances: Adrian, *Georgina Hogarth and Her Circle*, 80. For the assertion that Ellen Ternan responded coolly to Dickens, Adrian cites Thomas Wright's 1935 *Life*. Wright had gathered most of his information about Ellen from an Anglican clergyman, William Benham, who had met her after Dickens's death. Somewhat as *Great Expectations'* Pip ends his memoir by returning to the subject of Estella, Wright ended his biography of Dickens by returning to Ellen: "Miss E. L. Ternan continued, after Dickens's death, to brood over her connection with him. At last she disburdened her mind to Canon Benham. She told him the whole story and declared that she loathed the very thought of this intimacy" (*Life*, 356). In his memoirs, Wright elaborated: Benham ("Canon Benham," as an Honorary Canon of Canterbury), "seated in his study in Finsbury Square [in 1897 or '98], told me the whole story of Dickens's liaison with Miss Ternan. 'I had it,' said Canon Benham, 'from her own lips, and she declared that she loathed the very thought of their intimacy'" (*Autobiography*, 67). The Ternan-Benham-Wright connection proved fateful in exposing Dickens's secret, but some of the details may be suspect. Benham's conversation with

Ellen occurred some twenty years before Benham repeated it to the eccentric antiquarian and pedant Wright, who in turn waited more than thirty-five years to publish it (soon after the last of Dickens's children had died). Whatever Ellen told Benham of her affair with Dickens, moreover, was likely to have been colored by her situation at the time; she was by then Mrs. George Wharton Robinson, respectable wife of a clergyman schoolmaster and mother of two children.

All that alacrity: *Letters* 10:100 (2 July 1862).

very far from well: Letters 10:93 (13 June 1862).

a very long: quoted in Collins, *Interviews and Recollections* 2:282.

I have been so anxious: *Letters* 10:95 (20 June 1862).

on my way to Paris: *Letters* 10:95 (20 June 1862).

constantly disturbed: *Letters* 10:153 (4 Nov. 1862).

supposed to be: *Letters* 10:148 (22 Oct. 1862).

had a fancy: Forster, *Life* 2:245.

I cannot go now: Letters 10:153 (4 Nov. 1862).

been visiting in the country: *Letters* 10:201 (29 January 1863).

I went . . . to hear Faust: *Letters* 10:205-6 (1 Feb. 1863).

No! I want a treasure:

> Non! je veux un trésor
> Qui les contient tous; je veux la jeunesse!
> A moi les plaisirs,
> Les jeunes maîtresses!
> A moi leurs caresses!
> A moi leurs désirs!
> A moi l'énergie
> Des instincts puissants,
> Et la folle orgie
> Du coeur et des sens!
> (Gounod, *Faust*, 1.2)

After Marguerite: *Letters* 10:215 (19 Feb. 1863).

I read tonight: *Letters* 10:201 (29 January 1863).

You have never: *Letters* 10:205 (1 Feb. 1863).

We saw that the knocker: "The Four Sisters," *Journalism* 1:19.

go on a little: *Letters* 10:204 (1 Feb. 1863).

I don't want to pin: *Letters* 10:207 (1 Feb. 1863). During this ten-day holiday Dickens again kept himself almost *incommunicado*: "With the exception of letters to Georgina and Forster from Amiens on 12. Feb, no letters are recorded between 8 and 17 Feb" (*Letters* 10:201n.).

for good: *Letters* 10:201 (29 Jan. 1863) and 10:207 (1 Feb. 1863).

I do not come back: *Letters* 10:209 (4 Feb. 1863).

for good: *Letters* 10:218 (26 Feb. 1863).

on coming to town: *Letters* 10:224-25 (17 March 1863).

a hasty summons: *Letters* 10:230 (9 April 1863).

I have been away: *Letters* 10:235 (22 April 1863).

None of his letters: On April 22, 1863, after returning from his fourth mysterious absence in a month, Dickens wrote a long letter to Wilkie Collins which makes no mention of any recent trips to France (or anywhere else). Had he actually traveled to France four times in the previous four weeks, his silence on the subject would be curious in a letter to his old traveling companion Collins (who was himself in southern France at the time).

I am but in dull spirits: *Letters* 10:227 (31 March 1863).

I have been absent: *Letters* 10:245 (16 May 1863). In fact, he had been in London for at least the two days preceding, and apart from his own assertion there is no evidence that he had been out of England in the week prior.

I have not been anywhere: *Letters* 10:281 (9 Aug. 1863).

a short holiday: *Letters* 10:315 (15 Nov. 1863).

I am a dangerous man: *Letters* 7:545 (22 Feb. 1855).

My being on the Dover line: *Letters* 10:445 (25 Oct. 1864).

Charles Dickens was once: Byrne, *Gossip of the Century* 1:225.

his profits: Patten, *Charles Dickens and His Publishers*, 251-2, 391-93.

wavering between: *Letters* 10:153 (4 Nov. 1862).

I have had ambassadors: *Letters* 10:269 (6 July 1863).

I am always thinking: *Letters* 10:281 (9 Aug. 1863).

Think what a great Frozen Deep: *Letters* 10:238 (22 April 1863).

I am exceedingly anxious: *Letters* 10:300 (?12 Oct. 1863).

hard at work: *Letters* 10.341 (15 Jan. 1864).

She tried hard: *Our Mutual Friend*, ch. 3:6.

I love you: *Our Mutual Friend*, ch. 2:15.

with a bent head: *Our Mutual Friend*, ch. 2:11.

The more you see of me: *Letters* 7:224 (5 Dec. 1853).

an immoveable idea: *Our Mutual Friend*, ch. 2:11.

Far better that I never did!: *Our Mutual Friend*, ch. 2:15.

Do you suppose: *Our Mutual Friend*, ch. 2:6.

I have had stern occasion: *Letters* 8:608 (22 July 1858).

You could draw me: *Our Mutual Friend*, 2:15.

a large dark man: "Travelling Abroad," *Journalism* 4:88.

The feet were lightly crossed: "Some Recollections of Mortality," *Journalism* 4:224.

one under-lying expression: Ibid., 4:223

The air was black: "Down with the Tide," *Journalism* 3:114-15.

You will have read: *Letters* 8:598 (7 July 1858).

untreated sewage: Philpotts, *Companion to* Little Dorrit, 64-65

The rose and honeysuckle: *Oliver Twist*, ch. 32.

Pharoah's multitude: *Our Mutual Friend*, ch. 1:3.

Everything so vaunted: *Our Mutual Friend*, ch. 1:14.

The very fire: *Our Mutual Friend*, ch. 1:1.

Whenever I am at Paris: "Travelling Abroad," *Journalism* 4:88.

To please myself: *Our Mutual Friend*, ch. 2:1.

a dark girl: *Our Mutual Friend*, ch. 1:1.

rich brown cheek: *Our Mutual Friend*, ch. 1:3.

a deep rich piece: *Our Mutual Friend*, ch. 1:13.

fell in a beautiful shower: *Our Mutual Friend*, ch. 2:11.

loosened her friend's dark hair: Ibid.

pure of heart: *Our Mutual Friend*, ch. 2:2.

upon my soul and honour: *Letters* 8:741 (25 May 1858) (Appendix F).

there is no better girl: *Our Mutual Friend*, ch. 2:6.

She knows he has failings: *Our Mutual Friend*, 2:11.

Her heart—is given: Ibid.

has made a change: *Our Mutual Friend*, ch. 3:9.

So, in the rosy evening: *Our Mutual Friend*, ch. 4:6.

so earnest a character: Ibid.

you are in love: Hemingway, *Farewell to Arms*, ch. 35.

He was making love: Annie Fields Diaries, Massachusetts Historical Society. In 1869 Dickens wrote an article, "On Mr Fechter's Acting," which echoes these spoken remarks (probably dating from about the same time). The article's description of Fechter playing Armand, the lover in *La Dame aux Camélias*, suggests Dickens himself in love:

> There is a fervour in his love-making—a suffusion of his whole being with the rapture of his passion—that sheds a glory on its object, and raises her, before the eyes of the audience, into the light in which he sees her. . . . A woman who could be so loved—who could be so devotedly and romantically adored—had a hold upon the general sympathy with which nothing less absorbing and complete could have invested her. When I first saw this play and this actor, I could not in forming my lenient judgment of the heroine [a courtesan], forget that she had been the inspiration of a passion of which I had beheld such profound and affecting marks. I said to myself, as a child might have said: "A bad woman could not have been the object of that wonderful tenderness, could not have so subdued that worshipping heart, could not have drawn such tears from such a lover." ("On Mr Fechter's Acting," *Journalism* 4:406)
>
> Dickens first saw Fechter on stage in 1859, two years after meeting Ellen, and his admiration for Fechter's acting ("in the highest degree romantic") may have been owing in part to a vicarious participation in Fechter's stage passions.

Chapter 8

The older I get: *Letters* 12:268 (4 Jan. 1869).

He is known: Dickens's connection with Condette is explored in Carlton, "Dickens's Forgotten Retreat in France."

a visiting Methodist minister: Carrow, "An Informal Call."

Billiards, croquet: *Letters* 11:47 (26 May 1865).

Ellen Ternan came: Storey, draft TS, *Dickens and Daughter*, Storey papers, Dickens House Museum.

A friend of Ellen's: Helen Wickham, in conversation with Katherine Longley, Longley papers, Senate House Library. The daughter of a longtime friend of the Ternans, Helen Wickham became a sort of surrogate daughter of Ellen after Ellen's marriage, and a "sister" to Ellen's actual daughter, Gladys Robinson.

You know how: *Letters* 10:455 (17 Nov. 1864).

a little run: *Letters* 10:351 (3 Feb. 1864).

I expect to be: *Letters* 10:405 (17 June 1864).

a ten or twelve days: *Letters* 10:408 (26 June 1864).

I have been working: *Letters* 10:409 (26 June 1864).

a pretty little town: "Mrs. Lirriper's Legacy," *Christmas Stories*, 422.

What would you say: "Mugby Junction," *Christmas Stories*, 522-23.

I will turn over: *Letters* 10:409 (26 June 1864).

Every evening: "Mrs. Lirriper's Legacy," *Christmas Stories*, 428.

away for a week's run: *Letters* 11:12 (28 Jan. 1865).

The mysterious 'arrangement': *Letters* 11:13 (31 Jan. 1865).

away for 6 days: *Letters* 11:25 (7 March 1865).

a little uncertainty: *Letters* 11:33 (22 April 1865).

There is nothing: *Letters* 11:36-37 (28 April 1865).

I can throw anything: *Letters* 11:36 (27 April 1865).

I have been away: *Letters* 11:41 (17 May 1865).

Work and worry: *Letters* 11:48 (?End May 1865).

The moment I got away: *Letters* 11:48 (?Early June 1865).

The carriage was: *Letters* 11:54 (12 June 1865).

I have a—: *Letters* 11:57 (13 June 1865).

Two ladies: Ibid.

the breaks were applied: Letter to the Editor, *The Times* (London), 12 June 1865, 5.

A lady who was in the carriage: *Letters* 11:53 (12 June 1865).

I took to London: *Letters* 11:60 (17 June 1865).

other errands of business: *Letters* 11:60 (17 June 1865).

on my cause of anxiety: *Letters* 11:62 (18 June 1865).

Take Miss Ellen: *Letters* 11:65 (25 June 1865).

Patient immensely better: *Letters* 11:70 (12 July 1865).

Patient much better: *Letters* 11:83 (16 Aug. 1865).

Patient much the same: *Letters* 11:86 (25 Aug.1865).

Would you like to know: Fanny Ternan Trollope to Beatrice Trollope, 16 Feb. 1866, Trollope Papers, Princeton.

This is not at all: e.g. *Letters* 11:53 (12 June 1865) and 11:55 (13 June 1865).

I write two or three notes: *Letters* 11:58 (13 June 1865).

The noise: *Letters* 11:60 (17 June 1865).

My escape: *Letters* 12:175 (26 Aug. 1868).

the Railway travelling: *Letters* 12:232-33 (6 Dec. 1868).

offensive and disgusting details: "Report of proceedings in Arches' Court, Thursday, Jan. 20., Geils v. Geils," *The Times* (London) 21 Jan. 1848, p. 6.

I can hear no more: "Report of proceedings in Arches' Court, Saturday, Jan. 22., Geils v. Geils," *The Times* (London) 24 Jan. 1848, p. 6.

that adventure with the Doctor: *Letters* 10:281 (9 Aug. 1863).

the marriage: *Letters* 10:281 (9 Aug. 1863).

old friends: *Letters* 10:399 (26 May 1864).

Are you quite sure: *Letters* 9:288 (19 Aug. 1860).

I can not read it: *Letters* 12:441-42 (23 Nov. 1869).

black hair: Dixon, *As I Knew Them*, 29.

she takes a resentful bounce: *Letters* 10:462 (11 Dec. 1864).

I have not yet decided: *Letters* 11:166 (2 March 1866).

Don't come: *Letters* 11:310 (4 Feb. 1867).

a half hour's supper: *Letters* 11:325 (4 March 1867).

Judge how much: *Letters* 11:386 (1 July 1865).

his letter replying to Mrs. Dickinson: *Letters* 11:389 (4 July 1867).

I don't in the least care: As the widow of Thomas Ternan, Ellen's mother was also "Mrs. T. T." Thomas Ternan had died twenty years earlier, however, and his widow would by now more likely be addressed as Mrs. Frances Ternan. Dickens's use of "Mrs. T. T." seems to emphasize Fanny's recent acquisition of those initials, and the final paragraph of his letter, with its sharp animus against her, makes it almost certain that "Mrs. T. T." is Fanny herself and not her mother.

How it came to pass: McAleer, *Dearest Isa*, 348-49.

Browning admitted: To Isa Blagden's explanation of Dickens's connection with Fanny Trollope, Browning replied: "The relationship between Mrs T. [Fanny] and "Miss T." [Ellen] never crossed my mind: I must have heard it—very likely from yourself—but it took no hold of me: had it done so,—I should have been very 'green' indeed, to give no better a guess at the solution of the riddle" (McAleer, *Dearest Isa*, 348-49). Fanny Trollope was paid the substantial sum of £500 for *Mabel's Progress*.

chastity of honour: Edmund Burke, characterizing the age of chivalry in *Reflections on the Revolution in France*, 1790.

I must travel: *Bleak House*, ch. 36.

habit of suppression: *Letters* 7:543 (22 Feb. 1855).

Stanfield died yest: This and all subsequent references to the 1867 pocket diary are drawn from the manuscript in the Berg Collection, New York Public Library.

Felix Alymer: Aylmer explains his decoding of the abbreviations and train stations in *Dickens Incognito*, ch. 1.

The rate collector: Upton-Cum-Chalvey Ratebooks. The various names listed as householder for the two cottages in Slough in 1866-67 are tabulated in Longley, *A Pardoner's Tale*, Appendix A (Longley Papers, Senate House Library).

although I date: *Letters* 11:348 (2 April 1867).

a very trying week: Ibid.

in the worst: Ibid.

I cannot get down: *Letters* 11:364 (8 May 1867).

Jane [Wheeler] first went: Gladys Robinson Reece to Felix Aylmer, Aylmer Papers, Dickens House Museum. In early 1866 the Ternans let out their house at 2 Houghton Place, and Mrs. Ternan and Fanny moved to 14 Lidlington Place, Harrington Square N. W., "only a stone's throw from our old house" (Fanny Ternan Trollope to Beatrice Trollope, 16 Feb. 1866, Trollope Papers, Princeton).

a small black bag: *Letters* 11:357 (20 April 1867).

When walking: Dolby, *Dickens As I Knew Him*, 58.

a tiny ball of white fluffy fur: Mary Dickens, *My Father as I Recall Him*, 82.

little interest in more abstruse topics: In 1860 an unidentified guest made detailed notes on two separate Gad's Hill dinner-table conversations. Judging from these notes, Jerome Meckier, who first studied and printed them, concluded that "conversation at Gad's Hill was lively, literary, polit-ical, and anecdotal, seldom if ever speculative, theoretical, or philosophical" (Meckier, "Some Household Words," 19). What was true of the Gad's Hill table talk probably applies to Dickens's conversations with Ellen as well.

I think I mentioned: *Letters* 11:323-24 (2 March 1867).

Finlay's wife: *Letters* 11:341 (22 March 1867).

In the 1950s: Aylmer, *Dickens Incognito*, ch. 3.

For many years: Wright, *Autobiography*, 239-40.

Down the south side: Ibid., 243.

enormous: *Letters* 11:366 (10 May 1867).

knew all about the tradition: Wright, *Autobiography*, 242.

A book of verses: Edward FitzGerald, "The Rubaiyat of Omar Khayyam."

with the view: *Letters* 11:406 (2 August 1867).

I employed a job-master: Wright, *Autobiography*, 241.

Chapter 9

my wife's income: *Letters* 11:377 (6 June 1867).

The greatest pressure: Dolby, *Charles Dickens as I Knew Him*, 88-89.

has my instructions: *Letters* 12:6 (10 Jan. 1868). Dickens made a £1000 bequest to Ellen in the second sentence of his will. If he had been making annual £1000 contributions to an endowment for her, this legacy would have represented, apart from its symbolic value, a final, valedictory installment.

I really do not know: *Letters* 11:194 (2 May 1867).

I begin to feel myself drawn: Letters 11:366 (10 May 1867).

very miserable prospect: *Letters* 11:439n.

The prize looks: *Letters* 11:372 (?20-25 May 1867).

it would take years: *Letters* 11:375 (6 June 1867).

I am really endeavouring: *Letters* 11:374 (3 June 1867).

The Patient, I acknowledge: *Letters* 11:377 (6 June 1867).

I should be wretched: *Letters* 11:374 (?End May 1867).

you know I don't like: *Letters* 11:377 (6 June 1867).

cleared off one obstacle: *Letters* 11:382 (18 June 1867).

If I decide to go: *Letters* 11:389 (4 July 1867). As Dickens feared, Mrs. Dickinson saw Thomas and Fanny Trollope later that summer when they visited her Berkshire estate in August.

Madame sends you: *Letters* 11:410 (9 Aug. 1867).

I go!: *Letters* 11:441 (30 Sep. 1867).

Yes. Go ahead: *Letters* 11:441 (30 Sep. 1867).

I am sorry: Meckier, "Two New Letters," 180.

I have to fix: *Letters* 11:425 (12 Sep. 1867).

CUNARD LINE: *The Times*, 30 Sep. 1867, 2.

jotted a memorandum: 1867 Pocket Diary, Berg Collection, New York Public Library.

I don't worry you: *Letters* 11:410 (9 Aug. 1867).

like a pleasant voice: *Letters* 11:444 (3 Oct. 1867).

Dolby is charged: *Letters* 11:444 (3 Oct. 1867).

Now he wrote to Cunard's: *Letters* 11:455 (16 Oct. 1867).

very far from well: Frances Ternan Trollope to Beatrice Trollope, 20 Oct. 1867, Trollope Papers, Princeton.

for a time: Frances Ternan Trollope to Beatrice Trollope, 8 Oct. 1867, Trollope Papers, Princeton.

It may be a relief: *Letters* 11:455-56 (16 Oct. 1867).

all that I hold dear: *Letters* 11:425 (12 Sep. 1867).

a letter of instruction: *Letters* 11:475 (Early Nov. 1867).

Seven thousand: *New York Herald*, 21 Nov. 1867, 6.

a perfect ovation: Dolby, *Charles Dickens as I Knew Him*, 155-59.

discuss arrangements: *Letters* 11:481 (21 Nov. 1867).

Dolby! Your infernal caution: Dolby, *Charles Dickens as I Knew Him*, 388.

bubbled over with fun: Annie Fields Diaries, Massachusetts Historical Society.

a more central position: *Letters* 11:496 (1 and 3 Dec. 1867).

Your respected parent: Ibid.

Tremendous success: *Letters* 11:503 (4 Dec. 1867).

On the 14th the Cunarder: Aylmer, "Dickens and Ellen Ternan," 86.

Will you specially observe: *Letters* 11:483 (21 Nov. 1867).

I expect Mamma: Frances Ternan Trollope to Beatrice Trollope, 8 Oct. 1867, Trollope Papers, Princeton.

Mamma, I am sorry: Frances Ternan Trollope to Beatrice Trollope, 20 Oct. 1867, Trollope Papers, Princeton.

Mamma & Ellen: Frances Ternan Trollope to Beatrice Trollope, 23 Jan. 1868, Trollope Papers, Princeton.

in a red sleigh: *Letters* 11:515 (17 Dec. 1867).

dismal cold: *Letters* 11:521 (24 Dec. 1867).

I had a frightful cold: *Letters* 11:523 (26 and 27 Dec. 1867).

I am so very unwell: *Letters* 11:525 (26 and 27 Dec. 1867).

Catarrh worse than ever!: *Letters* 12:90 (1-3 April 1868).

It is a wearying life: *Letters* 12:57 (24 Feb. 1868).

I am beginning: *Letters* 12:67 (8 March 1868).

all his thoughts: Dolby, *Charles Dickens As I Knew Him*, 286.

Enclosed, another letter: *Letters* 11:522 (24 Dec. 1867). When Dickens's American
    letters to Wills were first edited for publication (in 1912), all references to
    Ellen were heavily canceled in the manuscripts. The manuscripts are now at the
    Huntington Library in Pasadena; in the 1950s infrared photography allowed an
    enterprising researcher, Ada Nisbet, to read the canceled passages.

You will have seen: *Letters* 12:55 (21 Feb. 1868).

I tell my sisters: Frances Ternan Trollope to Beatrice Trollope, 30 Jan. 1868, Trollope
    Papers, Princeton.

a very large: Frances Ternan Trollope to Beatrice Trollope, 20 Feb. 1868, Trollope
    Papers, Princeton.

The days are so short: Frances Ternan Trollope to Beatrice Trollope, 16 Dec. 1867,
    Trollope Papers, Princeton.

I have bought: Ibid.

Ellen's robin redbreast: Frances Ternan Trollope to Beatrice Trollope, 27 Dec. 1867,
    Trollope Papers, Princeton.

Ellen was very much amused: Frances Ternan Trollope to Beatrice Trollope, 8 Dec.
    1867, Trollope Papers, Princeton.

A girl who was here: Ibid.

I hear from Nelly: Frances Ternan Trollope to Beatrice Trollope, 26 June 1868, Trol-
    lope Papers, Princeton.

My literary success: quoted in Tryon, *Parnassus Corner*, 323.

She dazzled no one: Tryon, *Parnassus Corner*, 216-17.

singularly graceful: James, "Mr. and Mrs. James T. Fields," 164.

harmonious atmosphere: Cather, "148 Charles Street," 58.

Such kindliness as shines: Annie Fields's journals are held by the Massachusetts His-
    torical Society, Boston. Extracts are printed in Howe, *Memories of a Hostess*, and
    Curry, "Dickens and Annie Fields." My own reading of Annie's sometimes dif-
    ficult handwriting differs occasionally from Howe's or Curry's.

Eudora Welty recalled: Welty, *One Writer's Beginnings*, 7.

there was never: Cather, "148 Charles Street," 60.

a cult of adoration: Tryon, *Parnassus Corner*, 312.

cannot be expected: *Letters* 12:74n.

one of the dearest: *Letters* 11:518 (22 Dec. 1867).

she was willing to allow Dickens his mistress: Annie Fields rather disapproved of
    other irregular liaisons. When Charles Fechter came to Boston in 1870 he

brought his mistress with him—Carlotta Leclerq, the actress who often played the leading female roles opposite him. The Fieldses entertained Fechter (not Carlotta), but Annie later observed: "Fechter is not perfect, we could see that alas! only too clearly—but how far wrong only One must judge" (Annie Fields Diaries, Massachusetts Historical Society).

You may imagine: *Letters* 12:130 (10 June 1868).

Tomorrow I will come: *Letters* 12:109 (14 May 1868).

The early days: Dolby, *Charles Dickens as I Knew Him*, 338. A "saloon carriage" is a railway car "without compartments, furnished more or less luxuriously as a drawing-room" (*OED*).

I had such a hard day: *Letters* 12:161 (31 July 1868).

very restless: *Letters* 12:148-49n.

What with travelling: *Letters* 12:106 (11 May 1868).

Divers birds: *Letters* 12:119 (25 May 1868).

You wouldn't recognize: *Letters* 12:268 (4 Jan. 1869).

the train I have to drag: *Letters* 12:221 (16 Nov. 1868).

for ever and ever: *Letters* 12:82 (21 March 1868).

tearing about the country: *Letters* 12:320 (29 March 1869).

I am perpetually counting: *Letters* 12:235 (8 Dec. 1868).

I have a wild fancy: *Letters* 12:257 (26 Dec. 1868).

It seems as though: *Letters* 12:224 (19 Nov. 1868).

I murdered the girl: *Letters* 12:272 (6 Jan. 1869).

I have a great deal: *Letters* 12:285 (2 Feb. 1869).

I . . . tried it: *Letters* 12:248 (16 Dec. 1868).

as I do not leave: *Letters* 12:246 (15 Dec. 1868).

the other night: *Letters* 12:254 (25 Dec. 1868).

We propose: *Letters* 12:263 (31 Dec. 1868).

I MUST BE: *Letters* 12:271 (6 Jan. 1869).

I do not commit: *Letters* 12:277 (19 Jan. 1869).

Don't forget: *Letters* 12:288 (12 Feb. 1869).

For some time: *Letters* 11:168 (?Early March 1866).

four Murders: *Letters* 12:298 (26 Feb. 1869).

There was something: Charles Dickens, Jr., "Glimpses of Charles Dickens," 679.

Is it *possible*: *Letters* 12:336 (19 April 1869).

extremely giddy: Ibid.

a weakness and deadness: *Letters* 12:339 (21 April 1869).

greatly revived: Dolby, *Charles Dickens as I Knew Him*, 403.

immense exertions: *Letters* 12:431 (22 April 1869).

I was engaged: "A Fly-Leaf in a Life," *Journalism* 4:387-88.

Just as three days' repose: *Letters* 12:348 (3 May 1869).

I have had: *Letters* 12:391 (8 Aug. 1869).

all who loved him: [Hogarth & Dickens], *Letters of Charles Dickens*, 708.

A thousand thanks: *Letters* 12:350 (6 May 1869).

I am good: *Letters* 12:350 (5 May 1869).

She is a charming: Letters 12:299 (26 Feb. 1869).

Suppose we give: *Letters* 12:357 (19 May 1869).

In case Monday: *Letters* 12:358 (20 May 1869).

What a treat: Fields, *Yesterdays with Authors,* 237.

With a fine face: Longley, "The Real Ellen Ternan" 36.

In her next letter home: Mabel Lowell's letters from England are held at the
    Houghton Library, Harvard University.

we began with oysters: Hollingshead, *My Lifetime,* 1:99.

And perhaps you wouldn't mind: *Mystery of Edwin Drood,* ch. 11.

there was no sitting: Frederic Chapman, quoted in Collins, *Interviews and Recollec-
    tions* 1:113.

While so engaged: *Letters* 12:45 (9 Feb. 1868).

I need not tell you: *Letters* 12:187 (?26 Sep. 1868).

It was a hard parting: *Letters* 12:189 (End Sep. 1868).

When you come: *Letters* 12:190 (29 Sep. 1868).

a wasted life: *Letters* 12:208 (24 Oct. 1868).

I am truly grateful: *Letters* 12:207 (23 Oct. 1868).

belongs to my life: *Letters* 11:166 (2 March 1866).

any communication: *Letters* 12:395 (15 Aug. 1869).

he gave a little dinner: Dolby, *Charles Dickens as I Knew Him,* 436.

I shall not be able: *Letters* 12:407 (6 Sep. 1869).

I have a notion: *Letters* 12:408 (11 Sep. 1869).

In answer to your enquiry: *Letters* 12:445-46 (27 Nov. 1869).

The patient: *Letters* 12:470 (23 Jan. 1870).

I have just come back: *Letters* 12:475 (5 Feb. 1870).

a certain small dinner: *Letters* 12:482 (26 Feb. 1870).

In addition to: *Letters* 12:517 (2 May 1870).

having come here: *Letters* 12:541 (31 May 1870).

the best and truest friend: Dickens's will, printed in *Letters* 12:730-33 (Appendix K).

the little touch: *Letters* 12:466 (14 Jan. 1870).

For some fifteen years: Fielding, *Speeches,* 413.

In this brief life: Ibid., 378.

from these garish lights: Ibid., 413.

come back from: *Mystery of Edwin Drood,* ch. 14.

Dead? Or Alive?: Stone, *Dickens' Working Notes,* 381.

they look down: *Mystery of Edwin Drood,* ch. 12.

it has happened: *Mystery of Edwin Drood,* ch. 14.

a dark man: *Mystery of Edwin Drood,* ch. 2.

shadow on the sun-dial: *Mystery of Edwin Drood,* ch. 19.

Put those knives: *Mystery of Edwin Drood* (Clarendon edition), ch. 11.

Katie's husband Charles Collins: Collins designed a "charming" cover wrapper for
    the monthly numbers of *The Mystery of Edwin Drood,* "but having achieved

that success, instantly collapsed for the whole term of his natural life," Dickens reported with notable lack of sympathy. His sickly son-in-law simply lacked the will to get better, Dickens felt. "Charles Collins may be a shade better, but will never keep better or be well," he complained to Annie and James Fields in 1868 (*Letters* 12:212), and early the following year he observed that "Charley Collins is no better, and no worse. He can eat well, and that is about the only sign of a natural or healthy condition that can be detected in him" (*Letters* 12:268). Concerned for his daughter Katie, Dickens wished that her husband would either recover or die (though he never recovered, he outlived Dickens by several years).

After Dickens's death, Annie Fields recorded a conversation with Charles Fechter: "Dear Dickens took a strange dislike to [Collins] during the last year or two of his life. I think it was his [Collins's] dreadful and continued sickness which neither exhausted the frame to death, nor ever ceased in order to allow a return to health. He could not understand the prolonged endurance of such an existence and in his passionate nature which must snap when it yielded at all, it produced disgust" (Annie Fields Diaries, Massachusetts Historical Society).

The womanly qualities of sympathy and nurture that Dickens revered in his heroines and conceded to occasional male characters like *Great Expectations'* Joe Gargery were alien to his own impatient temperament. The only patient with whom he had much patience was *the* Patient—Ellen.

I see: *Letters* 12:449 (?Early Dec. 1869).

there are many points: *Letters* 12:467 (16 Jan. 1870).

a blooming schoolgirl: *Mystery of Edwin Drood*, ch. 2.

wonderfully pretty: *Mystery of Edwin Drood*, ch. 3.

a charming little apparition: Ibid.

an amiable, giddy: *Mystery of Edwin Drood*, ch. 9.

something untamed: *Mystery of Edwin Drood*, ch. 6.

when I lost: *Mystery of Edwin Drood*, ch. 7.

An unusually handsome: *Mystery of Edwin Drood*, ch. 6. "Gipsy" coloring or gypsy
    blood in a woman was a Dickens code for strong eroticism.

Mixture of Oriental blood: Stone, *Dickens' Working Notes*, 385.

a deep rich piece: *Our Mutual Friend*, ch. 1:13.

womanly feeling: *Mystery of Edwin Drood*, ch. 17.

My pretty one: *Mystery of Edwin Drood*, ch. 7.

sisterly earnestness: *Mystery of Edwin Drood*, ch. 9.

The lustrous gipsy-face: *Mystery of Edwin Drood*, ch. 7.

The Mystery in the Drood Family: Stone, *Dickens' Working Notes*, 381.

looks on intently: *Mystery of Edwin Drood*, ch. 2.

in the space of a few pages: *Mystery of Edwin Drood*, ch. 7.

pride and self reliance: *Letters* 11:389 (4 July 1867).

Every day and hour: *Mystery of Edwin Drood*, ch. 17.

Helena's admirer: It may (or may not) be significant that Crisparkle's name echoes one of Dickens's own epithets, "the Sparkler of Albion."

his heart and soul: Kate Perugini to G. B. Shaw, 11 Dec. 1897, British Library.

lost letters to Ellen: Lost or, more likely, destroyed.

Chapter 10

My dear father: Mary Dickens to Anne Cornelius, 9 June 1870, Dickens Family Correspondence, Huntington Library.

We were most thankful: quoted in a letter of Dickens's son Alfred, who was in Australia when his father died (Alfred Tennyson Dickens to G. W. Rusden, *Letters* 12:734, Appendix L).

four boxes: *Letters* 12:542 (3 June 1870).

Extending my hand: Kitton, *Supplement to Charles Dickens by Pen and Pencil*, 27.

he found his father strangely abstracted: Charles Dickens, Jr., "Glimpses of Charles Dickens," 683.

a better father: Storey, *Dickens and Daughter*, 133-34.

My father disliked: Perugini, "Edwin Drood and Charles Dickens's Last Days," 654.

much inconvenienced: *Letters*, Supplement 2, *Dickensian* 99 (2003), 163 (17 May 1870).

directed all the rehearsals: Merivale, "Last Days of Charles Dickens."

after the play: Fitzgerald, *Memoirs* 1.13-14.

her grief was "terrible": Longley, "The Real Ellen Ternan," 27.

Charles Dickens has died: Brooks diaries, Pierpont Morgan.

A telegram has just come: J. T. Fields to Annie Fields, Fields Addenda, Huntington Library. Fields's note is undated, but was probably written on June 10th, the day after Dickens's death. Dickens died at about six in the evening London time, but the news did not cross the Atlantic until the next morning.

will be felt by millions: *The Times*, 10 June 1870, 9.

a general and very earnest desire: [Hogarth and Dickens], *The Letters of Charles Dickens*, 750.

In his will: Dickens's will is printed in *Letters* 12:730-33 (Appendix K).

Our hands were . . . completely tied: Dexter, *Dickens to His Oldest Friend*, 258. Forster, Ouvry and Frank Beard were not the only non-family members of the funeral party, however; Wilkie Collins was also present.

Dickens's estranged wife: The day after Dickens's death Shirley Brooks "heard that Mrs. Dickens's sorrow was overwhelming." He was told by a family friend that she "wants to *see* C.D. but I think the permission would be cruel, & the scene shocking" (Brooks diaries, Pierpont Morgan). If requested, permission must have been denied; Mrs. Dickens did not view the body, which lay at Gad's Hill until the funeral.

When they entered: Adrian, "Charles Dickens and Dean Stanley," 153.

I have just come: Collins, *Collected Letters* 2:194.

The Times described: *The Times* 15 June 1870, 12.

The gardens along the way: Mary Dickens, in Kitton, *Charles Dickens by Pen and Pencil*, 49.

those fourteen mourners: *The Times* 20 June 1870, 14.

The will of Dickens: Bigelow, *Retrospections*, 383. Bigelow was reporting on a luncheon conversation with Collins about six weeks after Dickens's death. Though he seems to have mangled other of Collins's remarks, the gossip about Dickens's will is probably accurate.

Among the congregation: *The Times* 20 June 1870, 14.

We went when in London: Frances Ternan Trollope to Beatrice Trollope, 28 June 1870, Trollope papers, Princeton. Seventeen-year-old Beatrice, known as "Bice," knew that Dickens had been a particular friend of the Ternan family, but her stepmother Fanny's avoidance of any special mention of Ellen suggests that her relationship with him had been so far as possible kept from Bice.

a most devoted wife: Ethel Robinson to Felix Aylmer, Aylmer papers, Dickens House Museum.

ACKNOWLEDGMENTS

S ince 1870, scholars, editors, and enthusiasts have created a wealth of resources for those studying and writing about Dickens. There are many good editions of his novels and other fiction, from the scholarly Oxford Clarendon editions to student paperback editions; much of his journalism is reprinted and annotated in the Dent Uniform Edition; the Dickens Companions Series provides generous annotations of his novels; and there are of course many biographies and biographical studies. Three journals dedicated to Dickens studies—*The Dickensian, Dickens Quarterly,* and *Dickens Studies Annual*—contain a treasury of information and ideas. The most valuable resource to arrive in recent years has been the Clarendon Press Pilgrim Edition of Dickens's letters, to which anyone studying his life will be much indebted.

With respect to his affair with Ellen Ternan, a curious anomaly exists. No researcher has investigated the affair more assiduously than Katharine M. Longley, nor contributed more to our knowledge of it; her monograph on the subject, *A Pardoner's Tale,* remains the most complete collection and discussion of the evidence. Yet *A Pardoner's Tale* has never been published and can be read only in a typescript copy in the archives of Senate House Library of the University of London.

Miss Longley herself once called *A Pardoner's Tale* "unpublishable"; I hope this judgment will one day be proved wrong. Anyone studying or writing about Dickens's connection with Ellen Ternan owes her thanks.

Browsing bookstore shelves some years ago, I fortuitously came across another book by Miss Longley, a closely researched biography of the sixteenth-century martyr St. Margaret Clitherow of York—in print and conveniently available in paperback. Dickens would have scoffed at Miss Longley's admiration for the recusant saint, and would have deplored her tireless researches into his own quite different history. Despite her staunch Catholicism, Miss Longley was lenient on Margaret Clitherow's persecutors—"We cannot keep Heaven's balance-sheet, but looking back from this distance of time, we may judge that the rancour of the martyrdoms has been washed out, leaving only the joy"—and she was equally charitable to Dickens, arguing in *A Pardoner's Tale* that his connection with Ellen Ternan was simply an innocent friendship. My own views differ; but in disagreeing with Katharine Longley, I do so with gratitude and admiration.

Over the years, members of the Dickens Society have patiently listened to my notions about Dickens at the Society's annual symposia and provided both encouragement and corrective advice; I've also profited from their own ideas and discoveries. In particular, my thanks to Natalie Cole, Marie-Amélie Coste, Mark and Meg Cronin, Margaret Darby, Duane DeVries, Bert Hornback, Natalie McKnight, Goldie Morgentaler, Lillian Nayder, David Paroissien, Trey Philpotts, and Edgar Rosenberg. To three Dickens scholars especially—Joel Brattin, Robert Heaman, and David Parker—I owe special thanks for reading and offering helpful comments on an earlier (and longer) version of this study.

Many libraries have been generous in giving access to manuscripts or rare books, and in granting permission to print extracts from unpublished manuscripts: the British Library; the Dickens House Museum in London; Princeton University's Firestone Library;

Houghton Library at Harvard; the Huntington Library; Lauinger Memorial Library at Georgetown University; the Library of Congress; the Massachusetts Historical Society; the New York Public Library; the Pierpont Morgan Library; and Senate House Library, University of London. I was also helped by the collections of the University of Virginia's Alderman Library; Swem Library at the College of William & Mary; and the University of Missouri's Ellis Library. At Gettysburg College's Musselman Library, I'm grateful to Kerri Odess-Harnish for keeping the Dickens holdings current, and to the Interlibrary Loan office, and especially Susan Roach, for quickly and efficiently filling many requests, some of them arcane.

Gettysburg College extended travel grants for archival research, while several colleagues at Gettysburg College have lent moral support, sometimes without knowing it, especially Bill Bowman, Len Goldberg, Beth Lambert, Lani Lindeman, James Myers, Magdalena Sánchez, Suzanne Tartamella, and the late Ted Baskerville.

Pegasus Books and its impresario publisher and editor-in-chief Claiborne Hancock recall the happier days of independent publishing houses. I'm grateful to him, and also to Pegasus senior editor Jessica Case, copyeditor Phil Gaskill, designer Maria Fernandez, and proofreader Anna Van Lenten.

When the tally of Dickens's children reached a half dozen or so, and continued to mount, he began to think that he had, perhaps, a few too many. Though less prolific, I'm profoundly grateful both for and to my own children. And I am very grateful, too, to my wife Joanne for long tolerating my Dickensian preoccupations.

INDEX